Finland – A Cultural Guide

PIRKKO-LIISA LOUHENJOKI-SCHULMAN – KAIUS HEDENSTRÖM

OTAVA
PUBLISHING
COMPANY LTD.
HELSINKI

Wilderness,
Pekka Halonen 1899

Finland – A Cultural Guide

Second edition

Editors

Russ Hoyle
Cheryl Riggins

Printed by Otava Book Printing Company Co.
Keuruu 2005

ISBN 952-5490-00-9

Contents

Welcome to a Cultural Tour of Finland!

T ravel guides tend to promote Finland as a destination for nature tours to experience the thousands of lakes and the midnight sun as well as the blue dusk of midwinter's short days and the bright light of the spring sun on the snowy ski slopes. Finland is also the land of a thousand museums, of which over 300 are part of the Finnish Museums Association. The latest museum architecture is noted internationally and the collections are interesting.

Cultural associations are active in Finland, and in rural areas their traditional role in the community has always included a concern for cultural preservation. There are hundreds of local museums - one or more in every town – that portray farm life through their artifacts. The northern location of Finland, its waterways, and its sparse population

Nyländska Jakt-klubben – Harbor in Helsinki, Albert Edelfelt 1899

have had an effect in fishing, forestry, agriculture, and industry, illustrated by many cultural historical museums around the country. Fishing and seafaring traditions can be approached through the small museums of the coastal areas.

The first Finnish local museum, where the world's oldest diving suit is displayed, was founded by a Raahe district doctor in the year 1862. Museums preserving Finland's industrial heritage are located mainly in the southern part of Finland in the vicinities of Tampere and Helsinki. Environmental problems have recently led to a rise in interest to build new museums featuring science and technology. We can easily observe that museums tend to change along with general urban progress. Many historically significant buildings and former industrial plants have been converted to museum use. Many of the museums also have educational programs for children as well as museum shops and cafés.

The museums are often established in times of great social changes. Every new generation will start its own museums. Finland's awakening as a nation and the subsequent achievement of independence in 1917 heightened the effects of the National Romantic movement and its cultural symbols. Based on the collections put together by university students, the Finnish National Museum was founded in 1916. The oldest art museum, Ateneum, was founded in connection with an art school in 1888. The art museums are young and active, having for the most part been formed after the mid 1900s.

When visiting Finland's museums, you will get a good view of the cultural history of the Finnish people, both the history and the current state of arts, crafts, and technology.

Anja-Tuulikki Huovinen
Secretary General
The Finnish Museums Association

Acknowledgements

For many years of encouragement and support we wish to thank the following individuals and organizations:

Anja-Tuulikki Huovinen, Marja-Liisa Haveri-Nieminen, Jan Groth, Esko Koivusalo, Kari Poutasuo, Pertti Ripatti, John LaRocca, Laina Metsähuone, Ritva Mäkelä, Ellen Howe, Russ Hoyle, Ritva Müller, Kirsti Ala-Harja, Laila Williamson, Markus Aaltonen, Anne-Marie Dannenberg, Barbara Messick, Hilkka Rintamäki-Keisanen, Jussi Seppälä, Seija Virtanen-Beeh, Eva Reenpää, Marita Jaakkola, Kari Heliö, Marja Roth-Sopanen, Timo Maijala, Helen Pratt, Ann Markovich, Outi Hirvikangas, Alan Schulman, Nina Ilmolahti, Anu Seppälä, Sole Öhberg and Petra Kaminen-Mosher.

The Finnish Museums Association, The Kordelin Foundation, The Finnish Ministry of Education, The Nordic Cultural Fund, The American-Scandinavian Foundation, Nordea Pankki Suomi Oyj, Suomen Posti Oyj, Neste Oy, Kvaerner-Masa-Yards Oy, Oy Veikkaus Ab, Finnair Oyj, The Finnish Tourist Board, Finlandia Vodka, John Nurminen Oy, Sampo (Postipankki), Kymmene USA.

Introduction

Finlande is called a fayre Countrye, because it is more plesaunter then Swecia... Muche wyne is transported thither, out of Spayne, by the sea Balthic, which the people of the Country much desyreth, onely to exhillerat their myndes...The Finnons haue continual warres wyth the Muscouites in the arme or bosome of the sea Finnonicus: usyng in Summer the ayde of Shyppes, and in Wynter they combat upon the Ise.

The Description of Swedland, Gotland, and Finland,
George North, 1561.

History

S tones worked by people over 100,000 years ago have been discovered in Finland, but the first settlements by speakers of early forms of Finnish, began to appear following the retreat of the continental ice-sheet some ten thousand years ago. About two thousand years ago, the Finns who gave their name to the country, *Suomi*, began their migration from the southern shores of the Gulf of Finland. Later, the Åland Islands and coastal regions were settled by people from Sweden.

Christian influences gained a foothold in southwestern Finland through trading links. The Swedish conquest as a result of the First Crusade in 1155 brought the Catholic Church to Finland and made Finland part of western Europe. Finland became a battleground between its western neighbor Sweden and the Catholic Church on one side and its eastern neighbor Novgorod–Russia and the Russian Orthodox Church on the other.

The Treaty of Pähkinäsaari in 1323 set for the first time the border between Sweden and Novgorod, later Russia. Sweden built castles for defense against the Eastern power and as administrative centers. Six castles of national importance were built in the Middle Ages: Turku, Häme, Raasepori, Olavinlinna, and Kastelholm as well as Viipuri, now in Russia.

The Swedish legal and social system took root in Finland. Under the Swedish rule the Finnish peasants were never serfs, but always retained their personal freedom. Turku became in the 13th century Finland's most important town and the Bishop's seat. In 1362, Finns were given the right to send representatives to select the King in Sweden, and in the 16th century this right was extended to include representation in the Swedish Diet, giving Finland full political rights within the Kingdom of Sweden.

The Reformation started in Germany reached Sweden and Finland in mid-16th century, and the Catholic Church consequently lost out to the Lutheran faith, which was declared the state religion. During its period as a great power (1617–1721), Sweden extended its realm around the Baltic and managed, due to the weakness of Russia, to push the Finnish border further east. Uniform Swedish rule was extended to Finland in the 17th century. After Sweden lost its position of power, Russian pressure on Finland increased, and Russia conquered Finland in the 1808–09 war with Sweden.

During the Swedish period, Finland was merely a group of provinces and not a national entity. But when Finland was annexed to Russia in 1809 it became an autonomous Grand Duchy, and a sense of Finnish identity began to develop. Finland was allowed not only to retain Swedish laws, Swedish as the official language, and the Lutheran Church, but also its old form of government. Finland's highest governing body was the Senate whose members were Finns. It took, however, half a century before the Diet, a legislative assembly with four estates, started to meet. Helsinki was chosen as the new capital and rebuilt in a handsome fashion for the new Grand Duchy. The economy developed favorably, and the invention in the late 19th century of wood pulp for papermaking created a world market for Finnish paper. Finland received its own currency, the *markka*, in 1860, which it held onto for more than 140 years until it was superceded by the euro.

However, during the late 19th century, nationalism and chauvinism in Russia led to the curbing of Finland's privileges. During the years of oppression, nevertheless, Finland managed to get a unicameral parliament in 1906 and was the first country in the world to grant women full voting rights. In the turmoil of the Russian revolution Finland seized the opportunity to declare its independence on December 6, 1917, but had to fight a war to expel the 40,000 Russian soldiers still on its territory. When the radical left wanted revolution also in Finland, the ensuing conflict led to the tragic Civil War in 1918. It ended in the defeat of the Reds and victory for the government troops, led by General Carl Gustaf Mannerheim.

When Finland refused to allow the Soviet Union to build military bases on its territory, the Soviets attacked Finland in November 1939.

In this, the Winter War, Finland stood alone; only sympathy and modest assistance was offered, but Finland's survival against overwhelming Russian forces became legendary all over the world. Stalin expected the Red Army to be in Helsinki in a few weeks, but unlike all other countries on the European continent that were involved in the Second World War, Finland was never occupied by foreign forces. The peace treaty in March 1940 drawn by Moscow gave a tenth of the Finnish territory, western Karelia, to the Soviet Union, but Finland remained free. When Germany attacked the Soviet Union in the summer of 1941,

Finland joined the German side in hopes of winning back the lost land. When the war ended in September 1944, Finland had lost some 100,000 men out of the population of 3.5 million. She had to cede additional land, resettle 420,000 refuges from the lost territories twice, in 1940 and 1944, and pay a huge sum of war reparations to the Soviet Union.

After the war, Finland's position between the Western and Eastern blocs was delicate, but Finland managed to stay neutral, even though she was forced under Soviet pressure in 1948 to conclude a Treaty of Friendship, Co-operation, and Mutual Assistance. The collapse of the Soviet Union in 1991 and Finland's membership in the European Union in 1995 opened a new era.

Culture

The surviving seventy-three medieval stone churches, built during Catholic times, not only bear witness to the connections with the Catholic culture of Europe but also house the first Finnish artwork, primitive murals and wooden statues. New research, though not universally accepted, indicates that many medieval churches are younger than earlier thought.

As a result of fires and wars between Sweden and Russia, not a single medieval wooden building has survived to this day. The oldest wooden churches are from the 17th century. By the 19th century simple, rectangular plan developed into complex, even 24-cornered designs, built by local master builders. The oldest medieval stone manor dates from the 15th century. Manor houses include estates owned by the aristocracy, which enjoyed tax privileges in return for equestrian service, as well as officers' quarters and the manors built by ironworks.

During the Middle Ages there were six towns in Finland: Turku, Viipuri, Porvoo, Ulvila, Rauma, and Naantali. Because most buildings there were built of wood until the 19th century, the towns were destroyed repeatedly by fire. Today small coastal towns still have areas with well-preserved wooden houses.

The Reformation set in motion a rise in Finnish-language culture. The New Testament was translated into Finnish in 1548 and the entire Bible appeared in 1642, laying the basis for a Finnish literature. Education was greatly influenced by the Protestant faith. Even before the establishment of public schools, the Church required literacy of both men and women as a prerequisite for marriage. Even though the society now is secular, still about 85% of people belong to the Finnish Evangelical Lutheran Church and some 1.5% to the Finnish Orthodox Church, both of which are State churches.

The first newspaper in Finnish was published in 1776 and the first public library established in 1794. The first school, Turku Cathedral School, was founded at the end of the 13th century to train priests, even though the law about universal education was passed only in 1866. The first university was founded also in Turku in 1640, later moved to Helsinki after it had become the new capital in 1812.

The National Romanticism of the 19th century gave birth to a national spirit, national institutions, and a culture recognized as Finnish. The Finnish national epic, unique in the world, the *Kalevala* as compiled by Elias Lönnrot, was published in 1835 and acted as an inspiration for the birth of Finnish art, architecture, and music. Finally in 1863, Finnish became, alongside with Swedish, the official administrative language.

Both Finnish and Swedish are the official languages of Finland. Most Finns speak Finnish as their mother tongue and about 300,000 Finns, or 5.8% of the population of some 5,2 million, speak Swedish, mostly in coastal areas and on the Åland Islands. The languages are in no way related to each other; Swedish is a Germanic language, which belongs to the Indo-European group, whereas Finnish belongs to the Finno-Ugric language family.

Aleksis Kivi's novel *Seitsemän veljestä* – Seven Brothers – published in 1870 laid foundation of Finnish-language literature. Literature, music, art, and architecture were seen as a means of expressing Finnish nationhood and this period of the flourishing of the arts at the turn of the 20th century is often called the *Golden Age of Finnish Art*. The concept of the *national landscape* also developed in the 19th century. The Ministry of the Environment selected, in 1992, twenty-seven locations as national landscapes. They express Finns' mental image of their country and are key features of their identity.

The turns of history Finland has experienced have equipped it to adapt to new situations. While the land and enduring sense of Finnishness provide permanence, the lack of materials and economic possibilities have made Finns inventive. "…*the strength of civilization is its only salvation,*" said J. V. Snellman, the leading 19th century Finnish philosopher and statesman.

Provincial Museum Districts

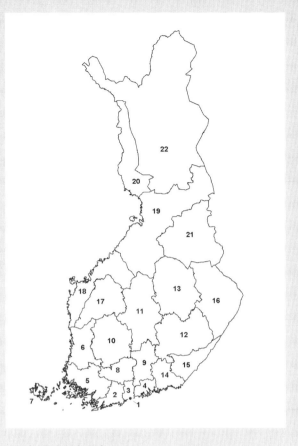

1. Helsinki – Helsingfors

During the time Finland was part of the kingdom of Sweden, King Gustav Vasa, the founder of a monarchy, systematically developed the country by concentrating trade in towns and denying the peasants the right to barter goods independently in the Baltic. The King founded Helsinki, then called *Helsingefors* or *Helsingeborgh*, in 1550 at the mouth of the Vantaanjoki River.

Helsinki was planned as a rival port to Tallinn on the south coast of the Gulf of Finland, a prosperous town of the Hansa League, a medieval free trade association based in North Germany. Burghers of Ulvila, the present day Pori, and Rauma on the west coast and Tammisaari and Porvoo in Uusimaa were forced to settle in Helsinki, but they kept running away from the miserable hamlet to return to their former homes.

The new town's monumental symmetrical plan was the first Renaissance design envisaged in Sweden but was never realized, and after six years the residents were permitted to move back to their homes. At most, the town amounted to about thirty blocks with houses irregularly placed along the main street.

A King's Manor was built on *Kuninkaankartanonsaari*, King's Manor Island nearby. Only after Helsinki was moved in 1640 to its present location, called *Vironniemi*, or Estonia Point, did the town start to grow.

King Gustav Vasa

The Senate Square, surrounded by Neo-Classical buildings, forms one of the world's most architecturally unified squares and serves as a dramatic setting for celebrations from New Year's Eve to Independence Day.

Senaatintori – Senate Square

When Finland was annexed to the Russian Empire in 1809 as an autonomous Grand Duchy, it ceased to be a conglomeration of provinces and became a state. Czar Alexander I, the Grand Duke of Finland, wanting to impress the Swedish king, declared the small town of Helsinki, practically destroyed in a fire a few years earlier, to be the new grand capital in 1812 to replace Turku. The courtier and diplomat Johan Albrecht Ehrenström, the head the reconstruction committee, planned the Square as the symbolic heart of the Grand Duchy of Finland. Carl Ludvig Engel (1778–1840), the Berlin-trained German architect, created the Square as an elegant example of Neoclassicism, called the *Empire Style*, in the Berlin neohumanistic and the St. Peterburg traditions. In 1816 Engel was appointed as the architect on the construction committee in charge of designing some thirty public buildings for the new capital.

Old Helsinki Map

C. L. Engel

Carl Ludvig Engel

The public buildings around the Senate Square are for the church, the state, and the university. The Lutheran Nicholas Church, for the Czar, today called the Helsinki Cathedral, rises majestically at the top of the hill, with the Senate Building, now called the Council of State (1822), on one side, and the University of Helsinki, originally established in 1640 in Turku and relocated in Helsinki in 1828, on the other. Because expensive stones were not available, the buildings were constructed of brick, stuccoed in pastel colors, often yellow, and trimmed in white with black roofs. Stylistically, they are reminiscent of the palaces of St. Petersburg, but on a smaller scale. For this reason, Helsinki has been a stand-in for St. Petersburg in films when the real locations were off limits in the former Soviet Union.

In the center of the Square stands a memorial to Czar Alexander II, who was assassinated in 1881. He granted Finland wider autonomy, for which the Finns remained loyal to him. It is the only statue of a Russian Czar still standing outside Russia.

Helsinki University Library – Helsingin yliopiston kirjasto – the National Library of Finland, was completed in 1844, after Engel's death. Its facade of Corinthian pilasters and columns is placed in the middle of

a long row of Classical facades along the street. The three large, barrel-vaulted halls with a central dome and 28 Corinthian columns are impressive and worth seeing. The vaulting and the cupola are skillful trompe l'oeil, painted to give an illusion of the relief. The interiors are said to be the most beautiful sequence of spaces in a secular building in Finland.

The Lutheran Cathedral still dominates the Helsinki skyline. The long flight of steps descending to the Square are a popular place for enjoying the sun and the great view.

Helsingin tuomio-kirkko – Helsinki Cathedral

Carl Ludvig Engel worked on the design of the church from 1818 until his death in 1840. The cruciform-shaped church has six Corinthian columns at each gable and it is capped with an imposing central tower. Engel's successor as head of the Intendant's Office, Ernst Bernhard Lohrmann, also a Berlin-trained architect, supervised the construction work and changed Engel's plans. The church was adorned with four small towers in the corners between the arms and twelve statues of the apostles made of zinc on the roof. The church was finally consecrated in 1852. The white interior with its diffused light still bears Engel's austere elegance. The altar painting was donated by Czar Nicholas I and it is surrounded by the frame arrangement designed by Lohrmann.

Suomenlinna – Suomenlinna Fortress Island

The major boost for the economy was the building of Suomenlinna on islands just off the southern shore. By the beginning of the 18th century, the Russian Empire had grown in strength and started to expand to the west. St. Petersburg was founded in 1703, and by 1714 the whole of Finland was occupied by Russia. The period known as the Great Wrath ended with the Peace of Uusikaupunki in 1721 under which Russia gained eastern Finland and the town of Viipuri. After a reprisal war, Sweden lost even more of Finland.

Suomenlinna Fortress, originally named Sveaborg, "Fortress of Sweden," and called *Viapori* in Finnish, was constructed to provide a stronghold close to the Russian border. It was a huge financial undertaking and the biggest public construction project in Sweden-Finland, financed by France, a military ally. The fortress was designed and the work supervised by Swedish-born Lieutenant-Colonel Augustin Ehrensvärd according to the Baroque ideals of the French fortress-builder Sébastien de Vauban.

Construction work began in 1748, and at its peak almost 7,000 soldiers were working on the fortress. Procurement of building materials provided employment and business opportunities for the burghers of Helsinki, helping the town finally to awake from its slumber. The fortifications formed enclosed strongholds with bastions, with the forts on the other islands forming an open line. The islands are characterized by high grass-covered earthworks, angular granite structures and Classical-

style barracks. The dry dock was built to provide the fortress with its own naval fleet – now the oldest functioning dry dock in Europe. The impressive ceremonial King's Gate of the fortress, *Kustaanmiekka*, "The Sword of Gustav," was regarded as the symbolic entrance to Finland: whoever passed through was the lord of the fortress and the whole country. The famous inscription on the wall reads: *"Posterity, stand here on your own ground and trust not help from outside."*

Russia, in alliance with France, attacked Sweden in 1808, and Sveaborg, "the Gibraltar of North" and captured all of mainland Finland, and Sweden surrendered it to Russia. The conquest of Finland ended Swedish rule and Finland became a Grand Duchy of the Russian Empire. Russia continued to expand and strengthen the fortress. During the Crimean War in 1855 people gathered on the cliffs to watch the English navy bombard the fortress, causing considerable damage to the structures, most of which were left unrepaired. The country's first Jewish prayer room was opened on the island in the 1830s, a common sanctuary for both Jews and Muslims was built in the early 1850s, although it was destroyed not long after during the Crimean War.

In 1918, a year after Finland gained its independence, the fortress was renamed Suomenlinna, "Fortress of Finland." The island's Russian Orthodox church was remodeled as Lutheran with an unusual tower that serves as a lighthouse. The fortress remained a Finnish garrison until 1973 when it came under civilian administration

Helsinki South Harbor

and restoration work began on this cultural site. Now the island is home to 900 permanent residents. Architecturally one of the finest fortresses in Europe, UNESCO added Suomenlinna to its list of World Heritage Sites in 1991.

When the ships sail in to the harbor past Suomenlinna, all but scraping the cliffs, the harmonious skyline of Helsinki center looms ahead. The unique maritime Helsinki has been nominated a National Landscape by the Ministry of the Environment.

Suomenlinna-museo – Suomenlinna Museum

The Museum and Visitors' Center is located in the new wing of the Inventory Chambers, built to house the Naval storerooms. The museum covers 250 years of Suomenlinna's Swedish, Russian, and Finnish history relating to the building of the fortress. The artifacts on display were discovered during the restoration work on the fortress and in attics of the houses on the island.

Ehrensvärd-museo – Ehrensvärd Museum

The Commandant's House, Count Augustin Ehrensvärd's residence, was built in 1752 flanking the Great Courtyard on Susisaari Island (*Vargö*), the first monumental Baroque square in Finland. The use of illusionist principles heightens its grandiosity. The museum is furnished as an 18th-century residence and shows the history of Suomenlinna fortress and the coastal fleet.

The **Manege Military Museum** – Sotamuseo, Maneesi – displays the heavy equipment used by the Finnish army in World War II. The **Coast Artillery Museum** – Rannikkotykistömuseo – in an old powder cellar illustrates the history of coastal fortifications and equipment during the past 300 years. The **Submarine Vesikko** – Sukellusvene Vesikko – a renovated 250-ton submarine built in 1933 in Finland and the last World War II submarine its this type, is open to the visitors.

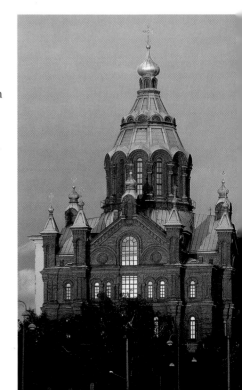

Uspenskin katedraali – Uspenski Cathedral

The red-brick Orthodox Uspenski Cathedral, consecrated in 1868, stands on a high rock facing Engel's Neo-Classical center. Dedicated to the Virgin Mary, the name of the cathedral comes from the Slavic word *uspenie*, "falling into the sleep of death." It was built for the growing Russian population, and also as a counterbalance to the Lutheran Nicholas Church that dominates the townscape and as a showcase of the Czars's power.

The cathedral is still the largest Orthodox church in western Europe. Designed by Aleksei Gornostayev, it is a combination of Bysantine Russian and Romanesque architecture. Its gilded, onion-shaped cupola, symbolizing the flame of the Holy Spirit, rises to a height of 42 meters with the 12 smaller cupolas representing Christ and the apostles. The cruciform church and its central cupola, painted blue with stars, is supported by four massive granite columns, carved from a single piece. The front part of the apse comprises an *iconostasis*, two rows of icons.

The church became Finnish Orthodox and independent from the Russian Orthodox Church in 1923. The church currently has about 17,000 church members in Helsinki.

When Carl Ludvig Engel arrived to Helsinki in early 1816 his first task was to draw up the plans for the new navy barracks on the rocky **Katajanokka** peninsula near the city center. Adjacent to the navy, Katajanokka was a shady neighborhood with humble fishermen's huts.

The whole central area of apartment buildings in the Art Nouveau style, unique in Europe, sprung up within a few years at the beginning of the 20th century; many of them were the artistic breakthrough for the young architects, Herman Gesellius, Armas Lindgren, and Eliel Saarinen. A shipyard occupied most of the peninsula until the mid-1970s; now the old warehouses have been renovated. Engel's navy barracks have been converted into the headquarters for the **Ministry of Foreign Affairs**.

Annankatu on a Cold Winter Morning, Magnus von Wright 1868

A good example of the distinctive Jugend style architecture is the **Eira** villa town based on the concept of the English garden town. The center of the city has many buildings in this National Romantic style, the Finnish interpretation of Art Nouveau, which bears influences from Finnish medieval churches, castles, and Karelian vernacular architecture, as well as the English Arts and Crafts movement, and the granite buildings of American architect H. H. Richardson.

The restrained Austrian and German-influenced Jugend is exemplified by the interiors of the **Helsinki Synagogue** (Jac. Ahrenberg, 1906) and the gray-granite **Kallio Church** (Lars Sonck, 1912). Saarinen's hand-some **Railroad Station** (1919) paved way to a more Classical architecture which, in common with similar work elsewhere in Scandinavia, is called *Nordic Classicism*. The powerful **Parliament House** (J. S. Siren, 1931) as well as large areas in the South Töölö district and the charming **Käpylä** garden town (Martti Välikangas), a wooden housing area from the 1920s, are built in this style. The rationality and the restrained, often elegant use of materials culminated in the International Style architecture, in Finland called the Functionalist style, from the late 1920s on. The various architectural styles over the decades are clearly visible in Helsinki's townscape as concentric rings going out from the old center.

Helsinki Railroad Station, Eliel Saarinen

Olympiastadion – Helsinki Olympic Stadium

The slender white tower of the Olympic Stadium became a Helsinki landmark immediately upon its completion in 1938 for the 1940 Olympic Games. The Stadium building, designed by Yrjö Lindegren and Toivo Jäntti, made the new Functionalist style a symbol of the young state which wanted to be modern and progressive. Sports were not only an important part of the Functionalist idea of body culture, but also played an important role in building the self-confidence of the emergent state.

The Olympic Games were canceled because of the outbreak of World War II, but they were finally held in 1952. For Finland, the Games were a major effort to show to the world that the country had survived the war, having just sent the last trainload of war reparations to the Soviet Union.

Sports Museum of Finland – Suomen urheilumuseo – is dedicated to the history of sports and exercise. The exhibitions cover 2000 years, from prehistoric skis to modern Olympic medals. Multimedia presentations about the Helsinki Olympic Games in 1952 and the Stadium and a video theater present the highlights of Finnish sports achievements.

Finlandia-talo – Finlandia Hall

Finlandia Hall by Finnish master architect Alvar Aalto, reflected on the waters of Töölönlahti Bay, holds proud memories for Finns when it was the venue for the 1975 Conference on Security and Co-operation in

Europe, which led to the signing of the Helsinki Accords. It takes its name from the symphonic poem by Jean Sibelius, a symbol of protest against oppression and censorship during the Russification of 1899–1905.

Finlandia Hall is the splendid culmination of Aalto's so-called white period, with its marble facades shimmering in the park and the massively sculptural form dominating the Helsinki skyline. Inside, the sequence of spaces resembling an open landscape, characteristic of Aalto, provides an excellent meeting place during intermissions. Aalto's Finlandia Hall from 1972 is the only building completed of his plan for "a string of pearls" along the western shore of the bay. The tattered landscape is now slowly being filled in after 80 years of planning and grand urban designs.

Several architectural competitions were from the 1930s onwards arranged to build a church on this rocky site lined by solid red-brick apartment buildings. When work began on a unique solution from the designs of architect brothers Timo and Tuomo Suomalainen in 1968, it was greeted nevertheless with protests by the younger generation.

This "Church in the Rock" has become the most visited building in Finland, attracting half a million guests annually. It is also a popular place for weddings, as well as concerts because of its excellent acoustics. The church is carved into the bedrock and lit through the central cupola, giving the space a mystical quality that touches people of all religions.

Temppeliaukion kirkko – Temppeliaukio Church

**Suomen Kansallis-
ooppera – Finnish
National Opera**

The Opera House is the first home built specifically for the Finnish
National Opera during its hundred year history. Designed by architects
Eero Hyvämäki, Jukka Karhunen, and Risto Parkkinen, it was completed
in 1992. The Opera House, in spite of its gleaming white modernity,
respects the tradition of grand opera houses with its elegant, yet intimate
1,400-seat horseshoe-shaped auditorium, clad in warm hues of wood.
The Finns are great opera lovers, and Finland has been fertile ground for
composers.

**Suomen kansallis-
museo – The National
Museum of Finland**

Some of the objects in the National Museum had already belonged to
the Turku Academy which was moved to Helsinki in 1828 and became
Helsinki University. The museum building, designed by the architects
Herman Gesellius, Armas Lindgren and Eliel Saarinen, was opened in
1916. As a symbol of the Finnish museum institution, the building
contains many references and allusions to the history of Finnish architecture, such as motifs from Finnish medieval churches and castles, to
highlight the various collections and to give them the appropriate
setting. The ceiling of the entrance lobby is vaulted in the style of Medieval churches and decorated with frescoes based on the *Kalevala*, the
Finnish national epic, and painted by Akseli Gallen-Kallela, the most
important artist of the time.

The exhibitions presents the culture and historical development of Finland from prehistoric times to the present. The prehistoric exhibition includes bronze and silver Viking jewelry, and silver treasures from the 12th century. Medieval art is represented by objects from churches and coats of arms. The period rooms depict life in an 18th-century manor. After Finland became an autonomous Grand Duchy of the Russian Empire, the gilded throne of Czar Alexander I was brought in 1809 to the Diet in Porvoo from Moscow, and was moved to the museum in 1917 after the Russian Revolution. A traditional chimneyless cabin, built around 1826, and a Finnish home from the 1990s are examples of everyday life.

Kulttuurien museo – Museum of Cultures

The Museum of Cultures is the first ethnographic museum based on scientific research in Finland. It has no permanent display but sets up temporary shows. The collections of the museum derive from all inhabited continents of the world, some of them unique and hardly to be seen elsewhere. They include a unique collection of objects, relating to the Fenno-Ugric peoples, many of whom are now close to extinction, was purchased during explorations in the late 19th century when the origin of the Finnish language and people was studied.

Seurasaaren ulkomuseo – The Seurasaari Open-Air Museum

In the 19th century the study of vernacular architecture was seen as an important component for recording the true Finnish heritage. Seurasaari Museum was established in 1909 with Skansen Museum in Stockholm as an example.

Seurasaari is a national open-air museum with 90 separate buildings, mostly from the 1700s and 1800s. The oldest building is the wooden church from Karuna in western Finland, built in 1686. It is still used during the summer and is especially popular for weddings. The farmsteads from western Finland and eastern Finland with their different ways of building provide an interesting picture of the local traditions. The village atmosphere is complemented by a parsonage, a manor house, a country store, mills, granaries, stables, and garden houses.

During the summer, there are work demonstrations, folk dance performances, and special events. The biggest event takes place on Midsummer Eve – for over 100 years Helsinki residents have come to Seurasaari to celebrate Midsummer with traditional bonfires, dancing, folk music and craftsmen's demonstrations.

Ateneumin taidemuseo – Ateneum Art Museum / Valtion taidemuseo – Finnish National Gallery	The ornate Neo-Renaissance Ateneum building is the oldest museum building in Finland, designed by Theodor Höjer and built in 1887 to house the collections of the National Gallery. The museum has the largest collection of art in Finland, including works which record the history of Finnish art from the late 18th century to the 1950s. It displays not only major works of Finnish art, familiar to Finns from their school lessons and important to the Finnish identity, but also offers well-known foreign art, including works by van Gogh, Cezanne, and Gauguin.
Nykytaiteen museo Kiasma – Museum of Contemporary Art Kiasma / Valtion taidemuseo – Finnish National Gallery	In 1993, the American architect Steven Holl won the design competition for the Museum of Contemporary Art, situated at the bottom of Töölön-lahti Bay, an area under planning since the time of Eliel Saarinen's proposals in the 1920s. Holl's design sparked controversy among the Finns, but after its inauguration in 1998, the museum became an immediate hit and popular meeting place.
	The museum exhibits Finnish and international art done after 1960, the turning point in Finnish postwar art. The core of the museum's works comprises works by some of the most prominent contemporary foreign artists. In addition to traditional exhibitions of paintings, sculpture, graphics, and installations, the museum specializes in interdisciplinary productions of art, dance, music, media art, and films.
Sinebrychoff taide-museo – Sinebrychoff Art Museum / Valtion taidemuseo – Finnish National Gallery	The museum is located in the former mansion of industrialist and brewer Nikolai Sinebrychoff, who had it built in 1840–42. The home has been restored to replicate the life style of this wealthy family. The exceptionally large art collection was donated by Sinebrychoff's descendants. It contains Italian, French, Dutch, and Flemish art from the 14th century to the mid-19th century, portraits, graphic art, miniatures, icons, furniture, silver, and porcelain.
Helsingin kaupungin museo – Helsinki City Museum	The Helsinki City Museum comprises eight museums around the city and functions as a center for the study of Helsinki's history. The museum on Sofiankatu Street provides glimpses of the city during its 450-year history and the lives of its inhabitants in a changing world.
	Sofiankatu Street has been restored as the **Street Museum** – Katumuseo –illustrating how a street in Helsinki looked in the early and late 19th century, as well as in the 1930s.
	The **Sederholm House** – Sederholmin talo – is the oldest stone building in Helsinki proper. The museum is dedicated to Johan Sederholm who built the house in 1757. Its construction mirrored the growth in the city's prosperity after years of occupation and devastation by Russian forces. The house was restored to its original appearance. Imaginative and well-executed exhibitions relating to the culture and history of Helsinki fill the museum.

talian Renaissance style **Hakasalmi Villa** – Hakasalmen huvila – was built in 1843–44 at Hakasalmi Bay, outside what were then Helsinki's borders. The English-style garden became the present Hesperia Park. The museum depicts the past and present of Helsinki from the city's foundation to independence telling the life stories of average Helsinki residents within the framework of the larger historical events.

Burgher's House – Ruiskumestarin talo – is the oldest wooden house in the city to survive in its original location. The small house was built in 1817–18 and functioned as a residence until 1974. The house is furnished and decorated in the style of a middle class home of the 1860s.

Three wooden houses, which remarkably survived in the center of the city, have been furnished as the **School Museum** – Koulumuseo. The interesting and illustrative exhibits portray the history of schooling in Finland and in particular in Helsinki, where the first public elementary schools opened their doors in 1867 to 224 pupils.

The main building of Tuomarinkylä (*Domarby*) Manor was built in 1790. Four side buildings were added to border the square courtyard. **Tuomarinkylä Museum** – Tuomarinkylän museo – has been restored to illustrate manor life in Helsinki.

Tram Museum – Raitioliikennemuseo – dedicated to the history of Helsinki public transportation, is located in the city's oldest tram depot (1900).

Worker Housing Museum – Työväenasuntomuseo – presents the life and living conditions of workers in Helsinki from 1909 to 1980 in one of the first rental apartments built by the city.

The restored water mills on Vantaanjoki River are a memorial to early industry in Helsinki. **Power Station Museum** – Voimalamuseo – is located near the original location of the town of Helsinki.

The museum has two locations. The older facility is in **Meilahti** just outside the center of the city. The newer gallery is downtown in the **Tennis Palace**. The collections consist mainly of Finnish art from the 1950s to the present. A large part is displayed in the city government's many offices and public spaces. The Tennis Palace houses changing exhibitions.

Helsingin kaupungin taidemuseo – Helsinki City Art Museum

The museum is housed in what was Amos Anderson's (1878–1961) private home and office, built in 1913. He was a patron of the arts and one of the most important cultural figures in Finland of the 20th century.

Amos Andersonin taidemuseo – Amos Anderson Art Museum

Coming from a humble background, Anderson built a financial empire that included printing presses, the largest Swedish-language daily newspaper, *Hufvudstadsbladet*, and the entire block of the Forum shopping center.

Anderson purchased a large amount of 19th- and 20th-century art, including works by French impressionists and by members of the Finnish *Septem* group which took its name from the number of its members, seven, favoring the pure and brilliant colors in the French tradition.

Designmuseo – Design Museum	The Finnish Society of Crafts and Design was founded in 1875 to support a design museum. The stunning success of Finnish design and crafts at the Paris Exposition of 1900 helped to heighten the importance of "Finnish design" among Finns. The museum's exhibition focuses on the high points of famous Finnish industrial design of the 20th century – furniture, textiles, glass, china, metalwork, jewelry, ceramics, and commercial art as well as unique pieces.
Suomen rakennus- taiteen museo – Museum of Finnish Architecture	The museum developed out of the Picture Archives maintained by the Finnish Association of Architects and exhibits foreign and Finnish architecture. The museum's archive has a collection of more than 100,000 photographs, 35,000 slides, and 300,000 original drawings by Finnish architects.
Luonnontieteellinen museo – Finnish Museum of Natural History	The museum maintains the national collections of zoology, botany, and geology. The exhibition takes the visitor through billions of years, starting from the Precambrian period and ending in the last Ice Age. It presents the history of the Earth with magnificent reconstructions and examples from zoology, botany, geology, and paleontology. Most of the animals are mounted in dioramas, showing them in their natural habitats. Besides Finnish fauna, there are African and Asian habitats.

The **Botanical Gardens** with its splendid 19th-century greenhouse in Kaisaniemi Park were restored in the late 1990s and are well worth a visit. |
| **Tekniikan museo – Museum of Technology** | The museum is situated on King's Manor Island at the mouth of the Vantaanjoki River near the location where Helsinki was established in 1550. The island is beautifully surrounded by rapids near a nature protection area, where the city built waterworks in the 1870s. When in 1969 the premises were no longer needed, the city renovated them for the museum. The museum features historical and modern-day technology and industry. |
| **Arabian museo – Arabia Museum** | The Arabia Factory, now part of the Hackman Group, has been making china for Finnish homes for more than 125 years. The museum displays pieces, many of them pure nostalgia for Finns, so intrinsic they have been |

o the Finnish household. There are also examples of Finnish design made famous at international design biennales in the 1950s.

Herttoniemen kartanon museo – Herttoniemi Manor House Museum

The Manor had been a freehold estate since the 1400s. The main building was reconstructed from the former china factory in a Neo-Classical style in 1814–20. The 17-hectare (42.5 acre) park includes a formal French garden traversed by tree-lined geometric paths and the more natural English style park with its two pavilions by C. L. Engel.

Postimuseo – Post Museum

The museum is an excellent combination of inventive application of multimedia and traditional presentation of authentic historical objects. The permanent exhibition intro-duces the 360-year history and current state of the Finnish Post Office. The collections comprise objects from post office signs and letter boxes, uniforms, and mail sacks to vehicles such as an old post boat and a bus. A complete old-fashioned post office is included in the exhibition; the larger-scale architecture of post office buildings is presented in the multimedia program.

Suomen valokuva-taiteen museo – The Finnish Museum of Photography

The Cable Factory, *Kaapelitehdas*, is a huge complex now renovated for artists and museums. The museum of photography is the oldest in Scandinavia and one of the largest in Europe. The "industrial" yet elegant interiors accommodate both the architecture of the building and the collections superbly. The exhibition covers Finnish photography from 1839 on and presents how, since the late 1960s, photography has come to be a respected field of the visual arts.

Teatterimuseo – Theatre Museum

The museum displays unique objects related to the history of Finnish theater and dance, and explores the magic of the theater. The exhibitions include costumes, scale models of sets, photographs, and also theater technology and equipment. *Arkadia Theater*, modeled on the first Fin-nish-language theater, *Esplanaditeatteri*, originally built in 1827 in the Esplanadi Park on the designs of C. L. Engel, displays the history of the Finnish theater. The stage and proscenium is painted according to the original designs.

Hotelli- ja ravintola-museo – Hotel and Restaurant Museum

The museum gives visitors a look at how the traditions of eating, drin-king, and manners have changed in Finland. The humble table of an inn, a fine festive dinner table from the early 20th century, and a restaurant kitchen with its handsome copper pots are all on view. Menus, postcards and photos intrigue us with the changing habits and etiquette.

Päivälehden museo – Päivälehti Museum

This museum dedicated to news presents its history in Finland using the news itself. The wall displays are set against the background of the general events in Finland and the world – the drama of more than alone hundred years of news illustrates the work of journalists and printers. The liberal *Päivälehti* newspaper was established in 1889, but in 1904 Russian authorities banned it and deported its founder Eero Erkko because of its strict constitutional line. It was soon reestablished as *Helsingin Sanomat* and grew to become Scandinavia's largest morning paper.

Suomen merimuseo – The Maritime Museum of Finland

The museum occupies a former pilot's station, off Helsinki harbor. It spans the history of boat and shipbuilding, the work of sailors and their lives aboard ship, the history of diving, merchant shipping, steam technology, and winter navigation.

The museum is responsible for archaeological sea research in Finland and has since the 1960s raised objects from shipwrecks. Seafarer' tools and everyday objects as well as ships' cargo found by divers illustrate everyday life on board ship. The museum has studied several interesting wrecks. The restored light ship the *Kemi*, built in 1901, is moored at the quay.

Sotamuseo – Military Museum

The collections cover the history of the Finnish army and the wars it fought from the 17th century to the present, the Finnish cavalry in the Thirty Years' War in 1618–48, called the *Hakkapeliittas* because of their battle cry, and today's UN peacekeepers.

Cygnaeuksen galleria – The Cygnaeus Gallery

The Cygnaeus Gallery was founded by Fredrik Cygnaeus (1807–1881), professor of esthetics and modern literature, historian, and poet. A patron of the arts, Cygnaeus supported Finnish art by buying and commissioning works. The collection is a good representation of Finnish painting and sculpture of the 19th century. The exhibition includes works depicting the nation's landscapes and people by major Finnish painters. The museum is housed in Cygnaeus' summer villa in Kaivopuisto Park, built in 1870, a rare surviving wooden house in downtown Helsinki.

Mannerheim-museo – Mannerheim Museum

The museum is the former home of Carl Gustaf Emil Mannerheim (1867–1951), Marshal of Finland and President of Finland. Born to a noble family, Mannerheim served in the Chevalier Guard of the Czar in St. Petersburg. He left the Imperial Russian army after the October Revolution in 1917 and returned to Finland to lead the White army against the Reds in the Finnish Civil War in 1918. Mannerheim was Commander-in-Chief during the Second World War against the Soviet

Union. He was awarded the title of Marshal of Finland, the only person in Finland ever to be given the honor. Mannerheim's symbolic importance as the defender of Finnish independence in the war was enormous. During the Winter War, the defensive positions of the Finns on the Karelian Isthmus became famous as the "Mannerheim Line." His grave in the military cemetery at Hietaniemi in Helsinki is a place of national homage.

An important part of the collections is the valuable scientific material, still used for research, which Mannerheim acquired during the military reconnaissance expedition he made on horseback through Asia to China between 1906 and 1908.

Carl Gustaf Emil Mannerheim

The Tamminiemi Villa was the official residence of President Urho Kekkonen (1900–1986) during his presidency (1956–81). Dr. Kekkonen, with his sharp intelligence and panache managed to keep Finland neutral between the East and West. The residence has been kept as it was when he lived there, including Finnish art and the gifts he received.

Urho Kekkosen museo – The Urho Kekkonen Museum Tamminiemi

The Didrichsen Art Museum is the result of the devoted interest in art of Marie-Louise and Gunnar Didrichsen. The collection comprises 20th-century Finnish paintings and sculpture. They also purchased a fine collection of modern international art, including Henry Moore's sculptures, rare outside Britain. The museum owns Finland's only collection of Pre-Columbian art by American Indians from 2000 BC to the 16th century AD. The unique collection of oriental art includes Chinese art from the Shang-dynasty to the Ming-dynasty. The modern Villa Didrichsen with a panoramic view of the bay was designed by Viljo Revell in 1959, a noted Finnish architect best known for the Toronto City Hall.

Didrichsenin taide-museo – Didrichsen Art Museum

Reitzin Säätiön kokoelmat – Collection of Reitz Foundation

The museum is the former home of Lauri Reitz, a contractor and successful businessman, who started collecting art when he was a boy. The museum contains paintings, many of them Finnish landscapes, by 19th- and early 20th-century Finnish masters as well as Finnish silver from the 17th to the 19th centuries, old china, and weapons.

Taidekoti Kirpilä – Kirpilä Art Collection

Originally the private home of physician Juhani Kirpilä, who collected art by Finnish artists, from the late 19th-century works to the 1960s informalist work, as well as sculptures, graphic art, and drawings and a collection of Russian porcelain.

Villa Gyllenberg – Villa Gyllenberg Art Collection

The museum, originally the home of the successful banker and celebrated art collector Ane Gyllenberg and his wife Signe, is one of the finest private collections in Finland. The collection covers the high points of Finnish art from the mid-18th century to the mid-20th century and represents all the well-known Finnish artists. Foreign art includes 16th- and 17th-century masterpieces by Titian and Tintoretto among others.

Aallon talo ja Studio Aalto – Villa Aalto and Studio Aalto

Villa Aalto was built in 1936 by architect Alvar Aalto (1898–1976) as his studio and home. The two-story house, made of red and white-painted brick and complemented with dark and white wood, has features which distinguish it from the pure International style of its time. Studio Aalto was built in 1955. The horizontal building turns its back towards the street while the front opens onto the courtyard that slopes down to form an amphitheater.

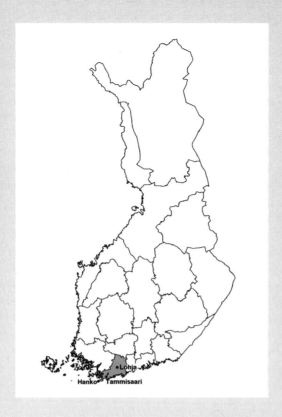

2
Länsi-Uusimaa
Western Uusimaa

The oldest travel itinerary, prepared by the Danes in 1219, describes the route through the western Uusimaa archipelago, with its numerous inlets and small islands. It has provided a protected seaway since ancient times for travelers and sailors, by which the Swedish Varangians could reach the Russian trade centers. The natural beauty of the archipelago attracted Czarina Maria Feodorovna, born Princess Dagmar of Denmark, who liked to stop at what is now called "the Empress's spring" near Tammisaari with Czar Alexander III during several summers of sailing in the Baltic during the 1880s and 1890s.

The coastal area between Helsinki and Turku is one of the oldest settled and most prosperous in Finland. The Finnish place names show that western Uusimaa, which in the early 1200s was still unsettled, was a fishing and hunting ground for the pagan Häme people from further north. From the 1240s onward, Swedish settlers migrated to the western parts of Nyland – New Land – in Finnish, *Uusimaa*. Still today, the coast is mostly Swedish-speaking.

The still extant stone churches dating from the 14th century on are witness to the early settlements. Raasepori Castle was built in the 1370s on the site of an older fort as the main bastion for the Uusimaa area and to counter Tallinn on the southern coast of the Gulf of Finland. The cultural landscape still conveys the importance of the region in medieval times, with the castle ruins rising from the sheer bedrock outcrop and the village north of the castle representing a landscape typical of coastal Uusimaa's cultivated valleys, dotted with well-kept buildings and farms interspersed with rocky forests. The Snappertuna – Fagervik area has been nominated a National Landscape by the Ministry of Environment.

In the 16th century, King Gustav Vasa established towns on the coast as trading rivals to compete for trade with Tallinn, such as Tammisaari and later Helsinki. Tammisaari residents were among those forcibly chosen to settle Helsinki. The irregular medieval street pattern is still visible in Tammisaari, which, along with Porvoo, avoided the "regularization" or grid plan that changed the appearance of Finnish towns.

Stone residential castles, freehold estates, numerous manors, and inns were built along the *Great Coastal Road*, also called the *King's Road*, the main road connecting Turku Castle in the west to Viipuri Castle in the east since the Middle Ages. The villages consisted of several farms with enclosed courtyards. The old industrial villages in western Uusimaa, with their handsome manor houses, workers' quarters and workshops, exemplify the history of Finnish industrialization, the source of wealth in the area. Twenty ironworks were set up in the 17th century, with the help of the Crown, at the access routes for shipping in the western part of the province. The ironworks communities not only provided a livelihood, but also introduced technical skills. The culture of the outside world spread through the owners' manor houses, which again reflected local ways of building and cooking. Many of the smiths at the ironworks were Swedes, Germans, Scots, and

Walloons who brought with them elements of a foreign culture. Many old buildings have survived, yielding insight into early industry and the communities, which grew up around it. Some have been renovated with state support and provide space for new kinds of businesses and residents.

Still during the 20th century the southern coast was militarily important. Under the peace treaty of 1940 following the Winter War, Finland was forced to lease the Hanko Peninsula to the Soviet Union as a naval base until 1941. In 1944, the Cape of Porkkala had to be leased and its 10,000 residents, farms and businesses had to be evacuated in eight days. Big farms and estates were split up and distributed to many of the evacuees from the area, as well as to many of the 400,000 Karelian refugees as well. The rebuilding after the war, and again in 1956 when Porkkala was returned to Finland, resulted in permanent changes in the landscape and social structure, leading to urbanization.

Hanko – Hangö

Because of its long peninsula stretching far out into the Baltic, Hanko has been important for seafaring and defense through the ages. The building of the fortifications on the islands protecting the harbor was started in 1656.

The town of Hanko was incorporated in 1878 with State support as a seaside resort, popular throughout Europe at that time. With its elegant spa and casino, Hanko as part of the Grand Duchy, became a fashionable resort for the wealthy from St. Petersburg who still were permitted to travel there after the Russian Czar banned travel abroad for Russians. Large, two- and three-story villas in the Neo-Renaissance fashion, sprung up during a construction boom in the late 1880s and early 1890s. They are some of the finest examples of this style in Finland, reflecting the wealth of their owners. Still today Hanko is a popular vacation town, having more than 30 kilometers of fine beaches and an annual regatta visited by more than 200,000 tourists.

Hanko, Villa Area

After the Winter War in March 1940, Finland was forced to lease Hanko Peninsula to the Soviet Union as a naval base until 1941. Both Finland and the Soviet Union built chains of fortifications across the peninsula on each side. The best preserved ones have been restored in

Lappohja village where the **Hanko Front Museum** – Hangon rintama-museo – illustrates the events of the war. The casino survived, but the spa was destroyed during the Soviet tenancy.

Linnoitusmuseo – Fortress Museum

The museum is located in the East Harbor in a graystone and brick barrack. The harbor now boasts the largest guest harbor in the country. Cruises to the tallest lighthouse in Scandinavia, the 52-meter high, magnificent granite **Bengtskär Lighthouse** in the outer sea, leave from the harbor.

The West Harbor, the oldest winter port in Finland, was the main port of departure for some 250,000 emigrants from all around Finland and Russia who left for the United States between 1880 and 1930.

Hanko East Harbor

Hauensuoli, "Pike's Gut," a narrow passage between the islands on the southern tip of Hanko, is the ancient port of Hanko. Sea travelers have engraved more than 640 marks or illustrations on the rocks, "the guest book of the islands." These were depicted as early as 1539 in the Swedish bishop Olaus Magnus's famous Carta Marina, published in Italy.

36

The old fishing village of Tammisaari grew up around the 13th-century settlement. King Gustav Vasa incorporated it in 1546 to concentrate foreign trade in the towns by denying the peasants the right to carry on independent trade on the coast. Tammisaari never grew to be an economically important town, but has had since 1601 a primary school, *pedagogio*, and a seminary, established in 1871.

The Old Town is one of the best-preserved wooden towns in Finland. Although the majority of the buildings are from the 18th and 19th centuries, the irregular medieval street pattern is still visible. The street names in the Old Town still reflect the many professions that were needed for self-sufficiency: *Linvävaregatan* – Linen weavers' street and *Hattmakaregatan* – Hatter's street. The Old Town remains a popular residential area, which has been protected by zoning since the 1950s. The charming harbor with old warehouses and yacht clubs is lively during the summer.

Tammisaari Old Town

Tammisaaren museo – Tammisaari Museum

The Museum encompasses a typical block in the Old Town with a courtyard and garden, surrounded by a tall fence. The two-story yellow main building built in 1802, the *Borgargården* or Burgher's House, is a fine townhouse of the Gustavian era of 1775 to1809, named for King Gustav III. It was the home of a prosperous craftsman, a watchmaker, now carefully restored. A house from the 1730s is furnished as a small-town photographer's studio.

Raasepori (*Raseborg*) Castle was built probably in the 1370s to oversee travel and trade by sea in the Gulf of Finland between Tallinn in Estonia, and Uusimaa province. Erected on a stone bluff, the horseshoe-shaped wall encloses the two forecourts, bailey, and the great round tower.

Raaseporin linna – Raasepori Castle

The castle did not become the center of political and military life in western Uusimaa, but around it grew the important marketplace of Tuna. The heyday of the castle was during the years 1465 to 1467, when the exiled King Karl Knutsson Bonde held court there. The castle was abandoned in the 1550s, after the founding of Helsinki and Tammisaari, because of its unsuitability as a base for seafaring. At present the castle is host to many activities in the summer.

Raasepori Castle

Tenholan kirkko – Tenhola Medieval Church

Tenhola (*Tenala*) Church, dedicated to St. Olof, the martyr king of Norway, was completed by the end of the 15th century. The octagonal columns are decorated with paintings on Lutheran themes, surprising for 1675, because the Reformation frowned on paintings as "papal." The church has many valuable objects such as the magnificent painted Baroque-style pulpit from the 1600s and the large 14th-century crucifix hanging from the vault. The walls are decorated with burial coats of arms, most from the 1600s, given by noble families from local estates to the church after funerals.

An old road leads along the beautiful ridge to the village of **Bromarv**, which has many summer villas and private estates.

Pohja – Pojo

Fiskarsin ruukki – Fiskars Ironworks

In 1649 a blast furnace, water-driven hammer forge, and a manufacturing shop was built in Pohja, which became one of the most important producers in Finland of iron products and which grew into the major industrial concern of today. As the need for charcoal increased, more and more of the surrounding lands were bought, so that by the late 1700s the ironworks consisted of 30,000 hectares (75,000 acres) of land.

When in 1757 copper was found nearby, for the first time in Finland

Canal. The cutlery mill has been famous since then for its high-quality products. However, the main product from the middle of the 1850s for the next century was ploughs, more than one million of them. Fiskars has since then become international, its most famous product being the ubiquitous and often-copied orange-handled scissors.

The office building for the engine shop now houses the **Fiskars Museum** – Fiskarsin

Fiskars Ironworks

smiths were able to supply copper hardware for the needs of the entire country. The impressive three-story Empire-style stone mansion of the ironworks, *Stenhuset*, the Stone House, by Charles Bassi, Pehr Granstedt, and C. L. Engel, was constructed from 1816 to 1818.

John Julin gained ownership of the ironworks in 1822 and established the first machine shop in Finland in 1837, bringing in Scottish and Swedish mechanics to provide technical expertise. He hired the most prominent architects of Finland to create factory buildings and workers' living quarters. Fiskars functioned as an independent community, serving its workers' needs through Julin's patriarchal concern.

The first Finnish steam engine was built here, in 1838, as were the iron columns for the six-story Finlayson textile mill in Tampere and the locks for the Saimaa

Museo. A designers' and craftspeople's co-operative functions and holds exhibitions in old factory buildings. The beautiful park along the meandering stream and surrounding the ironworks adds to the charm of the manorial grounds, the red-painted houses, and the old factory buildings.

Billnäsin ruukki – Billnäs Ironworks

The Billnäs Ironworks were founded in 1641 and a blast furnace and two bar-iron hammers built at the rapids. The production of electricity was started in the early 1900s. Billnäs was known not only for its iron products, which were manufactured until 1905, but from the end of 1900s also for its wooden office furniture, now collectors' items.

A stone mill and the pig-iron stores from 1788 are preserved. The castle-like *Villa Billnäs*, designed by Lars Sonck, the well-known Jugend architect, was built in 1917. The well-preserved, red wooden cottages still survive along *Hammarsmedsvägen*, Hammer Smith's Road. The road has retained its original appearance as part of the *King's Road*, which continues further to Tenhola through a most beautiful cultural landscape. The brick hydroelectric power plant from the 1920s is still functional and has been converted into the **Billnäs Power Plant Museum** – Billnäsin Museovoimalaitos.

The ironworks in Pohja offer a unique journey to the sources of Finnish industrialization. In recognition of this, the Ministry of the Environment has designated the area a National Landscape.

Pohja Medieval Church, dedicated to St. Maria, was built after the mid–1400s at the crossroads of the waterway and the medieval *King's Road*. The oldest object in the church is a small wooden sculpture of the Madonna and child from the 13th century. The imposing wooden Pietà-group was made in northern Germany in the early 15th century.

Karjaa – Karis

Mustion linna – Mustio Manor

Mustio (*Svartå*) Ironworks was originally established in the 1500s to process iron ore from the Ojamo mine in Lohja, but was active only a short time. Production started properly in 1616, when a blast furnace and a hammer forge were built.

A grand ironworks mansion called Mustio Castle, one of the finest Gustavian-era buildings in Finland, was built in 1783–92 in Palladian Neo-Classical style, designed by Christoffer Friedrich Schröder, Turku Town Architect, and Erik Palmstedt, the Stockholm Town Architect. The two-story palatial manor, the largest wooden secular building in Finland, is placed on a high slope. It has survived in its original appearance with fine formal interiors, restored by the seventh-generation owner. It now functions as the main attraction for the manor hotel.

A large, English-style park with many rare trees surrounds the buildings. The Neo-Gothic entrance portal as well as the stables and carriage house are from the 1850s. Along the lane, winding through a verdant park, stand the workers' dwellings.

Karjaa Medieval Church looks down from the hill over to the wide-open fields towards the lake. The church, dedicated to St. Katarina, *Catherine*, was built in the 1460s. A wooden Pietà was made in northern Germany in the early 15th century and several wooden statues of saints were probably made by the so-called Master of Karjaa in the 1300s.

Sammatti

Elias Lönnrot

Paikkari Croft, the gray cottage located on the shore of the beautiful lake, was given the name by writer Zacharias Topelius in his illustrated book *Finland framställdt i teckningar*, "Finland Presented in Pictures", published between 1845 and 1852. It is known by every school child as the birthplace and childhood home of Elias Lönnrot (1802–1884), a physician best known as the compiler of the *Kalevala*, the Finnish national epic. He was the collector of Finnish folk poetry, a researcher and journalist, the professor of Finnish language and one of the most important figures of the movement of national awakening. As early as 1889, the Senate decided to preserve it as a museum.

Paikkarin torppa – Paikkari Cottage

The small, wooden, oblong **Sammatti Church**, surmounted by a steep roof, was built in 1755. The church is surrounded by an old cemetery containing a memorial to Lönnrot.

Lohja – Lojo

In Ojamo iron ore was mined already at the beginning of the 1500s for the needs of the surrounding ironworks. Fine manor houses were built in the Lohja area.

The adventurous visitor not only can become familiar with a functioning limestone quarry, opened in 1897, but can also participate in an adventure tour 80 meters below ground in the **Tytyri Limestone Quarry Museum** – Tytyrin kalkkikaivosmuseo. Each summer an art exhibition enlivens the undergound caves.

The church of St. Lauri (*St. Lawrence*) is one of the most handsome medieval stone churches in Finland, profusely decorated with magnificent frescoes between 1514 and 1522, just before the Reformation. The murals, restored to their original glory, follow the sequence of events in

Lohjan kirkko – Lohja Medieval Church

the Bible and the ecclesiastical year. One of the pictures, the only one of its kind in any Finnish church, illustrates the Flood. The third largest medieval stone church in Finland, it was completed around 1510.

A few wooden sculptures have survived from the medieval times, such as the remarkable crucifix, believed to be the work of a Finnish sculptor from the late 15th century.

Lohja Medieval Church

Lohjan museo – Lohja Museum

The Lohja museum is situated on the property of an old parsonage. Surrounded by restored buildings and a well-manicured, large park as well as by a 1700s-style herb garden, it forms a beautiful entity.

The main building presents the culture of the manors and the gentry in Lohja. As a contrast, the house of the parish assistant shows how the peasants and workers lived during the 19th century. The nature, prehistory, and history of the settlement of the Lohja region is displayed in the old Lohja *pedagogio,* a grammar school, was established in 1659.

Inkoo – Ingå

Fagervikin ruukki – Fagervik Ironworks

Fagervik Ironworks are among the most impressive and best preserved in Finland. The manufacture of bar iron was begun in Fagervik in 1646. The operations were expanded after the Great Wrath (1714–21), with production continuing until 1902.

Fagervik

Under the direction of Christoffer Friedrich Schröder, the Town Architect of Turku, graygranite workshops including a drop forge, a bundle forge, and a tinning shed were built in the mid-1700s. Wooden workers' houses were constructed along the main lane of the village. The three-story manor was built in 1762–73 in the style of Rococo Classicism, flanked by two side wings, which complete the formal courtyard.

The formal, terraced French garden was laid in front of the manor and a 50-hectare (125-acre) English nature park, the finest in Finland, was planted in the back of the manor. A Chinese pavilion, unique in Finland, was erected on the lake in 1780–81. As early as in the 1780s, there were grapes, oranges, and lemons grown in the greenhouses and evidently the first potatoes in Finland were planted at Fagervik.

The small, wooden, cruciform **Fagervik Church** was built in 1737. A stone wall surrounds the well-preserved unity. The *Great Coastal Road* closely follows the original medieval route and is preserved as a museum road. The manor and the grounds are still privately owned, but the church and workshops can be visited.

The graystone Inkoo Church, dedicated to St. Nikolaus, the patron saint of seafarers, dominates the village on the bank of the Inkoonjoki River. The church is regarded as one of the earliest stone churches in Uusimaa; the crucifix inside dates from the 14th century. The gables are profusely decorated with unusual brickwork. The church was decorated in the late 1400s with wall paintings depicting popular subjects, such as the Dance of Death, inspired by the epidemic of the Black Death.	Inkoon kirkko – Inkoo Medieval Church

The graystone Inkoo Church, dedicated to St. Nikolaus, the patron saint of seafarers, dominates the village on the bank of the Inkoonjoki River. The church is regarded as one of the earliest stone churches in Uusimaa; the crucifix inside dates from the 14th century. The gables are profusely decorated with unusual brickwork. The church was decorated in the late 1400s with wall paintings depicting popular subjects, such as the Dance of Death, inspired by the epidemic of the Black Death.

Degerby Igor Museum in the village of Degerby reveals the secrets of those bitter and threatening times, called the *Parenthesis*, when Finland was forced to lease the Cape of Porkkala and the surrounding areas as a naval base to the Soviet Union during 1944–56.

Siuntio – Sjundeå

Siuntio Church bears the name of St. Peter, who is illustrated in the wooden sculpture on the pulpits where he carries the keys of Heaven and in the ceiling painting, crucified, his head hanging down. The church was built at the end of the 15th century. Karin Månsdotter's pulpit was donated by Åke Henrikson Tott and his mother Sigrid Vasa, the daughter of King Erik XIV (1533–1577) and Karin Månsdotter. During the Reformation, the wall paintings from the early 1500s were whitewashed, but most have been restored.

Siuntion kirkko – Siuntio Medieval Church

A tree-lined allée leads from the church to Suitia (*Svidja*) Manor, which Erik Fleming, deputy of King Gustav Vasa, started to build in 1541. It is one of the earliest examples of Renaissance culture in Finland, built by master builder Tomas Tomasson from Tallinn. The first floor was reserved

Suitian kartanolinna – Suitia Fortified Manor

for storage and cooking and the second floor for living. For defense, the walls of the first floor are about one meter thick and the windows small. The present Neo-Gothic romantic "castle-look" with Dutch-style steeped gables, pointed-arch windows, and the oak paneling in the medieval spirit, dates from the late 1800s. The University of Helsinki uses the restored manor as a continuing education center.

Kirkkonummi – Kyrkslätt

Hvitträsk

Hvitträsk, the home and studio of architects Herman Gesellius (1874–1916), Armas Lindgren (1874–1929) and Eliel Saarinen (1873–1950), rises on the cliffs above the lake. Built between 1902 and 1903, it is an example of *Gesamtkunstwerk*, a total work of art for its era, from landscaping to the smallest detail of furnishing. It represents the ideas, which were current in Finnish culture in the late 1900s, expressed in the National Romantic Style in which the artist sought to return to nature and a more authentic lifestyle.

The group of buildings rests on granite boulders, and was built from natural stone, brick, logs, and shingles. There are influences from vernacular Karelian architecture, medieval Finnish churches, the English Arts and Crafts movement, and from the American Shingle Style. The rooms

of varying size and height flow from one to another, with a gentle interplay of light and shadow. The main room, a *tupa*, in Saarinen's home draws its influences from Karelian farmhouses while the dining room, with its vaults, murals, and stained glass windows reminds of medieval churches. Eliel Saarinen designed the furniture, and his wife Loja, an accomplished sculptor and textile artist, designed many of the light fixtures and textiles. The Saarinens left for America 1923, but came back every summer until Saarinen's death. Both Saarinens and Gesellius are buried on the grounds.

Karkkila was born around **Högfors Ironworks**, founded in 1820. The heart of the blast furnace, built from stone in 1823, is the only preserved structure from the original ironworks. The log house that the ironworks owner had built in 1858 is the oldest preserved building. The first floor of the two-story building is made in an ashlar pattern to imitate a masonry structure.

By the 19th century, Högfors had become the largest foundry in Finland. Metal building materials and radiators for central heating were needed for the growing towns, and Högfors stoves and pots found their way into every Finnish home. In 1927, the first enameling plant in Scandinavia was established here and its new success article, the bathtub, was popular until the 1970s when it was surpassed in popularity by the shower because of the energy crisis. At the same time Högfors was affected by structural changes in the industry. The factory changed ownership in 1985, but iron manufacturing continues. Active residents' groups have started new types of enterprises and cultural and co-operative events, held in summertime in the machine hall.

The Museum features the history of the Finnish foundry industry. The exhibition displays hand tools, machines, and equipment from various iron, steel, and metal foundries in Finland. The making of molds both mechanically and by hand is demonstrated. There is an interesting collection of old cast iron products from Högfors Ironworks, such as stoves, ovens, cemetery crosses, and decorative objects. The restored blast furnace illustrates the making of pig-iron in Karkkila in 1823–1915.

Suomen valimomuseo – Finland's Foundry Museum

In the Fagerkulla open-air museum, houses have been carefully restored and furnished to convey workers' lives in different eras, ranging from the humble home of a factory worker from the 1890s to a nickeling master's higher class house. Small yards and gardens look as they once did, complete with hens, sheep, and horses.

Karkkila-Högforsin työläismuseo – Karkkila-Högfors Workers' Museum

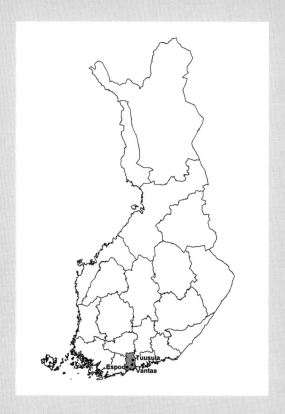

3
Keski-Uusimaa
Central Uusimaa

B efore the Crusades, eastern Uusimaa as far west as the present town of Vantaa had scattered settlements. In addition to the Swedes, settlers from Finland Proper, southwestern Finland, and Häme immigrated there. After the coast was abandoned residents from Helsingland in Sweden were ordered in the late 1200s to move to the valley of the Vantaanjoki River, giving the name *Helsinge* to the whole area, which then became Helsinki Parish. From the 14th century onwards, the *King's Road* connected Turku to Viipuri.

The coast of Uusimaa province was politically important to the Swedish Kingdom. In his campaign against Novgorod and the Orthodox Church, the Swedish king needed financial support and so in 1351 he donated the tenure of a chapel in Helsinge parish to a monastery in Estonia. The monks were also granted the right to fish salmon in the Vantaanjoki River. The main trade route went south to Tallinn which was closer and, as a Hanseatic town, was a more prosperous and international trade partner than Turku or Stockholm. The trade was two-way: from the 1400s there were merchant sailors in central Uusimaa who conducted trade. Lumber was transported as far as Stockholm, and was even used in the construction of the Royal Palace. The rivers and the road leading to Häme Castle carried the trade north.

King Gustav Vasa was interested in establishing a local administration in order to solidify the power of the Swedish crown in the region. He founded Helsinki in 1550 at the mouth of the Vantaanjoki River as a trading rival to Tallinn, but only when Helsinki was moved in 1640 to its present location did trade begin to concentrate in the town. As a result of his nearly year-long visit to Finland in 1555–56, he decided to establish a King's manor in every parish as a model farm to further agriculture and improve the country's defense. Many freehold estates were established, which were exempted from paying taxes in exchange for supplying soldiers and materiel for the continuous wars, and their owners were elevated to the nobility for their services. At the end of the 19th century a quarter of the present Espoo and Vantaa area was owned by the manor houses.

A severe famine, the Great Northern War, and finally the Great Wrath, the Russian occupation of Finland in 1714–21, ended the Swedish years of power. More than half of the estates and manors in the area were abandoned and the eastern part of the country was lost to Russia. The construction of Suomenlinna fortress, begun in 1748, however, boosted the economy around Helsinki and generated an industry of brick manufacturing, limestone mines, iron mines, sawmills, and distilleries. The officers purchased manors and estates built on French Classical models, still mostly in wood, but painted in light shades of gray and yellow. The rebuilding of burned Helsinki as the new capital of an autonomous Grand Duchy of Finland in 1812 provided work to people from the surrounding countryside.

The first railroad in Finland was built from Helsinki north to Hämeenlinna in 1862, and led to the growth of industry and the towns along the line. Summer villas and artists' residences were built in natural settings, inspired by the national romantic ideals of the late 19th century. Tuberculosis sanatoria, a new institution, were built on the Salpausselkä Ridge; its pristine pine forest was regarded as therapeutic. When regular steamship service started along the coast in the 1830s, Espoo became a summer villa haven for well-to-do townspeople, and remained rural until after the Second World War when suburbs with apartment houses started to crop up.

After the war, over 400,000 civilians who had been evacuated from the areas of Karelia that had been ceded to the Soviet Union had to be resettled. The resulting severe housing shortage united the nation in the enormous task of reconstruction. New suburbs based on the garden town idea were built in the immediate postwar years, a time of optimism. Much of the housing was built with low-interest, state-subsidized loans, but was designed by some of the most prominent architects of the time. Since then the population of the capital area has grown to over one million and new suburbs dot the land.

Espoo – Esbo

During his stay in Finland, King Gustav Vasa founded in 1556 **Espoo Manor** as an administrative center. The manor and its environment form a unified historical landscape, the *King's Road* crossing beside the manor mill over the oldest vaulted stone bridge in Finland.

On the *King's Road*, the **Espoo Medieval Church**, dedicated to St. Martinus, *Martin*, stands on the banks of the Espoonjoki River. The oldest parts of the structure date from the 1480s. When the church was restored, medieval paintings depicting the history of the world, and including everyday tasks, such as horse-trading and milking, were uncovered. The grounds around the church still preserve the old atmosphere even though they are surrounded by suburban sprawl.

Glimsin talomuseo – Glims Farmstead Museum

Further east on the *King's Road* is the former Glims farmstead, which functioned as an inn until the early 20th century. The museum arranges exhibitions and theme events.

One of the best preserved parts of the original *King's Road* winds for a few scenic kilometers from Bemböle to **Träskända Manor**. It was once owned by wealthy Aurora Karamzin, a maid of honor to Czarina Alexandra, known for her charitable works. An unusual "imperial latrine," complete with silk wall coverings and velvet upholstered seat built for the Czar's visit in 1863 still stands. The present Classical main building with a heavy Baroque stone portal is from 1921.

The museum is located in the former printing press building, the Wee-Gee Building, architecturally known for its unique structural solution, designed by Aarno Ruusuvuori in 1966. The permanent exhibition with its enchanting displays illustrates Espoo's long history, often ignored in this town known for its technological progress and high-tech companies such as Nokia.

Espoon kaupungin-museo – Espoo City Museum

In the same WeeGee Building the visitor can explore the wonderful collections of Helinä Rautavaara (1928–1998), a modern-day explorer and adventurer who traveled to South America, West and North Africa, and Asia. With an open and curious mind, she immersed herself in faraway cultures and reported on them for forty years for Finnish magazines. She not only collected experiences and objects, but also produced excellent documents. A mixture of ethnographically valuable objects and common tourist souvenirs reflective of her personal style, fill the museum.

Helinä Rautavaaran museo – Helinä Rautavaara Museum

After the Second World War there was an urgent need for housing and new suburbs sprang up around the capital city. The best example of them still today is the internationally famous garden town of Tapiola, which has been designated a National Landscape by the Ministry of the Environment. A nonprofit housing foundation built Tapiola, and the best architects of the time, designed the housing. They gave priority to single family and row houses, most of them built with State loans.

Tapiola Garden Town

Just a kilometer away in Otaniemi is the **Helsinki University of Technology** campus based on the plan by Alvar Aalto who also designed the university's main buildings. Kaija and Heikki Siren designed the intimate **Otaniemi Chapel** in 1957 with a large window opening up to allow the landscape to serve as an altarpiece. Raili and Reima Pietilä's bold **Dipoli**, the Student Union Building, built in 1966 of copper and rock, is already a landmark.

Examples of the extensive artistic output of Akseli Gallen-Kallela (1865–1931), the most famous Finnish painter, graphic artist, and designer of his time, are on display in his studio in Tarvaspää, preserved in its original condition. The castle-like studio home was designed by the artist himself and built in 1911–13. It resembles a Finnish medieval church, with its high vault connected

Gallen-Kallelan Museo – Gallen-Kallela Museum

Akseli Gallen-Kallela 1891

The Aino Myth Triptych, 1891

to the gallery, with the tower in between. The entrance, however, is through a Florence-inspired loggia.

Gallen-Kallela painted the frescoes for the Finnish pavilion in the Paris World's Fair of 1900. Finland having, for the first time, an exhibition in its own name despite increasing pressure by the Czar's government to Russify, was an enormous inspiration to the Finnish people. Gallen-Kallela also executed the wall paintings for the lobby of the National Museum of Finland. The images he created for the heroes of the *Kalevala* still dominate Finns' mental image of the story. His desire to depict real people, together with his interest in the late 19th-century National Romantic idea of Karelia, where the poems of the *Kalevala* were collected, inspired him to travel to Karelia.

The museum, owned by the Finnish Watchmaker Association, is unique in Scandinavia. Hidden in the basement is the spectacle of watches, clocks, and old tools. The museum collects and studies Finnish horology from everyday timepieces dating from the mid–1700s to unique examples of craftsmanship.

Suomen Kellomuseo – Finnish Museum of Horology

Vantaa – Vanda

The old center of the present City of Vantaa, the Helsinge Parish village, with its red cottages and old trees, has been settled since the 1200s at the confluence of the rivers. The well-preserved village contrasts with the surrounding highways and sprawling suburbs, and retains its atmosphere of a few hundred years ago.

Helsinge Parish Medieval Church, dedicated to St. Laurentius, *Lawrence*, was completed in 1494 in the eastern Uusimaa style, with an ornamental brick gable familiar from the Porvoo Cathedral.

The administrative center of the City of Vantaa is in Tikkurila along the country's first railroad line, going from Helsinki to Hämeenlinna and built in 1862. The oldest surviving station building in Finland from 1861 now houses the **Vantaa City Museum** – Vantaan kaupunginmuseo. The museum presents the cultural history of the city.

Helsinge Parish Village in the 18th Century

Heureka
Suomalainen Tiede-
keskus – Heureka,
the Finnish Science
Centre

Heureka is an interactive exhibition and activity center and one of the most popular attractions in Finland, visited to date by more than two million people since its opening in 1989. It has exhibits not only from the natural sciences but also on linguistics, archaeology, and the social sciences. The main exhibition has interactive displays from all areas of

science. Temporary exhibitions cover special subjects and later tour abroad where they are in high demand, with one million visitors in seven countries having seen those produced so far.

The building itself, designed by architects Markku Heikkinen and Mikko Komonen, dynamically expresses the spirit of science with its bold geometric volumes. The main hall is a great cylindrical space intersected by the ball-shaped, mirrored-steel planetarium and the hemispheric theater. Outside the painted steel columns create a spectrum of colors on the slanting, mirrored glass facade, particularly impressive when approaching from a distance.

Suomen Ilmailu-
museo – Finnish
Aviation Museum

The Museum specializes in civil and military aviation history, including the more than 75-year history of Finnair, the national airline. There are civilian and military aircraft on exhibit, including gliders and light planes, as well as engines, propellers, instruments, radio equipment, and scale models. The museum is located at the Helsinki-Vantaa airport, which was opened for the Helsinki Olympic Games in 1952.

The long, closed wall of Myyrmäki Church, built in 1984, is placed against the railroad tracks. The vertical panes of light brick and white wood blend with the white birch trees. For architect Juha Leiviskä, light creates the sacred atmosphere and brings out the richness of the interior. The rhythmic sequence of spaces of different heights has been compared to musical intervals, the light diffusing behind the overlapping planes of the altar wall. The textile work by Kristiina Nyrhinen hangs above the altar and hints of clouds with their shifting shadows and light.

Myyrmäen kirkko –
Myyrmäki Church

Tuusula – Tusby

Tuusula is known for the artists' houses along the Tuusula *Old Lakeshore Road*, which the artists of the Golden Age of Finnish Art at the turn of the 20th century, inspired by the ideals of National Romanticism and the works of Finnish national writer Aleksis Kivi (1834–1872), built there. The museum road, protected since 1982, starts from the wooden cruci-form **Tuusula Church**, erected in 1732–34 by Aleksis Kivi's great-great-grandfather. Kivi is buried in the cemetery.

*Lake Shore with Reeds,
Eero Järnefelt 1905*

The **Worker's Home Museum** – Tuusulan työläis-kotimuseo – an old church-warden's house, is furnished as a carpenter's home and a shoemaker's workshop. Work demonstrations from tar burning to smithery are arranged in the summer.

The **Klaavola Museum** – Klaavola – is located on what was once a prosperous farm. The compound includes a main building dating from the late 18th century, as well as barns, a carriage house, and a sauna.

Tuusula's industrial history is witnessed by the Mariefors Ironworks, founded in 1795, in the interesting **Kellokoski Industrial Area**. The workers' houses and production facilities now offer studios for craftspeople.

Halosenniemi – The Halosenniemi Museum

Pekka Halonen (1865–1933), one of the most beloved Finnish painters, designed for himself a studio home of logs, which was built in 1902 on a narrow rocky point on Lake Tuusulanjärvi. The house, one of the finest early 20th-century artists' wilderness studios, was inspired both by the National Romantic idea of traditional Finnish folk architecture and European Art Nouveau. The unspoiled nature surrounding the house was a lifelong inspiration for Halonen, who looked at the Finnish landscape and folk life through the eyes of both a realist and an idealist. His works played an essential role in the awakening of the Finnish people at the end of the 19th century. His snow-covered winter landscapes made him the "official landscape painter" of independent Finland.

Pekka Halonen

Washing on the Ice, Pekka Halonen 1900

Writer Juhani Aho (1861–1921), known for his socially realistic novels and short stories, and his wife, painter Venny Soldan-Brofeldt (1863–1945), were the first artists to move to a villa they named **Ahola**, in the artists' colony along the Tuusula *Old Lakeshore Road*. Now it houses an exhibition on Juhani Aho.

Järvenpää Art Museum – Järvenpään taidemuseo – in the center of the town exhibits paintings and drawings by Soldan-Brofeldt and Eero Järnefelt (1863–1937), master of the Golden Age of Finnish art, of Lake Tuusulanjärvi landscapes and family members.
The newest artist's house on the shore is **Villa Kokkonen** from 1969, designed by Alvar Aalto for his friend, composer Joonas Kokkonen (1921–1996), the leading personality of post-war Finnish music.

Jean Sibelius (1865–1957), Finland's greatest composer, sought inspiration in the *Kalevala* and in Karelia as did the other artists of his time. This is evident in the symphonic poem *Finlandia*, composed in 1899, which became a symbol of nationalism against the oppression and censorship of the period of Russification in the late 1800s.

Ainola

Jean Sibelius

Ainola

Jean Sibelius and family

Inspired by his brother-in-law, the painter Eero Järnefelt, Sibelius moved to the Lake Tuusulanjärvi shore. He had a house designed by his friend, architect Lars Sonck, known for his National Romantic style. The modest two-story log house, named for his wife Aino, was built in 1904 on a wooded hill facing the fields and lake. The house shares features from Karelian peasant architecture and Swiss cottages. The house is preserved as it was in his day, with memorabilia from his travels, performances of his music, and famous visitors to the house. The log walls are decorated with laurel wreaths and paintings, many done by his friends.

Kerava

**Keravan museo –
Kerava Museum**

The museum is a peaceful oasis right in the center of the town, located in the 18th- century main building of a farmstead. In addition to the main building, the museum area includes barns, a smithy, and farmhands' and tenant farmers' cabins. The museum has a collection of objects from the Stone Age to the present, while the exhibitions concentrate on life in Kerava from the mid-1800s to the 1930s.

**Keravan taidemuseo –
Kerava Art Museum**

When the town of Kerava celebrated its 50th anniversary in 1974, local friends of art channeled the donations mostly into Finnish modern art, to form the Kerava Art Museum. Mrs. Aune Laaksonen, a collector, established the Kerava Art Foundation, with the purpose of making quality contemporary art familiar to the average person. To further augment the collection, an annual Circus Fair was started in the town, reviving the old tradition. From small beginnings, this has developed into the town's most conspicuous public event and has helped to fund acquisition of the present collection of over 1,600 works of modern art; all in a town of only 30,000 residents. Until now the museum has relied on volunteer work.

The museum has a unique collection of original drawings of the Kerava Woodworking Factory, which was established in 1908 and grew into the most important cabinetmaker in Finland. The museum is located in an old red-brick rubber factory, protected as a historic site and renovated with sensitivity to its history.

Nurmijärvi

The birthplace is a museum dedicated to Aleksis Kivi (1834–1872), the Finnish national writer and pioneer of the Finnish-language novel and drama, who was the first major writer to be a native Finnish speaker. Kivi's masterpiece, the humorous and realistic epic novel *Seitsemän veljestä*, "Seven Brothers," is set in Nurmijärvi and has played a central role in developing the Finns' understanding of themselves.

The museum has been furnished as it might have been in Kivi's childhood, and includes some original pieces from the house. Nearby rises Mount Taabor, Kivi's favorite childhood playground, which he named himself. Now it has an open-air theater where local amateur actors have been performing popular stage adaptations of Kivi's plays.

Aleksis Kiven syntymäkoti – Birthplace of Aleksis Kivi

Aleksis Kivi

Hyvinkää – Hyvinge

At the end of the 19th century, Hyvinkää became popular as a spa town. Its location on the pine-covered Salpausselkä Ridge and its healthful air made it ideal, and it was a convenient trip by train to both Helsinki and St. Petersburg.

The expressively modern **Hyvinkää Church** (Aarno Ruusuvuori, 1961), made of two glass pyramids, dominates the townscape.

Suomen Rautatie-museo – The Finnish Railway Museum

The museum is located in the old station area for the Hyvinkää-Hanko line. The park-like grounds feature the restored station houses in addition to a roundhouse and the engine barn. Most of the buildings date from 1873 when the rail line to Hanko was built.

The museum brings to life the history of the Finnish railways starting from the building of the first rail line from Helsinki to Hämeenlinna in 1862. The rolling stock ranges from passenger cars to well-preserved steam engines, and rarities, such as the cars of the Russian imperial family with their original furnishings. Out of the more than one hundred cars the imperial family possessed, only the three in the Museum have survived, the Czar's and the Czarina's coaches and the Czar's saloon car. Those survived while the other cars were destroyed during the Russian Revolution. The steam locomotive park has 13 locomotives, the oldest of them built in 1869, and some of them still functional.

Hyvinkään taidemuseo – Hyvinkää Art Museum

The major part of the museum's permanent exhibition features paintings and drawings by Yrjö Saarinen (1899–1958), who lived in Hyvinkää for thirty years until his death. P. C. E. Sonck, a professor of medicine and a skillful amateur painter, botanist, and folklorist, and a close friend of Saarinen, acquired a considerable collection of his work. Besides Saarinen, Helene Schjerfbeck created many masterpieces while living in Hyvinkää.

For centuries most of the land in Mäntsälä belonged to big manors. For that reason there were more tenant farmers than in other towns in Uusimaa Province and only four independent farming villages. Historically the most interesting of the estates is Alikartano Manor, the childhood home of Adolf Erik Nordenskiöld (1832–1901), the world-famous explorer who was the first to sail the Northeast Passage. He came from a family of pioneers that included fortification officers, alchemists, economists, botanists, mineralogists, cartographers, and mathematicians.

The red-painted wooden main building was designed and built by Nordenskiöld's grandfather in 1805, based on plans in Rococo-era model books. A two-story, sky-blue parlor in the middle of the house, unique in Finland, is encircled by twelve rooms. Light enters from windows on the gallery level where the library is located. The older main building together with other buildings form a symmetrical layout stylistically typical of the early 18th century. Exhibitions illustrate the scientific interests and achievements of the Nordenskiöld family.

Sälinkää Manor at one time included 7,300 hectares (18,250 acres) of land, but later the lands were distributed to tenant farmers, refugees, and returning soldiers. The main building now houses a catering restaurant.

The main building of **Saari Manor** from 1929 ranks among the most remarkable of its era and is one of the last large residences built in Finland. The Classical white stuccoed building combines Italian and Scandinavian features, surrounded by beautifully symmetrical, terraced gardens.

The **Hirvihaara Manor**, built in 1918, is now restored and houses a handsome hotel and restaurant.

Sepänmäki, literally Smith's Hill, belongs to the public lands of the village and in the 18th century was given for the use of a smithy. Little by little, other craftsmen settled around, and it became a kind of service center not only for the village but also for the larger area. The last craftsman, a village smith, died in the 1950s and Sepänmäki was abandoned. At the initiative of the village residents, the buildings were restored. The museum tells in an interesting and entertaining way about life and work in bygone days. Every second year, the national folk music and dance festival *Sepän Soitto* fills the village with enthusiastic visitors.

Alikartano –
Alikartano Manor

Adolf Erik Nordenskiöld

Sepänmäen käsityö-
museo – Sepänmäki
Handicraft Museum

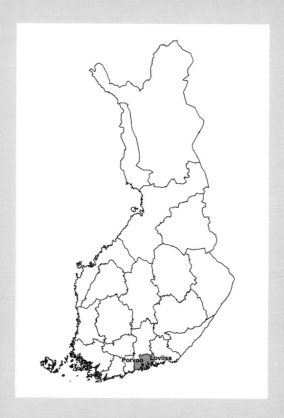

4
Itä-Uusimaa
Eastern Uusimaa

races of the earliest settlements, found in Askola in the Porvoonjoki River valley, are from the so-called "Askola Civilization" of 9000 years ago. Later Vikings and Hansa merchants from the west and the Varangians from the east traded on the coast. Around the year 1200 a strategic location at the mouth of the Porvoonjoki River was fortified as Castle Hill to protect the trade and later grew to become the town of Porvoo.

From the 1240s onwards, the eastern part of Uusimaa, populated at that time by Karelians politically allied with Novgorod, was settled by Swedish colonialists on order of the Swedish king to ensure his trade routes to the east. Politically and religiously, the area was unified with Sweden under the Treaty of Pähkinäsaari in 1323. The *King's Road* ran from Turku to Viipuri via Porvoo and Loviisa. At that time, the most important trading center, however, was Tallinn on the southern coast of the Gulf of Finland. Porvoo became a trading center. Goods from Central Europe traveled via Porvoo northward, and furs, timber, tar, dried fish, butter, and linen were transported via Tallinn to the south.

Eastern Uusimaa has played an important role in Finnish history, constantly the battlefield for border disputes. During the Great Northern War in 1700–21, the Russians burned down all the coastal towns. The Treaty of Turku in 1743 gave Russia the eastern part of Finland, all the way to the Kymijoki River which it started fortifying. As a result, Sweden started building fortifications in the present Loviisa, as well as Sveaborg, now called Suomenlinna in Helsinki and at the border crossing on the Kymijoki River. Loviisa became the capital of Kyminkartano and Savo provinces, and one of three towns in Finland permitted free access to foreign trade. The fortifications were never of any great military significance; instead Loviisa developed into a prosperous seafaring and spa town.

In spite of continuous wars, the eastern coast was continuously settled and farmed, as witnessed still today by the many medieval stone churches. By the end of the 16th-century, freehold farms, whose owners were exempted from land dues, were founded in Eastern Uusimaa. In the 17th century, the establishment of large farms worked by day laborers who were tenants and crofters was initiated by noble families, most of them from the Baltic lands. As a result of farming, and later prosperous trade and industry, some of the most magnificent manor houses in Finland were built in the region. As early as 1682 an ironworks in Koskenkylä, Pernaja, was established and contained a blast furnace and two hammer forges. After the ironworks closed, a sawmill and brickworks operated there.

Porvoo developed as a cultural center for the area. The building of the church was started in the 13th century, and the church is today the only structure surviving from the Middle Ages. Fine stone buildings were erected, including the town hall and the grammar school in the mid-

1700s. After the town of Viipuri was left on the Russian side of the border in 1721, the Viipuri Grammar School was transferred to Porvoo and reopened there in 1725. It housed the oldest completely preserved Finnish library, opened three years later. The Finnish national poet, J. L. Runeberg lived in Porvoo and taught in the school. His heroic poem, *Fänrik Ståls sägner*, "The Tales of Ensign Stål," published in 1848, includes the poem *Vårt land*, "Our Land," which later became Finland's national anthem, even though it was written in Swedish. It emphasizes love for Finland's nature. During the Russification campaign at the turn of the century, Porvoo was seen as the cradle of the nation. At that time, the popular movement to save the old town was initiated by Louis Sparre, the Swedish-born artist who settled in Finland.

Porvoo – Borgå

Children Playing on the Shore, Albert Edelfelt 1884

Porvoo, in Swedish literally "castle river," was named for the fortifications constructed there. Porvoo was granted its charter after Turku, probably in 1346 by King Magnus Eriksson when he visited the town. There were only six towns in Finland in the Middle Ages, and like others, Porvoo was

small and its wooden houses have burned down many times over the centuries. The only building to have survived from the Middle Ages is the graystone church, which still dominates the townscape. Even though most of the houses around the church date from after the fire of 1760, Porvoo alone in Finland has retained its medieval town plan which is still visible in the street layout. Vestiges of the earlier flourishing trade, the riverside storehouses, painted in red ochre and built in the late 1700s and early 1800s, are still an inseparable part of the Porvoo riverscape. The Ministry of the Environment has designated Porvoo and the Porvoonjoki River valley as a National Landscape.

The route mail from Turku to Viipuri was transported via Postimäki (*Postbacken*) – literally Postal Hill in Ilola (*Illby*) Village on the *King's Road*. Its dozen craftsmen's and small tenants' cottages are well-preserved.

Hörbersgården Museum on the island of Pellinki describes life in the archipelago in the late 19th century. Tove Jansson, the creator of the world-famous Moomintroll books, kept a summer cabin on the island of Klovharun, which is now part of the museum.

Porvoon tuomiokirkko –
Porvoo Cathedral

The Porvoo Cathedral was built around 1410 and expanded some years later to its present size under Carsten Nübuhr of Rostock who built the Gothic star vaults and rich brick ornaments of the gable, typical of Uusimaa province. The church was whitewashed on the outside.

The church was plundered many times during its history and the vaults were rebuilt. The unusual galleries on two levels as well as the Rococo-style pulpit were made by local artisans in the 1760s, painted in faux marble. Medieval frescoes from the end of the 15th century can be seen on some of the walls and vaults. The Finns, in turn, as a tax for not burning the town of Osnabrück in Germany during the Thirty Years' War

in 1633, confiscated an ornate guilt chalice made by silversmith Sifridus in the 1240s. Now this extremely fine artwork, one of the ten most valuable of its kind in the world, is brought to the altar during services.

The Porvoo church became a cathedral in 1723 when the Episcopal See moved from Viipuri to Porvoo. Today all of Finland's Swedish-speaking Lutheran congregations belong to the Diocese of Porvoo. It was in the Porvoo Cathedral that the foundation for Finland's independence was laid. After Sweden had lost Finland to Russia, the first Diet of Finland met in March 1809. Czar Alexander I ceremonially declared Finland an autonomous Grand Duchy of the Russian Empire, and speaking in the customary French, *"placée désormais au rang des nations"*–*"elevated Finland to membership in the family of nations"* by ratifying *"the religion and fundamental Laws of the Land..."*

Porvoon museo –
Porvoo Museum

The **Historical Museum** is located in the two-story Classical old town hall with a wooden clock tower, built in 1764. The museum presents the history and culture of the Porvoo area and eastern Uusimaa when trade prospered.

The **Edelfelt-Vallgren Museum** – Edelfelt-Vallgren museo – located next door in a merchant's house from 1762, is dedicated to Albert Edelfelt (1854–

1905) and Ville Vallgren (1855–1940). Edelfelt was the internationally best-known Finnish artist at the time, painting historical scenes, portraits, and also Finnish folk and landscapes. In France he became famous for his portrait of Louis Pasteur, the French scientist, for which he was awarded the Grand Prix d'Honneur at the World Exposition in Paris in 1889 and which was purchased by the French Republic. Every summer Edelfelt returned from Paris to Haikko Manor where he had a studio built in 1883, now the **Albert Edelfelt Studio Museum** – Albert Edelfeltin Ateljeemuseo.

Ville Vallgren

Ville Vallgren, a sculptor, also won a gold medal for his "Christ's Head" at the World Exposition. In Finland, he is known for his much loved fountain statue, *Havis Amanda*, in Helsinki's marketplace. Vallgren, too, lived in Paris.

A Swedish-born artist, Count Louis Sparre helped to set up the Iris Factory in 1897, inspired by the English designer William Morris, to produce contemporary utilitarian objects of high artistic quality. Sparre's simple but elegant furniture has influences both from international Art Nouveau and from the Finnish National Romantic style. He was inspired by the *Kalevala*, the Finnish national epic.

Iris Factory Ceramics, A. W. Finch

J. L. Runegergin koti – Home of J. L. Runeberg

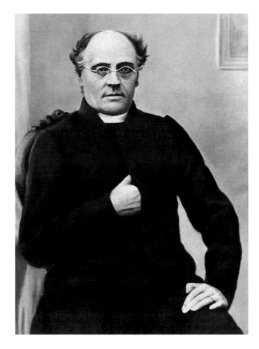

Johan Ludvig Runeberg

The national poet Johan Ludvig Runeberg (1804–1877) and his wife Fredrika, herself an accomplished writer, settled in the large burger's house in the Empire-style part of town. The authors and artists living in Porvoo, with Runeberg at the forefront, greatly contributed to the advancement of the national culture. Runeberg's home has been a museum since 1882. The interiors, furnishings, and objects are all original.

Walter Runebergin veistoskokoelma – The Walter Runeberg Sculpture Collection

One block from Runeberg's home is his son Walter's (1838–1920) sculpture collection of art, plaster casts, portraits, and sketches. Walter Runeberg became the first successful Finnish sculptor because of his Neo-Classical works which carry a spirit of idealistic lyricism. Even though he lived more than thirty years in Rome and Paris, he was the natural choice to sculpt statues of his father, one in Helsinki's Esplanadi Park and the other in Porvoo.

Runeberg also sculpted the statues of Count Per Brahe, Governor of Finland during the Swedish era, in Turku, and Czar Alexander II in Helsinki, rulers who were favored by the Finnish people.

Yrjö A. Jäntin Taidekokoelma – Yrjö A. Jäntti's Art Collection

Yrjö A. Jäntti, the former president of WSOY publishing house, passionately collected art. His collection of more than a thousand works decorated his house until 1984 when he donated it to the town of Porvoo. Love of beauty, in his own words, guided him in his acquisitions of Finnish paintings, graphic art, and miniature sculptures, a condensed survey of older Finnish art.

Sipoo – Sibbo

Sipoo Medieval Church, together with the new church, dominate the open river valley where the Sipoonjoki River and the *King's Road* meet. The graystone church, dedicated to St. Sigfrid, was built around 1450. The vaults and walls are decorated with medieval paintings of foliage, consecration crosses, solar emblems and trees of life. The medieval atmosphere is emphasized by the lack of balconies and pews, which were removed after the new church was built.

Since the Middle Ages, Pernaja has been distinguished by the most magnificent manor houses in Finland, still privately owned. **Suur-Sarvilahti Estate** (*Sarvlaks*), a three-story stone building in the style of Dutch Baroque Classicism, built in 1672–83, is one of the most impressive of Finland's fortified manors. **Tervik Manor**, built in 1710, has valuable interiors and one of Finland's most extensive private collections of portraits in its splendid halls.

Pernaja is called the birthplace of Finnish literature because Michael Agricola (ca 1510–1557), the creator of Finnish as a written language, was born there. He brought the Reformation to Finland after studying in Wittenberg in Germany and translated the New Testament into Finnish in 1548. The idea was to make the written Bible available to all Finns. The Church set the literacy as a prerequisite for marriage, both for women and men. Agricola became the Bishop of Turku.

The road to the **Rönnäs Archipelago Museum** – Rönnäsin saaristolais-museo – passes through the idyllic village of old Isnäs. The museum presents the life, culture, and boatbuilding in the eastern Uusimaa archipelago.

The **Koskenkylä** (*Forsby*) **Ironworks** operated from 1682 until the 1830s. The remains of a hammer works and quarried river bed have survived. The stone main building of Forsby Estate (1908) is surrounded by a garden.

The whitewashed graystone Pernaja Church, dedicated to St. Mikael, is located along the *King's Road* where the beautiful cultural landscape opens out onto the bay. Vaults are decorated by murals of clover leaves and sundials. The unusually fine altar screen is north German work from around 1500. The many funeral coats-of-arms of the local nobility reflect the grand history of Pernaja.

Pernajan kirkko – Pernaja Medieval Church

Adjoining the church is a park with a statue of Michael Agricola, originally located in Viipuri in present-day Russia, that was moved to the site in 1959. Agricola was buried in Viipuri Cathedral, which was destroyed in the Second World War.

Lapinjärvi – Lappträsk

The charming village of **Lapinjärvi** is unusually well-preserved. Traditional farm buildings line the birch-lined lane to Vasarakylä hamlet. Both wooden churches, the Big Church for the Swedish-speaking congregation, and the Little Church for the Finnish congregation were built in 1744 after lightning struck and burned the previous churches.

Loviisa – Lovisa

Loviisa

Loviisa, originally called Degerby, was founded in 1745 as Sweden's eastern outpost after the crown had lost lands east of Kymijoki River to Russia two years earlier. King Adolf Fredrik renamed the town after Queen Lovisa Ulrika.

A town plan was the first in Finland to be based strictly on Classical principles. In addition to the military installations, only the two-story **Commandant's House** and a few burghers' houses were completed. The Old Town around the Degerby Cavalry Estate luckily survived the great fire of 1855 and now ranks among the best-preserved wooden towns in Finland. After the fire, the town was rebuilt in the Neo-Gothic fashion. However, **Town Hall** (1862) was inspired by the Italian Renaissance. During the Russian period in the 19th century, Loviisa developed into a prosperous spa and seafaring town.

Svartholman linnake – Svartholm Fortress

Soon after the town was established, fortification of Loviisa was initiated by the Swedish Diet. The fortification of Svartholm Island, a square redoubt of 120 meters to the side, has sharply pointed bastions at the

corners complemented by vaulted casemates and two-story curtain structures. Additional work continued until the fortress was surrendered to the Russians in 1808 with virtually no resistance. By the time the English bombed the fortress into rubble in 1855, Svartholm had been abandoned. Now restored, it houses an exhibition describing the history of Svartholm and objects found during the restoration.

The Rosen and Ungern granite bastions, the foundations of the Adolf Fredrik bastions along the *Old Viipurintie Road*, and remnants of the earthern ramparts in various parts of the town are preserved.

The museum is located in the Commandant's House, built in 1755 as part of the fortress. The exhibitions illustrate life in the town, ranging from crafts and trade, seafaring and fortress life to Loviisa as a spa town. There is a remarkable collection of glass, china, and silver. An unusual tin workshop has molds and tin objects.

Loviisan kaupungin-museo – Loviisa Town Museum

Loviisan Merenkulku-museo – Loviisa Maritime Museum

The museum documents merchant shipping in Loviisa. It is located in a log structure built in the style of an old salt storage house in the historic harbor. The exhibitions detail Loviisa's seafaring history with scale models of ships, seamen's chests, naval paintings, and other maritime objects. The museum also owns the historic tugboat *Onni*, built in 1907.

Ruotsinpyhtää – Strömfors

Rod-iron was hammered in the Strömfors Ironworks on the shores of the Kymijoki River until the mid-20th century, longer than anywhere else in Finland. It is also one of the oldest ironworks in Finland, dating from 1698. When Pyhtää was left on the Russian side of the border in the Turku Treaty 1743, the area on the Swedish side was named Ruotsinpyh-tää – literally Swedish Pyhtää.

The appearance of the ironworks dates from "The Days of Her Grace," when Virginia af Forselles, who had inherited it in the 1780s as a

Strömforsin ruukki – Strömfors Ironworks

Strömfors Ironworks

young widow, ruled it. The ironworks grew into a prosperous industrial community. The handsome "Grace Castle," a two-story log building was built in 1824 for the manager and the office staff. Conservatism and a patriarchal way of life kept the village unchanged. The idyllic village with its red cottages, red-brick factories, and old trees reflected on the waters of the river has preserved its original atmosphere. The restored nail forge houses a drop forge and its machinery, and a portion of the furnace has been preserved. The restored buildings provide spaces for craftspeople and residents, making it a thriving village.

The unusual, octagonal wooden **Ruotsinpyhtää Church** was built for the community in 1772. The small church has a beautiful altar painting by the well-known artist Helene Schjerfbeck.

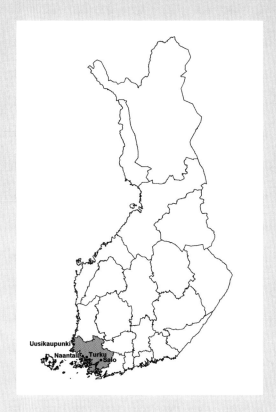

5
Varsinais-Suomi
Finland Proper

As the name "Finland Proper" connotes and its many archaeological sites bear witness to, this area is the historical center of Finland. Permanent settlements were established on the fertile banks of the Aurajoki River during the Iron Age. Trade later moved down to Koroinen when the sea level fell and the river upstream was no longer navigable. Trade brought Christian influences even before the so-called First Crusade to Finland, led by King Erik of Sweden and the English-born Bishop Henry of Uppsala, in 1155 according to popular legend. The recorded history of Finland can be said to have begun with the crusade. The seat of the first bishop of Finland, St. Henry or Henrik, was located in Nousiainen, north of present-day Turku, but was moved in 1229 to Koroinen.

As the land continued to rise, commerce centered on the site of the present Turku Cathedral. German merchants built a wooden church for their settlement in the 1250s, which was replaced by a larger brick church. The establishment of the Dominican monastery in 1249 and the consecration of the Cathedral in 1300, as well as the building of the citadel at the mouth of the river, made Turku the administrative and ecclesiastic center for the Swedish province of Finland, connecting the country to western culture.

The prosperity of the area is seen in the many noble estates and medieval stone churches. Most of the stone churches were built on the site of earlier wooden churches. The sturdy rectangular naves were built of large graystone blocks. The only features of the continental Gothic style are the high-pitched roofs and the brick ornamentation around the door and window openings on the gables. The first Finnish works of art – wooden statues, crucifixes, and wall paintings – embellished the churches. The age of these churches is currently debated, since recent research suggests that many of them are somewhat younger than originally thought.

Villages were heterogeneous after the 17th century, and included cavalry farmers, crown and freehold farmers, crofters, and cottagers. Houses were built around an enclosed square yard divided into household and livestock yards and separated by a fence. The floor plans of manors and parsonages with more than two rooms were adopted by the peasants by the late 18th century. The area is also called *Vakka-Suomi*, "wooden-box Finland," for the locally crafted wooden containers that were the most popular export article from the 15th to the 19th centuries.

The Archipelago Sea, one of the most extensive island systems in the world comprising 40,000 beautifully rugged islands and skerries, links the area to Sweden. It has been designated a National Landscape by the Ministry of the Environment. The archipelago has a long history of human settlement. Numerous antiquities, including stone labyrinths, ancient foundations, and ruins of chapels attest to the island's civilization.

The area around the imposing Turku Cathedral, the only medieval cathedral-size church in Finland, can rightly be called the cradle of Finnish civilization. Finland's first school, the Turku Cathedral School, was a seminary established here in the late 13th century. The newly appointed Governor General of Finland, the Swedish Count Per Brahe, established Turku Academy in 1640, the first university in the country. The magnificent basilica-like festival hall of the Academy, built in 1801–15, is one of the finest interiors of Gustavian Neoclassicism.

After Russia captured Finland from Sweden in the war of 1808–09, Turku lost its position as Finland's capital and was no longer the most important town when the Emperor ordered in 1812 that the seat of government was to be moved to Helsinki. The city suffered another crushing blow in the great fire of 1827, the largest fire ever in a Nordic country, which razed most of the city. Among the valuables lost in the fire was the library of the university with its irreplaceable archives. Adding insult to injury, the Czar ordered that the Academy, too, must go to Helsinki. Nonetheless, Turku's noble history is visible still.

Turku – Åbo

Turku Castle was established at the mouth of the Aurajoki River in the 1280s as an administrative stronghold of the Swedish crown and a residence for the governor. Originally a rectangular fortified camp, in the 14th century it was enlarged by dividing the large courtyard into a bailey and a keep. When the castle was rebuilt in the Gothic style, three-story wing buildings were added on all four sides and a King's Chamber and a Nuns' Chapel were built. With some 40 rooms, it became one of the largest castles in northern Europe. In the 1480s the eastern tower was heightened and the church was built.

Turun linna – Turku Castle

The most splendid period for the castle was in 1556–63 during the governorship of Duke Johan, King Gustav Vasa's son. His wife, Princess Katarina Jagellonica, the sister of the King of Poland, brought the culture of a Continental Renaissance court to Turku. Above the dark, medieval rooms a residence floor was built with grand King's and Queen's Halls, embellished by large glazed windows. The stairway tower and a wide Renaissance staircase were built, one of the first in Scandinavia. In 1568 Johan seized power from his brother Erik XIV and kept him imprisoned in the castle from 1570 to 1571.

In 1614, a fire destroyed the castle leaving only the graystone walls standing. It was rebuilt, but gradually fell into disrepair. Finally the castle was badly ravaged by bombing during the Finnish-Soviet War in 1941. The tedious restoration and rebuilding work, started already before the war, continued until 1980.

The castle houses the **Turku Historical Museum** – Turun kaupungin historiallinen museo – established in 1881 in the forecourt. It has exhibits on the history of Turku and its surroundings.

Turun tuomiokirkko – Turku Cathedral

Turku Cathedral is unique in being the sole medieval cathedral in Finland, the Archbishop's See for the Finnish-speaking congregations, and the most Magnificat record of Finnish architectural history.

A rectangular stone sacristy was built in the late 13th century on the foundations of an earlier wooden sanctuary. It was consecrated as the Cathedral Church of the Virgin Mary and St. Henrik, the first bishop of Finland, in 1300 when his relics were brought in a festival procession from Nousiainen. Soon after, in 1318, the church was destroyed by plunderers from Novgorod. The church was rebuilt and extended with a five-sided chancel in full Gothic style.

The Great Fire of Turku 1827

In the 15th century the chancel was replaced with a new, immense three-naved version surrounded by chapels dedicated to different saints, making the church in fact five-aisled. Since daylight in the church was virtually blocked, the central aisle was raised. The demanding work of building the high groin vaults in 1466 was directed by Pietari Kemiöläinen, or Petrus Murator as he was called in Latin, turning the church into a basilica that became the town's dominant feature. By the 16th century, the cathedral had taken on its current appearance. After the Reformation in 1524, the side chapels were converted into funeral vaults for bishops and military leaders. The only royal tomb in Finland is the sarcophagus of Queen Karin Månsdotter, the wife of imprisoned King Erik XIV, buried here in 1613.

The church suffered fire damage many times, and in 1827 the great fire of Turku destroyed the interior and the tower. The church was soon refurnished and a new spire on the tower, designed by C. L. Engel combining Neo-Classical and Gothic styles, was built in 1831. The Romantic style frescoes in the main chancel were executed in 1850 by the well-known court painter Robert Wilhelm Ekman.

Vanha Suurtori, the Old Great Square and the block surrounding it, is the only stone quarter in Finland that has retained medieval characteristics and is a remnant of Finland's oldest urban culture. The shape of the square itself speaks of international influences: it is of the Hanseatic type, similar to the squares in Danzig and Tartu. All the main roads in the country – the *Great Coastal Road*, the *Häme Oxen Road* east, and the Satakunta Road north – led to the square. The sea route to Åland began at the nearby quay on the Aurajoki River, extending onwards to Stockholm.

Vanha Suurtori – ‹
Old Great Square

After the great fire in 1827, the town was rebuilt following the Classical open plan of C. L. Engel. Around the square itself, new buildings were built on the foundations of the burned houses. The **Brinkkala House** was constructed atop a medieval first story in 1828. Turku is the only town in Scandinavia where the custom of declaring a public and special peace for Christmas has survived uninterrupted, except during the World War II, from the Middle Ages to the present day. On Christmas Eve Day, thousands of people gather in front of Brinkkala House to hear this medieval declaration, which has also been broadcast nationwide on radio since 1935, and is now also on television.

The two-story Neo-Classical stone structures around the square, stuccoed in pastel colors, form a unity. Several buildings were designed by Carlo or Charles Bassi, the Italian-born Swedish architect, first director of the Intendant's Office after Finland became part of Russia. Each July a colorful Medieval Market with more than a hundred performers, from musicians to merchants, fill the Square.

Turku Synagogue on the other side of the river has been preserved in its original 1912 Art Nouveau appearance.

Luostarinmäen
käsityöläismuseo –
Luostarinmäki
Handicrafts Museum

The only large area to escape the fire of 1827 was the *Luostarinmäki* wooden craftsmen's village, then on the edge of the town. In 1940, the area was opened as a museum for the crafts practiced by the people who had lived in the houses and to commemorate Turku as a handicrafts center during the guild period.

The museum area today comprises 18 modest wooden houses, with over thirty workshops. During the summer months, visitors can see craftspeople at work, continuing the traditions of the 18th- and 19th-century shoemakers, weavers, watchmakers, and saddlers, as well as of lace and violin makers. Its narrow lanes and small gardens complete a picture of life from another, distant era.

The Qwensel House is the oldest grand bourgeois house extant in Turku, built around 1700. The main building along the street is now restored as a fine upper class house from the late 18th century with rooms furnished in Rococo and Gustavian styles. It is an example of an urban yet self-sufficient life – an outbuilding in the closed yard included a bakery, a servant's hut, a stable, and a cowshed.

Apteekkimuseo ja Qwenselin talo – Pharmacy Museum and Qwensel House

A wing, added after the great fire, now has a 19th-century pharmacy with an herb room and two laboratories. The pharmacy has the oldest preserved original pharmacy interiors in Finland.

A major find was made when the Rettig Palace, built in a Baroque-inspired Classical style in 1928, was being renovated for the art museum. Beneath the garden, seven metres underground, an entire city block was unearthed. Building foundations and other items dating back as far as 1300 were left in place and the complex was expanded to include two museums. It was named for the famous academic work *Aboa vetus et nova* from 1700 by Daniel Juslenius, professor and later Bishop.

Aboa Vetus & Ars Nova -museot – Aboa Vetus & Ars Nova Museum

The **Aboa Vetus**, Old Turku, museum is built around the medieval cellars and alleys. One can walk around the old buildings, streets, and archaeological finds in their original locations. The excavation revealed over 40,000 objects. Interesting multimedia programs illustrate the Middle Ages.

The visitor steps into the present time above in the **Ars Nova**, New Art, which displays The Matti Koivurinta Foundation's collection of Finnish and foreign contemporary art. The multimedia programs present artists and their works.

Turku Drawing School, the first art school in Finland, dates from 1830 and played an important role in Turku's art life. Victor Westerholm, known for his Impressionistic landscape paintings, was the principal of the school and active in the founding of the Turku Art Society in 1891. The Society opened the museum in 1904 in the impressive granite castle built in Jugend style, influenced by American and Anglo-Saxon architecture popular in that day.

Turun taidemuseo – Turku Art Museum

Thanks to Westerholm, the museum can boast the second largest and most important art collection in the country. The collection of early 20th-century Finnish art, known as the Golden Age, is excellent. The purchases were progressive at the time and have since become national icons.

There are also samples of Scandinavian art and a considerable number of international graphics works.

The museum is temporarily housed in the Observatory, the oldest such building in Finland, while renovation of the museum building is being carried out. The Observatory was designed by C. L. Engel, one of his first works in Finland, in 1817.

Wäinö Aaltonen

Wäinö Aaltosen museo – Wäinö Aaltonen Museum

The city of Turku started to purchase art from Turku artists in 1937 in order to create its own art collection. The museum, established to honor the town's famous son, the sculptor Wäinö Aaltonen (1894–1966), and opened to the public in 1967, was designed by his son Matti Aaltonen and daughter-in-law Irma Aaltonen.

The museum contains mainly Finnish contemporary art and Wäinö Aaltonen's sculptures, paintings, graphic works, and drawings, donated to the museum. Jussi Mäntynen's sculptures were donated by the artist. Currently the museum has a total of 4,500 pieces of art, half of them in the museum and the remainder in city offices and public spaces. More than 50 sculptures are displayed outdoors in the city.

Sibelius-museo – Sibelius Museum

The museum is part of the Åbo Akademi University and the only music museum in Finland. It was established in 1926 with donations of instruments and historical material. It was named for Jean Sibelius, the renowned Finnish composer, whose manuscripts and first editions of compositions, as well as letters and notes, are exhibited.

Forum Marinum

Forum Marinum on the bank of the Aurajoki River is housed in a former crown granary. The **Maritime Museum** illustrates modern seafaring with exhibitions and through practical demonstrations on repair and restoration of vessels. The exhibitions at the **Finnish Naval Museum** present the history of the Finnish navy and equipment such as mines and gunboats. Since the Middle Ages, small boats and large vessels alike have been built in Turku; commercial shipbuilding started in 1737. The building of steamships started in 1862 and made Turku the leading dock in Finland.

Various museum ships can be visited during the summer months. The museum's flagship, the frigate *Suomen Joutsen*, "The Swan of Finland," was built in France in 1902 as a cargo vessel and then served as a training ship for the Finnish Navy and as a school for seamen. The mine carrier *Keihässalmi* was launched in 1957. The *Vetäjä V*, built in 1891, was the last steam-powered tugboat active in Finnish waters. Since 1939, the *Sigyn*, the world's last surviving three-masted wooden bark launched in Gothenburg in 1887, has been a museumship.

The museum is located in a beautiful Art Nouveau building from 1907. Its permanent exhibition combines natural science, art, and craftsmanship by displaying Finnish flora and fauna in their natural settings in three-dimensional dioramas with wonderfully painted backgrounds.

Turun Biologinen museo – Turku Biological Museum

Kylämäki village at Kurala has been inhabited continuously since the Iron Age. The village is a center for studies in experimental archaeological research. In the workshops children and adults alike can be archaeologists for a day, reconstructing objects based on archaeological findings.

Kuralan Kylämäki – Kurala Kylämäki Museum

Kaarina – S:t Karins

The Kuusisto estate was a center for administration and defense for the Catholic Bishops of Turku going back to the late 13th century. After the first wooden fort was destroyed by the Novgorodians in 1318, a new stone fort was built. At the beginning of the 15th century it was rebuilt to

Kuusiston piispanlinna ja kartano – Kuusisto Bishop's Castle and Estate

Kuusisto Estate

include living spaces. It was torn down in 1528, during the Reformation when the property of the Catholic church was confiscated by the Crown. The ruins of the castle, on the coast but protected by the archipelago, were unearthed in the 1870s, and reconstruction work has slowly been in progress since then.

A marked culture and nature path leads to the main building of the royal manor of **Kuusisto Estate**, one of the oldest surviving wooden manor houses, dating from 1738. It has an unusual steep Baroque hipped roof and fragments of Rococo interiors. It was built as the official residence for the commander of the Finnish Army, the colonel of the Turku Infantry Regiment. Its restored rooms house exhibitions on the history of the castle and the estate as well as on the rich flora and fauna of Kuusisto.

The small, wooden **Kuusisto Church** was built in 1792 and commands the landscape. The oblong sanctuary has unusual cloth wall coverings painted with large Corinthian columns.

Lieto – Lundo

Liedon Vanhalinna – Vanhalinna Museum

The museum, beautifully situated in the historic Aurajoki River landscape alongside the old *Häme Oxen Road*, was a former home of Mauno and Ester Wanhalinna, which they donated to the University of Turku. Vanhalinna Hill next to the house is the site of an exceptionally fine prehistoric hill fort. Several archaeological excavations have been carried out since the late 1800s, uncovering settlements from the Bronze Age to the 14th century, as well as an unusual abundance of artifacts from the Viking Age (800–1000 AD). The remains of a cemetery from the time of the Romans (100 AD) and one from the Viking period were unearthed. The Aurajoki River valley has been designated a National Landscape by the Ministry of the Environment.

The hill was named Vanhalinna, "The Old Castle," after completion of the new castle in Turku in the late 13th century. The estate has been settled since the Middle Ages. The present main building, built in 1930 in the Neo-Classical style, reflects the collectors' enthusiasm with its valuable furnishings. The exhibitions range from archaeology and the prehistory of southwestern Finland to agricultural and preindustrial Finland. The extensive ethnological collections provide a picture of Finnish folk life and serve as a teaching exhibition for the university. There are signposted nature and culture paths around the museum area through a varied and traditional flora.

Lieto Medieval Church, consecrated to St. Peter, was built in the early 16th century. The altar painting was done in 1908 by Eero Järnefelt, one of the masters of the Golden Age of Finnish art.

Nousiainen – Nousis

Nousiainen Church is significant in Finnish cultural history, rivaled only by Turku Cathedral. It is a burial place of St. Henrik, the first bishop of Finland, and the seat of the first bishopric. The church, dedicated to the Virgin Mary and to St. Henrik, is impressively located on a high bank of a river, constructed in the mid-1400s. The plan of the graystone church is unusual in that both the western gable and the narrower eastern chancel are three-sided. The nave is decorated with primitive murals of human, animal, and geometric figures.

Bishop Magnus II Tavast donated its most precious object, the sarcophagus of St. Henrik, to the church

Nousiaisten kirkko – Nousiainen Medieval Church

in 1429. However, his remains had been transferred to Turku Cathedral in 1300. Regarded the most splendid work of Finnish medieval art, the sarcophagus is made of black limestone and decorated with ornamental brass plates thought to be of Flemish origin, illustrating the life of St. Henrik.

Masku – Masko

Masku Medieval Church, dedicated to St. John the Baptist, was built in the late 15th century. The lower parts of the walls are decoratively painted as draperies. Medieval treasures include a well-preserved altar screen with carvings as well as crucifixes and wooden statues.

Naantali – Nådendal

The Order of St. Birgitta, named for St. Birgitta (1303–1373), an upper class Swedish woman, built numerous convents around Europe. The only one built in Finland was established in 1438 in Masku, in Latin called *Vallis Gratiae*, the Valley of Grace. In 1442 the convent, which housed both nuns and monks, was moved to the coast, where the town of Naantali was founded the following year. Its Finnish name comes from the town's Swedish name *Nådendal*, which also translates as the Valley of Grace.

The rich convent brought pilgrims and trade to the town. However, during the Reformation in 1527, King Gustav Vasa decreed that all cloisters were to be closed and their lands confiscated for the crown, leaving only the church standing. The town dwindled to a sleepy village, but the convent indirectly saved the settlement. A sock knitting industry developed from the art of making heels that had been taught by the nuns. Socks were the most important export of the town, with up to 30,000 pairs sold a year. Naantali's fortunes did not really rise until a spa was built in 1863, which became a popular health resort attracting visitors from as far away as Russia.

After the 1628 fire, the town's dwellings were rebuilt on their original medieval sites. The town is, nevertheless, an excellent example of medieval building traditions, with narrow streets following the contours of the land. Today, the yacht harbor and the well-preserved 18th- and early 19th-century wooden buildings make an idyllic view.

One of the best-preserved entities is the **Naantali Museum**, housed in the 18th-century houses and several outbuildings around the beautiful garden. The museum illustrates the history of the town through 19th-century merchants' and craftsmen's homes.

Naantali Museum

Naantali has the honor of being host to **Kultaranta**, which since 1922 has been the official summer residence of the President of Finland. The grand granite palace designed by Lars Sonck on an island opposite the monastery church, was built in 1913–15 for an entrepreneur. The magnificent gardens, designed by the well-known landscape architects of the time, Svante and Paul Olsson, can be visited.

The convent church was built in the late 1400s based on the rules and guidelines set down by the Birgittine Order and modeled on Vadstena church, St.Birgitta's own convent church. Together with Porvoo Cathedral, the church was the first in Finland to have the main aisle completely

Naantalin luostari-kirkko – Naantali Medieval Convent Church

Naantali Medieval Convent Church

covered by stellar vaults. After the Reformation the church became a community church. The foundation of the altar of St. Birgitta has survived, as well as the nun's chancel gallery columns located above. The German-style wooden altar screen depicting the Coronation of the Virgin Mary in heaven, flanked by St. Birgitta and her daughter Katarina, is of Swedish origin from the late 15th century.

Each June the church is a venue for the Naantali Music Festival, specializing in chamber music.

The **Art Museum** was established to exhibit the art of the Eero Ranta-nen Foundation, which includes some 3,000 works of art, mostly Finnish contemporary paintings, sculpture, and graphic art, and some from Estonia and Russia. The **Archaeological Exhibition** illustrates the rich history of Raisio since the late Iron Age (900s), as well as the excavations conducted in the town since the 1930s, both with actual findings and interesting multimedia.

Surrounded by heavy traffic, the nearby **Raisio Medieval Church**, dedicated to St. Martinus, was built sometime between the late 15th century to mid–16th century. The triumphal crucifix is by the so-called Lieto Master, the first Finnish artist known by name, who worked in the Turku area at the beginning of the 14th century.

Raision museo- ja kulttuurikeskus Harkko – Museum and Cultural Centre Harkko

The 15th-century, **Lemu Medieval Church**, dedicated to St. Olof, still dominates the village landscape. There are several examples of medieval art, including the large triumphal crucifix of Scandinavian origin and the limestone baptismal font, both from the 1200s.

The Baroque castle of Louhisaari is the most remarkable manor of the nobility in Finland during the Swedish empire. Finnish Baron Herman Clausson Fleming (1619–1673) was a notable member of the Swedish court during the reign of Queen Kristina and the Head of the Exche-quer. However, he fell out of favor with the aristocracy, and in 1664 he was, in effect, exiled by being appointed Governor of Finland.

Louhisaaren kartanolinna – Louhi-saari Manor

In 1655 Fleming had commissioned and evidently designed himself the three-story, white-stuccoed stone building, its high hipped roof built in

*C. G. E.
Mannerheim
as a young boy
with his brother*

the Dutch style. The first floor, used as a
kitchen and storage, and the festive floor above
have survived in their 17th-century style. The
castle still has noticeable medieval details:
there is only one entrance, it is surrounded by
a sturdy brick wall, and the windows of the
first floor are protected by iron bars. The

Louhisaari Manor

impressive sandstone portal of the entrance is the only one of its kind in Finland. The layout of the main building and the lower side buildings bordering the court reflects Renaissance influences.

The estate passed from the Flemings to the family of Marshall C. G. E. Mannerheim, who was born at Louhisaari in 1867. The Finnish government purchased it in 1961, had it restored and opened it as a museum.

A two kilometer-long park allée leads from Louhisaari Manor to Askainen Church, also built by Fleming in 1653. The white-stuccoed stone church is covered with a Dutch-style steep roof.

Askaisten kirkko – Askainen Church

The interiors reveal that the church was built by the nobility. The paneled wooden entrance door with its beautiful ironwork as well as the richly carved and painted Baroque oak pulpit were, according to tradition, brought as loot by Fleming from Germany during the Thirty Years' War. The 17th-century balconies for the gentry on either side of the chancel are decorated with coats-of-arms and the wall above is decoratively painted as draperies. There are many treasures in the church, including several 17th-century burial coats-of-arms of the noble families related to Fleming.

Merimasku

On a lush hill facing the bay is the small, unadorned wooden **Merimasku Church**, built in 1726. Inside, the walls are painted in faux marble and the Baroque pulpit, dating from 1658, is colorfully decorated.

Rymättylä

Rymättylä Medieval Church, dedicated to St. Jakob, the patron saint of fishermen, was most likely built between 1510 and 1520 and became a pilgrimage site. The walls and vaults are profusely covered with murals.

Mynämäki – Virmo

The large graystone church, dedicated to St. Laurentius (*Lawrence*) and St. Erik, is the second largest medieval church in Finland and was probably built in the mid–15th century. The chancel has a three-part pointed arch window, rare in Finland. The most

Mynämäen kirkko – Mynämäki Medieval Church

Mynämäki Medieval Church – St. Olof

magnificent piece in the church is the soapstone decorative memorial to Henrik Clausson Fleming and his wife Ebba from 1632.

St. Henrik's Road, the most popular path of pilgrimage during the Middle Ages, passes Mynämäki from Nousiainen to Köyliö, the place where Bishop Henrik was killed.

Taivassalo – Tövsala

Taivassalon kirkko – Taivassalo Medieval Church	The graystone church of the Holy Cross was built in the mid–14th century. Exceptionally skillful murals cover the vaults and most of the walls, painted in 1467–70 by the school of Petrus Henriksson, and possibly commissioned by a member of Bishop Tavast's family. The murals contain vines, other plants, heraldic devices, and unusually realistically depicted religious figures. Most of the paintings were covered after the Reformation, but restored according to the fashion in 1890 and provided with explanatory texts. A rare triumphal crucifix was made by the so-called Lieto Master.

Kustavi – Gustavs

A part of the *Old Postal Road* to Turku survives along the shore. The postal service between Turku and Stockholm was established in 1638 and followed a Medieval route. The old road winds its way to the harbor on Vartsala Island in Kustavi, from where the ferries even today start the trip through the idyllic archipelago to the Åland Islands. Kustavi, *Gustavs*, was named for King Gustav III.

The **Isokari Lighthouse**, built in 1831–33 on a ruggedly beautiful island, is open to the visitors. The island also contains old dwellings and the Archipelago Center, which organizes activities during the summer.

Piikkiö – Pikis

Pukkilan kartano- ja ajokalumuseo – Pukkila Manor and Vehicle Museum	The wooden, mansard-roofed, Rococo-style manor house of the old allodial estate of Pukkila in Piikkiö was built in 1762. It is an exquisite example of the manor architecture of its time. The building was restored to its original appearance and furnished as the home of the family who occupied it in the late 18th century. A vehicle museum in the stone cowhouse displays sleighs, wagons, and carriages. The kitchen garden is planted as it was at the time the house was built, with vegetables, herbs, and medicinal and ornamental plants.

Paimio

Paimio Sanatorium is a site of pilgrimage for everyone interested in the birth of modern architecture. Designed by Alvar Aalto when he was only 30 and built in 1929–33, the building introduced the International Style architecture in Finland. One of the rooms has been restored to its original state.

Sauvo – Sagu

The large graystone Sauvo Church was built in the 1470s. Its imposing high vaults are decorated by murals by the school of Petrus Henriksson and depict plant ornaments as well as prophets and apostles dressed in medieval outfits.

Parts of the medieval choir stalls were used to make a canopied bench for a bishop and a simpler one for a priest, decorated with exceptional wood carvings. An unusual number of burial coats-of-arms relating to the local noble families decorate the walls and indicate the strength of the manor culture in Sauvo.

Sauvon kirkko – Sauvo Medieval Church

Parainen – Pargas

In the center of Parainen and bounded by a canal, a charming old settlement of simple artisans' and sailors' huts, called the **Old Malmi** – Vanha Malmi – preserves the idyll of a country village. The area around the imposing old church became a flourishing marketplace.

The graystone church, dedicated to St. Simon, was built in the late 15th century at the crossroads of ancient trade routes. Brick decorates the arches and a porch, fashioned in a cross-and-lace pattern. The church was painted with murals by the school of Petrus Henriksson in 1486.

Parainen Funeral Chapel was built in 1929–1930 next to the church. The design by Erik Bryggman is an important example of Classicism in transition to minimalist Modernism.

Paraisten kirkko – Parainen Medieval Church

Nauvo – Nagu

Ferries nowadays connect the Nauvo islands, which were stopovers along ancient Viking sailing routes. The numerous Bronze Age burial sites attest to the age and density of the settlements on these islands, especially on Lillandet.

The graystone **Nauvo Medieval Church** and its ornamental brick gables was built apparently in the mid-15th century and dedicated to St. Olof. The nave and vaults were decorated with primitive paintings in the late 15th and 17th centuries.

On a bare rock nearby is a fine *jatulintarha*, a ring of stones used as a place for playing and dancing, probably as early as prehistoric times, to which its Swedish name *jungfrudans*, maiden's dance, refers.

The small, wooden **Nötö Church** in the verdant outer island in Saaristomeri National Park was built in 1756–57. It is a typical "boat-shape" island church, octagonal and oblong in plan.

King Gustav II Adolf ordered in 1619 that a leprosy hospital be established on the island which, as a result, was given the name *Själö* in Swedish, literally Soul Island, because of the fate of its residents. The island

Seilin hospitaali ja kirkko – Seili Hospital and Church

Sea Shore View,
Victor Westerholm, 1908

was chosen because of its isolated location. The last leper died in 1785; the buildings were then used as a mental hospital until 1962.

The grand Neo-Classical hospital buildings are an unusual sight amidst the idyllic scenery of the archipelago. The picturesque and peaceful island has been designated a nature preserve. The simple cruciform church, built in 1733, is painted red. The plain interior with unpainted, exposed wood reflects the isolation of the island. The high railing within the church separated the sick patients from the healthy people. The pulpit is decorated with wooden cutwork.

Korppoo – Korpo

**Korppoon kirkko –
Korppoo Medieval
Church**

The town of Korppoo comprises more than 2,000 islands and skerries. On the island of Jurmo there are half a dozen stone arrangements, known as "monks' rings," of unknown age.

The stone church with a tall tower, dedicated to St. Mikael, was built in the mid–15th century. The primitive wall paintings were revealed in the early 1950s and the unique medieval wooden choir loft returned to its original position.

The **Utö Lighthouse** is the oldest in Finland, built in 1753. It was blown up in the war in 1809, but rebuilt soon after. The tower includes a chapel, unique in a lighthouse. The harmonious village around contains pilots' houses and old wooden barracks.

The wooden church of Houtskari, dedicated to St. Mary, was constructed n 1703–04. It is the earliest 18th-century cruciform church to represent the type, which became common in the southwest of Finland. The red-painted church has low walls and a steep hipped roof surmounted by a slender banner pole. The altar painting was done in 1887 by the well-known impressionist landscape painter Victor Westerholm.

Houtskarin kirkko – Houtskari Church

The islands of **Björkö** and **Mossala** have preserved well their traditional village structure, old barns and boat sheds lining the shore. In the middle of Mossala village on the rock rises a traditional *majstång*, a midsummer pole.

Kemiö – Kimito

The old **Kemiö Medieval Church**, dedicated to St. Andreas, has experienced many construction phases after it was built around 1470. The murals on the high vaults, painted by the school of Petrus Henriksson in 1469, survived all the rebuildings.

The oldest and one of the largest local history museums in Finland, Sagalund was established by a village teacher in 1900 with a collection of over twenty buildings, historical objects, and books. The culturally interesting buildings include the *pedagogia*, one of the oldest grammar schools in Finland, established in 1649. The beautiful park and rose garden alone are worth the visit. The museum arranges special summer events and houses also a handicrafts center. The *Eugenia* carried freight from 1879 to 1951, the last wooden ship to do so. A copy was built in Kemiö and made its maiden voyage in honor of the museum's centenary.

Sagalundin Museo – The Sagalund Museum

Dragsfjärd

The town of Dragsfjärd is made up of thousands of islands and skerries. **Hiittinen Church**, built in 1685–86 on Hiittinen (*Hitis*) Island, is the oldest cruciform wooden church preserved in southwestern Finland. A massive square tower rises from the crossing, capped with a low pyramid roof and a sharp spire. Traditional island buildings have survived in the vicinity.

Stones of the encircling walls remain from a chapel dating back as far as the 13th century on a narrow strait, used by Viking ships. The strait separates **Rosala Village** from the rest of the island. The traditional villagescape and its numerous old houses and boathouses, sheltered around a cove, are well-preserved. In the **Rodeborg Viking Center** – Rodeborgin viikinkikeskus – the visitor can step into a reconstructed

Viking house and study exhibitions on the Vikings' Eastern Route from Scandinavia to Russia.

The idyllic **Högsåra Island** along the historic sea route to Jungfrusund has offered a sheltered harbor since ancient times.

The 52-meter-high, magnificent **Bengtskär Lighthouse**, the tallest in Scandinavia, has been important to Finland's security. This lighthouse on the outer sea was built from granite blocks in 1906. The large living quarters contain even a chapel.

Taalintehtaan ruukki – Taalintehdas Ironworks

The ironworks at Taalintehdas (*Dalsbruk*) was founded in 1686. After the smelting of bog ore ceased, a steam-powered sawmill and Finland's first Martin furnace for the casting of steel was built in the 1870s. Taalintehdas is now one of Europe's most modern rolling mills and the last historical ironworks in Finland where ore and scrap iron are still processed. Except for the chimney, the old blast furnace from 1850, with its granite lower section and brick arch opening, has survived intact. The brick foundry has been restored as a museum. The eleven slagbrick coke-stove buildings are unique in Finland.

The ironworks community came to include a church, school, and two still-private manors. Many of the old workers' quarters and officials' houses are still occupied; the most remarkable are the two-story wooden, galleried apartment houses from the turn of the 20th century. The old harbor front has an impressive Empire-style row of warehouses, complete with a Classical pediment and colonnade. In the summer the harbor with its guest harbor and annual Baltic Jazz festival is a popular spot.

The **Taalintehdas Ironworks Museum** – Taalintehtaan ruukkimuseo – encompasses workers' houses and several production buildings.

Björkbodan ruukki – Björkboda Ironworks

A hammer forge was established in 1732 at Björkboda rapids not far from Taalintehdas and in the 1880s started to make locks. Metal manufacturing is still done on the premises.

The well-tended grounds on the ridge on the narrow lake include numerous manufacturing facilities and workers' houses. The two-story wooden main building, one of the most imposing of the Gustavian-era manors in Finland, was built in 1783 according to the drawings of C. F. Schröder. Even the outbuildings are impressive with their the Classical-style stone granary. The manor is still private.

Söderlångvikin museo – Söderlångvik Museum

The Söderlångvik Estate was the summer home of Amos Anderson (1878–1961), who came from a humble home in a nearby village and rose to become a publishing magnate, building a financial empire he used to support culture, especially art.

Anderson bought 7000 hectares (17,500 acres) of land on the island. The main building of Söderlångvik, a former allodial estate, was constructed in 1870, but he had it rebuilt and enlarged in the Neo-Classical style. The house, surrounded by large gardens, stands on a hill with a beautiful view of the bay. Now a home museum, it contains Anderson's original furnishings and art, mostly Finnish, from the beginning of the 20th century.

Perniö – Bjärnå

Several enthusiastic individuals started collecting local historical artifacts in the late 1800s, which are exhibited in the **Perniö Museum** – Perniön museo. Today the collection sheds light on the rich prehistory of Perniö and also include interesting examples of weapons, tin, glass, copper, and textiles.

The early 15th-century sacristy is the oldest part of the handsome **Perniö Medieval Church**, dedicated to St. Laurentius (*Lawrence*). The rich paintings on the vaults were done by the school of Petrus Henriksson.

Teijon ruukki – Teijo Ironworks

A blast furnace, established in 1686, developed into a major ironworks. Teijo became the first in Finland to use sand to fabricate molds to make high-quality spades, ploughs, and anchors.

The Rococo-style stone mansion was built in 1770, designed by C. F. Schröder, as a center for the ironworks, surrounded by a symmetrical French garden. The unusual, small pagoda-like church on the top of the hill in the park, built in 1830, was designed by a self-taught scientist and owner of the ironworks at the time. The ironworks developed into an independent community. Many workers' quarters and production buildings made from slag-brick survive. Ships and machines are still being built, but the old blast furnace now houses an information center for the National Board of Forestry, which owns adjoining 2,300 hectares (5,750 acres) of recreational forest.

Mathildedal Ironworks was built nearby in 1852. There is still an impressive selection of original production buildings and workers' houses, which are being restored and developed into recreational uses.

Halikko

More than fifty ancient burial sites have been found at the end of the protected bay at Halikko, bearing witness to ancient settlements. The biggest silver hoard in Scandinavia, jewelry from the 12th century called the Halikko treasure, was uncovered there in 1887. The fortified **Rikalan-mäki Hill** was already a harbor and trading post a thousand years ago at the end of the Iron Age; there are interpretive signs at the site explaining its history. The old road from Turku to Halikko, following the course of the *Great Coastal Road*, winds through the beautiful landscape.

Magnificent estates, still private homes and now designated as landmarks, were built around the bay. The 16th-century main building of the **Vuorentaka Estate** and the Neo-Classical style **Wiurila Estate**, built in 1806–11, can be visited.

A three-story stone granary built in 1849 on the high bank of the river near the church now houses the **Halikko Museum** – Halikon museo. Small on the outside, it harbors a wealth of information on local history.

The **Trömperi Inn Museum** – Trömperin kestikievarimuseo – has preserved the original atmosphere of an 18th- and 19th-century inn along the *Great Coastal Road*.

Salo

Veturitalli – Salon taidemuseo – Roundhouse – Salo Art Museum	An old roundhouse was renovated for the Salo Art Museum. The turntable, now in the inner courtyard of the museum, still boasts a fine steam engine from 1921. Inside, the fan-shaped space creates an excellent backdrop for the art. The museum has in a short time established itself as an important center for modern art, presenting art and design of national and international quality.

Uusikaupunki – Nystad

The town, established in 1617 by King Gustaf II Adolf, was at first nearly destroyed by fires, then by modern construction in the 1960s and 1970s. Fortunately, many of the old, richly decorated, wooden Empire-style burgers' houses in the central part of the town survived and are now protected. The salt storage houses in the picturesque harbor date from when Uusikaupunki, literally, "New Town," was a prosperous center for seafaring and trade. Now the town is known for its annual woodwind music festival, named for composer Henrik Crusell, who was born in Uusikaupunki in 1775.

Uudenkaupungin kulttuurihistoriallinen museo – Uusikaupunki Museum of Cultural History	The Museum Cultural of History is housed in an old burgher's house, a fine example of the upper middle class architecture of the 19th century with its fine period rooms. Seafaring, always important to the town, and its history are illustrated by the deck of a ship, decorated with a figurehead from a bark, complete with maritime objects.
Pyhämaan uhrikirkko – Pyhämaa Votive Church	The church in Pyhämaa is one the best-preserved 17th-century wooden churches in Finland, located on an old sailing route outside of Uusikaupunki. Because of the treacherous waters, the place in ancient times was called Pahamaa, the "bad land." With the start of the Reformation, Franciscan monks who were forced

to abandon their monastery came to Pyhämaa, the "holy land," and were given shelter. A simple red-painted church was built in 1647–52. In the old tradition the chancel is separated from the rest of the church by a decorative choir screen. The church has been the recipient of anonymous donations from around the world as a sign of personal wishes or gratitude. The outward appearance is offset by splendidly rich allegorical paintings in the Baroque style, executed in 1667 by Christian Wilbrandt, a master painter from Vaasa. The illustrations are arranged as ornamentally framed pictures surrounded by lush floral and fruit details.

The graystone church of Kalanti, dedicated to St. Olof, was built probably in the 1460s. The church is famous for its abundant painted decorations of the so-called Kalanti school done in 1470–71 by Petrus Henriksson, the first known Finnish church painter. The realistic late-Gothic pictures illustrate legends of the saints separated by plant and other ornamental motifs.

Kalannin kirkko – Kalanti Medieval Church

The *Church Road* leads to the **Männäinen Ironworks** – Männäisten ruukki – established in 1741 at a waterfall. Despite its small size, the well-tended property with its restored buildings provides an unusually good picture of the ironworks of its times. Today, Männäinen is a private farm, but can be visited.

The **Kalanti Local History Museum** – Kalannin kotiseutumuseo – is located in the buildings of a traditional 19th-century farmstead by an ancient market site. There is a special collection of southwestern *vakka*s, wooden storage baskets made since the 18th century.

Laitila – Letala

Laitila is rich with Iron Age burial sites, sacrificial stones, and hill forts. The well-preserved village of **Untamala** is on a hill along the old road. From the old cemetery a path leads to the Roman-time burial site. The graystone **Laitila Medieval Church**, dedicated to St. Mikael, was built in the 1470s. The rich murals, made in 1483 by the so-called Kalanti school of Petrus Henriksson, illustrate evangelists, saints, plants, and animals.

The wealthy Kauppila Farmstead is the best-preserved example of an enclosed courtyard, based on the Renaissance model and common since the Middle Ages in Southwestern Finland. The yard was divided into household and livestock areas. The farmstead's old log buildings stem from the 18th and 19th centuries, but represent much older building traditions.

Kauppilan umpipiha – Kauppila House Museum

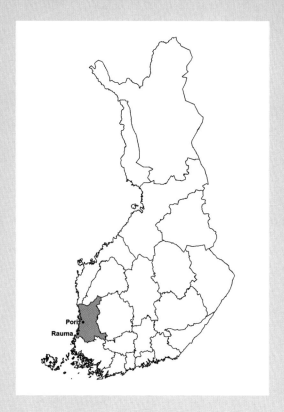

6
Satakunta

The unusual name of the province of Satakunta, literally "hundred district," unlike the ancient names of Finland's other provinces, is a historic remnant of the adoption of Swedish organizational measures in Finland. It is the Finnish translation of an administrative and juridical term that was applied in central Sweden to a regional division, *hundrade*. Political connections between Satakunta and central Sweden evidently antedate the first crusade in 1150. However, numerous burial finds bear witness to permanent habitation on the Kokemäenjoki River long before that, as far back as 400–550 AD, during the Iron Age.

Along the river, the settlements expanded during the Viking Era, 800–1050 AD. The fur trade from inland Häme was conducted on the river but, early on cultivation of the fertile fields of the coastal flatlands became the main occupation. One of the Viking kings, who made excursions to the area around 1000, was Olof Haraldson who suffered a martyr's death in 1030 and became the patron saint of Norway. His cult, which spread throughout the Nordic region and became especially strong in Satakunta, preceded the crusades. Olof the Holy is still portrayed on the coat-of-arms of Satakunta.

According to medieval tradition, Lalli, a peasant leader, murdered Finland's first bishop and patron saint, the English-born St. Henrik, in 1156 on the ice of Lake Köyliönjärvi. The earliest sources about Henrik are based on the "Legend of St. Henrik," which dates from the 1270s and is the earliest example of written literature in Finland. Henrik's cult was established at the time his remains were reinterred in Turku Cathedral in the 1290s. In the Middle Ages *St. Henrik's Road* from Nousiainen, where he was buried, to Köyliö became a lively pilgrim route. Lake Köyliönjärvi area has been designated a National Landscape by the Ministry of the Environment.

Evidently the second crusade was made via the Kokemäenjoki River to Häme province by the Swedish Earl Birger in 1239. Kokemäenkartano Manor was established on the river as a Swedish administrative center. Satakunta became a province in the 1300s, but only local, small feudal castles were built. German traders settled in Ulvila as early as the 1320s. From there, the great coastal road ran northwards to Oulu and Tornio.

Daily work and taxes levied as labor for building castles were heavy on the local peasants. Finally, after many complaints, the king ordered the castle in Kokemäki to be demolished in 1367. From the 1580s on, the king began to recruit cavalry by granting a tax exemption to estates or farms, which undertook to hire and equip a horseman. The Kokemäenjoki River region had 500 cavalry farms and also manors, owned not only by the nobility, but also by the wealthiest peasants. The tenant farm law of 1918 finally ended the tenant system. In Köyliö alone, a manor that owned more than half of the parish distributed 5,200 hectares (13,000 acres) of land to its 254 former tenants.

Since the Middle Ages, the traditional way of building farmsteads was to place the buildings so as to form an enclosed yard, with the household and cattle yards separated by a fence. The houses were in tight groups in the villages, separated from the fields further away. In addition to farming, the peasants also practiced maritime trade directly with Stockholm. A ship was usually owned by an association consisting mostly of wealthy peasants but also including some nobles and landless persons. This trade reached its peak in the 1810s, before a customs barrier was set up in 1817.

The Kokemäenjoki River also provided the preconditions for industry, which nowadays, together with agriculture, provides the main livelihood in the region. The first mills began operations in the 16th century and ironworks were founded the following century along the rivers. Large steam-powered sawmills were established at the mouth of the Kokemäenjoki River in the 1870s. Many of these were owned by the industrialist Antti Ahlström, a legendary businessman who expanded his empire across Finland. At the time of his death in 1896, he owned 14 sawmills, four ironworks, and 60,000 hectares (150,000 acres) of land.

Pori – Björneborg

In 1550, Ulvila residents were ordered to leave their town to settle Helsinki. When they returned home in a few years, Ulvila had been moved further down the Kokemäenjoki River and given a charter by Duke Johan under the name *Björneborg*. After the devastating fire of 1852, which spared only the town hall and a few other stone buildings, the town was rebuilt out of the ashes. Now the blocks on the southern bank of the river form one of the most impressive stone house districts from the end of the last century in Finland.

The grand old town hall was built in 1839–41 on C. L. Engel's designs, but was replaced by a new Italian Renaissance style **Town Hall**, originally a private palatial residence, in 1895. The oldest of the Finnish language theater buildings, the **Pori Theater**, built in 1883–84, has unusually fine interiors. Since the mid-1960s, Pori has been known best for the international Pori Jazz Festival, which draws up to 150,000 visitors every summer.

Pori Town Hall

Keski-Pori Church was built of red brick in the Neo-Gothic style in 1863 and has a 70-meter cast-iron spire, the only one of its kind in Finland.

Continuing postglacial uplift of the land has created a 6-kilometer long beach, Yyteri, and caused the harbors to be shifted westward. **Reposaari Island**, the biggest export harbor in Finland in the 1870s, is some 30 kilometers from Pori and connected to the mainland by a dike. The picturesque **Ahlainen Village** has retained its traditional appearance with a fishing harbor, small wooden houses, and large mansions. The altar painting of the village church was made by one of the first Finnish women artists, Elin Danielsson-Gambogi in 1888.

The Satakunta Museum was established in 1888 by the Finnish Society of Pori. The vast collection of 70,000 objects shows the local devotion to preserving the history of Satakunta.

Satakunnan Museo – Satakunta Museum

The Kokemäenjoki River gives the background for the exhibitions and archeological findings. The enchanting multimedia exhibition illustrates the province's prehistory and ethnography, nature, and culture. A scale model of Pori before the fire of 1852 illustrates the town's past. A history of styles and customs from the Middle Ages up to the beginning of the 20th century is presented through period rooms of the local industrial and cultural figures.

The tug boat *Santtu* moored on the island of Reposaari was built in 1894 and is one of the four museum ships in Finland dating from the 19th century.

The Pori Art Museum is located in a former bonded warehouse on a bank of the Kokemäkijoki River. Together with the old town hall, the museum premises and their restored Renaissance-style exteriors form an integral part of the riverside view.

Porin taidemuseo – Pori Art Museum

The core of the museum's works consists of the city's collection and the Maire Gullichsen Art Foundation's collection. The Foundation was set up by Maire Gullichsen (1907–1990), who was instrumental also in establishing the museum. Born into the Alhström family of industrialists, she was an influential patron of the arts. In 1939 she established an association, which brought current international exhibitions of abstract and constructivist art to Finland. The collections include mainly Finnish art from the beginning of the century to the 1980s, with the emphasis on abstract art. Exhibitions as well as research have put the museum at the forefront of the Finnish art scene.

The mausoleum was commissioned by industrialist F. A. Juselius as a memorial to his daughter Sigrid, who died when she was only 11. It was designed by Josef Stenbäck in the Neo-Gothic style and built in 1899–

Juselius-mausoleumi – Juselius Mausoleum

1902. The original frescoes by Akseli Gallen-Kallela, regarded as some of his most remarkable works, were destroyed by dampness after a few years, but Jorma Gallen-Kallela repainted them, following the outlines of his father. The paintings in the anteroom are by Pekka Halonen.

Juselius Mausoleum, Akseli Gallen-Kallela

Spring, Juselius Mausoleum, Akseli Gallen-Kallela 1902

Ulvila

Ulvilan kirkko – Ulvila Medieval Church

During the Middle Ages, the mouth of the Kokemäenjoki River was at Ulvila, the most important trading center in the region. It was incorporated in 1365, but by the beginning of the 16th century, ships were unable to sail to Ulvila due to the continuing rise of the land.

The church of red-tinged stone, dedicated to St. Olof, was probably constructed in the late 15th century. The brick gables are decorated with stepped ornamental niches. The triumphal wooden crucifix by the "Master of Ulvila" is from the 15th century.

The historic landscape includes old parsonages and manor houses surrounded by parklands as well as old villages, such as **Suosmeri Village**, which has retained its traditional look. **Kaasmarkku Village** still bears signs of its old industrial activities.

Kullaa

Leineperin ruukki – Leineperi Ironworks

The Leinperi or *Fredriksfors* Ironworks was established in 1771 on the Kullaanjoki River. The heyday of the ironworks in the 1860s saw the construction of the main building, surrounded by a park and workers'

quarters. In 1877 industrialist Antti Ahlström purchased the ironworks, but by the end of the century ironmaking was discontinued. Most of the lands were divided into smallholdings to resettle evacuees from Karelia after the Second World War.

Leineperi is one of the most interesting old ironworks because of the variety of its surviving structures and facilities, which have been carefully restored. The blast furnace is the best preserved of the 19th-century blast furnaces in Finland. Visitors can watch a blacksmith at work in the bar iron forge. Now craftspeople and artists have studios in the village.

Merikarvia

Ahlström also purchased the old **Lankoski** sawmill and paper mill in Merikarvia. The traditional village is well-preserved.

Noormarkku

The first sawmills were established in Noormarkku in the mid-18th century and a hammer forge in 1806, which Antti Ahström purchased in 1870. The mill and its machinery are unusually well-preserved. Besides the company headquarters, surrounded by extensive park-like grounds, there are many other architecturally interesting buildings.

Villa Mairea, together with Frank Lloyd Wright's Falling Water and Le Corbusier's Villa Savoye, is regarded architecturally as the most important private residences of the 20th century. Architects Alvar Aalto and Aino Marsio-Aalto were given by Maire Gullichsen, granddaughter of Antti Ahlström, and her husband Harry Gullichsen an opportunity to create a modern home and space for their art collection that includes Leger, Picasso, Arp, and Toulouse-Lautrec.

Villa Mairea

The house, finished in 1939, sits on top of a hill in the midst of a pine forest, its flowing series of spaces merging in harmony with nature. The influence of the rustic elegance of Finnish and even Japanese vernacular

Villa Mairea

architecture apparent in many details marked Aalto's move away from strict European Functionalism. The furniture designed for the house by the Aaltos makes it a total work of art.

Kankaanpää

The 55-kilometer road from Pori to Kankaanpää is named the *Art Road* for its dozen landscape art works. International sculpture symposiums have further embellished the town with modern outdoor sculpture, and now along the "Art Circle" and outside it there are more than eighty public art works – mostly permanent, some temporary landscape installations.

Kankaanpää Town Museum – Kankaanpään kaupunginmuseo – illustrates rural life and the history of an important local industry, shoemaking. A large collection of sculptures and paintings were given by the local artists, Kauko and Sinikka Räike. Kauko Räike is one of the first non-figurative sculptors in Finland, whose works complement the paintings by his wife.

Karvia

The wooden **Karvia Church**, built in 1789–98, is embellished inside with fanciful painted draperies.

Rauma

Since the last disastrous fire swept Rauma in 1682, it has survived as one of the largest and best-preserved wooden towns in Scandinavia. Rauma, one of Finland's four surviving medieval towns, was established in an old trading place and received its charter in 1442.

The old town has retained its irregular medieval plan, with narrow and twisting streets and alleys. The blocks are enclosed by residences facing the street and by outbuildings in the yards. Rauma took its current appearance in the late 19th century during an era of prosperity brought by

the great sailing ships when it had the largest fleet in Finland evident in Neo-Renaissance style houses with rich details. In 1991 UNESCO put Old Rauma on the World Heritage list as an example of a Northern European wooden neighborhood.

Bobbin lacemaking became by the 18th century the most common craft in Rauma. The lacemakers were known for their technically demanding lace, which was exported to Russia and Scandinavia from the end of the 18th century on. Now their skills have been revived and during Lace Week at the end of July, lace exhibitions and work demonstrations draw visitors both from Finland and abroad.

Old Rauma

The Franciscan brotherhood settled in Rauma and built a monastery in the 14th century. The Church of the Holy Cross was built as a monastery church in the next century, but during the Reformation in 1538 the Franciscans were exiled and the convent church became the town's main church. Franciscan regulations called for a nave divided into two aisles of different widths, which are covered with stellar vaults. The chancel was adorned with rich paintings in the early 1500s with themes of the Virgin Mary.

The church treasures include an altar cabinet with carvings, dating from the 1440s and a Renaissance-style pulpit decorated with carvings of apostles and saints made in 1625.

Pyhän Ristin kirkko – Church of the Holy Cross

The main exhibitions of Rauma Museum are located in the old two-story stone Town Hall, built in 1776 on the designs of Turku city architect C. F. Schröder. There is a large collection of fine Rauma lace and objects relating to the history of Rauma and seafaring.

Marela, the handsomest Neo-Renaissance house in Old Rauma, is furnished as an affluent shipowner's home from the turn of the century and is the best-preserved example in Old Rauma of the wealth brought by the maritime trade.

Rauman museo – Rauma Museum

103

Rauma Museum

Rauman taidemuseo – Rauma Art Museum	The Rauma Art Museum is located in Pinnala House, one of the best preserved architectural sights in Old Rauma. The buildings are grouped around a closed yard and give an idea of how prosperous burgers lived in the 18th and 19th centuries.
Teresia ja Rafael Lönnströmin koti-museo – The Teresia and Rafael Lönnström Home Museum	The Teresia and Rafael Lönnström Foundation's art collection is displayed at the former home of the Lönnströms. They were patrons of the arts and culture and filled their home with older Finnish art, a notable collection of silver, porcelain, glass, and sculptures. The original atmosphere of this elegant house has been preserved with its antique furniture and works of art. The paintings include well-known works from the Golden Age of Finnish art.
Lönnströmin taide-museo – The Lönnström Art Museum	The museum is a private art museum founded by the Teresia and Rafael Lönnström Foundation. It is located in one of the rare old stone buildings preserved in Old Rauma, originally built as a private home in 1912. The attic is specifically designed for music performances.

Harjavalta

Emil Cedercreutzin museo – Emil Ceder-creutz Museum	Artist, writer, and horseman Emil Cedercreutz (1879–1949), known for his sculptures of horses as well as skillful paper silhouettes, commissioned in 1914 a home in the popular National Romantic fashion. The villa displays the prosperous home of a nobleman with its Jugend-style furniture, old Satakunta *ryijy* rugs, and objects of art and design. Nearby Cedercreutz

built for his large ethnological collection the *Maahengen temppeli,* "Temple of the Earth Spirit," an eccentric, organically evolving wooden building. It has interesting folk art and objects connected to old crafts and livelihoods.

The separate art museum displays sculptures and silhouettes by Cedercreutz as well as art he collected. It includes mostly early 20th-century Finnish paintings and art.

The solid white **Nakkila Church** and its tall bell tower on a hilltop are visible from afar. It is the first and rare church in Finland in the International or Functionalist Style, designed by Erkki Huttunen and built in 1937. It contrasts with the low Congregation Center, by Juha Leiviskä (1970), below the church.

Emil Cedercreutz Museum

Kokemäki

On the site of the medieval trade center of Teljä stands St. Henrik's Preaching House where Bishop Henrik, according to legend, preached to the heathen Finns. The small room of logs has been dated, at least in part, from the Middle Ages, having 14th-century features, though not from St. Henrik's time. Tradition has it that St. Henrik spent the last night of his life here, 19 January 1156. The next day he was killed by the peasant leader Lalli on the ice of Lake Köyliönjärvi for demanding free hospitality. The Neo-Gothic brick chapel, which shelters the room, one of the oldest tourist sites in Finland, was consecrated in 1857.

Pyhän Henrikin saarnahuone – St. Henrik's Preaching House

Lalli

Kirkkosaari or **Köyliönsaari**, a small island in Lake Köyliönjärvi contains remnants of a memorial chapel built in the 14th century. Each June, the island is a pilgrimage site for Finnish Catholics. The Medieval pilgrimage road went from Köyliö to Nousiainen via Säkylä.

Eura

The history of Eura goes back to the Iron Age, about 600 AD, as indicated by the **Luistari** burial ground. It is the largest prehistoric grave site in Scandinavia, and more than 1,300 graves from Viking times have been excavated there since it was discovered in 1969. The stone foundations have survived of the log fortress Kauttuan Linnavuori, **Kauttua Castle Hill.** Twelve stones form a circle on the pre-Christian **Käräjämäki**, Court Hill, but the thirteenth stone, the so-called thief's stone, has disappeared. Graves have been found inside the circle.

Information about the archaeology of Eura and objects discovered in the excavations can be found in the **Laughing Dragon Information Centre of Prehistory** – Esihistorian opastuskeskus Naurava Lohikäärme. A marked path with imaginative descriptions leads from one site to another.

By the 16th century Eura became an important center for trade and mills were established. In spite of modern construction, the scale of a traditional village has survived in the center of town.

Kauttuan ruukki – Kauttua Ironworks

The Kauttua Ironworks was founded in 1689 on the Eurajoki River. By the mid-19th century the ironworks had become the biggest producer of rod iron in the country. Antti Ahlström purchased the works in 1873. Later a paper mill and a cardboard factory operated there.

The large wooden main building was built in 1802, surrounded by a garden with an unusual octagonal bell tower. On the edge of the falls are remnants of old mills and an old water sawmill. Ax smiths' shops as well as farm buildings and dwellings line the picturesque main street, which follows the medieval route.

In 1939 Alvar Aalto was commissioned to design a new kind of housing for workers. The War interrupted the plans, and only one terraced house was built on the hillside in a fan-like configuration. The roof of each apartment in the building acts as a patio.

Eurajoki

Eurajoki is known for the magnificent **Vuojoki Manor** whose history goes back to the 16th century. The impressive three-story manor and its side buildings were designed by C. L. Engel and built in 1836. It is one of the finest Empire-style manor houses in Finland, and has a large formal garden. It is now being restored as a cultural center.

The medieval **Irjanne Village** is surrounded by a historical landscape with wide-open fields. The charming oblong Irjanne Church from 1731, is the oldest wooden church in the province.

Lappi

The first archaeological site to be included in the UNESCO World Heritage List for Finland is the unique **Sammallahdenmäki** Bronze Age burial site in Lappi. The one-kilometer wide cliff contains 33 burial cairns from 1500–500 BC. Unusual in all of Scandinavia is a stone structure resembling a flat floor. The vegetation still reveals its ancient maritime location, even though the sea is now over 20 kilometers away.

Huittinen

Huittisten museo – Huittinen Museum

The museum, housed in a former graystone parish granary, concentrates on the cultural history of the area. The sculptor Lauri Leppänen (1895–1977) donated his sculptures, reliefs, medals, and sketches to the museum. He is known for his plastic and expressionistic portraits and numerous war memorials in the cemeteries around Finland where his standard subjects are an angel, child, mother, and a soldier.

Another interesting exhibition portrays the life of Risto Ryti, a local farmer's son and the Finnish president from 1940 to 1944, the difficult war years. He was imprisoned by the allied War Trials, in effect by the Soviets, in 1946 for his efforts to secure help from Germany in 1944, although, most Finns think he was charged unjustly.

Punkalaidun

Talonpoikaismuseo Yli-Kirra – Yli-Kirra Peasant Museum

Yli-Kirra is one of the best organized of the numerous local history museums in Finland. The original 19th-century main building faces a rectangular closed yard, divided into household and livestock yards. The complex includes some 30 buildings, most of them brought from other locations.

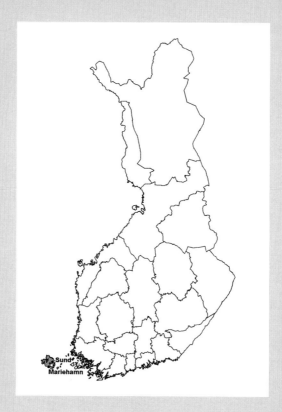

7

Åland
Ahvenanmaa

The Åland Islands between Finland and Sweden are a unique collection of some 6,500 islands, skerries, and rocks, in Europe comparable only to the Greek archipelago. Nature in Åland is also unusual compared to the rest of Finland. Because of its mild climate, many deciduous trees and an abundant flora, even orchids, grow in the wooded meadowlands, not found on the mainland Finland. The islands have only 25,000 residents, but attract visitors from all over Finland and Sweden.

Permanent residents came from the west 4,500 years ago. In the 6th and 7th century, settlers from the Lake Mälaren region of Central Sweden started migrating to the islands. By the Viking era, around 800–1050 AD, the islands were already densely populated. Christianity also came to the islands via Sweden in the 11th century, evident in the Christian burial customs in use by then. The oldest stone churches in Finland can be found in Åland and traces of even older wooden churches have been excavated there. They were often built on pagan cult sites, as were many mainland medieval churches. The first ones were probably built in the 13th century, mainly based on models in Östergötland and Gotland Island in Sweden, which, in turn, were influenced by Germany. The oldest wall paintings in Finland can also be found in Åland churches.

The islands have been a vital communications link across the Baltic ever since antiquity. Sea routes passed by Åland even before the Ålanders joined the Vikings on their excursions to the east. The islanders were frequently obliged to provide meals and lodging for travelers, especially for soldiers. In 1623 men in the most western town of Eckerö later received exemption from military service and tax relief. After the Swedish Postal Administration was founded in 1638, the so-called Old Postal Route ran from Stockholm across Åland to Turku. The farmers of Eckerö were divided into seven *rota*s, each of which included eight men who had the duty of maintaining mail services across the hazardous Åland Sea.

The fishermen and peasants shipped goods such as salted herring, fresh fish, firewood, timber, and butter to Stockholm and even further south. Peasant trading reached its peak in the 1810s before a customs barrier was set up in 1817, after which the trade was directed to the Baltic countries and even to Denmark and Germany. The ships were owned by associations of mostly wealthy peasants, but also of nobles and even the landless. By the end of the 19th century maritime trading by peasants had evolved into commercial freight trade. Mariehamn, the capital of Åland, was the home port of Gustaf Erikson's famous fleet of windjammers, the last in the world. The big sailing ships have been replaced by ever larger luxury ferries and cruise ships, most of them still operated by Åland shipping companies.

Åland is unusual among the Finnish provinces in that it is an autonomous area with its own government. While the rest of Finland is officially bilingual, the only official language in Åland is Swedish. After Sweden lost the war of 1808–09, Åland even tried to appeal to Napoleon, but Russia announced that the province belonged to Finland and would thus become part of Russia. After the Crimean War, both the Black Sea area and Åland were ordered to be demilitarized as stipulated in the Paris Peace Treaty of 1856. The unrest in the Russian Empire in 1917 gave Ålanders a chance to try to restore the union with Sweden, which was supported by a mass petition. When Finland gained independence later the same year, Finland instead offered the Ålanders a form of self-government. Sweden took the matter to the Paris Peace Conference in 1919, but finally the status of the islands was resolved at the newly-formed League of Nations in 1921 in Finland's favor. The islands were, however, to remain neutral and demilitarized and the Åland residents were exempt from military service. Finland guaranteed Åland autonomy, which gives the Ålanders the right to pass their own laws, apply the rules of regional citizenship and keep the island unilingually Swedish.

Mariehamn – Maarianhamina

Övernäs fishing village was given town rights in 1861 by Czar Alexander II who named it Mariehamn (*Maarianhamina*) for his consort Maria Alexandrovna. At that time the town had only 33 inhabitants, but has now grown to some 11,000. The town was built according to a novel Swedish idea, uncommon in Finland, where houses stand apart from each other and are separated from the street by a lawn and a row of trees. The entrance is from the street side via an "American"-style porch. Many of these houses, some of which still stand, were designed by Hilda Hongell, a female building master. Lars Sonck (1870–1956), also a native Ålander, designed many buildings in the town, including **Mariehamn Church**, dedicated to St. Göran, *George,* which was built in 1927 on a donation by a wealthy shipowner.

Mariehamn became a fashionable spa at the end of the 19th century. The **Maritime Quarter** – Sjökvarteret – in the Eastern Harbor continues the seafaring traditions of the town with a shipbuilding museum and a smithy. It boasts the biggest marina in Scandinavia.

Ålands museum – Åland Museum

The Åland Museum is the island's "national museum." Its interestingly arranged exhibitions provide an excellent survey of the history of Åland and offer a good introduction to a tour of the islands. The exhibitions are organized thematically from prehistory to the present and depict developments in everyday life, culture, and industries, as well as social and political events.

Ålands konstmuseum – Åland Art Museum

The museum was born from the works of art with impressions of Åland, purchased by the Åland Art Society. The exhibition shows the developments in Åland from the mid-19th century on, with a view to the trends, which influenced the artists. Annual purchases of both new and old art also concentrate on the themes of Åland.

Ålands sjöfartsmuseum – Åland Maritime Museum

The Maritime Museum has gained an international reputation for its collections encompassing the time of Åland's great sailing ships. The enchanting exhibitions include sculptural figureheads from old ships, one of them an unusual male head, as well as ship portraits commissioned by captains from local artists, and meticulous scale models of ships executed by one of the world's most skillful model-builders.

A unique attraction is a captain's saloon and its authentic furnishings from the four-masted bark Herzogin Cecilie, which ran aground in the English Channel in 1936. The ship set a world record in the so-called Grain Race from Australia to England around Cape Horn in 86 days.

Museifartyget Pommern – Museum Ship Pommern

The museum ship Pommern is the only remaining four-masted steel bark in the world that has been preserved in her original state. Built in Glasgow, Scotland, in 1903, it was bought by shipping magnate Gustaf Erikson in 1923. She sailed the grain trade route between Australia and England until World War II broke out in 1939. The wooden pavilion of the **Åland Yacht Club** was originally a private villa designed in the "expressive" style by Lars Sonck in 1896.

Jomala

Jomala kyrka – Jomala Medieval Church

The red-granite church of Jomala with a sturdy defense tower is believed to be one of the oldest churches in Åland and in Finland, built in the late 13th century. It is surrounded by a beautiful landscape, including one of Åland's biggest Viking burial grounds and remnants of dwelling sites from both the Iron Age and Middle Ages.

Jomala church is dedicated to the Norwegian Saint Olof or Olof Haraldson (ca 990–1030), an important Viking chief who made "excursions" all the way to Finland. With its unusual architecture and elaborate workmanship, it is one of the most remarkable churches in Åland. Some finely executed early Gothic paintings of human figures, animals, and ornaments, probably the oldest in Finland, have survived. A rare Romanesque limestone sculpture shows a lion's head swallowing a human being.

Knutsboda Hills,
Victor Westerholm 1909

The museum tells the story of the "Önningeby Colony," established in 1886 by Victor Westerholm (1860–1919), the Finnish pioneer of Impressionist landscape painting. He collected together artist friends from Finland and Sweden in his summer place in the charming village of Önningeby. During these golden years of outdoor painting, artists came to paint landscapes, *midsommarstångs* or maypoles, and people at their daily chores. The Colony members arranged group exhibitions in Turku, which helped inspire establishment of the Turku Art Society in 1891 with Westerholm as its spokesman.

The Colony was active until 1914, but had been almost forgotten by the time the museum was opened in 1992 in an old stone cowshed. The exhibitions display objects and pictures relating to the environment where the colonists' art was created.

Önningebymuseet – Önningeby Museum

Hammarland

The fortress-like **Hammarland Medieval Church**, dedicated to St. Katarina and surrounded by open fields of prehistoric graves, guards the Old Postal Route on the way to Eckerö. The massive 14th-century nave was expanded by an unusually placed, squat tower, which was used for defence and refuge during periods of unrest. A baptismal font from the 14th century in the style of Gotland Island has survived to the present day.

Eckerö

Eckerö Post och Tullhus – Eckerö Mail and Customs House
A traveler will be astonished to find a lonely palatial Empire-style building, designed by Carl Ludvig Engel, on the open rocks facing the sea. The Eckerö Customs House and Postal Station was built in 1828 by Czar Alexander I to show off Russian might on the westernmost shore of his empire after Finland had

The Mail Boat Jetty at Eckerö, Victor Westerholm 1885

become a Grand Duchy of Russia in 1809. Eckerö served as a major transit point on the ancient postal route between Sweden and Finland.

The imposing two-story building with two low wings now houses a small **Mail Boat Museum** – Postrotemuseet – which sheds light on the history of mail transportation on the route. On display is a mail boat from the 1860s, a so-called ice boat, which was built so that it could be dragged over smooth ice. When the ice was thin or the sea was open it could also be rowed or sailed.

Åland Hunting and Fishing Museum – Ålands Jakt- och Fiskemuseum – in the traditional, but still functioning, fishing harbor of Käringsund conveys not only local hunting and fishing traditions, but also a sense of the daily life of country people.

Eckerö Medieval Church, dedicated to St. Lars, *Lawrence,* is surrounded by an Iron Age burial place. The rectangular hall was probably built at the turn of the 14th century to which a massive west tower was added in the mid-15th century. The wooden Madonna and the baptismal font date from the early 14th century.

Signildskär Island on the open sea was for centuries the first outpost for sailors coming to Finland and a resting place for mailmen. An optical telegraph was built on the island in 1796. The ruins of the small medieval chapel are surrounded by a round stone wall.

Finström

Finström kyrka – Finström Medieval Church

Unlike the other churches on the main island of Åland, the red granite structure in Finström was not built on an ancient burial site. The sacristy and nave of the church, dedicated to St. Mikael, was built in the early 15th century. The primitively charming wall paintings of birds, stars, and human figures date from the late 15th century; the more refined saints' portraits are some two hundred years younger. There is an unusual abundance of Medieval wooden sculptures of saints, including a lively St. Göran, *George,* and a colorful altar cabinet, both from the late 15th century. A wooden sculpture of the *Giant Finn*'s head evidently originates from the earlier, 12th- century wooden church.

Saltvik

Saltvik's stone church, dedicated to St. Maria, rises in the middle of an ancient, important administrative center and marketplace. Saltvik has yielded innumerable, scientifically important findings from Åland's prehistory extending back to the first Åland settlers of 6,000 years ago. During the Viking period, the most important harbor was in Saltvik, "salt bay," a trading place for salt. In the Middle Ages, *landsting*, the first parliamentary assembly of Åland, was held in the open field south of the church.

Saltvik kyrka – Saltvik Medieval Church

The oldest part of the church, the nave, was probably built in the late 13th century. The finest pieces of art are the triumphal crucifix from the late 13th century, the smaller altar cabinet "Altare Domini" from the 1400s, and the larger three-part altar cabinet executed in 1666 in a naively colorful Baroque style. Saltvik Church probably was the cathedral for the autonomous diocese of Åland, since the limestone baptismal font from the 13th century is hewn in foil-leaf form, usually found only in the cathedrals.

The reconstructed **Långbergsöda Stone Age Village** – Långbergsöda stenåldersby – is located on Stone Age and Bronze Age dwelling sites.

Sund

The town of Sund is the site of Åland's ancient seat of government. Kastelholm Castle was first mentioned in historic documents from 1388, but the construction work evidently had started about a century earlier. It was built on a small island surrounded by water, as the farthest maritime outpost for the defence of Stockholm and to monitor the trade routes on the Baltic.

Kastelholms slott – Kastelholm Castle

Following the practices of central Europe, the castle comprises an older bastion, the central main castle with its mighty five-story tower in the center, and a newer, outer ward. The fortress became an administrative castle for the Åland Islands where the bailiff resided. In 1556 Duke Johan, Gustav Vasa's son, became the ruler over Åland, and later kept his brother King Erik XIV and his wife imprisoned in the tower. The castle

Kastelholm Castle

grounds were a favorite for royal elk hunts. The historic area has been designated a National Landscape by the Ministry of the Environment.

Jan Karlsgårdens friluftsmuseum – Jan Karlsgården Open-Air Museum

The main building of the Jan Karlsgården Open-Air Museum was moved in the 1930s from the village of Finström. A traditional maypole, *midsommarstång*, stands near the dance pavilion.

Across from the museum is the **Vita Björn Prison Museum** – Fängelsemuseet Vita Björn – the only prison on the Åland Islands, built in 1784 and used as a prison until 1975. It used to be customary to give names to public buildings, thus the name the White Bear.

Sund kyrka – Sund Medieval Church

From the castle one can see the sharp spire of the sturdy west tower of the large red- granite church, dedicated to St. John the Baptist. The oldest parts of the church were built possibly in the 1280s. In front of the choir is an old limestone cross, called the Wenni Cross because of the runic inscription bearing the name of Archbishop Wenni of Hamburg-Bremen. The 14th-century triumphal crucifix and wooden statues of saints and a magnificent altar cabinet of North German origin from the early part of the 1400s grace the church.

Construction of Bomarsund fortifications, a grand chain of forts with naval bases, was established in the 1820s by order of Czar Nicholas I at a strategic location on the *Old Postal Road*. After Sweden surrendered Finland to Russia in the Finnish War of 1808–09, it had strategic importance on Russia's new western border.

Bomarsunds fästningsruiner – Bomarsund Fortification Ruins

The semicircular fort differed from the earlier bastion designs. The

double walls were built of brick and faced meticulously with irregular polyhedrons of red granite. Only three turrets were completed by the time the Crimean War broke out in 1853. Turkish, British, French, and Sardinian allied forces fought on the Crimean peninsula against Russia who had initiated the conflict. The war spread even to the Finnish coast, and Bomarsund was destroyed by explosives by English-French naval forces

Bomarsund Fortification

the following year. The remnants of the skillful stonework, executed by some 2,000 builders brought from all over Russia, can be still admired.

On nearby **Prästö Island** is an unusual ecumenical cemetery in the middle of the forest, where the Russian Orthodox, Roman Catholic, Lutheran, Jewish, and Muslim workers and soldiers were buried.

Lemland

Lemböte kapellruin – Lemböte Chapel Ruins	Lemböte Chapel was built in the 12th century on the major international sea route from the coast of Sweden to the coast of Finland. The route is described in the Danish Itinerary mentioned in King Valdemar's land registry from the later part of the 13th century, the oldest preserved document on a Northern European sailing route. The small one-room chapel, built of gray granite blocks, is consecrated to St. Olof. **Pellas Shipmaster's Home** – Pellas Skeppargård – is an original shipowner's house from 1884, owned by the most prosperous of the farmer-sailors in Åland.
Lemland kyrka – Lemland Medieval Church	The Lemland red-granite church is also located along the old sea route, now on the ingrown bay. The unusually handsome early Gothic wall paintings are some of the oldest in Finnish churches, dating from around 1300. The portraits of the Apostles and Biblical scenes are refined and expressive. Several naturalistically sculpted triumphal crucifixes and wooden statues from the 14th century decorate the church. Especially fine is the so-called Lemland Madonna by the Master of Gotland with its expressive face and detailed rendering of clothing.

Kumlinge

Kumlinge kyrka – Kumlinge Medieval Church	This stark, rocky island in the outer sea reveals a surprising treasure inside the small graystone church of St. Anna, built in the late 15th century. Its magnificent paintings cover the walls and vaults with colorful images of the Passion, saints, angels, and garlands. The paintings are unusual in that they depict mostly women saints and include only two men. The Franciscan-style paintings from the beginning of the 16th century bear a relation to Byzantine iconography, maybe an influence from the Franciscan monastery on the island of Kökar. They have no direct parallels either on mainland Finland or Sweden. There are other medieval treasures in this small church, such as the French-style altar cabinet, which dates from the mid-13th century and is the oldest in Finland.
Museigården Hermas – Hermas Farm Museum	Hermas farmstead with its old, gray, weathered buildings scattered on a small hill, stands in its original place on the island of Enklinge. The first known resident on the island was mentioned in 1430. During the Finnish War in 1809 the village was burned on the order of the king to make it

difficult for Russian soldiers to spend the winter on the island. The residents, however, returned in the spring and rebuilt the houses, usually on the old foundations. The farmstead includes some twenty buildings around the household and livestock courtyards, connected by a gateway in the stable building standing in between.

Brändö

The interesting **Lappo Archipelago Museum** – Skärgårdsmuseet – on the main island is located on the shore in fine but unpretentious small wooden buildings, resembling traditional boathouses. The eye-catching exhibitions display handsome old boats and fishing equipment, as well as a photo exhibition on life in the archipelago.

Kökar

Kökar Island is mentioned as early as the 13th century in a Danish itinerary describing the route from Denmark to Estonia. Franciscan monks started coming to this windswept, remote island probably in the following century and established a monastery in the harbor, mentioned for the first time in 1472. During the Reformation the monastery was ordered by King Gustav Vasa to be closed in 1527, and the church fell into disrepair.

Kökar kyrka – Kökar Church

The present church of St. Anna was built from the stones of the monastery in 1769–84. According to the local tradition, a model hanging from the ceiling was made by a sailor from Kökar Island and portrays a Turkish ship, which captured the vessel he was on. From the foundations of a refectory, recent studies have uncovered many signs of the life there: glass, ceramics, and coins.

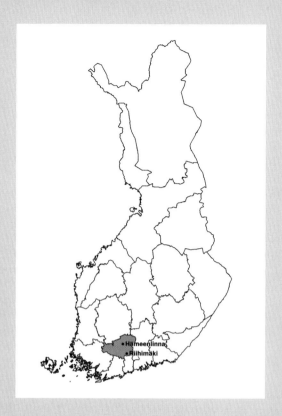

8
Kanta-Häme

In the southern part of Häme Province, Kanta-Häme, a traveler can find history and culture, scenic old roads, manors, and prosperous farms. Settlement in Häme concentrated around Lake Vanajavesi where Iron Age culture had spread along the Kokemäenjoki River. The Häme wilderness, *Tavastia*, was the border land between East and West, continuously attacked by Novgorod who tried to establish its rule and the Eastern Church. Swedish kings secured Western faith and new taxpayers by encouraging settlement eastwards. In order to avoid taxes and building churches, Häme peasants rebelled against their Swedish rulers in 1237 and returned to paganism. At the time of the so-called crusade by the Swedish nobleman Birger, later nominated as the Earl of Finland, possibly in 1249, Hakoinen Fortified Hill in present Janakkala was reinforced with a ring wall and a bailey surrounded by a fosse, along with an upper second ring wall encompassing a main inner bailey.

To provide stronger defense against attacks from Novgorod, Häme Castle was initiated by order of Earl Birger to establish Swedish rule firmly in Häme. The Swedish *Eriks krönika* or Erik's Chronicle from the early 14th century tells how, "*...the Christians built the stronghold, providing it with soldiers hold, Häme Castle is its name.*" Häme was one of the three major 'castle counties' in Finland under bailiffs subject to the King in Stockholm.

The spread of settlements towards the east led to Swedish colonization all the way to the Kymijoki River in present eastern Finland. The hunting grounds of the Häme people spread north to the Oulu and Savo areas. The importance of Häme Province increased towards the end of the 15th century when the region was part of the fief of the powerful Erik Axelsson Tott of Viipuri Castle. No less than twelve stone churches were built there, Hattula Church becoming one of the most famous pilgrimage sites. Beginning in Viking times, in the 9th century, the Swedish traders from Birka had purchased valuable furs from the wilderness of Häme. The *Häme Oxen Road* became a main route connecting the Aurajoki River Valley to Lake Vanajavesi and by the Middle Ages it became a vital administrative connector between the Turku and Häme Castles. After King Gustav III toured Finland in 1775 he decided to divide Finland into provinces and move the governor's residence from Helsinki to the small town of Hämeenlinna. Lake Vanajvesi valley with its many historic sites has been nominated a National Landscape by the Ministry of the Environment.

The prosperity of the province is visible in the traditional farmsteads and imposing manor houses, many of which were once old royal and cavalry estates. Artist Hjalmar Munsterhjelm (1840–1905), who was born in Tuulos and owned a manor there, drew inspiration from the surroundings. His romantic Düsseldorf-style paintings came to epitomize the tranquil Häme landscape. At one time Jokioinen Estate was the biggest manor in Finland. The manors furthered new ideas in cultivation.

Experimental farms and agricultural institutes were established; the first one in Finland was established in 1840 in Mustiala Estate in Tammela near Forssa. The Lepaa Gardening Institute was opened in the Lepaa Manor in Hattula in 1912.

From the 18th century on, paper and sawmills, spinning mills, iron and brick factories, and glassworks were founded along the rivers. Forssa became one of Finland's important industrial centers with the establishment of the spinning mill in 1847. Early industrialization led to the birth of the labor movement and the Social Democratic Party at a meeting in Forssa in 1903. The building of the first train line from Helsinki to Hämeenlinna in 1862 helped industry to thrive; Hämeenlinna, however, long remained a charming wooden town. Well-preserved old factory areas with manor houses and workers' quarters are witness to its industrial past – many are still thriving, such as the Tervakoski Mill in Janakkala, the oldest functioning paper mill in Finland, established in 1818.

Hämeenlinna – Tavastehus

Hämeen linna – Häme Castle

Häme Castle (*Tavastehus*) was founded by Birger Jarl on an island in Lake Vanajavesi near an ancient Viking trading place. The oldest parts of the castle are from the 1260s when it comprised a square fortified camp with a deep moat and massive graystone walls with three corner towers. During the following century it was built into a residential castle. A series of vaulted

rooms along the outer wall and a projecting gatehouse, *Kukkotorni*, Rooster Tower, were built. The main room is the oldest ceremonial hall in Finland.

Häme Castle is the only castle where brick, a rare material in Finland at the time, was used for construction. It made possible the more advanced vaulting and the use of Gothic decorative features. By the mid-15ᵗʰ century the castle comprised two accommodation stories around the rectangular courtyard and a chapel as well as the King's Hall and Queen's Chamber. During King Gustav III's time in the late 18ᵗʰ century, the castle's defensive system was modernized with ring walls and ramparts.

Häme Castle

The castle had been used as a prison since its founding. Now the prison has moved away and the impressive Gothic vaults of the royal hall returned to their original form. There is an exhibition on the prehistory of Häme, *Terra Tavestorum*, as well as exhibitions about medieval church art and the restoration work of the castle.

The **Artillery Museum** – Tykistömuseo – in the adjoining garrison was built for the Russian troops in 1850. It provides a fascinating look at the history and technical development of artillery from the 15ᵗʰ century to the present day.

The permanent collections of the museum are located in the former Kronoborg House of Correction, adjacent to the Castle. The objects illustrate the history, culture, and the life of the town and the province. Temporary exhibitions are mounted in the so-called museum block of fine 19ᵗʰ-century wooden houses offering a charming view of the castle.

Hämeenlinnan kaupungin historiallinen museo – Hämeenlinna Historical Museum

The **Prison Museum** – Vankilamuseo – is housed in the first prison with cells in Finland, completed in 1871. The prison operated until 1993 and was the only one in Finland that also detained women. Part of the building has been left untouched, while part of it has been renovated to house the museum.

The **Palander House** – Palanderin talo – was built in 1861 and is now restored as a bourgeois home in an authentic late 19ᵗʰ-century spirit. The rooms are splendidly furnished down to the smallest object.

The **Birthplace of Sibelius** – Sibeliuksen syntymäkoti – is a small wooden house where Johan Julius Christian Sibelius, later known as the world-famous composer Jean Sibelius, was born on 8 December 1865. The Empire-style house from 1834 has become a place of pilgrimage for music lovers from around the world. In the parlor the visitor can sit and enjoy his music. Documents and photos of the family are displayed, even Sibelius's guitar.

Jean Sibelius as a child, 1866

House of Cards – Korttien talo – in another charming wooden house is an example of how personal documents and private messages have become an accepted source of history writing.

Hämeenlinnan taide-museo – Hämeenlinna Art Museum	The nucleus of the collections in the Hämeenlinna Art Museum was formed by the works of art evacuated from the Viipuri Art Museum in 1939 at the outbreak of the Winter War. The museum, the former town granary drawn by C. L. Engel houses fine works of Finnish art from the 19th century to the present day and of foreign art from the 17th century. The granary on the other side of the courtyard was renovated to receive the Contemporary Art Collection of Henna and Pertti Niemistö Art Foundation. Their collection comprises Finnish and Nordic art from the 1950s to the present day.
Hämeenlinnan kirkko – Hämeenlinna Church	A settlement grew on the northern side of the castle and was given town rights by Per Brahe in 1638, as the first inland town. Because of the widespread interest in antiquity, circular churches became popular, influenced by the King Gustav III's tour of Italy in the 1780s where he had seen the Pantheon in Rome. The king's Neo-Classical dream of a Nordic Pantheon became a reality in 1798 in the round Hämeenlinna Church, which he ordered his court painter, French-born Louis Jean Desprez to design. The entrance is embellished with a Doric gable and columns.

The town square is surrounded by the church, by the handsome, two-story **Hämeenlinna Provincial Government Building** by C. L. Engel (1837), and by the palatial Neo- Renaissance **Town Hall** by C. A. Caven

(1887). Nearby, a number of wooden houses has survived as the last vestiges of one of the most uniform Empire towns in Finland.
The 152-hectare (380-acre) **Aulanko Park**, one of the most remarkable parks in Finland was established in 1883. It includes many man-made attractions, such as artificial ruins and a granite observation tower.

Vanajanlinna Manor, a splendid red-brick "hunting lodge" flanked by side buildings and numerous workers' residences, was built in 1924. In 1942 a German businessman bought the estate, but after the Second World War all German property was confiscated as war reparations by the Soviet Union. It then transferred it to the communist Sirola Foundation to serve as their educational facility, but the financial collapse of the Communist Party in the early 1990s led to its sale. It is now a conference center.

The small graystone **Vanaja Medieval Church** nearby was built in the 15th century. Its western gable is richly ornamented in brickwork with a rare outside pulpit, fashioned also from brick.

Hattula

The Church of the Holy Cross is, besides Turku Cathedral, the only medieval church constructed entirely of brick. It was built probably in the 14th century, at the same time as the red-brick Häme Castle. Bricks for the church and castle were manufactured in a workshop near the Castle.

Pyhän Ristin kirkko – Church of the Holy Cross

The church has high gables and brick buttresses in High Gothic fashion. The abundant murals of the nave and vaulting from the 1510s illustrating 180 stories from the Bible are unique in Finland. Hattula ranks, together with Lohja Church, as the most important decorated Finnish churches. The oldest of some forty wooden statues of saints was done by the so-called Lieto Master, the first Finnish artist known by name, who worked in the Turku area at the beginning of the 14th century.

Church of the Holy Cross

The Finnish Armour Museum – Panssarimuseo – has armored equipment used in Finland during both the past wars and peace time. The most valuable objects are the vehicles taken as booty from the Soviet Army during World War II. Parola has been a drill field for the army since 1777, where both Swedish kings and Russian emperors have inspected maneuvers.

On the shores of Vanajavesi Narrows north of Hattula, there are traces of settlement going back to the Iron Age. On **Retulansaari Island** there are some dozen sacrificial altar stones and more than a hundred Iron Age barrow graves.

Hauho

Unusually well-preserved **Hauho Village**, with its narrow lanes and old peasant houses is surrounded by a traditional Häme landscape.

Kalvola

Iittalan lasitehtaan museo – Iittala Glass Museum

The Iittala Glass Factory is the largest in Finland and its artists, such as Alvar Aalto, Tapio Wirkkala, and Timo Sarpaneva, enjoy a worldwide reputation. Its designs led to the world success of Finnish glass at the Milan Triennales in the 1950s and created the concept of "Finnish Design." These pieces became classics both in Finland and abroad and made the small red letter "i" world famous. It was established in 1881 and since 1991 Iittala, as well as the Nuutajärvi factory, are part of Hackman Designor Ltd.

A number of old brick factory buildings and red-painted workers' houses have been preserved. An old stone cowhouse has been converted into a museum that illustrates the history of glassmaking, and displays the art works by Iittala designers. The visitor not only can see how master glass blowers craft their magnificent products, but can experiment with glass blowing themselves under the guidance of professionals.

Renko

Renko Church, dedicated to St. Jaakko (*Apostle Jacob the Elder*) is charmingly surrounded by bays. It was built in the mid-15th century and soon became the center for the cult of St. Jacob, attracting pilgrims from as far away as central Europe. It is rare among Finnish medieval churches in having an octagonal floor plan.

Renko served as an important stopover along the 162 kilometer long *Häme Oxen Road*, with its church and inn established during the reign of King Gustav Vasa. Part of the road in Renko is preserved as a museum road, and marked with signs and information boards.

Rengon kirkko – Renko Medieval Church

Country Road, Hjalmar Munsterhjelm 1865

Janakkala

One of the finest scenic vistas in Häme Province can be found on the steep and rocky **Hakoinen Fortified Hill** where innumerable Iron Age grave finds and sacrificial altar stones have been found. The hill was evidently used for defensive purposes even in prehistoric times.

The **Tervakoski Mill** is the oldest still-functioning paper mill in Finland, established in 1818. From 1887 to 2000 before the euro was adopted the mill had specialized in making banknote paper. The main building of the Tervakoski Estate, enclosed by a park, was built in 1802.

Riihimäki

Riihimäen kaupungin-museo – Riihimäki Town Museum

Riihimäki was born around the railway and still bears signs of the town's importance as a major junction. The oldest buildings date from the beginning of the construction of the Helsinki-Hämeenlinna railway in 1857. The exhibitions of the museum illustrate the people of Riihimäki through history.

Suomen lasimuseo – Finnish Glass Museum

The Museum is located in the former factory of Riihimäki Glass, which was founded in 1910. The exhibition presents both the 4000-year history of glass and glassmaking in Finland. Besides glass, there is a large collection of sculptures and paintings by Wäinö Aaltonen (1894–1966) who was the most famous Finnish sculptor of the 20th century, known for his monumental art.

Near the factory buildings has survived a charming block of old workers' houses where craftspeople and glassblowers have opened shops.

The museum introduces Finnish hunting culture and the Finnish wilderness through hunting and fishing equipment, extending to hunting-related ex-libri and hunting club symbols. A unique collection of Finnish and foreign weapons is exhibited.

Suomen Metsästysmuseo – The Finnish Hunting Museum

Riihimäki Art Museum was established to house a lavish gift of art and antiques by Pentti Wähäjärvi, a legendary art and antique dealer. He knew many artists active at the beginning of the 20th century and was, therefore, able to acquire a true cross section of Finnish painting and sculpture from 1900–70. The works by artists of the post-Impressionist so-called *Septem* group and of the *November* group advocating the coloristic ascetism of Cubism form the core of the collection.

Riihimäen taidemuseo – Riihimäki Art Museum

Loppi

The old church of Loppi, dedicated to St. Birgitta and called in Finnish *Santa Pirjo* Church, was built in the mid–17th century, making it one of the oldest wooden churches in Finland. A short stretch of the *Häme Oxen Road* runs through the village, which has many well-preserved vernacular buildings.

Lopen vanha kirkko – Loppi Old Church

The **Hunting Lodge of Marshall Mannerheim** – Marskin Maja – was built by soldiers in Karelia in 1942 during the war as a 75th birthday gift to C. G. E. Mannerheim, commander of the Finnish army. It was disassembled with its furniture before the war ended and rebuilt in Loppi. Now it is a museum and restaurant.

Forssa

In 1847 a spinning mill was established on the banks of Loimijoki River, starting an important industrial center. The workers' quarters date from

Kaukola Ridge at Sunset,
Albert Edelfelt 1889

the time of the mill's founding, making them one of the oldest of their kind in Finland. The town bought the mill area and converted many of the former mill buildings into new uses. The **Southwest Tavastia Museum** – Lounais-Hämeen museo – is located in a brick cotton warehouse. **Forssa Museum** – Forssan museo – in the former foundry displays machinery needed for manufacturing and printing cotton cloth as well as samples of fabrics.

Mustiala Agricultural Institute, the first of its kind in Finland, was established in 1840 in an old King's Manor. Most of the buildings, surrounded by a large beautiful park, are from that period.

Jokioinen

Jokioinen Museum Railway is a part of the former private railway that opened to traffic in 1898. The 750-mm gauge, 23 kilometer-long railway was built to connect the towns of Forssa and Jokioinen with the wide gauge State Railways. It was one of the 13 public narrow gauge railways in Finland and carried passengers until 1954. The Museum Railway Association runs scheduled summer traffic from Jokioinen to Humppila. It also operates the Narrow Gauge Museum at Minkiö station where old engines are being restored to their original glory.

Jokioisten Museo-rautatie – Jokioinen Museum Railway

A woolen mill was founded in **Jokioinen Manor** in 1796 and four years later the first spinning machines in Finland were installed there. A stone main building, a remarkable example of early Neoclassicism in Finland, was built in 1794–1802 on the design of Stockholm town architect Erik Palmstedt. It is surrounded by a large English-style park. At its largest it constituted 32,000 hectares (80,000 acres) of land, which were mostly divided into small farms after the Finnish State took ownership in 1918. The manor is now a research institute.

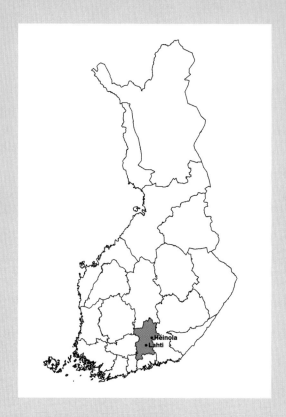

9

Päijät-Häme

Päijät-Häme, part of the larger historical Häme Province, wraps around the southern part of Lake Päijänne, the deepest and second largest lake in Finland, which divides the country down the middle. Its rocky and scenic shores were formed by the Ice Age, some 10,000 years ago, which also gave shape to the sandy Salpausselkä Ridge in the southern part of the area. Excavations have revealed signs of one of the earliest settlements in Finland of about 10,700 years ago, at the upper reaches of Porvoonjoki River, in present day Orimattila. Among the oldest settlements belong Ristola and Renkomäki in Lahti, but the permanent habitation centered in Hollola around the year 1000.

Most of the present day Päijät-Häme area used to belong to the large Hollola parish. Sysmä on the other side of the lake was the most eastern parish of the Häme area, marking the border between east and west. Many Iron Age burial sites and sacrificial altars testify to the old habitation. It was known for its grand manors where residents were said to have abundant bread even during the years of famine, not to mention the famous local homemade beer.

Since the waterways in older times were the main mode of transportation, Anianpelto in Vääksy at the narrow ridge between Lake Vesijärvi and Lake Päijänne became an important marketplace in Päijät-Häme in the 17th century. In 1727 the rights to have a market twice a year were transferred to Anianpelto from Lahti, which it had held since the 1670s. Trade prospered, so that even King Gustav III was inspired during his visit to establish a town there that, however, was never built. In memory of his visit there is still an imposing ancient pine forest, which the King ordered be preserved.

As a result of the increasing need for lumber products, Päijät-Häme became an important supplier of raw material, and Lake Päijänne was essential for its transportation. Industry took advantage of birch wood stemming from the old custom of slash-and-burn cultivation. Lahti developed into the center of the Finnish furniture industry. Since medieval times Lahti has functioned as a crossroads: the so-called Upper Viipuri Road, the Great Savo Road to Mikkeli, and the road south to Porvoo met there. The opening of the railroad from St. Petersburg to Helsinki via Lahti in 1870 and the Vääksy Canal in 1871, connecting Lake Päijänne all the way to the sea, made the rapid development of Lahti possible. In the late 19th century the need for sawmill products grew further, making the Lahti freight station the biggest in Finland.

Lahti grew rapidly as landless people moved to work in the sawmills and factories. During the Civil War in 1918, Päijät-Häme was the scene of many fierce battles. When the fighting ended, thousands of Reds were sent to the notorious Hennala prison camp in Lahti. Present day Lahti is very much a result of the over 10,000 Karelian refugees who resettled in Lahti after the Second World War, giving a fresh stimulus to its economy. Many cultural institutions moved with them from Viipuri, including the Art Museum and the Music Academy.

Lahti became symbolic of the modern city when the lattice steel radio masts were built in 1928 on Radio Hill, which still dominates the cityscape. The symbols of another kind of culture, sport, give a presence to the city in three ski jumping hills. Since 1923, the Salpausselkä Skiing Championships and later several World Nordic Skiing Championships have made Lahti an international sports center.

Lahti

The Lahti townscape is dominated by the radio masts and ski jumping hills, symbols of the city's modernity and vigor. The red-brick **Town Hall** by Eliel Saarinen from 1912 occupies a prominent position on a hill in the center of the town. Lahti is not only known for sports, but also has become a center for music as well. Literature lovers know Lahti for the International Writers' Reunion, held every second year for over 40 years in the **Mukkula Manor**, surrounded by a beautiful, protected park.

Lahden historiallinen museo – Lahti Historical Museum

The Lahti Historical Museum is located in the Lahti Manor, which was built in 1897 in the Revival style, combining Northern Renaissance and German brick Gothic features. It is surrounded by a beautiful park in the center of the city.

The permanent collections include objects relating to the history and culture of the province and those from the Viipuri Historical Museum, evacuated during the war from Viipuri, which was ceded to the Soviet Union.

Lahden taidemuseo ja julistemuseo – Lahti Art Museum and Poster Museum

The Lahti Art Museum was built around the 72 works of Finnish and foreign art from the 19th and 20th centuries, received as a permanent deposit from the former Viipuri Art Museum. Since then the museum has purchased mostly Finnish modern art and has now some 1,500 works altogether. An excellent collection of 1,400 drawings was donated by the Finnish Graphic Artists Association.

The Poster Museum on the same premises has a collection of some 50,000 Finnish and foreign prints and posters, covering a variety of fields from commercial to ideological and artistic subjects. The largest event arranged by the museum is the Lahti International Poster Biennale to which hundreds of designers from some 50 countries submit posters.

Radio- ja tv-museo –
Radio and TV Museum

The Finnish Broadcasting Company, YLE, was established in 1926, but amateur broadcasts were started in Lahti two years earlier. Lively exhibitions cover the century of progress in radio technology through receivers, equipment related to broadcasting, and amateur and DX listening receivers. Interactive installations allow visitors to hear old radio programs and even do their own broadcasts in the studio. They can test the newest technology by recording and performing in the TV program on view in the museum. An amateur radio station, OH3R, is operated by a local club and lets you visit stations around the world.

Hiihtomuseo –
Ski Museum

Skis were vital to the ancient Finns, clear from the fact that the Finnish word for a ski, *suksi* dates back 6,000 years. During the wars the army skiing troops were trained to scout intelligence by skiing behind the enemy lines. The ranks of the famous Winter War (1939–40) skiing patrols, clad in white and called "The White Death" by the Russians, were often filled by active skiers.

As early as at the end of the 19th century recreational skiing became popular among the upper classes. The first official skiing competition in Finland was held in 1879 and since 1923 the annual Salpausselkä Skiing Games have been held in Lahti. The permanent exhibition displays the development of skiing and ski jumping, including changing fashions in skis and ski clothing

over the last hundred years. Visitors can experience the thrill of ski jumping, minus freezing temperatures and icy winds, in a simulator.

Ristinkirkko – Church
of the Cross

Alvar Aalto won the architectural competition for the Lahti church in 1950. The Church of the Cross forms an axis through the marketplace with Saarinen's Town Hall at the other end. The common material, dark red brick, also unites the two landmarks. The sanctuary was only completed in 1978, two years after Aalto's death. The floor plan of the church is triangular, focusing and descending towards the altar.

Hollola

Hollolan kirkko – Hollola Medieval Church

Greater Hollola used to be the ancient center of the region. The old roads, the medieval Upper Viipuri Road, Great Savo Road, and the old road to Porvoo lead to Hollola Church. Nearby rises the high **Kapatuosia Fort Hill**, settled almost 8.000 years ago during the Stone Age. The graystone church, the third largest in Finland, was dedicated to the Virgin Mary and completed in the 1480s. Its gables are decorated with especially fine brickwork ornamentation, a sign of the importance of this unusually magnificent church.

The church is known for its many well-preserved wooden statues, such as a Finnish version of St. George and the dragon, several 15th-century descriptions of saints as well as a Finnish 14th-century limestone baptismal font. The porch walls were covered with colorful paintings in the 16th century. The pulpit and altar painting date from the 17th century and are decorated with richly painted carvings.

Across the road stands the old **Town Hall**, one of the first rural public buildings in Finland constructed in the National Romantic style. Designed by Vilho Penttilä, it was built in 1902 of exposed logs and painted red, its steep roof covered with wooden shingles. It is now a restaurant.

Pyhäniemen kartano – Pyhäniemi Manor

The Upper Viipuri Road leads from the church to Pyhäniemi Manor, one of the many old estates still found in the area. During the 19th century it was a prosperous estate of some 10,000 hectares (25,000 acres) of land with its own cheese factory, sawmill, and a wheel factory. Its two-story wooden main building dates from the 1820s. The owner lost the entire estate to gambling debts in Monte Carlo. During the 1930s it was a popular location for many Finnish historical and romantic films. Now the manor hosts high quality art exhibitions in the summer.

Orimattila

Orimattilan taide-museo – Orimattila Art Museum

The Art Museum, located in an old renovated factory building, grew from a private collection. Among the works of Finnish paintings and drawings spanning the beginning of the 19th century to the 1960s, one can make surprising discoveries of works by well-known Finnish painters and sculptors.

The exhibition "The Erkkos of Orimattila" describes the life history of three brothers, poets and newspaper men. Eero Erkko founded during the Czarist censorship a liberal Finnish-language newspaper, later to become *Helsingin Sanomat*, Finland's largest and unrivaled daily newspaper. It still belongs to the Erkko media family who also owns the extensive Helsinki Media Company.

Asikkala

Surrounded by the idyllic lake scenery typical of the province, the Urajärvi Manor dates from 1653 when it comprised 10,000 hectares (25,000 acres) of land. Some twenty years later it was purchased by the Heideman family. The last owners, sister and brother, bequeathed the

Urajärven kartano-museo – Urajärvi Manor

buildings of the manor to the Department of Antiquities in 1915.

The facade of the yellow wooden main building is turned away from the entry road to allow view to the beautiful scene. The rooms are furnished as they were during the von Heidemans tenure. They were enthusiasts of music, literature, painting, and were progressive and liberal in social matters. The courtyard is faced with the older mansard-roofed main building from the mid–18th century, where the von Heidemans collected old objects. A romantic English-style garden is decorated with animal figures, gate ruins, bridges, and an artificial island.

The canal through the narrow ridge providing a lake passage from Lahti all the way to Jyväskylä was built in 1868–71. Because of its beautiful scenery and good traffic connections the area became a popular vacation destination for artists and scientists. The canal is still popular – the 15,000 boats passing through each year make it the busiest lake canal in Europe. Vääksy waterfall has been an ancient location for watermills. The surviving mill functioned until 1950 and is now restored.

Vääksyn kanava ja Vääksyn vesimylly- ja piensähkölaitosmuseo – Vääksy Canal and Vääksy Watermill Museum

The road along the ridge leads to the western side of Lake Päijänne and to Padasjoki where a traveler still finds traditional village scenes. A breathtakingly beautiful scenic road further north to Sysmä follows a long, narrow ridge, *Pulkkilanharju*, crossing Lake Päijänne.

Vääksy Canal

Heinola

As a result of King Gustav III's inspection tour of Finland, the seat of the provincial government of Kymenkartano, *The Residence*, was relocated from Loviisa to Heinola village in 1776. A town plan was drawn up, and the settlement provided with a park avenue, *Perspektiivi*. It was one of the first town parks in Finland, now called Maaherranpuisto, Governor's Park. Heinola itself was given town rights in 1839, but only incorporated in 1843 after the governor's seat moved to Mikkeli. Even though Heinola did not become a major city, from the end of the 19th century on it flourished as a spa town and was known for its schools and a seminary. Some of their buildings still survive.

Heinolan kaupunginmuseo – Heinola Town Museum

The museum is located in a wooden late Empire-style house, built in 1872 and later used as a town hall, now restored to its original state. The town history from the time of Governors, called the Residence, is presented through objects, photographs, and scale models.

The period rooms, the Green Parlor with its the popular Biedermeier-style mahogany furniture, the Dining Room of a bourgeois family, and the late Empire-style Blue Bedchamber with its articles from the Governors' time, describe the life of the townspeople.

The **Heinola Art Museum** – Heinolan taidemuseo – is located in a wooden 1820s Empire-style house decorated with rare original ceiling paintings. On permanent display is the Empire-style library and one of the largest collections of Baltic silver in Europe.

Lääninkivalteri Aschanin talo – The Aschan Residence

The chief provincial policeman Lars Adolf Aschan built his house in a coveted location next to the planned Governor's House along the Perspektiivi Park in the early 1780s. The one-story wooden house with a mansard roof was built in the typical fashion of the times. The town's oldest house, it has been skillfully restored as a museum to illustrate life at the time of the Residence. The visitor enters the house through the peaceful courtyard and is transported 200 years back in time. The house looks as if the residents had just left; the furniture and objects are from the time of the Aschan family.

Sysmä

Sysmä was a major center of habitation on the eastern shore of Lake Päijänne from the 10th to 12th century, as seen in the many Iron Age burial sites and sacrificial altars. Because of the long history of settlement, prosperous Sysmä was always known for its many stately manor houses, still privately owned. The local cultural life is strong and offers the traveller many interesting surprises. Sysmä was the first Scandinavian Book Village in the international network of book villages. Concerts of the annual *Sysmän Suvisoitto*, music festival, fill the church and the manor houses. **Suvi-Pinx** is one of the largest and best-known and ever popular summer art exhibitions in Finland. It has also become a small, but interesting museum of vernacular architecture.

The graystone **Sysmä Medieval Church**, dedicated to St. Olaf, was built towards the end of Catholic times in the early 16th century in the easternmost location of the country.

Hartola

Itä-Hämeen Museo – Eastern Häme Museum

Hartola has a curious Swedish-language name: *Gustav Adolfs*, "Parish of Gustav Adolf," who was the King of Sweden and received the parish as a gift from his father Gustav III.

Eastern Häme Museum was founded at the initiative of Maila Talvio (1871–1951), a writer and a well-known cultural figure. The wooden green main building that houses the museum was constructed in 1828 in the Empire-style and is flanked by red side buildings. At one time it was one of the biggest manors in Eastern Häme, comprising about 25,000 hectares (62,000 acres) of land and some two hundred tenants. On the other side of the main building is a beautiful garden planted in the 1880s. Talvio's sister was the manor's last owner. The carefully restored rooms in the museum are furnished to reflect 19th-century manor culture. The kitchen, storage rooms, barns, and farmhands' quarters tell their own stories of servants' life at the time.

10
Pirkanmaa

Pirkanmaa was for a long time a borderland between the settled province to Häme in the south and the wilderness stretching northwards. Sääksmäki was the tribal seat of Häme where during prehistoric times local men built a defensive outpost, now regarded as the finest in Finland. The Christian religion was adopted slowly; even after more than a hundred years, the Sääksmäki peasants striked against the taxes imposed by the church. In response, Pope Benedictus XII issued in Avignon in 1340 a bull to excommunicate 25 peasants. In the same spirit of independence, in 1596, the local peasants joined a rebellion, called the Club War, which had started further north against the Governor of Finland, Klaus Fleming, for imposing excessive taxes and billeting troops.

In the early 1600s a well-known marketplace grew beside the mighty 18-meter-high Tammerkoski (*Tammerfors*) Rapids, which cut a passage between Lakes Näsijärvi and Pyhäjärvi. Industrial development started in the Middle Ages when one of the largest mills in Finland operated there. With the establishment of the Finlayson engineering works on the banks of the rapids to make machinery for processing wool and linen, Tampere, called "the Manchester of Finland," became a pioneer in Finnish industrialization. Later Finlayson became a cotton mill, which by the 1840s was the biggest industrial enterprise in Finland and employed a third of all factory workers in the country. It was its own kingdom, providing housing, a hospital, a fire brigade, a school, and a parish with a church in the Quaker spirit of James Finlayson. Now the historic rapids area has been declared a National Landscape by the Ministry of Environment.

Tampere naturally became a center for the workers' movement in Finland. After the declaration of Finnish independence, the Tampere area was in 1918 the location of bitter battles during the Civil War. The government White forces crushed the Red forces, joined by the Russian Bolsheviks. The Central Union of Finnish Workers was established there, as well as also many cultural organizations, such as theater groups, which developed into the professional theaters for which Tampere is well-known.

In spite of its industry, the Tampere area is known for its natural beauty. In 1775 King Gustav III was taken to the Pyynikki Ridge to admire the views over the two lakes. The hill was protected as early as 1830 from further tree felling and became a popular recreational area. Pyynikki was made a public park in the 1930s.

Southern parts of Pirkanmaa are dominated by old cultivated fields, small lakes, and hills. Both King Gustav III and Czar Alexander I visited the beautiful esker in Kangasala, later named Emperor's Hill. Zacharias Topelius was so inspired by the vistas that while there in 1853 he wrote one of his most beautiful poems, later set to music in the song "Summer Day in Kangasala," familiar to generations of schoolchildren. King Gustav Vasa had established there in 1556 a King's manor, Liuksiala, which was

later given by Duke Johan as a residence to Queen Karin Månsdotter, his
sister-in-law and the widow of Erik XIV, the brother he had murdered.
Her neighbor was Karin Hansdotter, Johan's former mistress, to whom,
when king, he donated Vääksy Manor.

North of Tampere one can still experience the wildernesses in the
Seitseminen and Helvetinjärvi National Parks, which with their gorges,
eskers, and creeks are some of the most rugged forests in western
Finland. It was here that J. L. Runeberg, the Finnish national poet, while
working as a tutor, was inspired to write *The Tales of Ensign Stål*, as well as
many poems praising the natural beauty of the landscape. Albert Edelfelt,
who later illustrated the Tales, used the steep shores and dark waters of
the wilderness lakes as a model for one of his poems. In these forests in
Virrat lived the famous bear hunter Martti Kitunen who during his
lifetime killed some 200 bears and who Topelius, in 1875 in his *Boken om
vårt land*, The Book of Our Land, raised to the status of national hero.

Tampere – Tammerfors

The town of Tampere was founded "for trade, industrial activity, and
crafts" in 1779 by King Gustav III after his visit there. The settlement
started to prosper only after the Scottish James Finlayson in 1820 set up
an engineering works
and the enormous
Finlayson Factory,
called the *Kuusvoonin-
kinen* or the "six-
storied," was built. The
wooden floors of this
brick Old Factory were
supported by 90 cast-
iron columns made by
the Fiskars Ironworks.
It was here that electric
lights were turned on
for the first time in
Scandinavia in 1882. In

addition to its famous entrance portal and clock, the area is still domina-
ted by large weaving and spinning mills. Now it is a lively center of
theaters, restaurants, and shops.

Finlayson was the only textile mill in Finland until the **Tampella
Factory** was established in 1856 to manufacture linen. A portion of the
five-story old mill survives as well as many turn-of-the-century buildings. The handsome smokestack from 1874 serves as the landmark of the
Frenckell Factory where the first Finnish paper machine was taken into
use in 1842.

The Tampella Bell Gate

The Hämeensilta Bridge, decorated with four statues by Wäinö Aaltonen, the foremost Finnish sculptor, leads to the **Central Square**, which has preserved its unified look. Tampere boasts unusually fine commercial buildings in the international Jugend and National Romantic Styles, commissioned by wealthy businessmen. Many of them were designed by Wivi Lönn (1872–1966), the first woman architect in Finland to practice independently.

Tampereen tuomiokirkko – Tampere Cathedral

The cathedral, originally called the Church of St. John, *Johannes*, was designed by Lars Sonck (1870–1956) and completed in 1907. It is the main monument of the National Romantic style, a synthesis of international ideas and a personal vision of Finnish architecture. Outside it is built

The Wounded Angel,
Hugo Simberg 1903

from rusticated sturdy gray granite blocks using the squared-rubble technique, influenced by the Scottish architecture of the time.

Inside the church is capped by an immense medieval style vault, supported by thick granite columns. Artist Hugo Simberg's idiosyncratic, symbolist watercolor-like frescoes of naked boys, serpents, and skeletons so shocked the townspeople at first that the church had to be kept closed. Simberg's favorite subjects, which he had studied earlier, were the frescoes "The Garden of Death" and "The Wounded Angel," where two poor working class boys with Tampere chimneys in the background carry a wounded angel on a stretcher.

The collections of six previously separate museums are under one roof in the former 19th-century engineering workshop of Tampella. The name comes from the Swedish for factory, *fabrik*, commonly called *vapriikki* in Tampere. The subjects range from archaeology to modern art and from crafts to technology and nature.

The 100-meter-long factory hall brings the history of the province and the town of Tampere to life. The archaeological and ethnological treasures come from the Häme Museum, founded in 1904, and include

Museokeskus Vapriikki – Museum Centre Vapriikki

145

folk textiles and wooden objects, some of the best examples found in Finland. The exhibition of Tampere's industrial history is based on technical collections started as early as the 1880s. They range from vehicles to household appliances and machines, from examples of industrial processes to samples of products made in the Tampere mills.

The **Finnish Ice Hockey Museum** – Suomen jääkiekko-museo – displays the history of probably the most popular sport in Finland.

Tampereen taide-museo – Tampere Art Museum	The Tampere Art Society, founded in 1898, established the art museum in a renovated former crown granary built in 1838 of red brick, a rare style for its architect, C. L. Engel.
	Today the collections comprise over 6,000 works, mostly Finnish paintings, prints, drawings, and sculptures from the early 19th century. The emphasis is on 20th-century artists from the Tampere area. The collection of 1,300 medals is one of the most significant in the world and presents a wide overview of the development of medal art during the 20th century.
Sara Hildénin taide-museo – Sara Hildén Art Museum	The museum is notable for its collection of modern Finnish and foreign art, owned by the Sara Hildén Foundation, which was established by Sara Hildén (1905–1993), a well-known Tampere art collector and businesswoman. The collection gives an excellent cross-section of the development of modern art since the 1960s.
	Sara Hildén was active, with the help of leading Finnish art experts, in expanding the collection to include modern international art, infor-malism, the dominant trend in European art at the time, kinetic and geometric abstract art, Neo-Realistic, and Pop Art. The collection is augmented by a solid collection of early masters of modern art from Pablo Picasso and Fernand Léger to Alberto Giacometti and Henry

Moore. Finnish artists are represented in large numbers with a wide selection of works.

Kustaa Hiekka (1855–1937), a successful goldsmith, can be regarded as the founder of the Finnish precious metals industry. He was an avid collector of not only art, but also ethnographic objects. The museum he established houses his collection of paintings, sculpture, and other artworks, including antique furniture, mirrors, clocks, silver, tin, coins, and glass objects.

Hiekan taidemuseo – Hiekka Art Museum

There are fine works from the Golden Age of Finnish art as well examples of he international influences on Finnish art at the beginning of the 20th century. The silver collection has fine examples of German, Baltic, Swedish, Finnish, and Russian silver from the 16th century on. Hiekka had worked as a journeyman in St. Petersburg before earning his master's diploma.

A palace-like private villa built in 1929 houses both Mr. Antti Salovaara's home and his private collection of Finnish art from the past 20 years. He started building his fine collection of 800 works in 1988 by purchasing them directly from artists, but after buying a single larger collection, decided to display the artworks in the house.

Willa Mac

The Central Museum of Labour in the old Finlayson dye works presents, through the story of a fictional family from the 1830s to the 1920s, the development of workers' lives, the labor movement, and social conditions framed by historical events. Twelve special objects have been selected to illustrate the colorful history of the workers' movement.

Työväen keskusmuseo – The Central Museum of Labour

Amurin työläismuseokortteli – Amuri Museum of Workers' Housing

The unusual name *Amuri* was derived from the Amuri colony in Siberia, which received its first Finnish immigrants in the 1860s. In the eyes of the Tampere people, the suburb of Amuri was so far from the city center as to earn it this metaphorical name. Amuri was zoned for workers' housing and by the 1890s included 29 blocks each comprising 4 plots. Now it is a reminder to posterity of the history of Amuri and Tampere in general, through the residents' lives, social and economic conditions,

important events, and articles from their homes. The museum consists of five houses in their original locations with 32 meticulously furnished small apartments.

Further along on the idyllic *Pispala Hill* overlooking Lake Pyhäjärvi, workers put up their small houses haphazardly on the slopes. In Finnish literature, Pispala has come to connote the independent initiative of the worker who builds his own home.

Lenin-museo – Lenin Museum	The Lenin Museum, the world's only permanently open museum dedicated to Vladimir Ilyich Lenin, portrays his life, the history of the Russian revolution of 1917 and Lenin's relations with Finland. The museum is situated in the historical Workers' Hall where the Russian revolutionaries met secretly in December 1905 and in November 1906. It was there that Lenin and Josef Stalin met for the first time. Lenin had promised that Finland would have the right to leave Russia once the Bolsheviks gained power. Finally, during the Russian Revolution, on 6 December 1917, Finland declared herself an independent republic.

There are photographs, documents, and paintings, as well as items from the apartment where Lenin lived in Helsinki while hiding from the Russian police. Many of them are made after original works, which during the Soviet times were in the V. I. Lenin Central Museum in Moscow. Now that the Soviet Union no longer exists, many previously restricted documents are becoming accessible.

Nukke- ja puku-museo – Museum of Dolls and Costumes	The museum is located in the splendid Neo-Renaissance main building of the Hatanpää Estate. It is surrounded by an English-style garden from the 18th century, now enlarged to include a rose garden with more than a hundred varieties of roses, and the City Arboretum. The museum returns the visitor to the enchantment of the past with its magical and antique toy dolls, theater and souvenir dolls, paper, costume, and religious dolls, as well as doll houses and toys. Hundreds of costumes, textiles, and accessories reflect the history of ideas, costuming, and civilization. The costumes from the 17th century up to the present day are set in the original furnishings of the estate.
Vakoilumuseo – Spy Museum	This unusual museum, in an elegant former factory owner's residence, reveals the secret activities of espionage, its history and present state, as well as famous spies and agents with their fascinating stories around the world. The equipment illustrates the exciting stories. The museum has been able to purchase secret maps belonging to the KGB. Today's techniques are represented by highly developed electronic devices.
Kalevan kirkko – Kaleva Church	The church was the major early work of Reima Pietilä (1923–1993), the great individualist of Finnish architecture, and his wife Raili, built in 1966. Standing high on a hill, it has one of the most impressive interiors found

in modern Finnish architecture. Walls soaring to the height of 30 meters are made of concave concrete slabs, all of different dimensions. Light shimmers through the narrow ribbon-like vertical windows between the concrete slabs, intensifying the powerful space.

The library is called *Metso*, wood grouse, because of the shape of its floor plan. Designed by Reima and Raili Pietilä and built in 1986, it has become one of the best-known architectural sights in Tampere. The curving rib-like concrete structure dominates the low interiors, lit by a huge skylight.

Tampereen pää-kirjasto Metso – Metso Tampere City Library

The first floor is occupied by the enchanting **Muuminvalley** exhibition of Moomin books, original ink drawings and watercolor illustrations by Tove Jansson (1914–2001), as well as the Moomin House. The internationally known and very popular Moomin books, first published in the Evening News (the UK) in 1953 as comics and translated into 33 languages, are now adapted into a TV series.

Initially, Jansson wrote about the adventures of the Moomintroll for children. The family grew to include an assortment of unusual members. When it became more complex, the books started to fascinate adults; analyses of the characters' relationships have been studied even in academic circles. Jansson's message, never obvious but always present, is to show consideration for one's fellow human beings and tolerance for those who are different. The pearl of the collection is the 2.5 meter-high scale model of the blue, turreted Moomin House, meticulously constructed in a kind of Carpenter Gothic style.

In the **Mineral Museum** – Kivimuseo – in the same building the visitor can admire some 4,000 specimens from precious stones to building stones and fossils.

Ylöjärvi

The art collection of the Urpo and Maija Lahtinen Foundation is located in the former home of the publisher Urpo Lahtinen. The imposing granite edifice was built in 1976 and commands a beautiful view of Lake Näsijärvi and the surrounding property of 16 hectares (40 acres). The collection is bold and original, reflecting Lahtinen's colorful personality, and currently comprises nearly 500 works of Finnish and foreign contemporary art.

Museo Villa Urpo – Museum Villa Urpo

Kangasala

Mobilia is the largest museum of its kind in Scandinavia. Its collections cover the history of road traffic and include more than a hundred horse-drawn vehicles, bicycles, cars, motorcycles, and steam engines. In the workshop connected to the exhibition hall, the visitor can follow the daily conservation and restoration work on the museum's cars and equipment as well as work done on cars.

Mobilia, Auto- ja tiemuseo – Mobilia, the Automobile and Road Museum

Mobilia, the Automobile and Road Museum

Lempäälä

An ancient road once crossed the Kuokkalankoski Rapids in the village of Kuokkala, at one time an important trading place. The traditional houses along the narrow village road have been preserved and now contain five special museums, called **Kuokkala Museum Route** – Kuokkalan museoraitti.

Toijala

The **Locomotive Museum** – Veturimuseo – in the old roundhouse at the Toijala train station displays steam locomotives and diesel railcars as well as photos, drawings, and scale models.

Valkeakoski

The earthworks of the Rapola hill fort along the Rapolanharju Ridge in Sääksmäki are the most magnificent of Finland's prehistoric fortifications with signs of human activity some 1,400 years ago. Several Iron Age settlements and burial grounds lie nearby. The historic Lake Vanajavesi valley, extending all the way to Hämeenlinna, has been nominated a National Landscape by the Ministry of the Environment.

From the hill, there is a beautiful view of a unique historical landscape and Lake Vanajavesi, which has inspired both tourists and artists. The graystone **Sääksmäki Medieval Church** was built in the 1490s. The most remarkable of the wooden sculptures from an earlier church is the statue of St. Olof by the so-called Master of Sääksmäki from the late 14th century.

By the mid-15th century there were several mills operating at Valkeakoski rapids. The wood-processing industry started on Myllysaari, literally "mill island," in 1873 when a groundwood mill and paper factory were established. In 1886 it started to utilize the sulfate cellulose method, which made paper stronger. The **Myllysaari Museum** – Myllysaaren museo – illustrates papermaking and the town's history. **Kauppilanmäki Museum** - Kauppilanmäen museo, an outdoor museum in a park-like setting in the middle of the town, introduces the other side of the story, the life of paper mill workers during the century from 1870 in five furnished houses and outbuildings.

In the summertime the many manors in beautiful Sääksmäki used to be frequented by artists. Sculptor Emil Wikström (1864–1942) designed for himself a studio, called Visavuori, built in 1893 on a picturesque peninsula of the lake. Following its destruction by fire only a few years later, he designed a new wooden Karelian-inspired dwelling, built in 1899–1902, and later a detached studio of stone.

Now the museum displays sculptures, sketches, and models of his mostly public sculptures. The home with original furnishings provides a fascinating insight into the lifestyle of the artists of the time. A separate pavillion features an exhibition of cartoons and paintings of Wikström's grandson, Finland's most famous cartoonist, Kari Suomalainen.

Visavuoren museo – Visavuori, Emil Wikström Museum

Urjala

The Nuutajärvi Glassworks, Finland's oldest functioning glass factory, was established in 1793. In the 1850s, production was expanded by training local men and bringing in foreign experts to manufacture pressed and filigree glass. Brewers from Germany were brought to make beer for their compatriot glassblowers. Now on weekdays visitors can watch craftsmen and glassblowers at work.

The charming village, with its red-painted Swiss-style wooden buildings decorated with fretwork, has preserved its old atmosphere. **Nuutajärvi Glass Museum Prykäri** – Nuutajärven lasimuseo Prykäri –

Nuutajärven lasitehdas – Nuutajärvi Glassworks

is located in a former brewery, converted into a museum by the famous designer of glass and china, Kaj Franck. The museum displays the history of the village and of Finnish glass design and production.

Vammala

The shores of Lake Rautavesi have a long history of habitation, witnessed by many Iron Age burial grounds and the two medieval churches, linked by an old road. The area has been designated a National Landscape by the Ministry of the Environment.

The old **Tyrvää Medieval Church** is one of the most imposing medieval stone churches in Finland, standing on a remote peninsula. It was built in the early 16th century and has especially rich brick gable decorations of stepped friezes and a four-leafed recess. The roof of unusually patterned wooden shingles had been just rebuilt in its original shape through the cooperative efforts of the parishioners when the church was virtually destroyed by arson in September, 1997. The rebuilding of the church back in its original style continues again, mostly by volunteers.

Hämeenkyrö

The harmonious landscape of **Hämeenkyrö**, shaped by centuries of cultivation, was nominated a National Landscape. Many of the houses are well-known from the novels of Frans Emil Sillanpää, the only Finnish winner of the Nobel Prize for Literature, in 1939.

Orivesi

Sculptor Aimo Tukiainen (1917–96), known for the equestrian statue of Marshal Mannerheim in Helsinki, started exhibiting in 1967 with six artist friends at his summer place and studio, called **Purnu**. This was the first in the continuing national tradition of popular summer art shows, which attract many people who might not otherwise visit exhibitions of "high" art.

Orivesi Church contains the first abstract altar piece made in Finland by Kain Tapper. It sparked much publicized debate about abstract art in the Christian faith. The church itself, designed by Kaija and Heikki Siren in 1961, was also novel for its time. The five curved walls overlap, allowing indirect light to enter.

Juupajoki

Kallenautio Inn, familiar from Zacharias Topelius's tales, operated as a halfway inn until the 1920s on the old Vaasa Road in Juupajoki, along what was then a notoriously difficult stretch of the road. The old, red-painted buildings grouped around the closed yard have been turned into an inn museum.

The idyllic natural scenes of Ruovesi have been a favorite landscape for many artists. Akseli Gallen-Kallela (1865–1931), at that time still called Gallén, had a wilderness studio built in 1895 on a beautiful rocky peninsula at Lake Ruovesi. He

Kalelan taiteilijakoti – Kalela Artist's Home

The Great Black Woodpecker, Akseli Gallen-Kallela 1893

designed it himself, inspired by the historical and national romantic movement in European art in the late 19th century. In Finland the movement was expressed by an interest in Karelian culture, impelled by the *Kalevala*, the Finnish national epic.

The exposed beams and fireplace of the two-story studio give it similarities to the family room of a Finnish farmhouse or an American Shingle Style house. The steep gables and unclad log walls resemble both a Karelian house and a Swiss chalet. In Kalela, Gallen-Kallela created his most significant works, including the well-known *Kalevala* paintings and the murals for the Finnish pavilion at the Paris World Exposition in 1900.

The environs around the wooden **Ruovesi Church** retain their traditional appearance. The church was built in 1777–78 and is one of only three 24-cornered

cruciform churches in Finland, with both the interior and the exterior corners beveled.

Kuru

The red-painted wooden **Kuru Church** is one of architecturally most impressive churches of the Southwestern type, built in 1781. The oblong church is adjoined by a stately onion-domed bell tower. **Kuru Open-Air Museum** – Kurun ulkomuseo – displays what is known as Ensign Stål's Cabin, which belonged to an ensign who fought in the Finnish War and who Runeberg used as a model for the main character in *The Tales of Ensign Stål.*

Mänttä

Gösta Serlachiuksen taidemuseo – Gösta Serlachius Museum of Fine Arts

The museum has one of the most significant private collections in the Nordic countries, uniquely posessing some of the central works in Finnish art history. G. A. Serlachius founded a groundwood mill at Mäntänkoski Rapids in 1868. He was an important patron of Akseli Gallen-Kallela and Emil Wikström. His nephew and son-in-law, Gösta Serlachius (1876–1942), the president of the company, became an important collector of Finnish art. The art works are now housed in Joenniemi Manor, designed by Jarl Eklund and completed in 1935 as the private residence of Serlachius.

Among the works in the permanent collection are national icons of the Golden Age of Finnish art, such as Edelfelt's best-known painting of Finnish soldiers in the Finnish War (1808–09) executed as an illustration for J. L. Runeberg's collection of poems, *The Tales of Ensign Stål*, in 1892. Serlachius also had a talent for collecting old Dutch, Italian, Spanish, and French art.

The **G. A. Serlachius Museum** – G. A. Serlachius museo – in the former company headquarters, which itself is a unique work of art, illustrates in interactive means the history and people of the factory town.

The **Honkahovi Art Center** – Honkahovin taidekeskus – is the heart of the Mänttä Art Festival and displays works by some of the best contemporary Finnish artists.

Virrat

The museum consists of farm buildings moved from the nearby village. The main building of a farm from 1843 and its authentic furnishings illustrate rural life at the turn of the 20th century. The yard includes a granary, storage barns, and a smoke sauna. The logging camp museum relates the hard life of forest workers between 1930 and 1960. The museum area adjoins the lock canal of Herraskoski, built in 1903–07, to complete a 135- kilometer route from Tampere.

Virtain perinnekylä – The Heritage Village

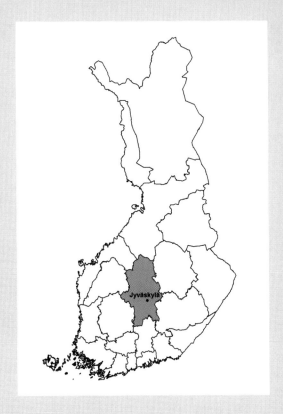

11
Keski-Suomi
Central Finland

Lake Päijänne, extending from Lahti to Jyväskylä, splits the country in half down the middle, and encompasses around its northern end an area aptly named Central Finland. Central Finland is not one of the historical provinces, but is made up of settlers from both east and west. It is said, in fact, that the Finnish language spoken in Central Finland is closest to standard Finnish. The early settlers left their mark in the rock paintings of Saraakallio in the town of Laukaa. The permanent residents came from Häme in the south, but the area received a great wave of migrants in the 16th century when farmers from Savo in the east pushed northwards into the vast uninhabited wilds. The forests provided land for slash-and-burn farming, still evident in the beautiful birch woods.

The central Finnish landscape is characterized by pockets of fields surrounded by forested hills and numerous glittering lakes in-between. Farmsteads used to be mostly lonely settlements or groups of a few houses on the southern side of the hills, as was the custom in the east. The building traditions were influenced by the west, such as the tendency to have an enclosed courtyard and two-story dwelling houses in the Ostrobothnian custom.

Until the 20th century Central Finland was sparsely populated, even though the town of Jyväskylä was founded in 1837 in an old marketplace on a ridge between two lakes. The first decades of the small town were so quiet – there were only two inns and thirtytwo illegal drinking establishments – as to provoke a remark of surprise in 1853 by *Suometar*, a major Finnish newspaper: *"Jyväskylä – call it a town?"* The development of the town was soon greatly helped by the establishment of the first Finnish language high school, *lyceum*, in 1858 and the first Finnish seminary, the Teachers' Training College, five years later. According to the Estonian example, the first singing festival was arranged in Jyväskylä when the Society for Culture and Education was founded there in 1881.

These events contributed to the Finnish language finally becoming the second official language of the country by 1883. The district doctor Wolmar Schildt, who had been influential in establishing the *lyceum*, had presented a wish, what he called "a whim," to found also a Finnish language university. The dream was finally realized when the College of Education became a full university in 1966.

In 1956 *Jyväskylä Summer* was arranged; the first of the summer arts festivals, which since have become increasingly popular in Finland. Jyväskylä is aptly called the Athens of Finland because it is a center for Finnish culture and enlightment. Alvar Aalto dreamed already in 1925: *"Central Finland is very reminiscent of Tuscany, where it is customary for towns to be built on hillsides. Indeed, Tuscany offers a fine example of how beautiful we could build our own province."*

The large forests provided the main source of livelihood. Small sawmills had been operating along the waterways, but only after restrictions on them were lifted, the founding of steam sawmills became permissible in 1857. When timber pulp began to be used instead of rag pulp to make paper, paper mills and in the 1880s also sulfite mills were built, such as those in Jämsänkoski, Lievestuore, and Äänekoski. They grew into industrial communities that were later to develop into real towns. The boom in the sawmill industry brought prosperity and turned the slumbering small town of Jyväskylä into a Klondyke, helped by the new railroad and bigger steamships. Handsome Neo-Renaissance buildings were built for the seminary, as well as for the church and the town hall, all in red brick. The merchants and craftsmen built decorative wooden houses for themselves.

After the Civil War in 1918 Jyväskylä was deemed to be the only safe location for arms manufacturing, which the expected enemy bombers would not be able to reach. As a result of the arms industry the population of Jyväskylä tripled during World War II, and further increased after the war with the resettling of 25,000 Karelian refugees in Central Finland. Jyväskylä can certainly call itself a town and Central Finland a province.

Jyväskylä

Nowhere can an enthusiast of modern architecture find such a wide range of Alvar Aalto's works as in Jyväskylä. Aalto opened his first office in Jyväskylä in 1923 at the age of 25, and there he designed his first major works, including the **Worker's Club** two years later, one of the most remarkable examples of 1920s Finnish Classicism. The city is very much shaped by Aalto's hands: he was commissioned to design the focus of the center, the **Cultural and Administrative Center** (1970–82), which includes the Town Hall and City Theater.

Another important example of the 1920s Classicism is **Taulumäki Church** from 1929 by a successful woman architect Elsi Borg, who beat Alvar Aalto in the architectural competition.

The campus for the **University of Jyväskylä** is one of Aalto's major works (1952–71). The red brick buildings, grouped on a hill along both sides of a park-like dale, form a continuation of the old seminary buildings. Many buildings on Seminaarinmäki, **Seminary Hill,** were designed by Wivi Lönn, the first woman architect in Finland to have her own practice.

The Museum of Central Finland, built in 1961, represents Alvar Aalto's later white period. It features many classical themes in his architecture from the undulating wooden paneling to galleries lit from above. Permanent exhibitions illustrates in a lively fashion how the marketplace developed into a center for Finnish culture, an industrial city, and the capital of Central Finland.

Keski-Suomen museo – Museum of Central Finland

A few steps down the hill the adjacent Alvar Aalto Museum specializes in the architecture of Alvar Aalto (1898–1976). The museum building itself,

Alvar Aalto -museo – Alvar Aalto Museum

finished three years before Aalto's death, is not only a testimony to his work, but also the permanent exhibition sheds light on his life and work, from town planning to furniture and glass and jewelry design, from architecture to painting and sculpture.

The former Civil Guard Building, designed by Alvar Aalto and completed in 1929 for the volunteer defense guard, houses now the art museum. The permanent exhibition displays part of the Ester and Jalo Sihtola Art Foundation's French, Italian, and Finnish art from the 17th century to current times as well as the collections of the Association of Finnish Graphic Artists. The museum has a separate space for the Center for Printmaking and the Center for Creative Photography as well as *Galleria Harmonia*.

Jyväskylän taide-museo – Jyväskylä Art Museum

The museum presents handiwork and its history in Finland, a country where work done with one's own hands has always been held in high esteem. It was in Jyväskylä that handiwork was for the first time anywhe-

Suomen käsityön museo – The Craft Museum of Finland

re included in the school curriculum as early as in the 1860s. There was a great interest to discover the "national" culture, and as a result a museum for handiwork was established in 1888. Handiwork and crafts are presented as a profession, hobby, and an art by displaying all possible techniques. The oldest part of the permanent exhibition was collected in 1906–45 and it gives an interesting view of what was then regarded as typical and valuable Finnish handiwork. Now the emphasis is on purchasing contemporary Finnish crafts.

The museum houses the National Costume Center, displaying the traditional festive dress worn by peasants in the 18th and 19th centuries and revived in the late 19th century.

Keski-Suomen Ilmailumuseo – Central Finland Aviation Museum	The exhibitions make visible the hundred-year history of aviation. The airplanes, mainly from the Finnish Air Force, excellently represent the history of airplane building, both in Finland and abroad. Engines, equipment used by flight crews, as well as scale models and dioramas detail aviation history.
Säynätsalon kunnantalo – Säynätsalo Town Hall	Anyone who has studied this shrine to Finnish modernism by Alvar Aalto from photos will be surprised to discover how unassumingly intimate, while also monumental, this small town hall is. The town hall was finished in 1952 and marked the beginning of a new era for Aalto, the use of red brick, here used also extensively inside. The town hall stands among the pines like a small castle, enclosing a courtyard, which is raised to the level of the second story. The outside staircase leads to the piazza-like courtyard with a pool.

On the island of Muuratsalo Aalto built himself a summer house, the so-called **Experimental House**, where he tested different methods of bricklaying. Here, too, the house encloses an atrium court, contrasted with the untouched forest around.

Muurame Sauna Village – Muuramen saunakylä – is a unique tribute to the Finnish sauna tradition. The park-like village contains not only old sauna buildings but an exhibition from the sauna's earliest origins to modern baths.

Petäjävesi

Petäjäveden vanha kirkko – Old Petäjävesi Church	The old Petäjävesi Church, built in 1764, is one of the most significant of Finland's wooden churches and is registered on the UNESCO World Heritage list as representative of Scandinavian wooden church architecture and long tradition of log building. Typical of the lake district, the church was built by the water, its high-pitched roof is a landmark for churchgoers who would come by boat or over the ice road.

The church is entered through the Ostrobothnian Renaissance-style bell tower and connected by a low passageway to the church. Both the exterior and the interior are of bare, unpainted wood. The naively executed, endearing pulpit is infused with four apostles and several angels carved in a folk-like fashion. St. Kristoforus, carrier of the Christ, with a severe expression on his face from bearing the weight, holds the pulpit up.

Keuruu

Kamana Keuruu Museum – Keuruun museo Kamana – includes the Art Museum, which located in an imposing stone cow shed. The charming area includes the protected main building of the parsonage and the parish house.

The wooden Keuruu Church, finished in 1759, is entered through a small gatehouse. The vaults and walls are painted white and decorated with frescoes in Rococo style. The beautiful pulpit is painted sky-blue. One of the longest church boats, 21-meters, to survive in Finland is kept in the churchyard. It was built by farmers to be used on Sunday mornings to row to church.

Keuruun vanha kirkko – Old Keuruu Church

The traveler must take a long, winding road through the wilds to find an unclad log church and a cemetery hidden in the wilds, which the farmers of this remote village built for themselves in 1783. A bell tower with a handsome onion dome rises from the west end where one enters the oblong church. The walls are joined with locked short joints, left unboarded and still fragrant with tar.

Pihlajaveden vanha kirkko – Old Pihlaja-vesi Church

Haapamäki Steam Engine Park

Old Pihlajavesi Church

Haapamäki village became an important hub when the rail line was opened in 1879. **Haapamäki Steam Engine Park** – Haapamäen höyryveturipuisto – preserves old steam engines and has the largest display of model trains in Finland.

Hankasalmi

Pienmäen talomuseo – Pienmäki Farm Museum	The Pienmäki farmstead represents the old way of building in Central Finland, with its rectangular courtyard and alleyways flanked by rows of barns leading up to the main building. The buildings have occupied these sites for several hundred years in a traditional landscape of slash-and-burn woodland clearings and a glittering lake a short distance away. They are filled with appropriate furnishings and household objects, vividly recalling life on the farm.

Saarijärvi

Saarijärven museo – Saarijärvi Museum	The museum presents the cultural history and art of the region. **Gentry Home Museum** – Säätyläiskotimuseo – is furnished on the Kolkonlahti Estate, where the 19-year-old J. L. Runeberg, later designated the national poet of Finland, worked as a tutor. During his stay in 1823-25 he became familiar with country folk whose toughness and endurance he so idealistically described in his first collection of poetry in 1830.
	Stone Age Village – Kivikauden kylä – is the largest reconstruction of a Comb Ceramic village in Finland, based on archaeological research. It presents concretely how people lived 6,000 years ago, the kind of dwellings they built and the methods they used for hunting and fishing. The main building has an exhibition on the current research and its background to the findings.

Kannonkoski

There were only a few churches in the new Functionalist or International Style built in Finland in its heyday in the 1930s. **Kannonkoski Church** is a fine example of the early period, designed by the architect couple Pauli and Märta Blomstedt and completed in 1938.

Luhanka

Peltolan mäkitupalaismuseo – Peltola Croft Museum

This rare museum records the history of crofter families who lived on the farmstead land, paying rent to the owner with their work. They were allowed to build their humble huts and cultivate a small piece of surrounding land. The village was constructed over the centuries; In 1960 the owners of the farmstead donated the houses, the oldest of them from the 18th century, to the local history association, which restored them. The buildings are furnished as if the original residents were still living there.

Peltola Crofter Museum

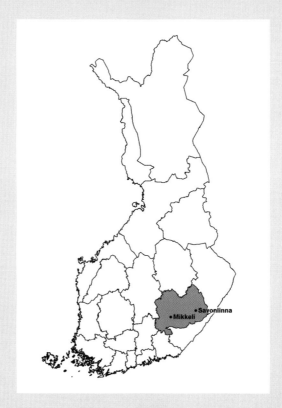

12
Etelä-Savo
South Savo

The landscape of southern Savo – bordered by Häme province to the west and south and Karelia to the east on Finland's border with Russia – is dominated by water. *"Savoland is an archipelago in the middle of the lakes,"* wrote Zacharias Topelius in his *Boken om vårt land,* The Book of Our Land, a well-thumbed reader familiar to generations of Finnish schoolchildren. As early as 900 A.D., during the Viking era, settlers from Häme and Karelia started to migrate to the area of the present-day Mikkeli. Several Iron Age hill forts, built on lake shores to guard and protect the settlers from enemy attacks, can still be seen.

Although Mikkeli where a 15th-century stone sacristy still stands was a busy medieval trading center, the first important town in the region was Savonlinna, "Savo Castle", founded when Sweden was a super power in Europe and when much of Finland was a part of the Swedish Kingdom. Savonlinna began life as a trading settlement on the islands surrounding the imposing Olavinlinna Castle. The castle itself, named for St. Olof, the patron saint of Christian knights, dates back to 1475 and was the last Medieval castle built in Finland – and the first in Scandinavia designed for use of cannon and firearms. In 1639, Count Per Brahe, Governor of Finland, granted town status to Savonlinna, which had become the home of the first grammar school, or *pedagogio*, in eastern Finland. Mikkeli was only incorporated in 1838 when it became the seat of the provincial government, but has grown into a bustling town.

Most early settlements in southern Savo comprised clustered log houses built around open courtyards. Land was cleared by slash-and-burn cultivation, signs of which are still visible in the beautiful birch forests. The peasant population was socially homogenous. By the 18th century, the culture of the gentry began to flourish in scattered country parsonages, freehold estates, manor houses, and military residences. After 1781, when the Haapaniemi Military Academy was relocated from Kuopio to Rantasalmi, noble families moved to Rantasalmi and Joroinen, where the town's social life was so lively and elegant it was called "Little Paris." Savo people still have a reputation as smart businessmen, which they earned during the booming trade in tar, extracted from the pine forests and used for waterproofing roofs and treating ships. Transportation of goods, especially dairy products in the late 19th century all the way to St. Petersburg, was made possible by the good water routes. Because of the small size of farms and the rocky, broken landscape, dairy farming is still an important source of revenue for farmers.

Dominated by the soaring keep of Olavinlinna Castle and the natural beauty of the nearby Punkaharju Ridge, Savonlinna became a booming tourist town in the mid-19th century. But it was the opening of the Saimaa Canal in 1856 that put Savonlinna on the map. A spa was opened in 1896, and in 1912 a summer opera festival was started in the courtyard of Olavinlinna Castle. Today Savonlinna is a popular summer resort, an international opera town, and a bustling center for lake traffic where old steamers still call. The spectacular canal route from Savonlinna north to Heinävesi is famous for its park-like surroundings, lakeland views, and narrow passages.

For Finns, Punkaharju Ridge has long represented the ideal image of Finnish nature, designated as a National Landscape by the Ministry of the Environment. *"The traveler never tires of nature's delightful play, constantly discovering new details he had not been aware of, and wherever he goes, finding new, open, smiling views,"* commented Topelius. The main road from Viipuri to Olavinlinna has run along the narrow glacial esker, or ridge, since the Middle Ages. Visiting the area in 1803, then part of Russia, Czar Alexander I was moved to ban the felling of trees. Forty years later, Punkaharju Ridge was designated a Crown park, Finland's oldest managed nature conservation area. Tourism is still important; the southern part of the province is the most popular summer cottage area of Finland. Only one in three residents live there permanently, the rest return to spend the summers.

Savonlinna

Olavinlinna – Olavinlinna Castle

Olavinlinna Castle is the world's northernmost medieval fortress, proudly rising on a rocky island with its round towers reflected in the dark waters of the strait. The last of six medieval castles built in Finland, it was established in 1475 to protect the eastern border of the Kingdom of Sweden-Finland and the new settlements of Savo. In 1714, the fortress and the town were conquered by the army of Czar Peter the Great, then for a while governed by Sweden. The castle was returned to Finland when Finland became a Grand Duchy of the Russian Empire in 1809, but by then it had lost its military significance.

Its round towers give Olavinlinna a different look from other castles in Finland. Sixteen foreign stonemasons worked on the fortress, including master craftsmen from Tallinn and Gotland. The walls of the main keep, three towers, and the forecourt were completed in 1496. Two of the three medieval towers survive: the Church Tower and the Bell Tower. The third tower was built in 1604–08, though its present appearance reflects repairs done by the Russians in the 1790s. The medieval appearance of the tower rooms, with their round shooting ports for firearms, is well preserved. Stone coats of arms still decorate the towers' outer walls. The chapel in the Church

Count Per Brahe

Olavinlinna Castle, Hjalmar Musterhjelm 1870

Olavinlinna Castle

Portrait of the Singer Aino Ackté,
Albert Edelfelt 1901

Olavinlinna Castle

Tower, with its carefully preserved side altar and fragments of painting, is a popular place for weddings.

Each July, the Savonlinna Opera Festival, the best-known cultural event in Finland, is held in the castle courtyard, featuring international opera stars. Founded in 1912 by the famous and beautiful Finnish soprano Aino Ackté (1876–1944), it lasted only four years, but has been going strong since it was revived by a new generation of Finnish opera singers in 1967.

Olavinlinna Castle and the Lake Pihlajavesi, dotted with islands separated by narrow straits, were designated a National Landscape by the Ministry of the Environment.

The town was built around the castle. In 1846, the so-called **Little Church** was built as an Orthodox sanctuary, which the Lutheran congregation bought in 1938. Red-brick **Savonlinna Cathedral** was built in 1874–78.

In Lehtiniemi on the lake stands the decorative wooden **Rauhalinna Villa**, which a lieutenant general in the Russian army commissioned for his wife on their silver wedding anniversary. Constructed in 1898–90, the building is an unusual mixture of Russian, Oriental, and Swiss styles, lavishly decorated in fretwork. It is now a summer restaurant and hotel.

Savonlinna Provincial Museum is located on an island in a two-story brick building designed by E. B. Lohrmann and built in 1852 to serve as a crown granary. It was the first building to be protected under Finland's historic landmarks legislation in 1964 and was restored twenty years later as a cultural history museum. Inside, the original structure can be seen clearly in the wooden columns of the exhibition room.

Savonlinnan maakuntamuseo – Savonlinna Provincial Museum

The permanent exhibition illustrates the people and life on the shores of Lake Saimaa since the Stone Age. Water is the theme that runs through the entire story; from it people have earned their livelihood through the centuries and it has provided a means of communication and transportation in both summers and winters. A meticulously executed miniature model of Savonlinna at the time of its 300th anniversary right before the Winter War in 1939, when the town had about 8,000 residents, is on display.

The museum prides itself on having three unique old steamers as well as a reconstructed traditional freight boat *Vappaa Savo*, "Free Savo", moored at a jetty behind the museum. The last surviving wooden steam barge, the *Mikko*, built in 1914, was in regular service until 1967. Such barges, nicknamed "tar steamers" because of their tarred sides, were a common sight on Lake Saimaa carrying timber and firewood to St. Petersburg, Helsinki, and Stockholm. A steam schooner *Salama*, "Lightning", was built in 1874 and regularly carried passengers from Joensuu to Viipuri and St. Petersburg. In 1898 she sank in 30 meters of water in Lake Saimaa, and finally in 1971 was raised

and restored as a museum ship. The passenger steamer *Savonlinna*, built in 1903 and known as the Saimaa Express, was the fastest passenger ship on Lake Saimaa. After the Saimaa Canal was closed in 1939 because of the war, the golden age of its steamers ended.

The Savonlinna Art Museum provides exhibition space for painters, sculptors, and photographers, as well as graduates of the Savonlinna Art College. During the Savonlinna Opera Festival the museum invites an artist to mount a private exhibition. The museum purchases art, which is then displayed in the town offices in Savonlinna.

Savonlinnan taidemuseo – Savonlinna Art Museum

Punkaharju

Punkaharju Ridge

The narrow, winding Punkaharju Ridge is the most spectacular of the glacial eskers in eastern Finland: "*...between shadows are tied silvery belts to each other; a lake next to another lake glistens as far as the eye reaches,*" as Topelius admired. The breathtaking, some seven kilometers long road, part of the ancient road from Viipuri to Savonlinna along the high ridge, threads its way between two lakes. The ridge itself was acquired as the first Crown park in Finland in 1843. Among its most stunning views are from **Runeberg's Hill**, where J. L. Runeberg, the national poet of Finland, in 1838 is said to have been inspired to compose lines for the national anthem while contemplating its majestic vistas.

The wooden, Swiss-style **National Hotel** on the ridge, was built in 1845 as a foresters' dwelling with guest rooms for travelers. The former **Hotel Finlandia**, now renovated as a health spa, was built in 1914. Serious scientific studies of Finland's forests began in the Punkaharju area in the 1870s. An arboretum and an old-growth forest is complete with nature trails.

Punkaharju's pine forests offered an ideal location for the architecturally distinctive **Takaharju Sanatorium**, originally built in 1903 for treating tuberculosis patients. With separate pavilions connected by light wooden balconies, its early Rationalist architecture is reminiscent of Viennese Jugend. The Takaharju facility was the first of several famous sanatoria in Finland, and is now used as a rehabilitation hospital.

The idyllic **Putikko Village**, south of the town center, grew up around the local sawmill in the late 18th century. Putikko Manor, besides renting rooms to travellers, operates a farm museum and craft exhibition.

Lusto Suomen metsämuseo – Lusto Finnish Forest Museum

Lusto gathers, preserves, researches and exhibits forest culture in many forms, from ancient beliefs, folklore, and ecology to conservation and industrial resources. Its distinctive circular design is the work of architects Rainer Mahlamäki and Ilmari Lahdelma, completed in 1994.

Located on the scenic Punkaharju Ridge, the museum is partly hidden by the forest, enveloped by the dappled light and shade of the trees. Its impressive round exhibition space, echoing the form of the museum's namesake – *lusto* is the Finnish word for the annual growth rings of trees – houses a permanent exhibition. The space is covered with thin battens of local tamarack treated with tar and linseed oil, the old Scandinavian method of treating boats, giving both the color of the surrounding pine trunks and the fragrance of pine tar. In the workshops

woodworkers exhibit their many skills, from making *virsut*, birch-bark shoes, to cutting *vasta*, a birch-twig whisk for the sauna. The gift shop is a visual treat, with wooden handcrafted kitchen utensils, toys, and decorations of every type imaginable.

The Retretti Art Center, the largest in Scandinavia, is not only famous for its hugely popular summer art exhibitions, which attract up to 120,000 visitors each year, but for its spectacular grottos, underground lakes, and rivers quarried twenty-five meters deep into the bedrock below the site. Its primary purpose is to make the fine arts available to people who otherwise might not be enticed to visit an art museum. Retretti's emphasis is on modern artists, and it attempts to reach beyond well-established European art. In addition, lasers, lights, sound, and color add excitement to the exhibits of design, sculpture, glass, and ceramic art in the underground galleries.

Taidekeskus Retretti – Retretti Art Center

Concerts and theater performances are staged in conjunction with the Savonlinna Opera Festival in the underground concert hall.

Kerimäki

Why would the 10,000 parishioners of Kerimäki build the world's largest wooden church, which seats over 3,000 worshippers and provides standing room for two thousand more? No one really knows. The parish was large and the minister wanted half of the parishioners to be able to fit into the church. Designed by architect Anders Fredrik Granstedt, and built by master builder Axel Tolpo, the church was completed in 1847

Kerimäen kirkko – Kerimäki Church

Kerimäki Church

after only three years of construction.

Two floors of balconies complement the church's huge sanctuary beneath a 27-meter high cupola. The church is a masterful testimony to the skill of the carpenters; here the structural potential of wood is taken to its extreme. The building represents an idiosyncratic mix of influences including Gothic Revival and the round-arch style known as Byzantine Revival that was popular on the Continent at the time. Since the State had tried to curb small congregations from building stone churches, some of the interiors were painted in faux marble.

The church is said to be like a "deep-timbred cello," and because of its special acoustics it is a popular location for concerts, some of them given in connection with the Savonlinna Opera Festival.

Mikkeli

Along the 16th-century Porrassalmi Road south of Mikkeli, now preserved as a museum road, traces of Savo's oldest settlements can be found. It is also a memorial to the illustrious Porrassalmi battle of 1789, where 650 Finns defeated the 5,000 attacking Russians. Handsome manor houses and villas were built on the shores of Lake Saimaa. Incorporated only in 1838, it became the seat of the provincial government of the new Mikkeli province.

Mikkeli's central Administration Square is dominated by the two-story stone Empire-style **Provincial Administration Building** designed by C. L. Engel in 1843, flanked by single-story wings built in the 1850s and 1938. The wooden **Mikkeli Parish Church**, located outside the central square, was built between 1815 and 1817 under the direction of master builder Matti Salonen on the designs of Charles Bassi from the Intendant's Office. It is a double cruciform structure, covered with a shallow pyramid roof with a wide lantern, typical of eastern Finnish churches of the time. **Mikkeli Cathedral**, a few blocks from the square, was built in 1896–97 in Gothic Revival style by Josef Stenbäck.

The town takes its name from St. Michael, the patron saint of the 15th-century sacristy. Once part of the easternmost medieval stone church in Finland, the building survives as an indication of Mikkeli's role as an ancient trading center. The lower section is part of the original structure, which was built on the site of a 12th-century Orthodox church whose patron saint was Archangel Michael. A 1.5-meter deep wooden crypt lies under the sacristy.

Savilahden kivi-sakasti – Savilahti Medieval Stone Sacristy

The sacristy was repaired and the upper portion reconstructed in the prevailing new Gothic style in 1897. Now it is a church museum displaying objects collected from local churches. Among them are a 17th-century Baroque pulpit and the so-called Black Seat, a shame bench for sinful parishioners and a verger's spear, used to wake up sleeping worshippers.

Sturdy and rectangular in shape, the granite building of the Suur-Savo Museum was built as a communal granary in 1848. Restored in 1960 as a museum, the building is itself an interesting historical sight.

Suur-Savon museo – Suur-Savo Museum

The exhibitions provide a museum-within-a-museum – well-preserved objects once used by farmers and fishermen, as well as by the gentry and officials, are not displayed in glass cases, but openly, as in older museums. Reconstructions of the fine ancient costumes, based on objects and resplendent jewelry found in a Viking grave circa 1100–1200 in Tuukkala, near Mikkeli, is a testimony to the all but vanished settlement there.

Mikkelin taidemuseo – Mikkeli Art Museum

The museum, originally housing a collection of works by sculptor Johannes Haapasalo (1880–1965), became the Mikkeli Art Museum when it received a bequest from a private collector. The permanent exhibition showcases Finnish paintings from the 1870s to the 1970s. The Neo-Impressionist works of the *Septem* group from the early 1900s and the works from the *November* groups in the Expressionist style from 1915 to 1925 form the core of the collection. Finnish illustration art is another speciality of the museum.

Päämajamuseo – Headquarters Museum

In December 1939, when the Winter War broke out, the Finnish army headquarters for Commander-in-Chief Marshal C. G. E. Mannerheim

was moved to the Central Elementary School of Mikkeli, which was convenient to the battle front.

On the 5th of January 1940, Mikkeli was bombed by Soviet planes. Mannerheim's headquarters was located outside the town until the end of the war in March. Peace lasted only 15 months before a new war broke out. From June of 1941 until September 1944, during the so-called Continuation War, Mannerheim's headquarters were again located at the school. The museum includes Marshall Mannerheim's office with its original furniture, the office of the infantry, and a multimedia exhibit.

Near the school is Naisvuori Hill, where Finnish troops started to quarry an underground command bunker, before the war broke out in 1939, to use as a headquarters in anticipation of a Soviet attack. This cave in nearby Naisvuori Hill became the famous **Communications Center Lokki** – Viestikeskus Lokki – where coded messages and telephone and teleprinter messages were processed by all-women auxiliary services. It is restored to its original state.

Jalkaväkimuseo – Infantry Museum

Mikkeli became the center of military administration for eastern Finland as early as 1775. Indeed, the museum itself is located inside two barracks of the Finnish 6th Mikkeli Sharpshooter Battalion. The artfully restored wooden barracks, built in the 1880s, surround a symmetrical courtyard and well-tended grounds.

This compact little museum is filled with interesting material on the history of Finland's many wars for visitors interested in military history. The exhibitions display weapons, original photos, objects from everyday life on the home front as well as from the theaters of war spanning the 18th century until the present. In addition to the Finnish infantry, the museum also exhibits Soviet and German war equipment.

Kenkävero, with the curious literal translation of "shoe tax," sits on the shore of Lake Saimaa. Known as an ancient Iron Age dwelling place, where many interesting archeological finds have been made, it has been the site of a parsonage since the Middle Ages. The present unusually handsome main building, designed by Carl Alfred Cavén, was built in 1869. The stone cowshed, farmhands' quarters, and storehouses predate the main building. The wooden single-story parsonage has exceptionally decorative fretwork ornamentation on the large, open porch.

Kenkäveronniemi pappila – Kenkäveronniemi Parsonage

A protected historic building, it is a good example of a prosperous 19th-century parsonage as a center of cultural and farming life. Though the building now functions as a local crafts center, some rooms are set aside and furnished as a parsonage museum.

Hirvensalmi

Workers houses, two villas, a still-functioning water power station, and an artfully restored factory, now housing businesses, survive from the old paper mill in Hirvensalmi along the **Kissakoski Canal**, built between 1831 and 1854.

Ristiina

Ristiina is a typical southern Savo church village. From the 1640s until 1682, when the region's alienated baronies and earldoms were returned to the control of the Swedish crown, Ristiina was dominated by the Governor of Finland, Count Per Brahe. Per Brahe named the town for his wife Kristina Stenbock and built his seat of government, the Brahelinna Castle, in the village of stones, logs, and bricks in the years 1646–69. The derelict edifice was demolished in 1802 and only the foundations of the castle are left today.

The wooden cruciform **Ristiina Church**, built in 1773–75, is located in the harmonious villagescape. The portraits of Per and Kristina Brahe are displayed in the church.

The **Pien-Toijola Farmstead Museum** – Pien-Toijolan talonpoikaismuseo – is situated on a beautiful site on a lake. The museum includes over twenty farm buildings, the oldest an 18th-century granary. The farm has been in the same family since 1672.

| Astuvansalmen kallio-maalaukset – Astuvansalmi Rock Paintings | Rock paintings, dating as far back as 3500 B.C. to 500 A.D., have been found on the sheer cliffs and boulders along the channel that ran from Lake Saimaa into the Gulf of Finland thousands of years ago. So far, 61 |

primitive rock paintings have been discovered, mostly in central and eastern Finland. Out of a total of some 450 known images, 65 have been found at Astuvansalmi, located south-east of the center of Ristiina. Because the images are located on walls rising straight up from the water, historians believe they were painted in the winter from the ice on the lake, or in the summer from boats.

The rock paintings at Astuvansalmi are the largest in Scandinavia and are regarded as the most valuable in Finland. They measure more than 15 meters across and are good examples of Stone Age Comb Ceramic culture. The illustrations depict mainly elk, but also show people, shamans, and boats. Human images are typically painted as stick figures. The paintings appear to have had a ritualistic connection to hunting, perhaps ensuring control over prey and guaranteeing the success of the hunt through the ritual shooting of the painted images. An unusual figure of a woman with a bow suggests that also women hunted.

Mäntyharju

The old town center of Mäntyharju has retained its traditional appearance with a church, many old public buildings, and houses. The handsome former town hall, built in 1823 as two separate houses from the logs of an old church, now functions as **Salmela Art Center** – Taidekeskus Salmela – a summer art gallery.

Pieksämäki

Among the many cultural centers built in Finland in the 1980s, the **Poleeni Cultural Center** – Kulttuurikeskus Poleeni – in Pieksämäki designed by architect Kristian Gullichsen in 1989, expresses the refinement of a classic modernist work. The visitor is welcomed by a row of trees, a forecourt, and a long wall that define the center as the civic building for this town of less than 15,000 people. The airy lobby opens into an exhibition space, leading to the library, the theater, and the café.

Because of the Military Academy, **Joroinen** had many estates of noble families. Several of its handsome manor houses are still privately owned. The center of the town has retained its traditional scale and old public buildings.

The **Heinävesi Canal** route is one of the most picturesque and impressive in Finland, nominated a National Landscape by the Ministry of the Environment. The canal is lined with parks, occasionally opening onto vistas of the wide lakeland.

The Karvio Canal is the oldest, dating from 1895–96. During the following twenty years, the canal network, with its several locks, was expanded. Many canal watchmen's huts built at the beginning of the last century still stand today. The canal master's house and the canal hands' quarters at the Varistaipale locks, with a rise of 14.5 m, the highest in Finland, are now a museum. The old steamers still carry passenger from Savonlinna all the way to Kuopio. Heinävesi Village has retained its character with its old harborside dwellings, cemetery and oblong wooden **Heinävesi Church** by Josef Stenbäck, built in 1890–91 on a high hill.

When the Orthodox Valamo Monastery, which originally stood on an island in Lake Ladoga, was evacuated during the war in 1940, the monks

Valamon luostari – Valamo Monastery

retreated 200 kilometers westward to a new home in Heinävesi. A new Byzantine-style church, dedicated to the Transfiguration of Christ, was built in 1976. It has a remarkable collection of 18th-century icons and religious objects from the Old Valamo. The modern monastery has new living quarters for the monks, a hotel, a library, and Lay Academy, and the Art Conservation Institute for icons and church textiles, designed during the 1980s in a modern adaptation of the Byzantine style.

The Monastery, the only Orthodox monastery in Scandinavia, has become a lively tourist site and Orthodox cultural center attracting more than 100,000 visitors a year. Even non-Orthodox visitors appreciate its importance as a place for contemplation and prayer. Courses at the Lay Academy are available throughout the year on various subjects, from Orthodox theology and holistic medicine to icon painting and silver-smithery. Organic produce is cultivated in the fields around the monastery, and the old tradition of winemaking has been revived. There are cruises to the nearby Orthodox **Lintula Convent**.

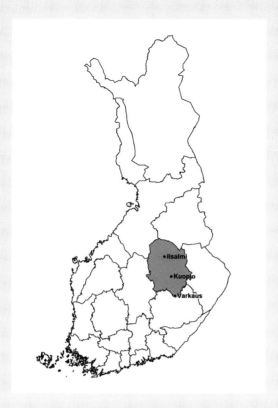

13

Pohjois-Savo
North Savo

"*A full understanding of the beauty of Kuopio cannot be received until one has climbed the ridge visible in the back of the picture, Pujo Mountain, which rewards the labor of climbing with the loveliest view over the open Lake Kallavesi plus those hundreds of islands, rocky islets, sounds, bays, grassy shores, smoke puffing steamships, and sails shining far away,*" wrote Zacharias Topelius in *En resa i Finland – Matkustus Suomessa*, Travel in Finland, published between 1872 and 1874. One can still see Topelius's views of northern Savo, now from the tower at the top of Puijo Hill.

Even though northern Savo only became part of Finland under the treaty of Täyssinä in 1595, culturally the area belonged to the west. Until the 19th century, northern Savo, peripheral to Western Finland, preserved the ancient Karelian culture of the east. The old chimneyless log cabin, with its origins in Karelia, survived in remote areas. Inside, smoke rose from masonry cooking stoves up to the ceiling and escaped through a vent or flue in the wall or roof. Settlement spread along the water routes from the south. Isolated small farms brought the wilderness areas into cultivation by slash-and-burn agriculture, signs of which are still visible in the landscape. Buildings line roads along ridges, offering views of the lakes, meadows, and woodland pastures. Farms are separated from one another by stands of forest.

Slash-and-burn farming made Savo people mobile, looking for new opportunities in the Häme wilderness, northern Satakunta, and the lake area of southern Pohjanmaa. Some went all the way to Värmland in central Sweden, from where they were sent in 1638 to establish the colony of "New Sweden" what became Delaware, the United States. Besides slash-and-burn farming, the major contributions of the early Finnish settlers were a skill of building log cabins and a way of living in peace with the Indians.

Most of northern Savo's small farmers were dependent on secondary sources of income, such as tar burning and logging. In 1782 King Gustav III divided Finland into smaller provinces and reestablished Kuopio as the governor's seat and the new center of farming for the new Savo and Karjala province. He also built roads that finally connected Savo and eastern Finland to the west. The Greater Saimaa waterway extended all the way from the Kuopio-Iisalmi region to the south coast on the Gulf of Finland, along which tar and timber were transported to the Viipuri area. Even today Kuopio harbor testifies to the importance of the town as a center of waterborne trade.

The first ironworks in Finland to smelt lake ore, taken from local lakes and bogs, was established in 1746 at Juankoski Rapids, near Kuopio. Although use of lake ore, mostly for cast-iron cookware, ended in the early 20th century, the ironworks still stand as a reminder of those flourishing times.

Varkaus, south of Kuopio, was founded in the 16th century as a trading center. It became the first freehold estate in Savo and during the

19th century grew into a busy marketplace and industrial center. The ironworks there was established in 1820. At the beginning of the 20th century, the Ahlström Company purchased the area and built a wood-processing factory. The water route via the Saimaa Canal gave Varkaus, too, a connection to the sea.

Northern Savo had few manor houses, but its parsonages functioned as centers of culture and innovation. In spite of its remoteness and smallness, Kuopio became a seat for progressive and national ideas. In the 19th century, during Finland's autonomous period, J. V. Snellman, the Finnish philosopher and statesman, published two newspapers in Kuopio, one in Finnish for the country people, the other in Swedish for the educated classes. Later, Minna Canth, the writer and women's rights advocate, was active in the town's social life.

Kuopio

The first efforts to establish Kuopio in 1652 by Count Per Brahe, the Governor of Finland, failed. Only when King Gustav III incorporated the town in 1782 as a seat for the governor of the new Savo and Karelia province did it start to grow. The opening of the Saimaa Canal in 1856 hastened its development as a center of commerce and made Kuopio the

The Kuopio Marketplace,
Ferdinand von Wright 1850

focus of inland water traffic. In the harbor, the old warehouses and factories survive.

The famous Kuopio marketplace is still the heart of the town's life. The **Town Hall**, with its richly painted interiors, is one of the handsomest Renaissance Revival public buildings in Finland, completed in 1885. Around stand **Kuopio Lyceum**, the center of which was designed by C. L. Engel (1826) and the Jugend-style **Market Hall** (1902). Kuopio's progressive architectural tradition is still alive and well.

Kuopion kulttuuri-historiallinen museo – Kuopio Museum of Cultural History

When the Kuopio Patriotic Society started collecting objects for the Cultural History Museum in 1884, there were only five ethnographic collections in Finland. The museum displays the cultural history of Northern Savo from prehistory to the present day, covering everyday life, festivals, and livelihoods. Life on the farms as well as in the town is richly illustrated with many objects.

View from Haminalahti, Ferdinand von Wright 1853

The Museum of Natural History was founded in 1897. Its exhibits cover the variety of Northern European flora, fauna, and mineral specimens that make up Finnish ecosystems. The exhibitions are embellished by the late 19th-century Biedermeier-inspired landscapes and bird paintings of the well-known artist brothers Magnus, Wilhelm, and Ferdinand von Wright who lived in the nearby Haminalahti Manor.

Kuopion luonnon-tieteellinen museo – Kuopio Museum of Natural History

Although wooden houses still dominated Kuopio's town center in the early 20th century, their gradual destruction and replacement by modern stone buildings sparked a lively debate on preservation. In 1973, a block of old buildings was restored for display as an open-air museum.

Kuopion kortteli-museo – Old Kuopio Museum

The Old Kuopio Museum consists both of buildings on their original sites and those transferred from other sites in Kuopio reflecting the 19th-century Neo-Classical style. The museum traces the changes in people's lives between the late 1700s and the 1930s. Lilacs, rose-bushes, and jasmines decorate the court-yards.

The writer Minna Canth (1884–1897), an early feminist and social critic, lived in Kuopio from 1880 until her death. One of the houses has a room furnished to replicate her workroom with her original objects and furnishings.

Across the street is a yellow wooden house that used to be a studio for Victor Barsokevitsch (1863–1933), a photographer of Polish origin. His house, surrounded by a garden, is now **VB Photographic Centre**, one of the major photographic galleries and research centers in Finland.

Johan Vilhelm Snellman (1806–1881), the philosopher and statesman, lived from 1845 to 1949 in this wooden townhouse. He was the leading philosopher of the mid–19th-century national awakening in Finland. Yet, due to his role in a dispute over the right of authorities to intervene in internal university decision-making, his early university career was curtailed. After spending four years abroad, he returned to Kuopio where he took a position as a grammar school headmaster.

J.V. Snellmanin koti-museo – J.V. Snellman Home Museum

Johan Vilhelm Snellman

J.V. Snellman Home Museum

His Swedish-language newspaper, *Saima*, published in 1844 through 1846 in Kuopio, was distributed primarily to Finnish intellectuals. The paper played a fundamental role in generating public awareness of the Finnish language at a time when Swedish was the dominant language of literature and business. The paper was often censored because of his nationalist opinions. Snellman went on to become a professor of philosophy, a senator, and the director of the Ministry of Finance. The original 19th-century exterior of the house remains largely intact. The interior, still full of objects that belonged to Snellman, has been redecorated many times.

Kuopion taidemuseo – Kuopio Art Museum

Kuopio Art Museum is located in a Jugend-style former bank building from 1904. Its collections provide insight into Finnish art history of the 20th century, ranging from the expressionism of the early 1900s and the coloristic ascetism of cubism to the new realism and the international styles. Besides its own collection, the museum is the repository of private collections, among them drawings and graphic art.

Suomen Ortodoksinen kirkkomuseo – The Orthodox Church Museum of Finland

The rich and beautiful exhibits of the Orthodox Church Museum not only mirror the history of the Finnish Orthodox Church, the second state church of Finland, but are unique in western Europe. The

Orthodox archbishop's seat and the seminary are also located in Kuopio.

The Orthodox tradition extends back to the ancient monasteries of Valamo, Konevitsa, and Petsamo in Russia, as well as to the religious culture of Karelia, the easternmost province and the one ceded to the Soviet Union after World War II. More than three thousand of its existing old icons and gold and silver sacred objects were gathered at the monastery of Valamo in 1911 by order of the church authorities. Many more were destroyed during the war.

Construction of the Kuopio Cathedral began in 1806, but work was interrupted for four years by the Finnish War of 1808–09. The stone church was completed in 1815 according to new plans in a more simplified style. When the sanctuary was restored in 1961, the church commissioned new silverware and textiles from Bertel Gardberg and Dora Jung, famous for their modern designs exhibited at the Venice Biennales.

Kuopion tuomio-kirkko – Kuopio Cathedral

The **Männistö Church**, dedicated to St. John, was built in 1992. It was designed by architect Juha Leiviskä, acclaimed for his sensitive use of natural light and rhythmically opening interior spaces. The ethereal interior of the sanctuary contrasts with the robust red brick of the foyer and the facades. Paintings by Markku Pääkkonen on the altar wall, exploiting the reflected light, complement the architecture.

Rautalampi

Rautalampi was first settled by migrants from southern Savo in the 1550s. In the 16th and 17th centuries, many of its residents emigrated first to Värmland in Sweden and then to Delaware in North America. One of them was Jussi Marttinen whose descendant, John Morton, was a signer of the U.S. Declaration of Independence.

The many old manor houses around attest to the rich cultural tradition in Rautalampi. Already in 1828 and 1831, while collecting folk poems for the *Kalevala* Elias Lönnrot advised the visitors to travel to the beautiful Rautalampi village. It is still charming and well-preserved.

Rautalampi Church was built between 1842 and 1844 from plans by C. L. Engel's son, Carl Alexander. The wooden structure is the second largest wooden church in Finland and seats 1,700 parishioners.

The museum was built in 1938 by Aina Peura, the owner of an estate and a local businesswoman, to house the objects she collected from the area at a time when the old farming and manor house culture was giving way to contemporary 20th-century life.

Rautalammin museo – Peura Museum

On display are exhibits representing the interiors and furnishings of local estates as well as peasant cultural traditions. In addition, the museum has a fine collection of some 150 paintings from North Savo. The adjoining outdoor museum includes a traditional chimneyless cottage, a windmill, storerooms, and a late 19th-century church boat, a communally-owned wooden rowing boat used by villagers on Sunday mornings to travel to church.

Karttula

Riuttalan talonpoikais-museo – The Riuttala Peasant Museum

The prosperous farmstead of Riuttula, proudly standing on the shores of Lake Riuttasjärvi, is a well-preserved example of a 19th-century Savo farm that was chosen to represent Finnish country life at the 1900 Paris World's Fair. It was the only independent farm in the village; all other houses were tenant farms of Riuttala. The 19th-century farmstead buildings cluster around the rectangular yard. The log buildings are restored to their early 20th-century appearance when the farmstead was at its largest with 2000 hectares (5000 acres). With its furniture and household objects made in the house, it looks as if the residents had just stepped out for while.

Each August, the Finnish rye scything championship is organized in Riuttala. Original tools, farming equipment and live domestic animals bring the museum to life, as do demonstrations by local craftspeople of old farming methods.

Vesanto

Vesanto Croft Museum – Vesannon torpparimuseo – illustrates the history of the tenant farm system that started in the early 18th century when also farmers, not only the nobility and ministers of the church, were given the right to establish them. A tenant cleared land and built his house on the land of a farmer and paid the rent with labor and farm produce. The system gave the ever-growing landless population a means of livelihood. In 1922, after Finland became independent, the tenant farmers were given the right to purchase their farms.

Nilsiä

Paavon pirtti – Paavo's Cabin

The old log cabin on Aholansaari Island was a home of religious leader Paavo Ruotsalainen (1777–1852). Born a peasant and self-educated, Ruotsalainen attracted a large following as a preacher. A widely publicized 1839 court case, in which Ruotsalainen was fined for holding illegal revival meetings, cemented his reputation as a champion of the common folk. Later he became an important symbol of Finnish nationalism during the Russification period from 1899 to 1905, when Finnish autonomy was threatened by the Czars. Due to the support of the clergy, his revivalist movement stayed within the church and is still a vital force.

Even in contemporary times Ruotsalainen's story has been an inspiration: Finnish composer Joonas Kokkonen based his opera *Viimeiset kiusaukset*, The Last Temptations, on his life. When it was first produced in 1975, it helped to reignite the popularity of modern opera in Finland. Singing the lead role brought Finnish bass Martti Talvela great fame.

Iron ore is found in Finland's thousands of lakes as beads, utilized already 1,000 years ago. Because of the abundance of firewood and water power, several ironworks were established in Savo, bringing prosperity

Juankosken ruukki – Juankoski Ironworks

Juankoski Ironworks, P. A. Kruskopf 1845

and international influences to these remote corners. The Juankoski Ironworks, also called Strömsdal, is Finland's oldest and best preserved ironworks originally using lake ore. Founded already in 1746, the heyday of the ironworks started after the opening of the Saimaa Canal in 1856 linking the inland lakes to shipping routes south. Juankoski became known as the "Pot Works" because of its main product, pots and kettles.

Most of the late 19th-century ironworks buildings still stand. The two charcoal furnaces from 1890 are unique, and the last of their kind in Finland. The Empire-style residence of the director dates from 1826, and a foreman's house and wooden church from 1864.

The **Workers' Museum** Juankosken tehtaan- ja työväenmuseo – exhibits manufacturing and farming equipment. Each August "Brynolf's Night," an annual celebration named after the ironworks' original founder, Brynolf Bronou, is celebrated.

Vieremä

The handsome Empire-style main building of Herrala Manor from around 1840 and said to be designed by C. L. Engel himself, attests to the importance of **Salahmi Ironworks** in Vieremä. The first blast furnace was built there in 1807 and operated until 1909.

Sonkajärvi

In 1831 a blast furnace and bar-iron forge was established at Jyrkkäkoski Falls in Sonkajärvi. After **Jyrkkäkoski Ironworks** was purchased by a large company, a new Scottish-type blast furnace of English brick was erected in 1874. The works produced pig and bar iron, as well as nails and cast iron products.

Maaninka

Maaninka Canals

Old Vianto Canal was built between 1847 and 1852 to connect Maaninkajärvi and Onkivesi Lakes at the site of canals first dug by the Russians earlier in the century. When it proved too narrow for traffic, it was replaced by the enlarged **Ahkiolahti Canal** in 1874.

The **Korkeakoski Falls**, a popular tourist sight already in the 19th century, was made famous by Zacharias *Topelius's Finland framstäldt i teckningar* (Finland in Pictures) from 1845, a book which in many ways influenced Finns' views of their country. Its name means "high waterfall" and it is indeed the highest unharnessed waterfall in Finland with a vertical drop of 46 meters. The water cascades down the rocky slope to a ravine, echoing thunderously through the steep canyon.

Lapinlahti

Eemil Halosen museo ja Lapinlahden taidemuseo – Eemil Halonen Museum and Lapinlahti Art Museum

Eemil Halonen (1875–1950) was born in Lapinlahti to a peasant family who later produced many well-known artists. Originally a carpenter, he was attracted to art. His works met with immediate success and, in 1900, he was commissioned to carve six wood reliefs with subjects from Finnish folk life for the Finnish Pavilion at the Paris World's Fair. Halonen became one of the most successful Finnish sculptors of the early 20th century.

Even though Halonen's rarefied occupation met with criticism from locals, in 1908 he purchased a home in Lapinlahti and founded an art studio where many of Finland's finest sculptors came to work. **Eemil Halonen Museum** – Eemil Halosen museo – exhibits hundreds of sculptures ranging from works in plaster to finished metal pieces, including original works by Halonen. There are also sculptures by Arttu Halonen, Eemil's brother, who established Finland's first art foundry in 1912. The foundry cast virtually all of Finland's major public statues of the period, including the equestrian memorial to Marshall Mannerheim in Helsinki in 1960.

The **Lapinlahti Art Museum** – Lapinlahden taidemuseo – includes collections of works by Eemil Halonen's cousins, Antti and Pekka, as well as local modern artists. Pekka Halonen became the most famous them, known as a master of winter landscapes and illustrator of local peasants.

Now the town is not only known for the art in its museums, but for its art schools and interesting public art found along the streets and squares.

West of the town center is the well-preserved northern Savo village of **Väisälänmäki**, its buildings lining the road along the top of a hill. Open courtyards offer sweeping views of the lakes and the grazing pastures, meadows, and birch woodlands descending towards the lakeshore. Few villages in Savo have retained so well the traditional look shaped by early slash-and-burn farming. A guided culture and nature trail leads through the area, designated a National Landscape by the Ministry of the Environment. It was here that Finnish peasants and landscapes, so important to the national identity in the late 19th century, were painted by Eero Järnefelt and the Halonen brothers, Antti and Pekka.

Iisalmi

The **Koljonvirta Bridge** was the scene of the Koljonvirta Battle, from a tactical point of view the most illustrious victory in the Finnish War. By October 1808, the Russian troops had forced the Finnish army to retreat to Iisalmi where the battle began on October 27, 1808 at noon and ended in the evening. The Russian force of 3,000 men set out to attack the Finns. The outnumbered Finnish troops of 1,100 men mounted a successful counterattack. The Finnish victory was decisive in forcing a cease-fire that ended the war. Yet, only a month after the cessation of hostilities, Sweden was forced to cede Finland to the Czar.

The memory of the battle was revived forty years later by J. L. Runeberg, the national poet of Finland, in a heroic romance *Fänrik Ståls sägner*, or "The Tales of Ensign Stål." Regarded as his masterpiece, in the poems Runeberg celebrated the courage of the Finnish soldiers and credits victory in the Koljonvirta battle to Sven Dufva, a lone soldier who, with stubborn naivety, defended the bridge. The events of the battle can

Juhani Aho

be relived both on the battlefield and in the multimedia theater in town.

Juhani Ahon museo – Juhani Aho Museum

Juhani Aho (1861–1921), a writer noted for his realistic descriptions of Savo and its people, spent his childhood in the Mansikka-niemi Parsonage. Built in 1841, it is now a home museum with original artifacts. Besides the parsonage, the museum includes a "war shed," an old granary, that stood on the western side of the Koljonvirta River during the Finnish War. Its outer walls are still pockmarked by bullets.

Juhani Aho Museum

The wooden cruciform **Iisalmi Old Church** was completed 1779. Framed paintings on the balcony railing, which Mikael Toppelius made in 1748 for the earlier church, were moved to this church.

The **Evacuation Center** – Evakkokeskus – built in Iisalmi in 1989 in the Russian- Byzantine style, commemorates the wartime evacuation of Karelia in the 1940s, and serves as a testament to Orthodox Karelian culture. The walls of the great meeting hall are covered with Greek Byzantine-style frescoes. Its stained glass window, the largest in Finland, was made in St. Petersburg according to 19th-century Russian Orthodox tradition. The exhibitions include a unique collection of models of

Karelian churches destroyed during the war, which provide an intriguing historical overview of Orthodox church architecture in Karelia from the 1600s to the 1900s. The collection of icons and other religious objects were recovered from churches in the territories ceded to the Soviet Union.

The adjoining **Iisalmi Orthodox Church** – Iisalmen ortodoksinen kirkko – dedicated to the prophet Elijah, was built in 1957. The huge wall paintings, unique in Scandinavia, were completed in 1995 according to the Slavic style from the 12th to 14th centuries. The icons on the wall separating the church hall and the altar are framed by a magnificent wooden *iconostasis* carved in the ancient Bulgarian style, a type built nowhere else in the world during the past hundred years.

Varkaus

In the 16th century Varkaus was the first freehold estate in Savo to develop into a trading post. The lake-ore ironworks began operations in 1820. The Taipale Canal, built between 1835 and 1840 and 1867 to 1871, opened up a shipping route via Lake Saimaa south to the Gulf of Finland and boasted the first state-operated locks in the country.

When iron production ended in 1908, the **A. Ahlström Company** started a successful wood-processing industry by constructing a wood pulp plant and sulfite pulp mill as well as paper and plywood mills. Walter Ahlström also commissioned a general plan for the town with a central park surrounded by symmetrical, Classical-style buildings. Architect Alvar Aalto was hired to design offices as well as workers' houses and a number of industrial buildings in the 1940s, including a sawmill, which was unfortunately demolished.

Varkauden museo – Varkaus Museum

The museum is located in the former hotel of the Ahlström Company, built in 1914. The collections illustrate the history of shipbuilding as well as the wood and metal industries that have dominated Varkaus since the early 1800s.

Varkauden taide-museo – Varkaus Art Museum

Varkaus Art Museum's permanent exhibition comprises the collection established by a local merchant, Pekka Kansanen, a patron of modern art, and donated to the museum by his daughter Rakel. It includes treasures by Finnish modernist painters from the *November* group.

Mekaanisen Musiikin "Museo" – "Museum" of Mechanical Music

This is the largest museum in Scandinavia specializing in music produced by mechanical instruments – and the only one in Finland. The collection covers the entire history of mechanical music from the 1850s to the present. It not only must be seen, but heard, with its player-pianos, music cabinets, amusing stereo gramophones, old juke boxes, a self-winding violin, as well as "Popper Goljat," the world's biggest orchestrion, a giant

"Museum" of Mechanical Music

4,000-kilo box that reproduces the sound of a 75-piece symphony orchestra.

The instruments are displayed in nostalgic "sets" conveying the spirit of various musical eras. Visitors are shown around by guides who are familiar with the instruments and well-versed in the social history and customs of mechanical music. The museum is private and was inspired by the owner's interest in mechanical music.

14
Kymenlaakso
Kymijoki River Valley

The medieval *Great Coastal Road*, the *King's Road*, connected Turku on Finland's southwest coast and Viipuri in the easternmost reaches of the Gulf of Finland. The road allowed exchanges of trade, new ideas, and culture between the Swedish west and the Russian-oriented east. Granite churches and handsome houses, such as the Kyminkartano Estate on the Kymijoki River, were constructed along it. Between Vehkalahti and Virolahti the road still follows its old route, preserved as a museum road.

By the 14th century Vehkalahti had become an important trading post, nowadays known as the town of Hamina. Farmers and fishermen on the coast enjoyed direct contacts with the northern coast of Estonia and thus with traders of the Hansa League, the medieval trading alliance with northern Germany and countries around the Baltic. Signs of the old fishing and farming culture are still visible in the picturesque island villages along the Finnish coast.

The terms of the Treaty of Uusikaupunki, following the Great Northern War (1700–21) and the Russian occupation of Finland from 1714 to 1721, known as the Great Wrath, meant a harsh future for Finland, exhausted by war. Sweden had to cede southern Karelia, including the town of Viipuri, to the Russians. Sweden set about strengthening the new eastern border by building forts in Hamina and Lappenranta. Hamina's distinctive town plan, with its octagonal central plaza at the hub of eight streets radiating outward like spokes, was based on Renaissance ideas of town planning and fortification. Both the Swedes and Russians applied the general European fortification theory of the time, the Swedes confining themselves to a restrained Rococo Classicism while Russian Classicism was quite grand.

Reconstruction was interrupted by yet another war known as the Lesser Wrath in 1742. The Treaty of Turku in 1743 dictated that more land had to be surrendered: the Kymijoki River formed a new border when all the land east of what is now Kotka had to be ceded, including the towns of Savonlinna, Lappeenranta, and Hamina. The river became also the cultural boundary between east and west. The area east of the river became known as Old Finland for which Russia promised to guarantee freedom of religion, maintain the existing school system, and keep the local village administrations intact. The Russians rebuilt the fortifications at Hamina and Lappeenranta. The Military Academy for training Finnish officers was moved to Hamina from Rantasalmi in 1819, and became the Finnish Cadet School.

After the Swedish victory in the so-called Gustav's War of 1788–90, waged by King Gustav III, his cousin Empress Catherine II of Russia ordered the construction of fortresses at the Kymijoki River to protect St. Petersburg, a new capital established by Peter the Great in 1703. Transport to Hamina and Viipuri was closed off and exports of tar from the Swedish side to Viipuri halted. The extensive Russian fortress construction put local peasants to work, but lodging and feeding Russian troops to oversee these efforts was costly. The Russian policy of conscripting Finns into the army for up to 25 years led to large-scale desertions and migrations.

Thanks to the good water connections, the wood and timber industry began to flourish at the mouth of the Kymijoki River. After Finland became part of the Russian Empire in 1809, the sawmill trade was taken over by Viipuri merchants. The boom after the Crimean War, the opening of the Saimaa Canal in 1856, and the later expansion of the canals between northern Savo and Karelia, made possible the great industrialization of the Kymijoki River valley. Landless peasants from Savo migrated south to work in the mills, where people were able to ride out economic downturns and readily absorbed influences from other cultures. Granite quarries in Vironlahti providing valuable stone for the building boom in St. Petersburg, gave Karelian peasants another opportunity to earn a living.

Kotka

The mouth of the Kymijoki River, where Kotka is now situated, has been known for its excellent salmon fishing since the 1300s. But beginning in the mid–19th century, the city became better known as the center of the Finnish pulp industry. The new red-brick factory buildings of the **Ahlström Company** were drawn in 1949 by Alvar Aalto, who also designed glass objects for the Ahlström glass factory. The young Aalto had earlier been commissioned to design a sulfate pulp mill and housing area for Ahlström in the nearby **Sunila Factory**. Built in 1936–39, it is one of his early masterworks of International-style industrial architecture. The residences became a model for progressive housing for workers.

Kyminlinna Castle

The prospering industrial town built a cathedral-size church. For a town of 5,000 people, the red-brick **Kotka Church** seating 1,600 was constructed in the popular Neo-Gothic style in 1897–98. **Maretarium**, the largest aquarium in Finland, is the latest attraction in Kotka. Its 22 theme aquariums introduce 50 Finnish fish species and the 500,000 liter cylindrical pool holds Baltic specimen.

Haapasaari Island, twenty-five kilometers south of Kotka, has been guarding the sea route east since the 1600s when pilots came to the island. The closely spaced houses, surrounded by boat houses and docks, relate its long history as a fishing and trading village.

Kyminlinna – Kyminlinna Castle

Catherine II of Russia ordered Kyminlinna Castle built at the mouth of the Kymijoki River to control the main east-west land routes to Russia. After the construction of the earthworks, the large caponier fortifications were begun in 1803 amidst rising political tensions between Russia and Sweden. The pentagon-shaped fort with its five bastions guarded the river crossing.

Ruotsinsalmen linnoitus – Ruotsinsalmi Fortifications

The Ruotsinsalmi coastal fortifications were built in the late 18ᵗʰ century at the same time as Kyminlinna Castle as a base for the Russian Navy. The fortifications were built on the islands and included about 30 different structures. Kotkansaari Island constituted a town of its own with military buildings. Fort Elisabet was built on Varissaari Island where the memorial to the Ruotsinsalmi Naval Battle of 1790, the biggest naval battle ever in Scandinavia and Sweden's most glorious naval victory, was later raised. The salvage from the Russian frigate *Sankt Nikolai* is exhibited. The outermost fortification, now the restored ruins of

Slava on Kukouri Island, was an unusual round fort built of polished stone and red brick in 1791–94. During the Crimean War in July 1855, the British Navy destroyed the empty ramparts and buildings of Ruotsinsalmi. Most of the structures, with the exception of St. Nicholas Orthodox church, survive only as ruins.

The Provincial Museum of Kymenlaakso specializes in the life of the coastal archipelago as well as the history of Kotka. Artifacts on exhibit from the frigate *Sankt Nikolai* range from spyglasses to ropes and small arms. The *Tarmo*, the world's oldest functioning icebreaker, built in England in 1907, is displayed in the Central Port.

Kymenlaakson maakuntamuseo – The Provincial Museum of Kymenlaakso

Kotkan ortodoksinen kirkko – St. Nicholas Orthodox Church

St. Nicholas Orthodox church is the most remarkable example of Russian Neoclassicism in Finland. Consecrated to St. Nicholas, the church was built in 1801 as part of the Ruotsinsalmi fortress. The church was designed by a St. Petersburg admiralty architect. The church is embellished by floral ornaments and an unusual curved iconostasis.

After the Czar of Russia Alexander III, Grand Duke of Finland, and Czarina Maria Feodorovna, the former Princess Dagmar of Denmark, saw salmon fishing at Langinkoski Rapids they wanted to have a hut there. The lodge, designed in the romantic Swiss-style by Finnish architects Sebastian Gripenberg, Magnus Schjerfbeck, and Jac. Ahrenberg was built in 1889. The imperial family felt safe at Langinkoski. The royal couple led a simple life, doing carpentry work and preparing food in the kitchen. Authentic household objects are impeccably preserved.

Langinkosken keisarillinen kalastusmaja – Langinkoski Imperial Fishing Lodge

Langinkoski Imperial Fishing Lodge

Hamina – Fredrikshamn

Count Per Brahe, Governor of Finland, had established in 1653 a town on the site of the medieval trading post of Vehkalahti. After the town was burned in the Great Wrath, it was reestablished as Fredrikshamn, "Fredrik's Harbor," named for the King of Sweden, to protect the eastern border between Finland and Russia. The town became known as Hamina in Finnish.

A radial town and fortification plan for, unique in Finland, was based on the 16th-century Renaissance fortress. From the central octagonal plaza with a town hall, eight streets, intersected by ring streets, radiate out towards the ramparts. By 1742 the fortress work was barely finished when Hamina was burned by the Russians. In 1809 a peace treaty was signed in Hamina by Sweden and Russia making Finland an autonomous Grand Duchy of the Russian Empire. The Finnish Cadet School, where generations of Finnish officers were trained, many of whom would become prominent leaders in both countries, was established in 1819.

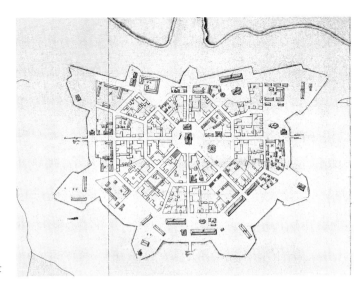

The unusual design of Hamina, one of less than ten circular fortress towns built in all of Europe, has remained intact despite fire, siege and, during the last century, public indifference. Many fine 19th-century stone buildings remain, including the fine three-story **Town Hall** with a monumental bell tower and C. L. Engel's Neo-Classical **Town Church**, in the form of a Greek temple. The unusual, round **Orthodox Church** in the Neo-Classical style has a detached bell tower, capped with a Russian-style onion dome.

The idyllic **Tammio Island** off the coast is made of some forty closely-built houses, the oldest from the early 1800s, with boathouses and storage sheds on the shore.

Never has such splendor been seen in Hamina before or since as on the 17th of June 1783, when dozens of carriages carrying Catherine II, Empress of Russia, and her entourage rolled into the little border town. She settled into an 18th-century stone house, now the **Hamina Town Museum**. The arrival of her cousin, Gustav III, King of Sweden, was a much more modest affair. The King, disguised as the Count of Gotland, reached the town the next evening to "secretly" negotiate with her. The museum's exhibits are mostly related to Hamina's history. Two rooms are furnished in period style: the blue Biedermeier room and Catherine's room.

Haminan kaupungin-museo – Hamina Town Museum

The **Merchant's House Museum** – Haminan kauppiaantalomuseo – was built in 1841 after the great fire and used as a dwelling and merchant house until 1977. The museum with its period rooms and objects celebrates the work and lifestyles of craftspeople and merchants in Hamina.

Anjalankoski

The mighty rivers and sturdy paper mills still bear signs of Anjalankoski's past. The first mechanical pulp factory in the Kymijoki River Valley was established in Anjalankoski in 1872. The riverscape is dominated by the handsome red-brick hydroelectric plant. In the 1930s the Tampella Company invited Alvar Aalto to design a paper mill, several housing areas, and the still amazingly modern school.

Anjalan kartano- museo – Anjala Manor

Anjala Manor dates from 1605, when Henrik Wrede of Livonia, in present-day Latvia, sacrificed his life to save King Carl IX in battle near Riga. The King rewarded Wrede's valor by giving his widow the Elimäki lands, which included the village of Anjala. It was here during Gustav's War in 1788 that the revolt of the Finnish officers, the so-called Anjala League, attempted to force the King to make peace with Russia. Plans were outlined for an independent Finland.

The two-story manor was built in the 1790s in the Neo-Classical style, popular after Gustav III's trip to Italy. Now a museum, one of its rooms is dedicated to Mathilda Wrede (1864–1928), a legendary friend of prisoners and the poor.

Nearby is **Wredeby Manor**, where the constitution for independent Finland was drafted in the summer of 1917.

The wooden **Anjala Church** was completed in 1756. The wooden pulpit, altar railing, and the columns framing the altar painting are executed in faux marble. The altar painting is set in an unusual, blue-painted "drape" on the wall.

Elimäki

Elimäen kirkko – Elimäki Church

The simple Elimäki Church, built in 1678, is one of only sixteen surviving 17th-century wooden churches in Finland and the best-preserved in the eastern coastal area. The interiors reveal treasures: the finely executed pulpit from the 1650s is the work of the Master of Pernaja, a craftsman from the coastal town, and a rare Baroque-style choir screen from 1666 separates the altar from the rest of the nave.

Elimäki is well-known for its many manor houses. The present Neo-Classical **Moisio Manor**, a two-story stone structure, was designed by C. L. Engel and built in 1818. The manor now houses a collection of works by prominent late 19th- and 20th-century Finnish painters and sculptors.

Moisio Manor

The 120-hectare (300-acre) **Arboretum Mustila** was established in 1902. It is unique in the whole of Northern Europe with its 100 different species of coniferous trees, 150 deciduous trees, and more than 100 different species of rhododendrons.

Pyhtää

The well-preserved white-stuccoed stone church of Pyhtää, dedicated to St. Henrik, has since the 15th century stood at the point where the *Great Coastal Road* crosses the Kymijoki River. The original Gothic so-called lancet windows, divided by brick staffs, are unique in Finland. The walls and vaults display colorful paintings dating from the end of the 15th century.

Pyhtään kirkko – Pyhtää Medieval Church

Ten kilometers off the coast is **Kaunissaari Island**, settled since Viking times. The island truly lives up to its name, Beautiful Island. The picturesque fishing village is well preserved. The lighthouse at the northern end of the island is from the 1880s.

Kouvola

Kouvolan kaupungin-museo – Kouvola Town Museum	The Kaunisnurmi Historic District of wooden Jugend-style houses in Kouvola is the home of three small museums depicting various aspects of life in the town. The **Kouvola Pharmacy Museum** – Kouvolan apteekkimuseo – has a late 19th-century apothecary's shop, laboratory, and pharmacist's office. The nearby **Kouvola Tube Radio Museum** – Kouvolan Putkiradiomuseo – exhibits period furnishings and radios from the 1920s to 1950s. The **Museum of Railway Worker's Home** – Rauta-tieläiskotimuseo – built in the 1890s, depicts how railroad workers and their families lived a hundred years ago.
Kouvolan taidemuseo – Kouvola Art Museum	The Kouvola Art Museum is housed in Kouvola House, the cultural center of the town. The collection includes Finnish modern art after 1960 and nationally recognized local artists.

Kuusankoski

Työväenasuntomuseo – Workers' Museum	The buildings at the Kettumäki Workers' Museum are good examples of one- or two-room log cabins factory workers built for themselves. The interiors reproduce the living quarters of a stableman, and a paper factory worker, and a paper mill master.

The well-preserved **Iitti Village**, surrounded by three lakes, has been called "the most beautiful village in Finland." Old houses line the country road that continues to the charming village of Radansuu with its handsome, old farmsteads.

Valkeala

The Verla rock paintings are among the most notable Finnish examples of rock art. Fifteen out of the 61 rock paintings in Finland are located in the northern Kymijoki River Valley. The red-clay paintings cover an area six meters long and more than one-and-a-half meters high. Among the figures depicted are elks, humans and an angular creature, probably a snake. The unusually realistic depiction of elks indicates that the Verla paintings belong to the oldest period of Finnish rock art, the early Comb Ceramic era about 6,000 years ago.

Verlan kallio-
maalaukset – Verla
Rock Paintings

Jaala

Verla is an idyllic mill village, which since 1972 has been an industrial museum. In 1996 Verla was added to the UNESCO World Heritage List. The village is the only remnant left of the early wood products industry

Verlan tehdasmuseo –
Verla Mill Museum

in the Kymijoki River valley. The mill, established in 1872, produced handmade white cardboard from groundwood, or mechanically made pulp. The factory has been kept as it was when the operations ceased in 1964; only the workers are missing. The park-like area with decorative Neo-Renaissance style brick buildings retains its authentic late 19th-century appearance.

Miehikkälä

Salpalinja-museo – Salpa Line Museum

When the Winter War with the Soviet Union ended in March 1940, the outbreak of another major war was imminent. Already in April, frenzied construction of fortifications began along Finland's eastern border. By 1944, the defensive Salpa Line, *Salpalinja*, stretched from the Gulf of Finland in the south all the way to the Arctic Ocean. The 1,200 kilometer system of trenches, anti-tank barricades, and field fortifications was the largest such undertaking in Finnish history.

Portions of the Salpalinja defences, built by more than 37,000 Finnish men and women, have been restored. According to military historians, the Salpa Line was the best defense line of World War II. Although no major battles were fought along the line, its existence during the defensive battles of the summer of 1944 boosted Finnish morale and influenced Stalin's decision to halt attacks on the Finnish front.

Virolahti

Virolahden graniitti-louhokset – Virolahti Granite Quarries

The shores of Virolahti Bay are surrounded by granite hills and provided stone from quarries for over 200 years for the buildings, canals, bridges, and streets of St. Petersburg. They were the source of stone for the 48, almost 17 meter-high columns for St. Isaac's Church. The most ambitious project was cutting a giant, 25 meter-high monolith base for the statue of Alexander I in the Winter Palace square. They also provided the red granite for Napoleon's tomb in the Invalides Church in Paris. A landscaped path leads the visitor through the quarry area, now being restored.

Also in Vironlahti there are restored Salpa Line fortifications. Weapons and equipment are displayed in bunkers.

15
Etelä-Karjala
South Karelia

*K*arjala, or Karelia, the easternmost province of Finland in what used to be a much larger area, is considered the primal origin of the Finnish people. Epic folk poetry, the oral tradition once common in the whole of Finland, survived longest in Karelia where most of its runes, collected to form the *Kalevala*, were finally written down in the mid-19th century.

Karelia was always a battlefield between East and West, between Russian and Swedish influences. In the 9th century, the Swedish Vikings conducted raids into the east via the Åland Islands and the Gulf of Finland to Lake Ladoga in Russia. From the 11th century on, the Orthodox Church and Novgorod brought eastern influences to Karelia. The Karelians allied with Novgorod, which fought against the Finns in Häme province, then in the Swedish sphere of influence. Thanks to the fur trade, the late medieval period was a prosperous one for Karelians.

During the third crusade to Finland in 1293, the Marshal of Sweden, Tyrgils Knutson, invaded Karelia and built a castle in Viipuri. The Pähkinäsaari (Schlüsselburg) Treaty between Sweden and Novgorod in 1323 divided what is now Finland along a southeast-northwest axis between Sweden and Russia and made the region increasingly a battlefield of power politics.

After the Uusikaupunki Treaty of 1721, Karelia became part of the Russian Empire and was referred to as Old Finland. The war had impoverished the area. Most of the towns on the coast were burned by Russian soldiers. The Czars rewarded the loyalty of local officials by donating land to their favorites, a time-honored method of ruling in the Viipuri area. The estates were run by a bailiff with a work force of peasants virtually reduced to serfdom. Authorities had to crush several peasant revolts before they were persuaded to rescind a hated daily labor requirement in 1858. By 1891 the Finnish State purchased the estate lands and allowed peasants to buy plots for themselves.

At the end of the 19th century, when Finland was part of the Russian Empire, the importance of Karelia increased. Karelians moved to St. Petersburg as workers and traders, and villas built by Russians on the Karelian Isthmus meant new opportunities for local tradesmen. After the opening of the Saimaa Canal in 1856, the transport of tar and sawmill products also boosted the area's economy.

Lappeenranta, now a lively commercial center at the northern end of the Saimaa canal, was once a medieval trading center. The Swedes began building fortifications in Lappeenranta after the Uusikaupunki Treaty and the Russians continued the work after the Turku Treaty of 1743. When Finland became a Grand Duchy of Russia, Lappeenranta developed into a popular spa and garrison town with a lively social life. The natural attractions of the area even drew Russian royalty.

As early as 1772 Empress Catherine II of Russia, accompanied by her entourage, stopped to admire the famous Imatra Rapids. Her example even inspired the emperor of Brazil to visit, among other illustrious tourists. In 1842 Emperor Nicholas I declared the Imatra Rapids a Crown park, inns were built and tourism boomed, thanks to the Saimaa Canal and rail connection with St. Petersburg. However, there was a darker side. The rapids became such a popular spot for would-be suicides that policemen had to patrol the bridge at all times. Eventually the construction of a power plant at the rapids significantly reduced that gloomy appeal. The rapids area has been designated a National Landscape by the Ministry of the Environment.

The legendary Karelian character of the area diminished after World War II as more and more people settled in Karelia from other parts of Finland. Once again, since the collapse of the Soviet Union in 1991, the border is beginning to attract trade and tourism from the east.

Lappeenranta – Villmanstrand

The town of Lappeenranta was founded by Count Per Brahe in 1649 at the site of the medieval trading post. In the 19th century it became a flourishing garrison and spa town located centrally on the waterway. The opening of the Saimaa Canal in 1856 brought new life and opportunities

to Lappeenranta. The **Lappeenranta Spa**, established in 1870, as well as the charming **Casino**, built in 1913, are located in a beautiful shorefront park. The Neo-Classical wooden **Town Hall**, embellished with an Empire-style bell tower was built in 1828–29.

Lappeenrannan linnoitus ja Ratsuväki-museo – Lappeenranta Fortress and Cavalry Museum

The original fortifications around Lappeenranta were built by the Swedes after the Uusikaupunki Treaty of 1721. The town was all but destroyed in 1741 after a fierce battle that resulted in Russian rule. The fortress was reinforced with newly constructed ramparts in the 1770s by the Russians. The fortress buildings have been restored and are now used as museums

and workshops for artists and craftspeople. Next to the entrance to the fortress is the guardhouse, built in 1772, which houses the **Cavalry Museum**, dedicated to the famous cavalrymen during the Thirty Years' War and their successors, the cavalrymen of the Finnish Dragoon Regiment.

Cavalry Museum

Etelä-Karjalan Museo – South Karelian Museum

During World War II, the city of Viipuri, the second largest city in Finland, was taken by the Soviets and its inhabitants and museum collections were evacuated to other areas of Finland. The museum, located in a graystone former gunnery depot in the fortress, illustrates Karelian life, complete with an interesting collection of folk costumes and an extensive photographic archive.

Etelä-Karjalan taide-museo – South Karelian Art Museum

The art museum is located in two Neo-Classical yellow barracks buildings, built in 1798 for the fortress. The permanent collections include older Finnish art from the 1850s on, as well as modern art by nationally known artists. The museum received valuable works by well-known artists, evacuated during World War II from Viipuri Art Museum.

Wolkoffin talomuseo – Wolkoff House Museum

Until 1812 Lappeenranta was part of the so-called Old Finland, ceded to the Russian Empire in 1743. Many Russians moved to Finland and succeeded in trade. Three sons of a Russian serf came to Lappeenranta and soon established a flourishing merchant's house. Their house, built in 1826, is one of the oldest wooden houses in town and sheltered four generations of the Wolkoff family until 1983. Full of historical objects and interior decorations, the house is a unique example of the life style of the Russian merchants and Orthodox traditions in Lappeenranta.

The Orthodox Church of the Virgin Mary, built in 1785, is the oldest standing Orthodox church in Finland. It is built in the style of 18th-century military and country churches, mixing Russian church architecture with Western Baroque and Neo-Classical influences.

Lappeenrannan ortodoksinen kirkko – Lappeenranta Orthodox Church

The large wooden Lappee Church was built in 1792–94. Its plan is a so-called double cruciform: in order to gain more space, the center part of the cross was enlarged by extending the inner corners outward, in essence superimposing a square on the cross. The altar piece was painted by Aleksandra Frosterus-Såltin, one of the most productive altar painters of the time.

Lappeen kirkko – Lappee Church

Saimaan kanava ja Kanavamuseo – Saimaa Canal and the Canal Museum

Only after Finland had become an autonomous Grand Duchy of the Russian Empire, was the canal connecting Lake Saimaa and the Gulf of Finland finished. The Saimaa Canal, 58 kilometers long and consisting of 28 granite locks, opened on the coronation day of Czar Alexander III in 1856. The drop in the water level from Lake Saimaa to the Gulf of Finland was a huge 76 meters.

At the turn of the century a special vessel, or the "tar steamer," was developed to negotiate the canal. The steamers carried tar and lumber from the north and brought back the international sophistication of St. Petersburg and Viipuri on their return. Now the

Lappee Church

Old Saimaa Canal

Saimaa Canal

border between Finland and Russia bisects the canal. In 1963 Finland leased the Soviet part of the canal for 50 years, and in 1963–68, a new, wider and deeper canal, 43 kilometers long, was built to replace the old canal. The **Canal Museum** – Kanavamuseo – is located in an 1840s canal manager's residence on the eastern side of the locks.

Lemi

Lemin kirkko – Lemi Church

The wooden Lemi Church, built in 1786, with its beautiful wooden vaults, curved in cloverleaf shapes and covering the cross arms and the cap of the dome, is unique in Finland. The ribs on the seams are painted in red diagonal stripes.

Taavetti

The massive **Taavetti Bastions** in Luumäki were built by the Russians in 1773–96 in order to close the Hämeenlinna-Viipuri road.

Suomenniemi

Lyytikkälän talo – Lyytikkälä Farmstead

The grand Lyytikkälä farmstead belonged to the same family for 200 years when the National Board of Antiquities purchased it with all its furnishings in 1984. The buildings and the interiors comprise one of the best-preserved farmsteads in the province, and reflect 19th-century vernacular rural architecture in southern Karelia.

Imatra is best known for its rapids, which travelers at one time conside-red Finland's chief natural attraction. For artists, the rapids represented unharnessed beauty – Albert Edelfelt, Akseli Gallen-Kallela, and Louis Sparre came to paint outdoor winter scenes, considered exotic at the time. In 1926, however, the Imatrankoski Power Plant was constructed to harness the churning rapids and is still the largest hydroelectric plant in the country. Once a day each summer, the water is allowed to thunder through the dam.

Imatra Falls in Snow,
Akseli Gallen-Kallela 1893

The advent of hydroelectric power in Imatra gave rise to a sawmill and pulp industry. The Enso-Gutzeit Paper Company commissioned Alvar Aalto in 1953 to draft a general plan for Imatra. Though little of Aalto's design was realized, Imatra has become an internationally known architectural town.

The Imatra Art Museum was born as a result of work by Jalo Sihtola (1882–1969), who collected mostly 20th-century paintings. As the director of the Enso-Gutzeit paper company selling timber in Europe, he became

Imatran taidemuseo –
Imatra Art Museum

acquainted with the latest movements in art. The museum's collection of 800 pieces of art is located in the Imatra Cultural Center.

Valtionhotelli
There are few Finnish hotels with as proud a tradition as Imatra's *Valtionhotelli*, or "National Hotel." The handsome castle-like building opened in 1903 on the banks of the foaming Imatra Rapids. The hotel was designed in the National Romantic style and reflected the yearning for spectacular and romantic sights popular at the turn of the century. Prior to the hotel's construction, the site was already a popular location for visiting notables; Count Per Brahe, the Governor of Finland, visited as early as 1638. The skillful renovation has preserved the old spirit of this famous hotel.

Vuoksenniskan kirkko – Vuoksenniska Church
Vuoksenniska Church, called the Church of the Three Crosses, is considered one of architect Alvar Aalto's preeminent monumental designs of the 1950s. Consecrated in 1958, the church's interior is a freely flowing volume made up of concave forms that narrow and expand into one continuous space, animated by both reflected and direct light.

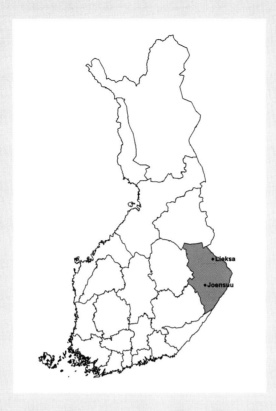

16
Pohjois - Karjala
North Karelia

P hotographer and writer I. K. Inha, an early recorder of the Finnish landscape, in *Suomen maisemia*, Finnish Landscapes, of 1909 poetic ally characterized North Karelian scenery: "...*strange projecting rocks; whispering spruce forests along the hillsides, the tops of trees rising from sheltering ravines; in the barest places, pine trees twisted into the most wonderful shapes, ravaged by the winds.*"

The North Karelian landscape is dominated by rolling *vaara*s, hills covered by green forests, with glittering lakes and rivers in the valleys. Settlements consist of handful of houses surrounded by cultivated fields with sweeping views of lakes and spruce forests. Slash–and–burn farming still marks the landscape with reforested stands of birch and alder and natural meadows. The traditional villages were nominated a National Landscape by the Ministry of the Environment in 1992.

Since the late 1800s the scenic Koli Hills at Lake Pielinen had attracted artists, such as painters Pekka Halonen and Eero Järnefelt, whose

painting of the hills, among them the large wall painting for the Helsinki Railway Station restaurant in 1922, came to define national landscape painting. The first inn was built in the Koli Hills in 1896, and eventually this breath–taking sight grew into a major tourist attraction. In 1991 the hills were designated the Koli National Park and also given a nomination as a National Landscape. In a new, elegant nature center, *Heritage Centre Ukko*, a visitor can learn about projects how to preserve the unique nature and the traditional landscape of the hill area.

Generations of Finnish artists, writers and composers have been inspired by the Finnish folk epic, the *Kalevala*, to explore Karelian villages and landscapes. Compiled by the physician Elias Lönnrot from folk poetry he collected in Karelia and published in 1835, it became the cornerstone of Karelianism, a late 19th–century national romantic belief in a mythic national golden age and a primeval Finnish home. Jean Sibelius took names for many of his compositions from the *Kalevala*. He and also the painter Akseli Gallen–Kallela made their honeymoon trips to northern Karelia and were both deeply influenced by their visits.

As early as the 12th century, eastern Finland was a battleground between the Eastern Orthodox and the Roman Catholic churches. The Orthodox Karelians, whose territory stretched from the Karelian Isthmus to Lake Ladoga in what is now Russia, were allied with Novgorod and the Eastern church against the Swedish crown and the Finns from Häme Province.

Autumn Landscape from Lake Pielisjärvi, Eero Järnefelt 1899

Karelian folk culture was brought by settlers from the shores of Lake Ladoga to the Mikkeli area and to northern Karelia, then inhabited by the Sámi, or Lappish people. Over the generations, Karelian culture survived in this remote easternmost region, which is now considered the ancestral home of Finland's small, now about one–and–a–half percent, Orthodox population. Even today, the differences in eastern and western traditions are reflected in many North Karelian village churches.

The traditional 17th–century Karelian house was a large two–story rectangular building made of round logs, with the living quarters and animal shelters under the same roof. The family rooms were on the second floor at one end of the house above the storerooms. At the gabled front of the house a decorative balcony formed the facade of the second–story living quarters. The horizontal blockwork technique, or corner–timbering, was adapted from Russian–Byzantine builders and remained the dominant construction method in the region up to the 1930s. Southern fashions came slowly to these remote areas.

In the early 19th century, many old marketplaces at the junctures of rivers and lakes in North Karelia grew into towns and small industrial centers where sawmills and ironworks using lake ore had brought prosperity. The most famous of the local industrialists was Nils Ludvig Arppe who controlled the sawmill industry in the big lakes area. He not only bought sawmills and developed them by establishing ironworks and machine works, such as Möhkö in Ilomantsi, Utra in Joensuu and Puhos in Kitee, but purchased large areas of forest land. Here and there, remnants of that industrial heritage is still visible, such as many hand-some manor houses.

Joensuu

Once a trading post at the mouth of the Pielisjoki River, Joensuu means literally "river mouth" in Finnish. Its central north–south street is anchored by a red–brick Neo–Gothic **Lutheran Church** at one end and a wooden **Orthodox Church** at the other. The massive tower of the monumental red–brick **City Hall** by Eliel Saarinen from 1914 dominates the townscape. The old wooden houses have been largely replaced by commercial buildings, but one can still

Kullervo's Departure,
Akseli Gallen-Kallela 1901

feel the 19th–century atmosphere among the houses of wealthy burghers on Rantakatu Street.

The Carpenter Gothic **Utra Church**, an unusual vertical log structure, was built in 1894–95 at the Utra Canal on the Pielisjoki River, the site of a once important sawmill.

The museum is part of the Carelicum Cultural and Tourist Center. Its exhibitions present a comprehensive view of old Karelia stretching from Finland into Russia. They illustrate the history of the border areas not only as a product of the power struggle between East and West, but also as a beneficiary of influences from the Byzantine architecture of the Orthodox churches, as well as from the Lutheran faith and Swedish culture, especially in western Karelia. Some of the collections were rescued from the Ladoga Karelian Museum in Sortavala, a town ceded to the Soviet Union after World War II.

Pohjois–Karjalan museo – North Carelian Museum

The Joensuu Art Museum's collections give an excellent view of Finnish art. There is a significant collection of Finnish works from the 19th and early 20th century. The sophisticated and harmonious works by the group called *Viiva ja Väri*, literally Line and Color, are an example of the art of the 1950s. The unusual collection of foreign art includes Classical art, Greek, Etruscan, and Roman works from the Hellenistic period, as well as paintings and sculpture from the 14th century. There are also examples of Chinese art from the Tang period, a rarity in Finland.

Joensuun taidemuseo – Joensuu Art Museum

Kontiolahti

The Jakokoski Museum Canal, the 700–meter section of the large canal system in the Pielisjoki River, was built in 1879 to speed traffic on the river past the treacherous Jakokoski Rapids. The canal buildings were constructed on sturdy granite foundations. The old Lake Saimaa log boom and the steam–operated tugboat *Utra*, which operated on the Pielisjoki River from 1935 to 1969, are restored to their original condition.

The old Tohmajärvi road towards Kiihtelysvaara offers magnificent views of traditional *vaara* settlements, ribbon–like along the road.

Jakokosken museokanava – Jakokoski Museum Canal

Outokumpu

Outokummun kaivos-museo – Outokumpu Mining Museum

The Outokumpu Old Mine is where Finland's modern mining industry got its start in 1913. It is also the birthplace of the Finnish multinational mining company Outokumpu Ltd. Most of the copper mine's old buildings survive. After mining activity ceased in 1989, the area was converted to recreational use. The museum at the Old Mine, the only one of its kind in Finland, exhibits in detail how copper ore was discovered as well as the means and techniques of prospecting, mining, and dressing ore. Former miners proudly lead tours of the Old Mine, with its shaft and restored machines and equipment.

Ilomantsi

Ilomantsi parish became part of Sweden after the victorious war of 1609–17 with Russia. Sweden attempted to establish Lutheranism in all its domains and as a result, many Russian Orthodox residents fled to Russia. The Swedish crown responded by importing settlers from Savo to cultivate the abandoned Orthodox farms in northern Karelia. Nonetheless one–third of the Orthodox population remained, and Ilomantsi's Orthodox Congregation, incorporated in the 14th century, is now the oldest in Finland. Under the peace treaty following the Second World War, Finland was forced to cede a third of the town of Ilomantsi to the Soviet Union. There are many memorials and restored military sites from the wartime years.

Ilomantsi became known for its rune singers when Elias Lönnrot, who compiled the *Kalevala*, collected songs there for the *Kanteletar*, a lyrical work of Finnish folk poetry published in 1840.

Ilomantsin kirkot – Ilomantsi Churches

A wooden **Lutheran Church**, built in 1796, is one of the last so–called "picture churches," decorated by Samuel Elmgren in 1830–32 with paintings of a total of 116 angels and other inspiring subjects, replacing the conventional medieval religious themes of gloom and doom.

The yellow–painted wooden **Orthodox Church**, dedicated to the prophet Elijah, was built in 1891–92 in northern Russian style. It is the largest wooden Orthodox church in Finland.

Hattuvaara Orthodox Prayer House – or *tchasouwnia* – in the idyllic hill village is the oldest and most representative of northern Karelia's Orthodox prayer rooms, built in 1796–1844. Nearby is a typical small village graveyard with log crypts and humble wooden crosses.

Ilomantsi Orthodox Church
Pörtsämö Wilderness Cemetery

Möhkön ruukki – Möhkö Ironworks

Since the 17th century, Möhkö Ironworks refined iron from lake ore. At its heyday the ironworks produced a quarter of the county's lake–ore iron and employed 2,000 people. They were even paid with the ironworks' own currency, which the locals trusted more than money minted by the Czars. The ironworks closed in 1907 and during the Second World War most of the factory buildings were burned. The ruins of the blast furnace have been excavated, and a six–meter high functioning water wheel has been reconstructed. The 700–meter canal, built in 1872, and its four

Möhkö Ironworks

Tuupovaara

wooden locks have been restored. The director's residence, known as *Pytinki*, or squire's abode, survives from 1849.

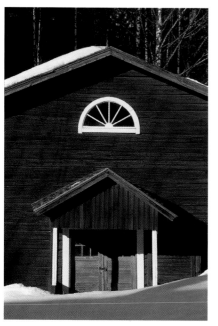

Koskenniska Mill and Inn Museum

In Öllölä Village in Tuupovaara, **Koskenniska Mill and Inn Museum** – Koskenniskan mylly- ja kievarimuseo – displays restored inn rooms and the mill machinery. Another cemetery, **Pörtsämo Wilderness Cemetery**, in Öllölä is hidden in the wild forest.

Lieksa

Count Per Brahe, the Governor of Finland, established a town called Brahea in 1652 on Church Island in order to encourage trade and reinforce Swedish rule. The town, now called Lieksa, began to flourish in the 1800s with the rise of the lumber industry. A dozen buildings predating the fire of 1934 still survive.

Pielisjärven kirkko – Pielisjärvi Church
The church, built in 1982, was designed by Raili and Reima Pietilä on the stone foundations of the old church, destroyed by fire. The atmosphere of the old church permeates the modern structure, its large Palladian dome supported by crossed double arches, leaving skylights in between. The window in turn frames Engel's surviving 19th–century bell tower. The white–painted wood of the interior and the exterior is reminiscent of the old church.

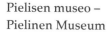

Pielisen museo – Pielinen Museum

The Pielinen Museum is one of the most remarkable open–air museums in Finland – and second only in size to Helsinki's Seurasaari Museum. It encompasses more than 70 old relocated buildings, providing an interesting history of life in northern Karelia. The influences of east and west are evident in the buildings and in the artifacts on display.

The studio of Eva Ryynänen (1915–2001) and a chapel was designed and built by her and her husband Paavo. A sculptor by training, Ryynänen for years was able to concentrate on her art only in her spare time after farming all day. She carved figures mostly from wood, depicting nature, children, animals, and life in the countryside.

Kuvanveistäjä Eva Ryynäsen studio ja Paaterin kirkko – Sculptor Eva Ryynänen's Studio and Paateri Church

The nearby **Paateri Church**, called the Chapel of Silence, was built of old pine logs. Eva Ryynänen carved each bench as a work of art.

Juuka

The old center of Juuka, on this site since the 1500s, is one of the few traditional village centers in northern Karelia that has its late 19th and early 20th century houses and shops preserved as an entity. The village is adjacent to the Herralankoski rapids, where a grain mill has been converted into **Juuka Mill Museum** – Myllymuseo.

Nurmes

Between Lake Pielinen and the town center, the old wooden houses climbing up the beautiful hill and large birches between them compose an idyllic scene.

Ikola Museum – Ikolan museo – is an open–air museum, which includes a prosperous farmhouse. The main building has a traditional *paritupa*, or "double cottage," consisting of two multipurpose rooms connected by a central hallway. On the other hand, the crofter's cabin vividly reveals the harsh life of the poor crofter.

Valtimo

Valtimo, located on the ancient road between Novgorod and Käkisalmi to Oulu, was first settled by immigrants from Savo and Kainuu in the early 17th century. Murtovaara is an impressive farmstead located on a hillside in the wilderness. It is one of Finland's best provincial museums of local culture. Exposed log dwellings and outbuildings are grouped around a central courtyard.

Murtovaaran talo-museo – Murtovaara House Museum

17
Etelä-Pohjanmaa
South Ostrobothnia

*T*he land, then, is flat and monotonous, but its fertility and cultivation arouses the traveler's admiration. As far as the eye can see, full ears of grain ripple in the gentle July breeze, like a green sea," wrote Zacharias Topelius in 1875 in *Boken on vårt land*, The Book of Our Country.

The flatlands and river valleys attracted permanent settlers in the 11th century from the south, Häme and Satakunta. The settlements are strung along the rivers, the fields reaching to "within two bowshots of the river." The population increased in the 16th century, when farmers from Savo pressed along the upper reaches of the rivers. The importance of the area is highlighted by the late Medieval graystone church of Isokyrö, commanding the great parish of Kyrö, which now makes up some thirty towns. The river valley and the plains have been nominated a National Landscape by the Ministry of the Environment.

Ostrobothnians are known for their stubborn independence, not willing to bend to others' rule. During the Peasant Revolt, the Club War of 1596–97, peasants lacked firearms, but they equipped themselves with spiked clubs. Their leader was Jaakko Ilkka, a prosperous farmer, whose memory is proudly kept alive in the name of the local newspaper, *Ilkka*.

Military service, the obligation to provide soldiers for the army, was finally semi-enforced in 1733 in Ostrobothnia. By the late 1700s Finnish peasants, except those in Ostrobothnia, were allowed to pay a fee to release themselves from supplying soldiers. During the Finnish War in 1808–09, the first full-scale battle in the field took place in Lapua on 14 July 1808, still celebrated as a provincial holiday in South Ostrobothnia.

*Burning Village –
A Scene from the Club War,
Albert Edelfelt 1879*

The farmers were independent because there were no cavalry estates or nobility. In the 18ᵗʰ century tar making had brought wealth to the province and provided even the younger sons of the farms a good living, but that ended early in the next century. The ensuing drop in social status led to dissatisfaction and violence, and the roudy Knifers, *puukkojunkkarit* or *häjyt*, terrorized the countryside in southern Ostrobothnia in the early 1800s. Many landless peasants and young men, afraid of being recruited into the Russian army, immigrated to America; half of the Finnish immigrants between 1860–1930 were from Ostrobothnia.

Ostrobothnia has been characterized by intense popular movements. When a large number of clergy participated in the religious revival movement in the mid-19ᵗʰ century, an evangelical crusade combined with social protest caused the government officials to become concerned. The Youth Association Movement was founded in 1881 and while not religious, it was concerned about the morals of young people. Because of the systematic opposition the Russian officials decided to free Finns from armed service in 1905. Young volunteers or *Jägers*, consisting not only of students, but mostly peasants and workers instead, went secretly to be trained in Germany during the First World War. They became the core of the White forces, centered in Ostrobothnia during the Civil War, which for the Ostrobothnians, was a war of freedom.

Tar making had brought wealth to the farmers. Handsome two-story red-painted houses were built according to the town models. The building culture displayed a high degree of technical skill learned in shipbuilding, influenced by the Renaissance style. Ostrobothnia is still famous for its furniture, espacially handmade period furniture. Folk art, costumes, and handicrafts, especially knives and grandfather clocks, are characteristic of the local spirit. Typical of Ostrobothnia are the touching-ly naive wooden figures, "poor boys," standing beside the church door collecting money into the charity boxes in their belly. The famous church building families such as the Kuorikoskis transformed the Continental styles into vernacular buildings.

The old country roads still follow the course of the rivers, passing handsome farmhouses, old watermills, suspension bridges and pastures, and numerous Finnish War memorials so dear to Ostrobothnians.

Seinäjoki

Aalto-keskus –
Aalto Center

In Seinäjoki Alvar Aalto realized his most grandiose town center. The light washes the pristine white walls of the **Cross of the Plain Church** (Lakeu-den ristin kirkko, 1960) and its lofty bell tower soars like a beacon in the flat landscape. The **Town Hall** (1965), the **Library** (1965), and the **City Theater** (1987) form a plaza, the Citizens' Square. The terracing, stairs formed in nature, is Aalto's idea of the stage. The library, with its fan-shaped plan, is classic: light reflecting through the ceiling down to the central space, a few steps below. The **State Office Building** (1968) encloses the area. The

Aalto Center, Seinäjoki

museum is located on the beautiful park-like grounds of **Törnävä Estate**, the former Östermyra Ironworks. The wooden two-story main building was built in 1806 and now, beautifully restored and furnished, serves as the town's banquet hall. The handsome stone cowhouse contains the museum and its exhibitions on farming life. A dozen old buildings have been moved from around the province to the museum area.

Etelä-Pohjanmaan maakuntamuseo – Provincial Museum of South Ostrobothnia

Alvar Aalto's first commission in Seinäjoki was the staff quarters for the Civil Guard organization in 1924. In spite of his youth, 26 years, Aalto showed an extraordinarily refined spirit of Classicism in both its overall design and splendid details.

Suojeluskuntatalo ja Lotta Svärd -museo – Civil Guard House and Lotta Svärd Museum

The restored buildings now house a museum dedicated to the volunteer defence work. The Civil Guard was started in 1917 before Finnish independence by activists among the *Jägers*, volunteers who were trained as light infantrymen in Germany. First a clandestine movement, the Civil Guards became important in training men when the official army was just being formed. The auxiliary women's organization, called *Lotta Svärd*, was named for the brave and sturdy soldier's wife who followed her husband to war in J. L. Runeberg's *The Tales of Ensign Stål* about the Finnish War in 1808–09. On the eve of the Winter War in 1939, the Civil Guards had 130,000 and *Lotta Svärd* 150,000 regular members as well as 70,000 young boys and girls. The Civil Guards were ordered disbanded by the Allied Control Commission in 1944. Some suggest this shows how decisive a role they had played in the wars, even though the official reason was to limit the number of men in the Finnish armed forces, as stated in the peace treaty.

The exhibition pays tribute to the Finnish women who served as nurses, cooks, telephone operators, and those in charge of the air defence service. In no other country during World War II did women have such a role in the war as the *Lottas* did in Finland.

Ilmajoki

Yli-Lauroselan talo-museo – Yli-Laurosela Farmhouse Museum

Yli-Laurosela is a fine example of the skillful log houses built in the area in the early 19th century, when tar burning and cultivation by drying marshlands brought prosperity. The two-story main building combines Ostrobothnian tradition with features adopted from the Empire style and

was built in 1848. The rectangular farmyard is bordered by outbuildings. The common room or *tupa* and the master's and mistress's rooms are furnished in the style of the early 20th century. The common room was the center of activity in the farmhouse, which besides functioning as a place to cook and eat, was in the winter a place to sleep and do crafts.

The unusual building for the **Ilmajoki Museum** – Ilmajoen museo – was modeled according to the second church of Ilmajoki. It is the oldest and one of the biggest local history museums in the area, beautifully sited on

the historical Museonranta shore of the Kyrönjoki River. The exhibitions include articles relating to the Könni masters, who were famous for their grandfather clocks, made for five generations.

Jalasjärvi

Further south the **Jalasjärvi Museum** – Jalasjärven museo – has one of the largest collections of its kind in Scandinavia. The vernacular buildings house a farmstead, textile, church, and war museums.

Kauhajoki

Hämes-Havunen Farmstead – Hämes-Havusen talo – is an impressive example of the handsome 19th-century Ostrobothnian dwellings. The buildings make two separate courtyards, the household and livestock enclosure.

Isokyrö

Still in the 16th century Isokyrö was the center of Great Kyrö Parish, which encompassed most of inland Ostrobothnia. The old stone church, dedicated to St. Lauri, *St. Lawrence*, stands by the Kyrönjoki River, an impressive monument to those times. The oldest part, the sacristy, was built in the late 1300s. It is the only church in Ostrobothnia to retain its medieval form. After the Reformation the walls were covered with sumptuous frescoes, thought to be painted by a German artist. The 114 large pictures in three rows were completed in 1560 and are the only surviving monumental paintings made during the Reformation.

Isonkyrön kirkko – Isokyrö Medieval Church

Isokyrö Medieval Church

Orisbergin kartano – Orisberg Estate

Orisberg is the only manor in Ostrobothnia, established in 1676 when an ironworks was founded there. The ironworks, however, foundered, but the new owner concentrated on developing machinery works and farming. Orisberg was marked by active construction: the magnificent new residence, a three-story stone building was completed in 1809 on a pond with a one-kilometer-long dam. The carpenters and painters came from Stockholm to furnish the interiors, which have been preserved in their original state. Many structures and ruins still stand from the time of the ironworks. Today Orisberg is still a private farm, owned by the same family.

Vähäkyrö

Further along the Kyrönjoki River stands **Vähäkyrö Church**, designed by Jacob Rijf and built in 1798–1803. Adjacent old storehouses, together with many well-preserved handsome two-story houses, are unique examples of Ostrobothnian riverfront settlements.

Lapua

The strong and independent people of Lapua have left their mark on Finnish history. On 14 July 1808, the Finnish army won the first full-scale battle in the field against the Russian army in Lapua, glorified by J. L. Runeberg in his poem *The Tales of Ensign Stål*. It is recognized in memorials, and to this day, is celebrated as a provincial holiday in southern Ostrobothnia.

In the early 19th century Lapua became known as a center for the religious movement led by lay preachers. The movement stayed within the Lutheran Church, but aroused concern among government officials because of its social protest. Lapua was also the home of the so-called Lapua Movement, a right-wing populist movement, which in the 1920s was so successful that the Communist party was banned in Finland.

Lapuan tuomiokirkko – Lapua Cathedral

The large wooden church with its cupola dominates the surrounding lowlands from the banks of the Lapuanjoki River. Heikki Kuorikoski, the master builder, followed C. L. Engel's plans independently. The church, completed in 1827, is capped by a magnificent tall octagonal cupola. The exterior, however, faithfully followed the new Empire style.

The town of Lapua has built an impressive **Vanha Paukku Cultural Center** – Vanha Paukku -kulttuurikeskus – in the buildings of the *Vanha Paukku*, Old Blast. The State used it as a cartridge factory, and during the war, production was at its height with the mostly female staff working in three shifts. The interiors retain the feeling of the old factory buildings as closely as possible. The city library, the adult education center, the music institute, a movie theater, galleries, and an auditorium have been fitted into the old structures. The gas plant, a fine small Jugend-style building, was converted into a chapel.

Kauhava

The wide plains north along the Lapuanjoki River bear signs of long settlement centered along the rivers. In Alajoki village, the endless expanse of the renowned "sea of barns" still bears the imprint of haymaking, the foundation of cattle raising, once the main source of wealth. Kauhava is also known for the traditional *puukko* knives, the handmade sheath knives that are not only necessary tools, but also, especially in Ostrobothnia, since ancient times the symbol of a free man – and woman on a smaller scale. The *puukko* with its sheath is the last relic of the folk costume of the Finnish man.

Ylihärmä

Ylihärmä village has retained its traditional villagescape, its wooden church and parsonage standing in the center. The trend to centralize the space and the desire to use shorter logs led to the observation that it was preferable to bevel an increasing number of corners within the cruciform plan. This development led to the 24-cornered church, three of which were built in Finland during Swedish rule. The new models also came from Sweden,

Ylihärmän kirkko – Ylihärmä Church

especially from mausoleum architecture influenced by St. Peter's in Rome.

The unusual 24-cornered church was built in 1787. All the corners, both exterior and interior, of the cruciform church are beveled. The walls of the cross arms lean outward, a custom often employed in South Ostrobothnian vernacular architecture.

Kuortane

The first 24-cornered church was **Kuortane Church**, topped by a large ridge turret with an onion dome. It was built in 1777 and later joined by an unusually handsome bell tower.

Lehtimäki

Suokonmäki Village in Lehtimäki, on an open hill surrounded by woods, is one of the oldest settled areas in Pohjanmaa and offers wide views of seven churches. **Lehtimäki Church**, built by Jacob Rijf in 1800, commands the villagescape from a hill.

Ähtäri

Pirkanpohja Art Centre – Pirkanpohjan Taidekeskus – in Ähtäri exhibits both indoor and outdoor works of the sculptor Eero Hiironen, stately steel monuments reflecting the light and surrounding nature.

Alajärvi

Alajärvi was a summer home for Alvar Aalto's family during his child-hood. There he also designed his first building while still a student of architecture, the **Civil Guard Building**, now the Youth Association House, a small wooden building with a high hipped roof and lantern that gives it an air of a manor house, completed in 1921. **Alajärvi Municipal Center**, even though the smallest of town centers designed by Aalto, has the same ennobling affect on its surroundings as his more monumental plans. The memorials to the war dead in the cemetery were designed by Aalto.

Nelimarkka-museo – Nelimarkka Museum

A Freezing Cold Day,
Eero Nelimarkka 1914

Eero Nelimarkka (1891–1977) was one of the classic landscape painters of his time. The wide, open luscious summer fields and quiet peasant life of Ostrobothnia acquire a pictorial identity through his art. He established the museum in 1964 adjoining his father's birthplace. Its solid stone building recalls the 1920s Classicism according to the tastes of Nelimarkka, contrasting to its rural setting. The museum exhibits Nelimarkka's paintings from 1910–75 and Finnish art from the end of the 19th century up to the present. The graphics collection of both Finnish and international works is remarkable.

Vimpeli

Vimpeli Church is an example of the interest in Antiquity inspired by Hämeenlinna Church, designed by Louis Jean Desprez, the court architect for King Gustav III, to be the Pantheon of the north. Jacob Rijf's most unusual design, the 12-cornered round Vimpeli Church became the crowning achievement of his career. It is built of logs with the corner-timbering technique. Here the centralizing of the space reached its extreme form, surmounted by a huge cupola, with a lantern on top.

Vimpelin kirkko – Vimpeli Church

The **Ski Museum** –Vimpelin Suksitehdasmuseo – the only one of its kind in Europe and probably in the whole world, is located in an old ski factory and displays wooden skies made in 1920–60. In the same yard is

Kortesjärvi

the **Museum of Finnish Baseball** – Suomen pesäpallomuseo – illustrating the local passion, Finnish baseball, evidenced also by the famous grand stadium and the statue of a baseball player.

Kaustinen

The fascinating **Finnish Jäger Museum** – Suomen Jääkärimuseo – in Kortesjärvi presents the history of the movement. In proportion to its population, more men from this town than anywhere else in Finland left as *Jägers* to be trained in Germany.

Kansantaidekeskus – Folk Arts Center

It is said that on the wall of every Kaustinen farmhouse you can find a violin, and everybody from small children to grandparents is a fiddler. The tradition has been revived and kept alive for over thirty years at the annual Kaustinen International Folk Music Festival, which attracts some 50,000 visitors each July.

The Folk Arts Center, designed by architects Mikko Kaira, Ilmari Lahdelma, and Rainer Mahlamäki, an elegant wooden building built partly inside the bedrock opened in 1997. The Museum of Traditional Folk Instruments was established with the collection of some one thousand unique instruments. Besides the basic exhibition, the visitor can see and hear the multimedia performance.

Kaustinen is also known for the Kuorikoski family of famous church builders. The fifteen building masters of four generations spanning 140 years not only built over 40 churches and 20 bell towers, but bridges, dwellings, and industrial buildings all over Finland.

Ullava

Vionoja Gallery in Ullava displays the life's work of Veikko Vionoja, born in 1909, the well-known and loved artist, whose paintings reflect the quietly harmonious mood of the Ostrobothnian landscape depicted on a summer night or in the blue-gray light of winter.

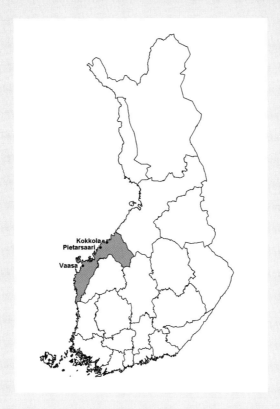

18
Pohjanmaa
Ostrobothnia

The fertile meadows and rugged islands on the Ostrobothnian coast have slowly emerged from the sea – and continue to rise at a rate of about one centimeter a year. Signs of prehistoric settlements now gone can be found, but permanent settlers, fishermen and hunters from Satakunta and Häme came to the mouth of the Kyrönjoki River in the late 12th century. After the mid-1200s Swedish settlers came to the coastal areas to clear land for cultivation. They had already converted to Christianity and had a profound influence on the area.

Albrekt of Meckelenburg, chosen King of Sweden, built in the 1360s a German-style castle near Vaasa, called Korsholm, *Kryszeborgh*, to house the administration for the western and eastern sides of the Gulf of Bothnia – *Västerbotten* in Sweden and *Österbotten*, Ostrobothnia, in Finland. It also functioned as a model farm to teach agriculture and animal husbandry.

Local fishermen and farmers maintained close contacts with Sweden for historical reasons and because of their common Swedish language. Still today the majority of coastal towns are Swedish-speaking and the language border between the towns is quite pronounced. Many cultural customs spread from Sweden that were not found in other parts of Finland. The peasants sailed all the way to Stockholm to trade Ostrobothnian products, such as fish, furs, train oil, butter, and later tar for grain and salt. The tar burning and exporting brought prosperity to the area.

With tar making and shipbuilding the economic importance of Ostrobothnia grew and the Government founded new towns in order to concentrate and control trade. King Karl IX founded Vaasa, naming it for the royal house, in 1606 on the island of Mustasaari, *Korsholm*, the site of the old port and trading center. A grammar school, *pedagogio*, was moved from Uusikaarlepyy to Vaasa in 1683 and in 1794 Finland's first public library opened there. In 1765 the towns on the Ostrobothnian coast, Pori, Vaasa, Kokkola, and Oulu, were given the status of staple towns, giving them the right to conduct trade directly with foreign cities, not just with Turku and Stockholm. Shipbuilding and freight traffic were important sources of wealth, to which the handsome town halls, burgers' houses, and treasures in the local museums attest. In the 1850s the small settlement of Kristiinankaupunki, with 50 ships, had one of the biggest merchant fleets in Finland.

As a result of King Gustav III's first journey to Finland in 1775 Ostrobothnia was divided into two administrative districts, Vaasa and Oulu. The King established a second Court of Appeal in Vaasa; the first was in Turku. King Gustav III was interested in the arts and was an eager participant in designing the impressive building for the Court. Vaasa became the provincial capital and center for the Swedish-speaking coastal population.

The technical skills acquired in shipbuilding and carpentry are evident in the skillful local crafts, such as traditional colorful textiles and the building trade. In the late 1400s an ingenious technical innovation in building wooden churches was developed in Pohjanmaa, the so-called block-pillar system. When building a larger oblong church of logs, the walls easily buckle if they are made from consecutive courses of logs. In the block-pillar system, the logs are of a single length and are reinforced by hollow pillars secured to the logs. The oldest surviving church built using this technique, is Vöyri Church from 1627. Jacob Rijf (1753–1808) from Pietarsaari was the first local church builder master to receive academic architectural training in Stockholm.

Vaasa was briefly the capital of Finland in 1918, when General C. G. E. Mannerheim and the senate were forced to flee there during the Civil War, still called locally the Freedom War, between the Reds who wanted to establish a socialist Finland and the White government. The spirit of those times is still alive in Ostrobothnia, memorialized in the statue of Freedom in the market square and a monument to the White Guard in the park at the Court of Appeal. Mannerheim granted the Cross of Freedom to Vaasa, seen in its coat of arms.

Vaasa – Vasa

Vaasa was established in 1606 where now stand the ruins of the Korsholm Castle, built in the 14th century as an administrative seat for the Swedish power, and of the stone church, dedicated to St. Maria. Nearby was built in 1776–86 the magnificent Vaasa Court of Appeal, designed by

Vanha Vaasa ja Mustasaaren kirkko – Old Vaasa and Mustasaari Church

Painting of the Frigate Europa 1877

Carl Fredrik Adelcranz in French Classical style. The two-story palace sits at the end of an avenue of trees in four lines. It was the most notable secular building of its time in Finland and the only one of its kind in Scandinavia. King Gustav III gave the new courthouse a portrait of himself in full coronation regalia.

The fire, which destroyed the town in 1852 fortunately missed the court building, but led to the rebuilding of the town 7 kilometers away closer to the shore. The courthouse with its impressive white-and-gold interiors was converted into **Mustasaari Church** and a tall belfry was added. The church is also home to the internationally known Korsholm Music Festival.

A two-story house built by the town's wealthiest citizen survived the fire. Called **The Wasastjerna House** – Vanhan Vaasan museo, it is furnished as an early 19th-century merchant's home with the offices of a shipping company.

The new town was planned by Swedish architect Carl Axel Setterberg who became the official architect for the province and the town. The town provided an impressive setting for the provincial capital with spacious, planted avenues and public buildings carefully placed to give visual grandeur. Setterberg brought the Neo-Gothic red-brick architecture of Scandinavia to Vaasa. The townscape has changed considerably, but the major buildings are all well-preserved and beautifully restored. The new **Court of Appeal** from 1862 is situated in a leafy park. The oblong **Vaasa Church** (1859, 1862–67) has richly

Mustasaari Church

King Gustav III of Sweden, H. Pasch

painted interiors. The palatial **Governor's House** was originally built as a private residence for an industrialist in 1863–65.

The museum with its vast collections presents the history of Ostrobothnia with special displays on the Middle Ages and the so-called War of Clubs (1596–97). Tar burning, seal hunting, and seafaring, so important in

Pohjanmaan museo – Ostrobothnian Museum

the coastal region, are richly illustrated. Peasant life, beautifully decorated furniture and textiles, and the gentry are all chronicled. The museum owns also Chinese and European china as well as coins.

Valuable art work collected by Dr. Karl Hedman (1864–1931) is displayed in period rooms of various styles, some from his private residence. The collection comprises Finnish art from the Golden Age at the turn of the 20th century and older foreign art, mostly Dutch and Italian. The natural history exhibition **Terranova** is found on the ground floor.

Tikanojan taidekoti – The Tikanoja Art Museum

The museum is the former home of Frithjof Tikanoja (1877–1964), a Vaasa businessman, whose love of art fills the house. In the 1920s Tikanoja began buying modern art by Degas, Gauguin, Matisse, and Picasso. His collection of international art was unique in Finland then and unusual to be found hanging on the walls of a small town bourgeois home. Tikanoja donated his large collection to the City of Vaasa.

Biarritz, Eemu Myntti 1928

For ten years Tikanoja supported Eemu Myntti, his brother-in-law, paying him for expensive sojourns in France where his palette brightened and became more expressive. His paintings now hang in the museum. Tikanoja bought Finnish art from the Golden Age at the turn of the 20th century and several works by Eero Nelimarkka, known for his harmonious Ostrobothnian landscapes.

Nandor Mikola Museo – Nandor Mikola Museum

The picturesque old Customs House today has large watercolors by Nándor Mikola, regarded as the Master of Finnish watercolors. Mikola was born in Hungary in 1911 and moved to Finland in 1936. He soon gained a reputation for his watercolors, stylistically close to the *November* group, using the blue-gray "Finnish" colors, which capture the lyrical spirit of Finland's nature. Travels south turned his colors brighter and the scale larger, and with age, Mikola's palette has become more abstract works of light and shadow, rhythm and tone.

Right beyond the bustle of the city center the visitor can enjoy the peace of **The Brage Open-Air Museum** – Bragen ulkomuseo – a typical Swedish-speaking area farmstead. The houses retain their original furniture and objects. Especially interesting is a bridal chamber decorated with textiles from a dowry, and a "bridal heaven," a canopy used in the wedding ceremony.

Mustasaari – Korsholm

Stundarsin käsityöläiskylä – Stundars Handicrafts Village

Stundars Village is a unique open-air museum and a center for Ostrobothnian culture. More than 50 traditional Ostrobothnian buildings have been relocated there and include craftsmen's workshops, which are busy during the summer. The handsome townhouse from Vaasa was moved to

the village and is now a center for art exhibitions and concerts. The village specialty is *kalas*, a festival meal of traditional foods served to some 700 people at long tables in the yard.

The nearby **Sulva Church** was built in 1783–86. The wooden, oblong building is capped by a small turret rising on the ridge of the roof. The church is known for its unusually handsome Baroque altar from 1696.

From the church is a view of a unique circular field, *Söderfjärden*, a depression thought by geologists to be the result of a meteoric collision some 550 million years ago. Initial efforts to drain the marsh were started in the 1800s and by the 1920s 1,400 hectares (3,500 acres) of arable land had been claimed. The field is a well-preserved example of the so-called "Ostrobothnian sea of barns."

The Quark, *Merenkurkku* in Finnish, *Kvarken* in Swedish, a narrow neck of water between Finland and Sweden, has long provided a quick route between the two countries. Permanent settlers came to the islands in the 14th century, dependent on the sea for their livelihood. In the 17th century, the islanders were charged with handling mail and passenger traffic to Sweden across the Quark. Finnish volunteer soldiers, the *Jägers*, trained secretly in Germany, slipped across the Quark to fight in the Finnish Civil War, on the White side.

A 1,045 meter bridge, the longest in Finland, connects the islands to the town. Luckily **Raippaluoto Island** (*Replot*) has preserved its rugged beauty, original scale and many old buildings. Since 1781, the small church has survived the stiff northern winds off the open sea. A quiet country road runs from the village to the picturesque fishing harbor and its old boathouses.

The road runs through the ruggedly beautiful landscape in **Björkö Island**. Still further away, lit by the most impressive lighthouses in Finland, are the rugged Valassaaret or Whale Islands. The steel grid structure was built in 1886 on the designs of the well-known lighthouse engineer, Frenchman Henry Lepaute.

The islands of the Quark have been nominated a National Landscape by the Ministry of the Environment.

Maalahti – Malax

The idyllic Åminne fishing harbor in **Maalahti** (*Malax*) has rows of boathouses numbering over a hundred on both banks of the river.

Korsnäs

The town of Korsnäs is characterized by low and rocky shores. The coastal heritage of Harrström and Molpe Villages with their idyllic fishing harbors has been well-preserved. The former parsonage was constructed in 1831 and is now furnished as **The Korsnäs Parsonage Museum** –

Korsnäsin pappilamuseo. The museum depicts the life of an Ostrobothnian minister's family at the end of the 1800s, and has meticulously restored surroundings. The adjoining **Korsnäs Local History Museum** – Korsnäsin kotiseutumuseo – has a large collection of unusually colorful traditional textiles and knitwear along with an exhibition on seal hunting, so important to the coastal people.

Närpiö – Närpes

Närpiön kirkko ja kirkkotallit – Närpiö Church and Church Stables

The medieval stone church of Närpiö was dedicated by Bishop Mikael Agricola in 1555. It was extended many times and is now cruciform in plan, reflecting the Ostrobothnian wooden churches of the 18th century.

Standing next to the church is an unusual "village" of some 150 church stables, built to shelter the horses of long-distance travelers attending church. Originally, there were double that number of red-painted wooden sheds.

Närpiö Church Stables

Kaskinen – Kaskö

With only 1,600 residents, Kaskinen is the smallest town in Finland. The Governor of Ostrobothnia ordered residents of Vaasa and Kristiinakaupunki to move to a new location where plans for a rectangular grid town, one of the grandest at that time, were made. By the time Kaskinen was incorporated in 1785, Vaasa had been given staple rights and residents were no longer willing to move to Kaskinen. Kaskinen never grew to fulfill the original plans, leaving the visitor to imagine only where the two enclosed squares would have been.

Kristiinankaupunki – Kristinestad

Kristiinankaupunki was established in 1649 as a result of Per Brahe's policy of collecting taxes from trade. He named the town after both Queen Kristina and his wife. Typical of the times the town was built on a grid plan with narrow streets and a central square at the river, surrounded by burghers' residences. Kristiinankaupunki boasts one of Finland's and Scandinavia's best-preserved traditional townscapes, having the distinction of being the only town in Finland spared from extensive fires.

Kristiinankaupunki was granted staple rights in 1792, which attracted merchants and craftsmen to the town. By the mid–19th century its merchant fleet was one of the largest in Finland. The town, however, never grew into a major center, saving most of the old structures.

The red-painted wooden church, built in 1700 and named for the queen, is one of the best preserved wooden churches of its time in Finland. The church is oblong in plan and its long walls are supported by block-pillars. The stiff western sea winds have caused its pointed, narrow western tower to lean. From the boarded barrel ceiling hang several ship models, typical of coastal churches, given in gratitude by sailors who survived a dangerous sea journey.

Ulrika Eleonoran kirkko – Ulrika Eleonora Church

Next to the church stands a unique customs hut from 1720, where everybody entering the town had to pay a fee.

The house with its yard and outbuildings have retained the authenticity of a well-to-do burghers' lifestyle in the 18th and 19th centuries. The two-story log main building was built in 1761 for the Lebell family and has been carefully restored.

Lebellin kauppiaantalo – The Merchant House Lebell

The unique Baroque-style hall, with ceiling frescoes, linen wall covers, and a green tile stove, is thought to be the oldest in Finland. The small decorative objects were imported and show the importance of foreign trade to the town.

The Maritime Museum – Kristiinankaupungin merimuseo – preserves and illustrates the maritime history of the town. It is located appropriately in a large Empire-style house at the market square, built by a shipowner in 1837. The attic space is built as a ship's deck complete with fittings and a captain's cabin.

Kiili Local History Museum – Kiilin kotiseutumuseo – is both an extensive outdoor museum in the old fishing village of Kiili (*Kilen*) and a place for cultural events and festivals. The buildings have been relocated from various villages, presenting the vernacular culture of the coastal villages of Swedish-speaking Ostrobothnia.

Vöyri – Vörå

Vöyrin kirkko – **Vöyri Church**	The center of the Vöyri settlement still sits on the banks of the Vöyrinjoki River. Built in 1626, it is the oldest Ostrobothnian block-pillar church. At the crossing of the wooden barrel vaults there is an octagon with paintings of the sun, sky and clouds. The walls were decorated by Thomas Kiempe, and the impressive pulpit was executed by Jacob Rijf. The beautiful altar cabinet, made in Lübeck in the 15th century, is regarded as the most impressive Medieval work of art found in Ostrobothnia.

Myrbergsgården Local History Museum – Myrbergsgården – is a treasure trove for those interested in traditional textiles, including complete festive costumes and bedding textiles. They are displayed in the museum's vernacular buildings, which include a farmhouse with traditional, skillfully decorated furniture. The wagons in the carriage house are beautifully decorated with painted flowers and were used only to ride to church in the summer.

Maksamaa – Maxmo

Nearby is Maksamaa (*Maxmo*), a town of beautiful islands and lush bays. The original settlement is mostly intact. A good example is **Klemetsgårdarna Museum** – Klemetsintalot – a collection of five handsome two-story Ostrobothnian houses from the 18th and 19th centuries.

Oravainen – Oravais

On the 14 September 1808, Finland's fate was sealed in Oravainen. Russian troops had pushed west to the Finnish coast where they encountered the retreating Swedish-Finnish army. In a bloody battle the Finns lost more than one-tenth of their men, the Russians even more. Finland was annexed to Russia as a Grand Duchy. The battle had a far-reaching effect also in Sweden where the king was imprisoned and replaced by a new king, Napoleon's general from France.

In the summer the visitor can follow the progress of the battle and the life of the soldiers through tours, films, and exhibitions on the battlefield and in **Fänrik Stål's Center** – Vänrikki Stoolin keskus – named after J. L. Runebergs's heroic romance, *Fänrik Ståls sägner*, "The Tales of Ensign Stål," which also later gave courage to the Finns in their struggle against Russian oppression.

Kimon ruukki – **Kimo Ironworks**	Kimo Ironworks, established in 1703, unusually has its buildings scattered long distances from one another along the course of the waterfalls. The blast furnace was built in 1740 closer to the seashore. The descendants of the highly respected Walloon blacksmiths who had moved to

Sweden in the 1600s found their way to Kimo. During the heyday of the ironworks it consisted of some one hundred structures, but in 1891 production ended because of its increasing unprofitability. The restoration of the area is ongoing.

The wooden, cruciform **Oravainen Church**, built in 1795–97, is one of the handsomest churches built by Jakob Rijf. His academic studies schooled him in Classical details, seen in the impressive entrance and its Doric gable and pilasters on the exterior walls. Crosses forged by the Kimo smiths are still intact in the cemetery.

Uusikaarlepyy – Nykarleby

The idyllic small town of Uusikaarlepyy was founded on the old trading post in 1617 by King Gustav II Adolf to further trade along the coast. Despite all the new construction, some of the richly ornamented old wooden houses have survived.

Uudenkaarlepyyn kirkko – Uusikaarlepyy Church

The wooden St. Birgitta Church standing on the bank of the Lapuan-joki River was one of the few structures to survive the fire that ravaged the town in 1858. It was designed by Elias Brenner from Stockholm, who modeled it after the Klara Church in Stockholm. The church was built in 1708–10 and its shallow vaults were skillfully decorated by Daniel Hjulström with colorful paintings and windows embellished by painted draperies.

Kuddnäs is the birthplace and childhood home of Zacharias Topelius (1818–1898), professor of Finnish history, who was known primarily for

Kuddnäs

his writings dominated by romantic idealism, moralism, and strong patriotic fervor. Few others have influenced the Finns' national self-understanding as Topelius has. Particularly important was a book on Finland's history, people, countryside, and geography, *Boken on vårt land*, A Book of Our Country. Since its publication in 1875 it was for many generations an essential primary school reader,

published in more than 60 editions. His numerous, well-loved children's novels and plays were popular also in Sweden, because he wrote in Swedish.

A beautiful, birch-lined allée leads to the white Mansard-roofed 18th-century main building. The museum illustrates the period's comfortable, bourgeois life style. In the yellow side building Topelius's library retains the original furniture from his later home.

Childhood Home of Zacharias Topelius

Luoto – Larsmo

The town of Luoto (*Larsmo*), comprising more than 360 islands and bays, rose from the sea only some 2000 years ago. The historic **Öuran Island** surfaced only in the 700s and was settled by fishermen. The idyllic fishing village is still active today. The handsome **Luoto Church**, built in 1785–89 by Jacob Rijf, and its surroundings are among the best preserved of their kind in Finland.

Kruunupyy – Kronoby

The **Torgare Parsonage** – Torgaren pappila – has been, since it was built in 1796, the center of culture in Kruunupyy (*Kronoby*). The buildings around the two yards have been preserved mostly in their mid–19th-century form.

Luoto Church

Pietarsaari is an old marketplace given as a fief to commander Jacob de la Gardie. His widow, Countess Ebba Brahe, established the town in 1652, which in Swedish bears his name, Jakobstad. The irregular town plan is still visible around the wooden **Pietarsaari Church**, which survived the fire in the southern part of the town in 1835. One of the oldest cruciform

churches in Finland, finished in 1731, it was erected on an important axis, separating the burghers' town from the workers' quarters. After the fire, the town was rebuilt with broad streets lined by burghers' homes and gardens.

Pietarsaari developed into an important seafaring town with a large shipbuilding industry. The monumental factory buildings and the tower, topped by a huge globular clock, still dominate the townscape, even though the Strengberg Tobacco Company closed in 1998. It was then the second oldest tobacco factory in the world, established in 1762, and by the beginning of the 20th century had become the largest in Scandinavia. The entrance to the workers' old neighborhood, *Skata*, goes through the factory's massive archway. Construction of the small wooden houses started in the late 1700s, and the area has survived as one of the most unified urban quarters in Finland.

**Pietarsaaren kaupun-
ginmuseo – Pietarsaari
Town Museum**

The museum is located in a handsome stone building, **Malm House** – Malmin talo – built by Peter Malm, one of the most successful shipowners in Finland, in 1836–38. Objects such as model ships, art work,

photographs, and textiles displayed in period rooms relate the maritime history and trading traditions of the town. The 19th-century shipowner's office illustrates the comfortable life style of the owner.

**Arktinen museo
Nanoq – The Arctic
Museum Nanoq**

Nanoq, the word for polar bear in Greenlandic, is the first arctic museum in Finland and research center on Arctic culture. The model for the museum's main building is a turf hut from Northern Greenland. It is surrounded by small cabins made from recycled, gray wood.

The museum has an unusual collection of equipment from Norwegians Fridtjof Nansen's and Roald Amundsen's famous Arctic explorations, and from engineer S.A. Andrée's tragic balloon flight. The oldest of the large number of hunting weapons and tools from Northern Scandinavia, Canada, and Greenland is from the 17th century. Arctic flora and fauna, textiles, art works, including a rare soapstone collection done by Canadian Inuits, illuminate the Arctic cultures.

The medieval stone church of Pedersöre is one of the oldest in Ostrobothnia, built in the mid–15ᵗʰ century. The narrow, tall west tower is typical of Ostrobothnian churches. The oblong structure was expanded into a cruciform shape under the supervision of a native son, Jacob Rijf in 1787–95. He designed also the monumental Doric entrance colonnade.

Kokkola – Karleby

Kokkola was established in 1620 by King Gustav II Adolf who wanted to concentrate all trade in towns in order to collect more taxes. After a big fire destroyed the town in 1664, it received a new grid plan. This has survived until today in the old town, *Neristan*, the lower part of town where sailors and workers lived. It comprises one of the most important unified wooden house districts in Finland. The golden age of shipping began in 1765 when the town was granted shipping rights to conduct trade to foreign countries. Kokkola soon surpassed Oulu as a major port. The burghers built their large homes in *Oppistan*, the upper town.

The Art Museum is housed in **The Roos House** – Roosin talo – a two-story stone building that was the grandest in town when it was built by Finland's richest man in 1813. Karl Herman Renlund (1850–1908) bequeathed to the town, his birthplace, works by many well-known Finnish artists from the turn of the 20ᵗʰ century. From a humble background he became a successful and generous businessman. The museum has also a large collection of works by Ostrobothnian Veikko Vionoja (1909–2001), known for his harmonious still lifes and landscapes.

The permanent collections of the Historical Museum are housed in the old **Pedagogio**, a school building from 1696, the oldest urban secular building in Finland. The wooden building has a so-called lantern roof, popular at the time, topped with a small ridge turret. The rooms illustrate the town's seafaring, shipbuilding, and tar trade. There are many finely detailed ship models built in Kokkola. The tools and photos illustrate the work of craftsmen who were members of the guilds, formed in the 17ᵗʰ century by trade regulations.

The English Gunboat – K. H. Renlund Museum

There is also an exhibition about an event during the Crimean War in 1854–55 when England and France allied with Turkey against

Russia. Because Finland was part of Russia the British navy destroyed shipyards and harbors along the Ostrobothnian coast. The people of Kokkola, however, decided to defend themselves. They were warned by optical telegraphs that were installed along the Finnish coast during the war. In the battle they managed to capture the gunboat now displayed in the English Park, *Englantilainen puisto*. The six English soldiers who died are buried in Maria Cemetery, and the Queen's administration sends a small sum of money annually for the upkeep of their graves.

Nearby the two-story wooden **Lassander House** – Lassanderin talo – built in 1748, has been restored and decorated in authentic materials as an example of the well-to-do burghers' life style in the 18th and 19th centuries.

Windswept **Tankar Island** has been the base for fishermen and seal hunters since the 1600s. Huge stone cairns and pilots have been guiding sailors from there; the present lighthouse was built in 1889. The landscape is still dominated by a small, gray fishermen's hut. **Öja Island** at one time was a summertime cow pasture. It is still a fishing village.

The traditional villagescape has survived around the medieval stone **Kaarlela Church** (*Karleby*), dedicated to St. Katarina. It was apparently built in the early 16th century, but later rebuilt in the ascetic Neo-Classical style. The tall west tower has an unusual "Palladian" window. The wooden main building of Kaarlela Parsonage, the oldest one still in use in Finland, was built in 1736–37 as a model parsonage.

Lohtaja

The wooden **Lohtaja Church** was built in 1768 and has a large three-part altar painting by Mikael Toppelius, famous in Ostrobothnia for his church decorations.

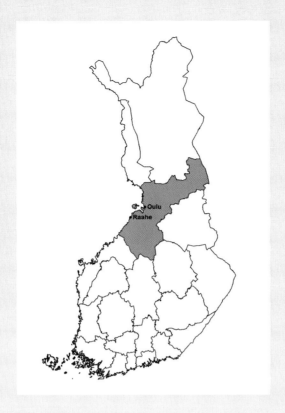

19

Pohjois-Pohjanmaa
North Ostrobothnia

Characteristic of the Ostrobothnian coast are the wide sandy beaches and low meadows which are slowly being exposed from the sea as a result of the rising land. The landscape is said to have been formed by *"the Creator, river, and Ostrobothnian labor."* Traditionally the houses were built ribbon-like along the many rivers. The scenery in the eastern hilly Kuusamo area differs dramatically from the coastal plains. The spectacular rapids and rocky ravines in the Oulankajoki River were nominated a National Landscape by the Ministry of the Environment.

The first signs of humans were the *jätinkirkot*, giant's churches, typical of Ostrobothnia, and from the end of the Stone Age, ca 3300–1300 B.C. and the Bronze Age, ca 1300–500 B.C. They are large encirclements with openings which probably functioned as seasonal shelters for hunters. The earliest permanent settlements were established at the mouth of the rivers where there was an abundant salmon catch. Some of the hunters from the south and east settled permanently, but from the 16th century onwards most of the permanent inhabitants came from Savo in the east.

Under the 1323 peace of Pähkinäsaari the areas north of the Pyhäjoki River belonged politically to Novgorod, but the bishop of Finland wanted to push the border up to the Oulujoki River. A fortress was built at the mouth of the river in 1375 to guard the passage to the north, but Northern Ostrobothnia was long a contested borderland. Life was made difficult by continuous attacks from Viena Karelia, followed by revenge attacks. King Karl IX was interested in expanding Swedish power all the way to Lapland where he sent the first scientific expedition in 1601. Oulu grew into an important trading center. The fortress was destroyed by an explosion in 1793, and having been built of logs, very little of it is left.

Already in the Middle Ages salmon was the most important export item from Ostrobothnia where it was caught by building salmon weirs in the rivers. Salmon fishing was taxed by both the church and state which also established their own fishing waters and rights. The last of the taxes were dropped only in 1925. Salmon was exported as far as Stockholm and St. Petersburg. It was caught in such a large quantities that farmhands signed an agreement that they were not required to eat salmon more than once a week.

Still in the 16th century tar was almost entirely a Central European product, but when the coniferous forest diminished, tar production moved further north. Tar was a major export of the Oulu area and needed for shipbuilding. By the middle of the 19th century most of the tar was produced in Kainuu, from where it was transported by special narrow tar boats down the mighty Oulujoki River to be sold to the "tar burghers" of Oulu. Oulu, together with Pori, Kokkola, and Vaasa, had been granted staple rights or the right to conduct trade directly abroad in 1765, and the "tar exchange" was set up for storing the tar in Oulu. Oulu was, in fact, at the time the leading tar exporting port in the world.

Even though the low wooden town did not make a very favorable impression, the life style revealed its prosperity to a traveler who in 1846 wrote: *"...here the peasants do not have a custom of bowing down before the lords...The reason for the lack of the custom might depend on the character of Ostrobothnian residents. Merchant spirit, wealth, and the resulting independence from the other estates can nowhere be without affecting the customs of the people."* During the Crimean War in 1854, the English fleet, led by Admiral Plumridge, captured ships and destroyed coastal towns. The English burnt the harbors of Raahe and Oulu as well as the shipyards and tar and pitch yards. The tar trade declined as the era of wooden ships, many of which were built in Oulu docks, came to an end. The final blow was the fire of 1901 which destroyed the tar exchange.

The sawmill industry and export of wooden products have not only laid the foundation for Oulu's later growth and well-being, but for the whole of Finland. The first steam-operated sawmill in Finland was established in 1857 by Oulu merchants in the town of Ii near Oulu. Now Oulu's wealth is underpinned by having Finland's second largest university and its high tech industry.

Oulu

Oulu – Uleåborg

The mouth of the Oulujoki River was an ancient trading center, the early traders having been drawn there by the rich hunting grounds and fishing waters as well as by the good natural harbors. Oulu was incorporated as a town in 1605. The big fire of 1822 destroyed four-fifths of the town's buildings. The town was quickly rebuilt and grew into a prosperous tar exporting port, still witnessed by the handsome "tar burghers" houses along Rantakatu Street and the market square. The grand Neo-Renaissance **Town Hall** was originally built as the social hall in 1887.

Oulun tuomiokirkko – Oulu Cathedral

Oulu Cathedral dominates the monumental center of the town. It was built in 1776 and like its contemporaries, was named after Queen Sofia

Magdalena, the wife of King Gustav III. After the fire it was completely rebuilt in 1832 on the designs of C. L. Engel in the new Neoclassic style, incorporating a large central dome and clean white walls.

The red-brick **Puolivälinkangas Church**, dedicated to St. Thomas, was built in 1975. Typical of Juha Leiviskä, the indirect light washes the walls which are decorated with symbolically rich paintings by Hannu Väisänen.

Pohjois-Pohjanmaan museo – Museum of North Ostrobothnia
The streamlined Functionalist museum building was built in 1931, but the museum was established already in 1896. The exhibitions cover prehistory, folk culture, cultural history and livelihoods of Oulu and North Ostrobothnia, presented in a captivating way. Interesting specialities of the museum are the displays of tar making and Sámi culture.

Oulun taidemuseo – Oulu City Art Museum

Oulu Art Museum has grown into an important supporter of art in Northern Finland. It is located in an old glue factory, now an interesting combination of the old and the new. It is one of the largest art museums in Finland with almost 2,000 works. The bulk of the collection consists of 20th century art from Northern Finland. In addition, the museum has received more than 200 works in donations including an important collection of naivistic art. The museum is known for its interesting and progressive changing exhibitions.

Turkansaaren ulko-museo – Turkansaari Open-Air Museum

The island of Turkansaari is thought to have risen from the sea almost two thousand years ago as a result of land uplift, at a time when the sea coast lay only a couple of kilometers away. As a busy trading center the island became an unofficial border post between Russia and Sweden.

The first written record of a salmon weir in Turkansaari dates from 1592.

In 1694 a simple wooden church was built for the fishermen, but after the island lost its importance as a trading place and salmon fishing diminished, it was abandoned. In 1922 the old church was restored on its original site, and since then some forty traditional buildings have been moved to the museum area to build a farmhouse complex typical of the Oulujoki River region. In the summer, theme days are organized to illustrate how tar is made in a real tar pit or how traditional crafts were done.

Kempele

Kempeleen vanha kirkko – Kempele Old Church

The small wooden Kempele Church was built in 1688–91. The long walls are supported by only one pair of block pillars, connected by a sturdy beam across the church hall. The wall paintings of Biblical scenes as well as the portraits on the skillfully carved pulpit were created in 1785–95 by Mikael Toppelius (1734–1821). The Ostrobothnian Toppelius was the most remarkable church painter of his time, who during his career decorated more than thirty churches. There is no altar painting, but the altar faces the window, surrounded by paintings illustrating the Crucifixion and the Resurrection.

Turkansaari Open-Air Museum

Liminka

The Card Players, Vilho Lampi 1929

Liminka is known for its wide open shore meadows and view of seven churches around the bay. **Liminka Nature Center** – Limingan luontokeskus – serves as a center for excursions for nature lovers.

Vilho Lampi (1898–1936) was the painter of poetic, yet powerful, meadow landscapes of Liminka and expressi-

Vilho Lampi -museo – Vilho Lampi Museum

ve, even haunting, portraits. The Renaissance-style old school building, located along a historically protected road, was restored to display works by Lampi and other Finnish painters.

Adjoining the house, now **Aabraham Ojanperä Museum** – Aabraham Ojanperän museo – was the summer villa and home of well-known opera singer, Abraham Ojanperä (1856–1916). The rooms are furnished with original Neo-Renaissance furniture, a grand piano, and many mementoes from his career.

Rantsila

The settlement in the village of Temmes follows the river like a ribbon. The handsome wooden cruciform **Rantsila Church**, built by master builder Simon Jylkkä-Silvén in 1785, boasts Mikael Toppelius's colorful triptych with painted Rococo frames on the altar wall and paintings on the Baroque pulpit.

Hailuoto

Ruggedly beautiful, windswept **Hailuoto Island** was settled only some 1000 years ago. Because of its isolated location, the harmonious villagescape and traditional houses have preserved many old features. It has been nominated a National Landscape by the Ministry of the Environment.

Raahe – Brahestad

Count Per Brahe, Governor of Finland, owned vast fiefs in East and North Finland and for them he established a town with a port in 1649. Brahe named the town *Brahestad*, "Brahe's Town," which became Raahe in Finnish. The town was given a regular grid plan and developed into a prosperous and handsome trading town, helped by staple rights in 1791

when direct foreign trade became possible. The famous **Pekkatori Square**, named for Pekka, the Finnish form of Brahe's first name, is not only the best preserved 19th-century square in Finland, along with Helsinki's Senate Square, but a rare example in Europe of the closed-corner type, conforming to the ideals of Italian Renaissance. Most of the Empire-style one-story

houses are handsome, angled buildings of the notable burghers, whereas side streets are lined with smaller craftsmen's and sailors' houses.

Raahe Museum is the oldest museum in Finland, established in 1862 by a local doctor. The museum is located in the customs warehouse, built of logs in 1848. The core of the collections is made up of objects of nature, exotic souvenirs, and everyday utensils from faraway. The town's prosperity, created in the late 19th century by a merchant fleet of 58 sailing ships at its height, is well described. Scale models, paintings of ships, and navigation equipment illustrate Raahe's maritime history. The museum boasts rarities among its collection, such as the world's oldest diving suit, the "Olde Gentleman," made of leather.

Raahen museo – Raahe Museum

Sovelius House is the oldest preserved house in Raahe, a typical bourgeois house of its time, built in 1714. The second floor is restored as a handsome late 19th century shipowner's home, rich with period furniture, decorative objects of the time, and paintings commissioned in foreign harbors.

Soveliuksen talo – Sovelius House

The famous Neo-Classical **Saloinen Bell Tower** is known because of its designer, King Gustav III himself, who was inspired by the Antiquities he saw during his trip to Italy. Jacob Rijf, however, made the designs more practical when he built the tower in 1786–87.

Pyhäjoki

Annala Local History Museum – Annalan kotiseutumuseo – is located in the old farmstead, first mentioned in documents in 1635. In the 19th century it was the largest estate in Pyhäjoki. It now encompasses 22 original farm buildings.

Kalajoki

Maakallan kirkko – Maakalla Church	Kallankari Islands, some twenty kilometers off the coast, have since the early 1500s served as a base for fishing Baltic herring along the coast. The islands still enjoy a special administrative and legal self-rule given by King Adolf Fredrik in 1771 to the fishermen, who to this day, meet each summer to decide upon joint matters and collect a harbor fee to maintain the church and museum on the island.
	The small wooden church on the barren island of Maakalla was built in 1780. It is surrounded by fishermen's huts, still occupied in the summer. The log walls are unpainted inside; only the pulpit and the cantor's pew are sparingly decorated. A lighthouse, built in 1781, stands guard on Ulkokalla Island.
	The picturesque village of **Plassi** at the mouth of the Kalajoki River was an important trading center since the 16th century, later settled by fishermen and artisans. South of the river and covering more than one kilometer are the famous Kalajoki sand dunes, the northernmost dunes in Europe.

Nivala

Kyösti ja Kalervo Kallion Museo – Kyösti and Kalervo Kallio Museum	President Kyösti Kallio (1873–1940) was a farmer who started his political career as a representative of the peasantry in the House of Estates and continued as a member of the Agrarian Party in the first unicameral parliament in 1907. During his term as prime minister in 1922 a law called *Lex Kallio* was passed allowing the state to purchase land to settle tenant farmers. Kyösti Kallio was elected President of Finland in 1937, the first person without a university degree to hold the presidency. The heavy responsibility of running the country during the Winter War ruined his health and he resigned in 1940. When leaving for his home in Nivala he dramatically died at the Helsinki Railway Station as thousands of well-wishers were on hand to bid him farewell.
	The museum displays Kallio's office and library with his personal belongings. The museum also exhibits some 70 artworks, original statues and casts, drawings and paintings, as well as metalworks by his son, the sculptor Kalervo Kallio (1909–1969).

Haukipudas

The wooden **Haukipudas Church** is famous for its vividly expressive painted decorations by Mikael Toppelius. The cruciform church, typical of Ostrobothnia, was built in 1762.

Kiiminki

Also **Kiiminki Church**, built in 1760, has paintings on the choir wall by Toppelius, the triptych placed in a Rococo-style frame.

Iin Hamina, **Ii Harbor,** at the mouth of the Iijoki River was a major harbor and marketplace in Northern Ostrobothnia, known since the 1300s. Old wooden houses line the shorefront along two narrow streets in a harmonious villagescape.

Further up the river excavations have revealed signs of prosperous villages from the Stone Age, 5000–3000 BC. Originally villages on the sheltered bay were moved every twenty years because of the land rising from the sea. In **Kierikki Stone Age Centre** – Kierikkikeskus – multimedia presentations provide an interesting view of an ancient way of life. The center itself is a magnificent castle, one of the largest modern-day log buildings, designed by Reijo Jallinoja and constructed in an ancient way from stacked wood.

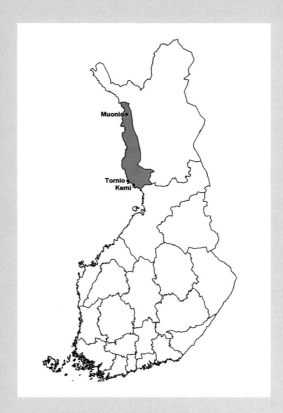

20
Länsi-Pohja

"*F*rom this mountain the prospect is very beautiful. Towards the south it is open and unbounded, and the river Torneå is seen to a vast extent. On the east, the eye traces the Teglio as far as its course through sundry lakes,"* described the Frenchman Pierre-Louis Moreau de Maupertuis of the views from Aavasaksa Fell. As early as in 1736–37 he led a surveying party along the Tornionjoki River valley to Lapland on assignment from the French Royal Academy of Science. The plan was to prove that the globe was flattened at the poles, but at the same time his entourage became familiar with life in the North. As a result of his journey Aavasaksa Fell and the Tornionjoki River valley became known to the world and the midnight sun attracted travelers from all corners of Europe to the summit of the fell which, along with the Imatra rapids, has long been one of Finland's celebrated natural sights. Now it is a National Landscape, nominated by the Ministry of the Environment.

In 1799 the Italian Giuseppe Acerbi followed in Maupertuis's footsteps to explore the valley and in 1802 published a widely-read travelogue, printed in four languages, *Travels Through Sweden, Finland and Lapland to the North Cape*, where he described the natural beauty, hospitality, toughness and inventiveness of the people in surviving the harsh winter conditions. In Oulu Acerbi met the Englishman Edward Daniel Clarke, who published the third part of his *Travels in Various Countries of Europe, Asia and Africa* in 1819 describing his travel in Scandinavia.

Hunters and fishermen from Häme and Finland Proper had wandered northward and by the 12th century the Kemijoki and Tornionjoki River valleys as far north as Ylitornio were settled permanently. For a long time, however, Lapland was a contiguous area between Sweden and Russia. The Pähkinänsaari Peace treaty in 1323 gave Novgorod influence over the land around Kemi and eastward, while the Tornionjoki River valley and large areas of Lapland came under Swedish control. The Swedish Crown gave rights to tax the Lapps and conduct trade and legal matters to *Birkarls*, first mentioned in 1328, a group of Swedish traders who in return recognized Swedish sovereignty. Later the mobile Savo people migrated, looking for new land, rich salmon rivers, fertile riverside meadows – and they levied taxes on the Lapps.

The Uppsala and Turku bishops competed for the establishment of dioceses, and especially for the rich salmon tithes. The Uppsala bishop established the Tornio chapel congregation and the Turku bishop established one in Kemi. Finally the bishops, both called Hemming, met at the Kaakamajoki River in 1346 and chose to set the border there.

Salmon fishing brought wealth to the north. The annual yield of salmon from the Tornionjoki River in the 1600s was on average 1,000 barrels and from the Kemijoki River 3,000 barrels. Tornio, an old trading post on the island with a narrow isthmus near the shore, became a major export town. The Swedish bishop Olaus Magnus had visited Tornio in

Salmon Fishing

1519 which, in his famous *History of the Northern Peoples* of 1555, he described as a town because of the abundance of the warehouses at the harbor, even though it was incorporated only in 1621.

After the Finnish War in 1809, the division between Sweden and Russia was drawn at the Tornionjoki and Muonionjoki Rivers and thus formed the still recognized border between Sweden and Finland. The town of Tornio, even though on the western side of the river, was now annexed to the Grand Duchy of Finland. The western part of the Tornionjoki River valley and its Finnish-speaking population was cut off from the rest of Finland. The establishment of a sawmill and later paper and pulp industry led to the founding of Kemi in 1869, and brought a livelihood not only to the town, but to the larger area. The building of steel mills and cross border trade have enlivened the economy and today Tornio and its twin town Haparanda on the Swedish side form a unified urban area. It may be the only place in the world where one is able to play golf on the border of two countries.

Kemi

During the past few years Kemi has gained fame for having the world's largest Snow Castle which includes not only a traditional castle with towers, but also a restaurant seating a couple of hundred guests, a hotel, and a chapel, which is popular for weddings.

The older history of the town is still visible in Meripuisto Park where the old warehouses mark the importance of Kemi as the main harbor of Lapland at the mouth of the wide Kemijoki River. The adjoining block of old wooden houses has been restored to tell the story of the prosperous life of a seafaring and merchant town.

Kemin kulttuuri-historiallinen museo – Kemi Museum

Kemi Museum is located a few blocks away in a Neo-Classical former bank building. The museum arranges exhibitions not only illustrating the history of Kemi and Lapland from their own collections, but also on various other cultural aspects.

Kemin taidemuseo – Kemi Art Museum

Kemi Cultural Center is the focus of the cultural life of the town and houses also the Kemi Art Museum. The museum's over 1700 works of art are regularly augmented with a focus on northern Finnish art, especially bold Surrealist paintings. Its specialty are comics, and in connection with the annual Arctic Comics Festival, the museum exhibits international comics art.

Keminmaa

Keminmaan vanha kirkko – Keminmaa Old Church

The Old Church of Keminmaa, dedicated to St. Mikael, is the most northern and one of the last of Finnish medieval churches. It was built in the early 1500s at a marketplace on the river and was the main sanctuary for the large and sparsely populated Kemi parish.

The graystone has modest brickwork decoration on the western gable. The boarded barrel vault was decorated with paintings in 1650. Wooden statues of saints on the walls, as well as the baptismal and holy water font survive from Catholic times. The fame of the church in the area comes from its Lutheran minister, Niko-laus Rungius, who died in 1629 and was buried under the church, as was the custom then. Rungius used to preach, "... *if my words are untrue, my body shall rot, but if they are true, my body will not rot.*" His intact corpse is still on view in the church.

Valmarin museo – Valmari Museum
The fertile banks of the wide Kemijoki River have been settled since ancient times. The river was an important means of transportation and also a source of salmon, and is now dominated by a large power station. Valmari Museum, on the

Valmari Museum

beautiful point, is a good example of the many handsome farmsteads still on the river bank. The same family lived on the farm from the 1600s until 1985, farming, fishing, and conducting trade.

Simo

The old postal road ran already in the 17th century along the shore, but it was finally completed in 1752 when King Adolf Fredrik visited Tornio. Now a 3-kilometer stretch in the village of **Simonkylä**, south of Kemi, is preserved as a museum road. The road is lined with handsome traditional farmhouses, known for their decorative porches.

Tervola

Tervolan vanha kirkko – Tervola Old Church

The small wooden church of Tervola was built in 1687–89 on the beautiful riverfront along the Kemijoki River. Because the interior is still without boarding and details of the original structure can be seen, it is regarded as one of the most genuine of the 17th-century wooden churches. The nave and sacristy were whitewashed only in 1818.

The church is of the Ostrobothnian block-pillar type with a high, wood-shingled roof. The interior is covered by a flat barrel vault. The pillars and the crossbeams are carved not only with builders' initials, dates, and other markings such as *hannunvaakuna*, Hans's seal or St. John's emblem, used as a protective sign, but also with special magical figures depicting a reindeer and a fish.

Tornio – Torneå

Tornio was nominated by King Gustav Vasa in 1531 as a legal marketplace and harbor and incorporated as a town in 1621. In March 1694 the townspeople were informed that King Karl XI will "mercifully" visit them in the most northern town of his kingdom and were ordered to fix their humble houses and clean the streets. The king came to see the midnight sun and spent the night in the recently finished, fine Gothic bell tower. The King's observations were later inscribed on a wooden plaque still displayed in the church. A commemorative medal was minted in memory of the royal visit with the rather pompous text, *"To the invincible sun from another favorable sun."*

After Finland became part of the Russian Empire in 1809, Tornio became a border town and, having lost its old trade areas, turned quiet. Later, during the First World War, Tornio became a gateway between east and west; it provided an escape route for political dissidents, both for *Jägers* going to Germany to be trained to fight for Finland's independence, and for Lenin, who in 1917, returned from Central Europe via Sweden to lead the revolution in St. Petersburg. Since independence, the border between Sweden and Finland has not separated the neighbors; instead, it has allowed a lively trade.

The church, finished in 1686, was named after the Dowager Queen Hedvig Eleonora. The oblong nave is supported by three pairs of block-pillars. The west tower has a tall, narrowing pinnacle, originally a land-mark for seafarers. The roof is covered with tarred shingles in a rhomboid pattern, continuing the Gothic roof decoration tradition.

The church is richly decorated with colorful frescoes. The ornate Baroque-style chancel railing dividing the nave, the window and door frames, and the pulpit, which alone took 11 years to finish, are magnifi-cently carved. An itinerant master painter, Diedrich Möllerum, decorated the pulpit and possibly also the old altarpiece.

The unusually imposing **Alatornio Church** stands on a peninsula on the river. The cruciform stone building with smooth stuccoed walls was designed by Jacob Rijf in the French Classical style and built in 1794–97.

Tornion vanha kirkko – Tornio Old Church

263

Aineen taidemuseo – The Aine Art Museum

The modern, airy museum building offers a breathtaking view from the bay of the river to Sweden. The museum annually arranges several exhibitions selected from the permanent collection of the Aine Pictorial Art Foundation, established by a local businessman, Veli

Self-portrait, Elin Danielson-Gambogi 1899

Aine. It represents Finnish art from the early 1800s until today, with an emphasis on the Finnish expressionists, such as the artists of the *Septem* and *November* groups at the beginning of the 20th century, the *Prisma* group from the 1950s and 1960s, and the art of Northern Finland.

Log Floating

Tornionlaakson museo – Tornionlaakso Museum

The museum's collections give a good overview of the history and culture of the Tornionjoki River valley or Western Lapland. The coin collection of more than 3,500 items reveal the importance of Tornio as a medieval marketplace. Scale models of ships and design drawings remind visitors of the prosperous 1700s when trade was at its height. Everyday objects used by hunters as well as displays of forestry and logging illustrate daily life in the countryside. The museum boasts valuable ethnographic objects of the Sámi people, such as their traditional *kota*, or tent, costumes, daily objects and skillful craftsmanship.

Tornionlaakso Museum

Ylitornio

Imperial Lodge

Since the 17th century the midnight sun has attracted travelers to the summit of Aavasaksa Fell. The oldest of the buildings at the top is the **Imperial Lodge** – Keisarin-maja – built by the Government in 1882–83 as a hunting lodge for Czar Alexander III. He actually never came to this ornate log pavilion; instead, it was soon taken over by crowds of tourists. The view from Aavasaksa is particularly impressive because of the powerful contrasts of the landscape: an endless succession of hills and ridges, great forests, and winding ribbons of glittering rivers.

Muonio

Muonio Local History Museum – Muonion kotiseutumuseo – is one of the few houses in the village which survived the war in 1944. The farmstead buildings and rare objects represent the traditional way of life in this part of Lapland.

If you have not seen the northern lights, you can catch them in a planetarium and also experience the Lappish sky in a three-dimensional multimedia show at **Kiela Naturium**.

The round-topped Pallastunturi Fells, one of Lapland's celebrated natural sights, have attracted travelers since the 18th century. Skiing on the fells became popular in the 1930s. Pallastunturi-Ounastunturi National Park was founded in 1938, and now fells have been nominated a National Landscape by the Ministry of the Environment.

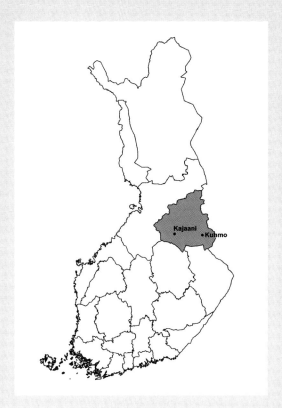

21
Kainuu

Located in central Finland between Pohjanmaa on the Gulf of Bothnia and North Karelia, Kainuu was dominated during the 16th century by the Swedish crown. Royal minions of King Gustav Vasa lured settlers from north and central Savo with promises of land, despite the fact that much of Kainuu lay on the Russian side of the border established by the Pähkinäsaari Treaty with Novgorod 200 years earlier. However, the area had been a hunting ground for Russian Karelians since the Iron Age. Major trade routes went through Lake Oulujärvi to the north and west of what is now Kajaani. Northern parts of Kainuu were inhabited by Lapps as late as in the 1740s.

Kajaani Castle

In the spring of 1552, the first wave of 140 families moved – or were forced by the Crown – to emigrate from central Savo to Lake Oulujärvi, 400 kilometers away. The settlers found themselves under constant attack by Russian Karelian raiding parties. By 1585, during the 25-year war with Russia known as the Long Wrath, some 300 settlers' farms were destroyed. Finally, in 1595, the area was attached to Sweden.

In order to protect lands in the west and serve as a base for Swedish expeditions to the Arctic Ocean, the construction of Kajaani Castle began in 1604 on an island above waterfalls on the Kajaaninjoki River leading to Lake Oulujärvi. In 1651, the town of Kajaani was established next to the castle and the fortifications were expanded by the Governor of Finland, Count Per Brahe. In 1716, during the Russian occupation known as the Great Wrath, the Russians blew up the castle, leaving only parts of the granite wall standing.

Large tracts of Kainuu are covered by vast marshes and treeless bogs, with forested hills in the east. The farms established on arable land were mostly small, pioneer holdings. The buildings and settlements were typical of eastern Finland, scattered about the hillside with sweeping views of the dark green forests and glittering lakes. Except for the clergy, there was no gentry to speak of. For many small farmers and peasants, a subsistence livelihood depended not only on cultivation of crops, animal husbandry, and reindeer herding, but also on tar burning, which until the 1860s in some areas of Kainuu, was the chief occupation. As the forests became more valuable, tar burning moved inland and away from coastal regions. At the beginning of the 20th century, 75% of all Finland's tar came from around the Kajaani region. Tar was transported west to Oulu via the Oulujoki River in special long, narrow tar boats.

Though Kajaani was the commercial and cultural center of the area, it long remained a humble and undeveloped outpost. Elias Lönnrot who, with J. L. Runeberg and J. V. Snellman, was an important figure in the Finnish movement of national awakening, collected and compiled the *Kalevala*, the Finnish national epic, while working in Kajaani as a district medical officer between 1833 and 1852. Lönnrot used the town as a base for his rune-gathering expeditions to Karelia. He also published other collections of folk poetry, as well as guides on health and hygiene.

The basic staples of life in Kainuu – farming, forestry, tar burning – remained unchanged well into the 20th century. Heavy fighting took place during World War II in the border areas, some of which were ceded to the Soviet Union. In the 1960s, when mechanization finally caught up with Kainuu's logging industry, widespread unemployment and migration led to the abandonment of whole villages. Today ski resorts, holiday villages, and spas attract tourists and vacationers to the region, providing jobs for local residents who offer local traditions, crafts, and unspoiled nature to visitors.

Kajaani

Kajaani Castle was among the last castles to be built by the Swedish crown in Finland. It was constructed on an island in the Kajaanijoki River to protect the inhabitants of Pohjanmaa from attacks by Russian Karelians and to support Sweden's expansion to the Arctic Ocean.

Kajaanin linnan rauniot – Kajaani Castle Ruins

The oldest part of the castle was built between 1604 and 1619 on the orders of Karl IX. The two round towers were encircled by a granite wall and reinforced by two rectangular bastions. A second level was added to the fortifications in 1661–66. In 1716 during the Great Northern War, the castle after five weeks of siege and bombardment finally surrendered to the Russians who then blew up the fortifications.

The Swedish historian Johannes Messenius, who was accused of heresy, was imprisoned in the castle in 1616. Messenius wrote his famous history of the Nordic countries, *Scandia Illustrata*, in the prisoners' tower.

The castle was left in ruins, and when in 1936 a bridge was built over the site, a historic landmark was spoiled.

The Ämmäkoski Canal, next to the rapids, was built in 1846 to transport tar. The **Ämmäkoski Canal Museum** –"Lussitupa"– or the lock keeper's house, features exhibits on the history of the waterways and the tar trade in Kainuu.

Kajaani Castle Ruins

The intensifying oppression of Finland by the Russian Czars from the 1880s onward made the traditional service by aristocratic young Finns in the Russian Army, once a respected pathway to prominent military and civil posts back home, increasingly distasteful. During the First World War, Finnish young men dreaming of complete separation from Russia began secretly making their way through Sweden to Germany to be trained as light infantrymen, known as *Jägers*, by the German army. When Finland declared independence in December, 1917 during the Russian revolution, *Jägers* returned to Finland to form the core of the independent Finnish army. The lock keeper's house was a favorite resting place for them.

The elaborate wooden **Kajaani Church**, designed by Jac. Ahrenberg and built in 1895–96, is the handsomest example of the Carpenter Gothic style in Finland.

The Kainuu Museum's exhibits depict life in Kainuu during the 19th and 20th centuries. Photographs, models, and authentic equipment illustrate how tar, a necessity for shipbuilding, was made by burning wood for several days in a covered pit.

The museum displays regional handicrafts, artifacts related to Elias Lönnrot's work on the *Kalevala*, and the Swedish Count Louis Sparre's donation of some forty drawings, and paintings, and traditional objects

acquired in Viena Karelia while following Lönnrot's route in 1892. While in Kajaani, Lönnrot founded the first Finnish language periodical, *Mehiläinen*, "The Bee" in 1836.

Elias Lönnrot

Kajaanin taidemuseo – Kajaani Art Museum

The Kajaani Art Museum is located in the International-style former police station, which was built in 1936. A sculpture garden connects the building with the Neo-Classical wooden former Town Hall by C. L. Engel from 1831. The museum's collection includes works of contemporary Finnish art.

Paltaniemen kirkko – Paltaniemi Church

Paltaniemi Church is located on the shore of Lake Oulujärvi on an unspoiled peninsula of fields and wind-bent pines. The wooden structure with an attached tower was built in 1726.

In 1778–81 the vaults were decorated by Emanuel Granberg with frescoes of biblical events, and are among the few Rococo paintings in Finland. Paltaniemi Church is thus often called "a picture church." The best preserved painting depicts the eternal bliss of the children of God as well as the torments of Hell. Part of the fresco was later painted over because the punishments were considered too graphic. The altar painting was painted by the first known Finnish woman painter, Margareta Capsia (1690–1759). The Rococo-style pulpit, the altarpiece, and the railing of the chancel with obelisks further embellish the sanctuary.

The so-called *Keisarintalli*, or Emperor's Stable, survives from 1819, when Czar Alexander I was served dinner in it, because it was the only decent structure as it had just recently been finished. An old museum road leads from the church to the parish graveyard.

Kuhmo

Juminkeko – Juminkeko Cultural Center

During a visit to Kuhmo in 1834, Elias Lönnrot gave the name *Kalevala* to the collection of folk poems he had been gathering in the remote villages of eastern Finland and Russian Karelia. Juminkeko, the information center for the *Kalevala* and Karelian culture, is a modern log building, designed by Mikko Heikkinen and Markku Komonen. Covered with a flowering grass roof and supported by 24 solid wooden columns, it incorporates an older building inside. Its name comes from an old Finnish riddle, still unsolved, *"What goes round a day, goes round the moon, but cannot go round the Juminkeko?"*

The exhibition on the *Kalevala*, its birth, the rune singing tradition, and on the influence of Karelia and the *Kalevala* in the arts, is related with the help of multimedia exhibits. The translations of the *Kalevala*, which by now have been made into 44 languages are displayed along with audio samples of runes. Among the many languages the visitor can choose are Fulan, Faroese, Hindi, Hebrew, Catalan, Moldavian, and even Yiddish.

Today Kuhmo is known for the Kuhmo Chamber Music Festival, visited by some 40,000 music lovers each summer.

Kainuu – Winter View

Kalevalakylä ja Talvi-sotanäyttely – Kalevala Village and Winter War Museum

Kalevala Village celebrates in an entertaining way the folk traditions and mysticism of the *Kalevala*. Along with having traditional buildings and historical exhibits, it is a lively tourist center.

Adjacent to the village, the Winter War Museum explains the battles that took place in Kuhmo in 1939 and 1940. The exhibits include photographs, scale models, computer-aided displays, and a 100-kilometer tour through the areas where many of the battles took place. During that unusually cold winter, the fighting in Kuhmo alone resulted in the deaths of some 1,350 Finnish and 10,000 Soviet soldiers. The peace treaty, signed 13 March 1940, forced Finland to cede Karelia and areas in the northeast, and to lease the Hanko peninsula to the Soviet Union.

Hyrynsalmi

Kaunislehto farm is a good example of a late 19th century Finnish farmstead. The 150-hectare (375 acres) farm is now a museum, which includes more than 20 buildings that have been moved to the site from around the region.

Kaunislehdon talomuseo – Kaunislehto Farm Museum

Named for the hillside birch grove nearby, the museum at Kaunislehto, literally "beautiful grove," focuses on traditional skills of past eras. Each June, a tar pit is burned in Kaunislehto as a demonstration of the manufacture of the once-dominant product of the region. The museum also maintains two reconstructed charcoal pits, based on an original plan dating from the early 16th century, where lake iron ore is burned.

Tar Pit

Suomussalmi

Suomussalmi, located along the old east-west trade routes, is well-known for its abundance of prehistoric artifacts. Stone Age dwelling places, tools, ceramic vessels, and jewelry have been discovered on the southern shores of Lake Kiantajärvi. One of the oldest such sites in Finland, more than 10,000 years old, was found on Kirkkosaari, Church Island. Some of the rich finds together with modern handiworks, continuing the long tradition of local craftsmanship, are exhibited in **Jaloniemi Handicrafts House** on the lakeshore in Ämmänsaari.

The decisive battle in Suomussalmi during the Winter War started on January 5, 1940 on the road from Suomussalmi to Raate. With only 1,100 men, the heavily outnumbered Finns were able to destroy two elite Soviet motorized divisions of 35,000 men. The Finns lost 800 men and the Soviets 23,000 in the fighting. The defensive triumph contributed to Moscow's willingness to discuss peace.

Raatteen museotie – Raate Museum Road

The Raate Museum Road begins about 18 kilometers east of Suomussalmi center. The **Raate Gate House Exhibition**, a memorial to both fallen Finnish and Soviet soldiers, displays Finnish and Soviet uniforms and personal objects of the soldiers. In the multimedia performance the visitor is taken back in time and put into the middle of the war.

The 18-kilometer museum road, lined with original and restored constructions and trenches, leads to the **Raate Outpost Museum** – Raatteen vartiomuseo – originally a guard station on the border. In addition to numerous local memorials, Alvar Aalto's famous nine-meter bronze sculpture, "Flame," dedicated to the Finnish soldiers who fought in the Winter War, stands near Suomussalmi town center.

Värikallion kalliomaalaukset – Värikallio Rock Paintings

The *Värikallio*, or "colored rock," paintings are located on a large rock face at Lake Somer in the sprawling Hossa state recreational area. They are the northernmost of Finland's 61 rock paintings, dating from the end of the Stone Age or the beginning of the late Comb Ceramic culture, or 2500 to 1500 B.C. Like all of Finland's prehistoric paintings, they were drawn on sheer rock escarpments rising from the water's edge. The paintings are more than 10 meters long and composed of more than 60 images. Unlike other Finnish rock paintings, they include representations of female figures giving birth, similar to figures found in Alta, Norway.

Vaala

Lamminahon talo – Lamminaho Farm

The Lamminaho farmstead, dating from the 1750s, is handsomely sited on the banks of the Oulujoki River in Vaala near the once-formidable Niskakoski rapids, whose turbulent waters were tamed by the construction of hydroelectric stations in 1945 and 1953. In the 19th century several generations of Lamminaho men served as rapidsmen or pilots, nominated by the Governor, who guided the boats through the rapids that extended for 9 kilometers downriver and dropped more than 33 meters along the way. Travelers, crossing Lake Oulujärvi on their way to or from Oulu in tar boats, often found comfortable accommodations at Lamminaho.

The buildings at Lamminaho Farm are exceptionally well preserved. The existing main farmhouse was built in 1813 and its original furniture and household objects are on display.

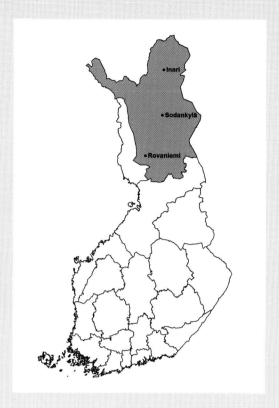

22
Lappi
Lapland

The mystical *Terra ultima*, the end of the world according to the Romans, has fascinated explorers and travelers for centuries. Lapland was written about as early as 1555 in Olaus Magnus's famous *History of the Northern Peoples* and in 1673 in Johannes Schefferus's *Lapponia*. For a long time, Lapland remained colored by prejudices, romantic ideas, and clichés that attracted travelers, such as Italian Guiseppe Acerbi and Swedish A. F. Skjöldebrand who recounted their impressions in words and drawings in 1799.

The earliest settlements in Lapland date from about 8,500 years ago. The Lappish people, or the Sámi, conducted trade all the way to Central Europe during the Stone Age. About one thousand years ago, population from the south started to move up the rivers to cultivate the land. However, hunting remained the mainstay up until the modern times.

Lapland remained for centuries the object of demands and power struggles between Sweden and Russia, and the residents were taxed by both powers. In 1323, the area came under Novgorod's sphere of influence, but with the advance of western Finnish resettlement and Swedish administration it turned more towards Sweden. In 1601, King Karl IX dispatched the first scientific expedition to Lapland to map the area and expand his power, also sending settlers and promising them major tax relief. The slash-and-burn farming practiced by the Finns drove off the Sámi's most important game, reindeer, forcing them to move northwards.

Ethnically, culturally, and linguistically the Sámi are a distinctly separate people, the only indigenous inhabitants of northern Scandinavia. They have derived from the same original Finno-Ugric population as the Finns. Under old laws covering Lapland, reindeer herding, fishing, and hunting were the recognized ecomic resources of the Sámi people on the land they owned. Lapland was first divided among the Scandinavian countries in 1751, guaranteeing the Sámi the right to cross national borders and to use state land regardless of national frontiers. Nowadays, the State owns 90% of the Sámi homelands in Finland, but the legality of this is now being challenged. The number of Sámi living in the northernmost part of Finland is around 7,000. The interest in reviving indigenous peoples that is seen throughout the world has also had an effect on the Sámi by increasing the use of their language.

During the past century, the Sámi way of life has undergone a marked period of transition. The Sámi have moved from their traditional *kota* or tent settlement into houses, which were later moved to roadsides. There are conflicts over land use because non-Lapps are also allowed to keep reindeer, the traditional Sámi way of life. Instead of intensive forestry and the construction of hydroelectric power plants, there are modern pressures to use the land for recreational purposes, tourism, and large-scale conservation.

At one time the Kemijoki River was Finland's main salmon river, providing a major source of income, but it quickly lost its value once hydropower plants were built starting at the end of the 1940s. The forests of the north were nearly pristine until the end of the 19th century when seasonal work, logging and floating grew as the wood processing industry expanded. Mechanization of forest work began in the 1950s and attracted people from outside the area. Year-round professional loggers gradually replaced seasonal workers and machines have reduced the need for lumberjacks. Log floating too, has passed into history.

During the so-called Continuation War from 1941 to 1944, German troops were based in Lapland as Germany fought against the Soviet Union. This alliance was severed when the Soviet Union signed a truce in 1944. Finns, exhausted from the war with the Soviets, were compelled by them to take military action to expel the German troops from Northern Finland. In retreating to the Arctic Ocean, the German soldiers razed much of Lapland, leaving only a few remote villages untouched. The last German troops finally left the country in April 1945.

Above all, Lapland is a land of natural grandeur and mighty land-scapes, of the *aurora borealis*, the northern lights, and a land of contrasts, from the darkness of winter or *kaamos* to the nightless days of summer.

Lappish Scenery

Rovaniemi

Rovaniemi has been an important focus for trade, which in the 19th century became the main logging center on the Kemijoki River and famous for its Winter Fair, still popular. In 1938 Rovaniemi became the administrative center of the Province of Lapland. The events of the Second World War brought a dramatic change in prosperity. The town was turned into a command center for German troops, but in 1944 the retreating German soldiers completely destroyed Rovaniemi.

During the last decades Rovaniemi has become known to the outside world primarily as the home of Santa Claus. The little cabin on the Arctic Circle, hastily built for the 1950 visit of the First Lady of the United States, Eleanor Roosevelt, still stands today. The adjoining **Santa Claus Village** has expanded into a theme park.

Aalto-keskus – Aalto Center

Alvar Aalto was commissioned to design the new plan for the town and its main public buildings. Here he repeated the themes familiar in his other urban centers: the square surrounded with public buildings. In the **Library**, finished in 1966, Aalto has masterfully considered the low northern sun, which bathes the lobby with light. The central part of the room is lower, with balcony-like spaces around. **Lappia Hall**, which serves as the city theater as well as the concert and congress center, with its silhouette of Lapland fells, was completed in 1975. The **Town Hall** was completed after Aalto's death in 1988.

Arktikum – Lapin maakuntamuseo ja Arktinen keskus – Arktikum – The Provincial Museum of Lapland and the Arctic Centre

Arktikum houses two independent institutions, a science center and a museum. The building is an attraction itself, designed by Danish architects Claus Bonderup, Sören Birch, and Ellen Waade. Built in 1983–84, it is constructed underground in the sloping bank of the Ounasjoki River. It symbolizes the harsh climate of Lapland that forces many plants and animals under the snow for protection. The visitor enters from the riverside into the 174-meter long tubular glass gallery, which, in lyrical contrast, rises above ground, ans is positioned directly north-south as a gateway to Lapland.

Arktikum

The Provincial Museum of Lapland researches and presents the Lappish wilderness and the cultural heritage it has shaped. The excellent multivision exhibitions provide a thorough insight into life in Lapland.

The Arctic Centre conducts research and houses a scientific exhibition relating life amid the exceptionally severe winters and brief, but intensely beautiful summers in the Arctic areas.

The Rovaniemi Art Museum is housed in the renovated post bus depot where the elegant details contrast with the robust red-brick surfaces. It was established with a donation to the city from the Jenny and Antti Wihuri Foundation art collection, which by now has grown to some 2,000 paintings, sculptures, drawings, and graphics. The collection is a survey of the most influential trends and developments of visual art in Finland since the 1940s, continuously augmented by both the city and the foundation. The museum covers the northern aspect in its exhibitions and publications.

Rovaniemen taide-museo – Rovaniemi Art Museum

Rovaniemi Local History Museum Pöykkölä – Rovaniemen kotiseutu-museo Pöykkölä – is located on the banks of the Kemijoki River. The fine Southern Lappish style main building from the 1840s, a barn, and two granaries are from the original farmstead.

Kemijärvi

Kemijärvi is known for the annual International Woodsculpting Sympo-sium, where artists from more than forty countries have created large outdoor sculptures made from old pine.

Pelkosenniemi

Suvanto Village in Pelkosenniemi on the bank of the River Kitinen is a rare, unusually well-preserved Lapland village, settled in the 1600s. A total of over one hundred log buildings survived the war and are now being restored.

Sodankylä

Sodankylän vanha kirkko – Sodankylä Old Church

Time has stopped in the hut-like Sodankylä old church, where the small lead-glass windows, set high as in medieval stone churches, allow dim light to reflect on the bare, unpainted silvery log walls. The roof is covered with shingles in a triangular pattern and provided with three weather vanes. The wooden barrel vault covers the small rectangular hall, supported by only one pair of block pillars. A simple railing separates the altar from the seats. The Baroque altar painting from 1730 illustrates the Last Supper.

The church is Finland's best-preserved and most completely intact wooden church, retaining the features typical of the Finnish medieval church building tradition and of Ostrobothnian block-pillar construction. The church was paid for by King Karl XI in 1689 as part of the colonialization of the northern regions. Until then, the vast area of Lapland had only two small chapels built to convert the Sámi to Christianity. However, the Sámi hung on to some of their old beliefs, though the ministers had worked hard to eradicate Sámi idols, the shaman's drums and the magical doors in the *kota*, the Lappish tent.

Kultamuseo – Gold Prospector Museum
Since the 1870s, Lapland has drawn gold prospectors from far and near. The legendary history of Lapland gold-digging has been

gathered and preserved in the museum, one of the most popular tourist attractions in Lapland and a respected institution for research and science. The exhibition gives the visitor a broad picture of the work and life of gold prospectors in Finland through pictures, documents, prospecting equipment and tools. The museum has one of the best collections in Finland of minerals and gemstones suitable for jewelry.

The museum started the World Gold Panning Championships, which initiated the idea of documenting the history of gold around the world. The unique Golden World exhibition in a round hall that symbolizes the world's largest prospecting pan introduces the history and traditions of gold panning for 22

*Oula Valle's Summer Place,
Andreas Alariesto*

countries. The outdoor exhibition, *Auraria*, features exact replicas of typical buildings from gold towns around the world, some representing the only historic buildings left, from Skagway in Alaska to a Chinese gold-diggers' shelter in New Zealand. Visitors can also pan for gold under the guidance of an experienced panner – and they get to keep any nuggets they find.

Andreas Alariesto (1900–1989) was a self-taught artist who wanted in his paintings to capture and preserve the old Samí way of life and culture, as well as his own experiences in his native village. For most of his life, Alariesto supported himself by various jobs, from logging to road building, and only after he retired was he able to devote more time to painting. His movingly naivistic paintings full of colorful details are displayed in the Gallery.

Alariesto-Galleria – Alariesto Gallery

Kittilä

The paintings of Reidar Särestöniemi (1925–1981) are an explosion of vibrant colors, taking an exotic departure from the quietly restrained mainstream of Finnish art. He is one of Lapland's most notable artists, who was born and spent most of his life on Särestö farm. Särestöniemi was best-known for his large, passionate paintings inspired by the enigmatic wilds of the far north, the dark winter nights of Lapland, and the brilliant white nights of summer. His love of nature is symbolized in the shapes of animals such as the lynx, willow grouse, and reindeer.

Särestöniemi-museo – Särestöniemi Museum

Architects Reima and Raili Pietilä designed a castle-like gallery, built with weathered logs, in 1972 and an adjacent studio in 1979, which became a major local attraction even during his lifetime. The original 18th-century farmhouse still stands next to the museum.

Inari

Saamelaismuseo
Siida – Sámi Museum
Siida

Siida, which means the winter village of the Sámi, is a center for Sámi culture and environment. Set in the oldest inhabited area of Northern Lapland,

it was established as an open-air museum after nearly all buildings were destroyed during the war, A new museum building, which combines natural materials with sleek but organic shapes, designed by Juhani Pallasmaa, opened in 1998.

The fascinating exhibitions present the story of the Sámi people's adaptation to the extreme northern environment and their culture. The nature exhibition is creatively displayed around the perimeter of the hall. It follows the influence of the four seasons displayed in the center, on Sámi culture, traditional work, social system, folk art, and religion. Northern Lapland Nature Center, one of 10 nature centers around the country, gives out information on the Finnish nature.

The small Pielpajärvi Church stands isolated on a lake, a 7-kilometer hike along a path from the center of Inari. It was built in 1754–60 on an old trade site and survived the Second World War because of its wilderness location. On the ridge of the shingled roof rises three weather vanes, decorated with incised ornaments. The simple interior is painted in pale colors.

Pielpajärven kirkko – Pielpajärvi Church

Utsjoki

Utsjoki Church, standing high on a hill, dominates the open landscape on the lake shore. The gray granite church was built by the state in 1850–53 as well as the fine Empire style parsonage. The church cottages on the market grounds were built for overnight accommodation during church holidays and markets, which were held in connection with the church services. Each Sámi family had their own cottage and market site. Several Lappish villages, some used only during fishing season, have survived along the Tenojoki River. The Utsjoki River in its narrow, deep valley and the open expanse around has been nominated a National Landscape by the Ministry of the Environment.

Notes

GENERAL NOTES

As a rule, the Finnish place name is here given first, even though there are some towns where the majority of the residents are Swedish speakers. The Åland Islands, where Swedish is the only official language, is an exception. The Swedish name is given when it is commonly used. The names of the rulers from the Swedish period are spelled in their original Swedish form.

The opening hours, especially of local museums and churches, can change annually and should be checked beforehand. The grounds of sites mentioned in this book as private are not open to visitors.

NOTES ON ARCHITECTURE

Gustavian (1775–1810)
The style is named for Gustav III, King of Sweden, who was inspired by Italian antiquity and had *Hämeenlinna Church* built. Later the style became stricter without columned gables as in *Turku Academy* or replacing Classical columns with flat pilasters as in *Mustio Manor*. Simple clarity and light colors as well as the harmony of forms and relationships made the style popular among vernacular builders and cabinetmakers.

Empire (1810–1850)
German-born Carl Ludvig Engel brought from St. Petersburg the Classical style, which is close to the English Regency and American Federal styles. Typical features in Finland are the central axis of the facade, a set of Classical columns to describe the usage of the buildings, pale yellow stucco walls, and shallow roofs. The buildings around Helsinki's *Senate Square* are the grandest example of the style. The towns were built with wide streets lined with mostly one-story wooden houses. The style had an impact on vernacular architecture, which adopted white corner boarding and ornamental details.

Neo-Gothic (1850–1870)
Typical of the style, also called Gothic revival, is the use of red brick, pointed arches, and corner towers. The best examples are the *House of Nobility* in Helsinki and the red-brick churches as well as public buildings in *Vaasa*. New industrial buildings often employed the Neo-Gothic style. Decorative fretwork was typical in wooden churches and houses.

Neo-Renaissance (1870–1890)
The style borrows from the Renaissance details in sculpturally articulated facades in an adaptation of the Renaissance *palazzo*. However, new techniques, such as the use of iron, were applied. The best examples are the *Ateneum* and the grand apartment buildings on *Esplanadi Street* in Helsinki, as well as the profusely decorated wooden houses of *Rauma*.

National Romantic (1890–1915)
The style arose as a revolt against the Classical and Eclectic styles, inspired by the interest in Finnish history, medieval castles and churches, and Finnish nature. Influences were taken also from Art Nouveau, the German and Austrian Jugend, and the British Arts and Crafts movement as well as from the American H. H. Richardson. The style strived to create "a total work of art" with furniture, textiles, and light fixtures designed specifically for the space. Examples of the style are the buildings by Lars Sonck as well as Herman Gesellius, Armas Lindgren, and Eliel Saarinen, such as *Hvitträsk*.

Nordic Classicism (1920–1930)
Simplified Classicism and its disciplined harmony and abstracted geometric forms were the foundation from which the Modernist movement arose. Classical decorative motifs and rules of proportion were eclectic, sometimes even ironic. Examples of the style are the *Parliament House* and the *Helsinki Art Hall* as well as the *Töölö* and *Käpylä* areas in Helsinki.

Functionalism (1930–1940)
Called elsewhere the International Style or Modernism, Functionalism demanded that the appearance of the buildings responds to their function. Influence for the streamlined, white buildings was received from Bauhaus in Germany, Le Corbusier, and the Swedish architects. Examples include Alvar Aalto's early works, such as *Paimio Sanatorium* as well as the *Nakkila Church*, and the *Olympic Stadium* in Helsinki.

Contact information

1 HELSINKI – HELSINGFORS

Helsingin yliopiston kirjasto – Helsinki University Library
Open: Jun and Aug: Mon-Fri 9am-6pm, Sat 9am-4pm,
             Sep-May: Tue 9:30am-6pm, Wed-Sat 9:30-4pm, Sun
             9:30am-3pm
Address: Unioninkatu 36
             00170 Helsinki
Phone: (09) 1912 2738, 1912 3190
Fax: (09) 1912 2719
Internet: www.lib.helsinki.fi

Helsingin tuomiokirkko – Helsinki Cathedral
Open: Daily 9am-6pm
Address: Unioninkatu 29
             00170 Helsinki
Phone: (09) 709 2455, 050 357 4540
Fax: (09) 709 2465
E-mail: tuomiokirkko.srk@evl.fi
Internet: www.helsinginseurakuntayhtyma.fi/tuomiokirkko

Suomenlinna – Suomenlinna Fortress

Suomenlinna-museo – Suomenlinna Museum
Open: May-Aug: Daily 10am-6pm Sep: Daily 11am-5pm
             Oct, Mar-Apr: Sat-Sun 11am-5pm
Address: Suomenlinna C 74
             00190 Helsinki
Phone.   (09) 668 120, 40501
Fax.   (09) 4050 9690
E-mail: matkailu@suomenlinna.fi
Internet: www.suomenlinna.fi, www.nba.fi/museums/slinna

Ehrensvärd-museo – Ehrensvärd Museum
Open: Early May-Sep: Daily 10am-5pm,
             Oct and Mar-early May: Sat-Sun 11am-4:30pm
Address: Suomenlinna B 40
             00190 Helsinki
Phone: (09) 684 1850
Fax: (09) 668 348
E-mail: matkailu@suomenlinna.fi
Internet: www.suomenlinna.fi

Sotamuseo, Maneesi – Manege Military Museum
Open: May-Aug: Daily 10am-5pm, Sep: Daily 11am-3pm,
             Oct and Apr: Sat-Sun 11am-3pm
Address: Suomenlinna, Iso Mustasaari
             00190 Helsinki
Phone: (09) 1814 5296
Fax: (09) 1812 6390
Internet: www.mpkk.fi, www.mil.fi

Rannikkotykistömuseo – Coast Artillery Museum
Open: May-Aug: Daily 10am-5pm, Sep: Daily 11am-3pm,
             Oct and Apr: Sat-Sun 11am-3pm
Address: Suomenlinna, Kustaanmiekka A 2
             00190 Helsinki
Phone: (09) 1814 5295
Fax: (09) 1812 6390
Internet: www.mpkk.fi, www.mil.fi

Sukellusvene Vesikko – Submarine Vesikko
Open: May-Aug: Daily 10am-5pm, Sep: Daily 11am-3pm

Address: Suomenlinna, Tykistölahti
             00190 Helsinki
Phone: (09) 1814 6238
Fax: (09) 1812 6390
Internet: www.mpkk.fi, www.mil.fi

Uspenskin katedraali – Uspenski Cathedral
Open: Tue 10am-6pm, Wed-Fri 10am-4pm, Sun 12-3pm
             and during the services
Address: Kanavakatu 1
             00160 Helsinki
Phone: (09) 634 267, 6844 0429
Fax: (09) 6844 0450
E-mail: hellevi.matihalti@ort.fi
Internet: www.ort.fi/helsinki

Helsingin synagoga – Helsinki Synagogue
Open: By appointment.
Address: Malminkatu 26
             00100 Helsinki
Phone: (09) 586 0310
Fax: (09) 694 8916
E-mail: srk@jchelsinki.fi
Internet: www.jchelsinki.fi

Kallion kirkko – Kallio Church
Open: Mon-Fri 12-6pm, Sat-Sun 10am-6pm
Address: Itäinen Papinkatu 2
             00530 Helsinki
Phone: (09) 753 2086, 5868 7058
Fax: (09) 763 656
E-mail: kallio.srk@evl.fi
Internet: www.helsinginseurakuntayhtyma.fi/kallio

Eduskuntatalo – Parliament House
Open: By appointment.
Address: Mannerheimintie 30
             00100 Helsinki
Phone: (09) 4321
Fax: (09) 432 2274
E-mail: eduskunta@eduskunta.fi
Internet: www.eduskunta.fi

Suomen urheilumuseo – Sports Museum of Finland
Open: Mon-Fri 11am-5pm, Sat-Sun 12-4pm
Address: Olympic Stadium
             00250 Helsinki
Phone: (09) 434 2250
Fax: (09) 434 22550
E-mail: urheilumuseo@stadion.fi
Internet: www.stadion.fi

Finlandia-talo – Finlandia Hall
Open: By appointment.
Address: Mannerheimintie 13
             00100 Helsinki
Phone: (09) 40241
Fax: (09) 402 4249
E-mail: finlandiahall@fin.hel.fi
Internet: www.finlandia.hel.fi

Temppeliaukion kirkko – Temppeliaukio Church
Open: Mon-Fri 10am-8pm, Sat 10am-6pm
Address: Lutherinkatu 3
             00100 Helsinki
Phone: (09) 494 698
Fax: (09) 496 366
E-mail: taivallahti.srk@evl.fi
Internet: www.helsinginseurakunnat.net/taivallahti

Suomen kansallisooppera – Finnish National Opera
Open: By appointment.
Address: Helsinginkatu 58
            00250 Helsinki
Phone: (09) 4030 2210
Fax: (09) 4030 2305
E-mail: opera@operafin.fi
Internet: www.operafin.fi

Suomen kansallismuseo – The National Museum of Finland
Open: Tue-Wed 11am-8pm, Thu-Sun 11am-6pm
Address: Mannerheimintie 34
            00100 Helsinki
Phone: (09) 40501, 4050 9554
Fax: (09) 4050 9400
E-mail: kansallismuseo@nba.fi
Internet: www.nba.fi/natmus/Kmeng

Kulttuurien museo – Museum of Cultures
Open: Tue-Sun 10am-8pm
Address: Salomonkatu 15 / Eteläinen Rautatiekatu 8
            00100 Helsinki
Phone: (09) 4050 9805
Fax: (09) 4050 9821
E-mail: kulttuurienmuseo@nba.fi
Internet: www.nba.fi/museums/kultmus/kumueng

**Seurasaaren ulkomuseo – The Seurasaari
Open-Air Museum**
Open: Jun-Aug: Daily 11am-5pm, Wed until 7pm,
            May 15-31 Sep 1-15: Mon-Fri 9am-3pm, Sat-Sun
            11am-5pm Sep 16-30: Sat-Sun 11am-5pm
Address: Seurasaari
            00250 Helsinki
Phone: (09) 4050 9660, 40501
Fax: (09) 4050 9665, 4050 9579
E-mail: riitta.ailonen@nba.fi
Internet: www.nba.fi/museums/seuras

Ateneumin taidemuseo – Ateneum Art Museum
Open: Tue, Fri 9am-6pm, Wed-Thu 9am-8pm, Sat-Sun
            11am-5pm
Address: Kaivokatu 2
            00100 Helsinki
Phone: (09) 1733 6401
Fax: (09) 1733 6226
E-mail: ainfo@fng.fi
Internet: www.ateneum.fi

Nykytaiteen museo Kiasma – Museum of Contemporary Art
Kiasma
Open: Tue 9am-5pm, Wed-Sun 10am-8:30pm
Address: Mannerheiminaukio 2
            00100 Helsinki
Phone: (09) 1733 6501
Fax: (09) 1733 6503
E-mail: kinfo@kiasma.fi
Internet: www.kiasma.fi

Sinebrychoffin taidemuseo – Sinebrychoff Art Museum
Open: Tue, Fri 10am-6pm, Wed-Thu 10am-8pm,
            Sat-Sun 11am-5pm
Address: Bulevardi 40
            00120 Helsinki
Phone: (09) 1733 6460
Fax: (09) 1733 6476
E-mail: sinfo@sinebrychoff.fi
Internet: www.sinebrychoffintaidemuseo.fi

Helsingin kaupungin museo – Helsinki City Museum
Open: Mon-Fri 9am-5pm, Sat-Sun 11am-5pm
            and by appointment.
Address: Sofiankatu 4
            00170 Helsinki
Phone: (09) 169 3933, 169 3949
Fax: (09) 667 665
E-mail: kaupunginmuseo@hel.fi
Internet: www.hel.fi/kaumuseo, www.helsinkiarena2000.fi/
            maailmat/virtmuse

Sederholmin talo – Sederholm House
Open: Wed-Sun 11am-5pm
Address: Aleksanterinkatu 16-18
            00170 Helsinki
Phone: (09) 169 3625

Hakasalmen huvila – Hakasalmi Villa
Open: Mid Sep-mid Jun: Wed-Sun 11am-6pm
Address: Karamzininkatu 2
            00100 Helsinki
Phone: (09) 169 3444

Ruiskumestarin talo – Burgher's House
Open: Mid Oct-mid Apr: Wed-Sun 11am-5pm
Address: Kristianinkatu 12
            00170 Helsinki
Phone: (09) 135 1065

Koulumuseo – School Museum
Open: Sep-May: Mon-Thu and Sun 11am-5pm
Address: Kalevankatu 39-43
            00180 Helsinki
Phone: (09) 3108 7066

Tuomarinkylän museo – Tuomarinkylä Museum
Open: Aug-Jun: Wed-Sun 11am-5pm
Address: Tuomarinkylän kartano
            00690 Helsinki
Phone: (09) 728 7458

Raitioliikennemuseo – Tram Museum
Open: Mid Sep-Jul: Wed-Sun 11am-5pm
Address: Töölönkatu 51 A
            00260 Helsinki
Phone   (09) 169 3576

Työväenasuntomuseo – Worker Housing Museum
Open: May-Sep: Wed-Sun 11am-5pm
Address: Kirstinkuja 4
            00510 Helsinki
Phone: (09) 146 1039

Voimalamuseo – Power Station Museum
Open: Jun-Aug: Wed-Sun 11am-5pm
Address: Hämeentie 163
            00560 Helsinki
Phone: (09) 3108 7064

**Helsingin kaupungin taidemuseo, Meilahden museo –
Helsinki City Art Museum, Meilahti Museum**
Open: Wed-Sun 11am-6:30pm
Address: Tamminiementie 6
            00250 Helsinki
Phone: (09) 3108 7031
Fax: (09) 3108 7030
E-mail: karri.buchert@hel.fi
Internet: www.hel.fi/artmuseum

Helsingin kaupungin taidemuseo, Tennispalatsi – Helsinki City Art Museum, Tennis Palace
Open: Tue-Sun 11am-8:30pm
Address: Salomonkatu 15 / Pohjoinen Rautatiekatu 18
            00100 Helsinki
Phone: (09) 3108 7001
Fax: (09) 3108 7010
E-mail: karri.buchert@hel.fi
Internet: www.hel.fi/artmuseum

Amos Andersonin taidemuseo – Amos Anderson Art Museum
Open: Mon-Fri 10am-6pm, Sat-Sun 11am-5pm
Address: Yrjönkatu 27
            00100 Helsinki
Phone: (09) 684 4460
Fax: (09) 684 44622
E-mail: museum@amosanderson.fi
Internet: www.amosanderson.fi

Designmuseo – Design Museum
Open: Jun-Aug: Daily 11am-5pm,
            Sep-May: Tue-Sun 11am-5pm, Wed until 8pm
Address: Korkeavuorenkatu 23
            00130 Helsinki
Phone: (09) 622 0540, 6220 5455, 626 733
E-mail: info@designmuseum.fi
Internet: www.designmuseum.fi

Suomen rakennustaiteen museo – Museum of Finnish Architecture
Open: Tue-Sun10am-4pm, Wed until 8pm
Address: Kasarmikatu 24
            00130 Helsinki
Phone: (09) 661 918
Fax: (09) 662 573
E-mail: mfa@mfa.fi
Internet: www.mfa.fi

Luonnontieteellinen museo – Finnish Museum of Natural History
Open: Mon-Fri 9am-5pm, Sat-Sun 11am-4pm
Address: Pohjoinen Rautatiekatu 13
            00100 Helsinki
Phone: (09) 1912 8800, 1912 8804
Fax: (09) 1912 8888
E-mail: info-fmnh@helsinki.fi
Internet: www.fmnh.helsinki.fi

Yliopiston kasvitieteellinen puutarha – University Botanical Gardens
Open: Gardens: May-Sep: Daily 7am-8pm, Oct-Apr:
            Daily 7am-6pm Greenhouses: Tue-Sun 11am-5pm
Address: Unioninkatu 44
            00170 Helsinki
Phone: (09) 191 24453
Fax: (09) 191 24454
Internet: www.helsinki.fi/ml/botgard

Arabian museo – Arabia Museum
Open: Mon 9am-8pm, Tue-Fri 9am-6pm, Sat-Sun 9am-3pm
Address: Hämeentie 135
            00560 Helsinki
Phone: 0204 2911
Fax: 0204 395180
E-mail: hannele.nyman@designor.com
Internet: www.sci.fi/~hts/arabia

Herttoniemen kartanon museo – Herttoniemi Manor House Museum
Open: May-Oct: Sun 12-3pm, Nov-Apr: First Sun of the
            month 12-2pm and by appointment.
Address: Linnanrakentajantie 14
            00810 Helsinki
Phone: (09) 298 9522, 789 874

Suomen valokuvataiteen museo – The Finnish Museum of Photography
Open: Tue-Sun 12-7pm
Address: The Cable Factory
            Tallberginkatu 1 G
            00180 Helsinki
Phone: (09) 6866 3621
Fax: (09) 6866 3630
E-mail: fmp@fmp.fi
Internet: www.fmp.fi

Teatterimuseo – Theatre Museum
Open: Tue-Sun 12-7pm
Address: The Cable Factory
            Tallberginkatu 1 G
            00180 Helsinki
Phone: (09) 6850 9150
Fax: (09) 6850 9121
E-mail: teatterimuseo@teatterimuseo.fi
Internet: www.teatterimuseo.fi

Hotelli- ja ravintolamuseo – Hotel and Museum
Open: Tue-Sun 12-7pm
Address: The Cable Factory
            Tallberginkatu 1 G
            00180 Helsinki
Phone: (09) 6859 3700
Fax: (09) 6859 3766
E-mail: hrm@kaapeli.fi

Postimuseo – Post Museum
Open: Mon-Fri 10am-7pm, Sat-Sun 11am-4pm
Address: Helsinki Main Post Office
            Asema-aukio 5 H
            00100 Helsinki
Phone: (09) 0204 51 4775, 0204 51 4980
Fax: (09) 0204 51 4777
E-mail: postimuseo@posti.fi
Internet: www.posti.fi/postimuseo

Päivälehden museo – Päivälehti Museum
Open: Tue-Sun 11am-5pm
Address: Ludviginkatu 2-4
            00120 Helsinki
Phone: 01 0519 5210
Fax: 01 0519 5208
E-mail: museo@paivalehdenarkistosaatio.fi
Internet: www.paivalehdenarkistosaatio.fi

Suomen merimuseo – The Maritime Museum of Finland
Open: May-Sep: Daily 11am-5pm,
            Oct-Apr: Sat-Sun 10am-3pm
Address: Hylkysaari, access via Korkeasaari Zoo
            00570 Helsinki
Phone: (09) 4050 9051, 4050 9052
Fax: (09) 4050 9060
E-mail: suomenmerimuseo@nba.fi
Internet: www.nba.fi/museums/maritime

Sotamuseo – Military Museum
Open: Jun-Aug: Tue-Fri 11am-6pm, Sat-Sun 11am-4pm

Sep-May: Sun-Fri 11am-4pm
Address: Maurinkatu 1
             00170 Helsinki
Phone: (09) 1812 6265
Fax: (09) 1812 6390
E-mail: maritta.partanen@mpkk.fi
Internet: www.mpkk.fi/muut

Cygnaeuksen galleria – The Cygnaeus Gallery
Open: Wed-Sun 11am-4pm, Wed until 7pm
Address: Kalliolinnantie 8
             00140 Helsinki
Phone: (09) 4050 9628
Fax: (09) 4050 9627
E-mail: cygnaeuksengalleria@nba.fi
Internet: www.nba.fi/museums/cygn

Mannerheim-museo – Mannerheim Museum
Open: Fri-Sun 11am-4pm and by appointment.
Address: Kalliolinnantie 14
             00140 Helsinki
Phone: (09) 635 443
Fax: (09) 636 736
E-mail: mannerheim@museo.pp.fi
Internet: www.mannerheim-museo.fi

Didrichsenin taidemuseo – Didrichsen Art Museum
Open: Sat-Sun 1-4pm, Wed 4-6pm
Address: Kuusilahdenkuja 1
             00340 Helsinki
Phone: (09) 489 055
Fax: (09) 489 167
Internet: www.didrichsenmuseum.fi

Reitzin Säätiön kokoelmat – Collection of Reitz Foundation
Open: Wed and Sun 3-5pm. Closed in July.
Address: Apollonkatu 23 B 64
             00100 Helsinki
Phone: (09) 442 501
Fax: (09) 497 490

Taidekoti Kirpilä – Kirpilä Art Collection
Open: Wed 2pm-6pm, Sun 12-4pm. Closed in July.
             By appointment for groups.
Address: Pohjoinen Hesperiankatu 7
             00260 Helsinki
Phone: (09) 494 436
Fax: (09) 447 658
E-mail: al@skr.fi
Internet: www.skr.fi/taidekoti

Villa Gyllenberg – Villa Gyllenberg Art Collection
Open: Wed 4pm-8pm, Sun 12-4pm. Closed in July.
Address: Kuusisaarenpolku 11
             00340 Helsinki
Phone: (09) 481 333
Fax: (09) 607 119
E-mail: stiftelsen@gyllenberg-foundation.fi
Internet: www.gyllenberg-foundation.fi

Aallon talo – Villa Aalto
Open: Tours daily 2pm, 3pm, 4pm, 5pm
Address: Riihitie 20
             00340 Helsinki
Phone: (09) 4243 3301
Fax: (09) 485 119
E-mail: foundation@alvaraalto.fi
Internet: www.alvaraalto.fi

Studio Aalto
Open: Mon-Fri 9am-4pm, tours 1pm and 3pm
             and by appointment for groups.
Address: Tiilimäki 20
             00340 Helsinki
Phone: (09) 4243 3301
Fax: (09) 485 119
E-mail: foundation@alvaraalto.fi
Internet: www.alvaraalto.fi

2 LÄNSI-UUSIMAA – WESTERN UUSIMAA

HANKO – HANGÖ
Hangon rintamamuseo – Hanko Front Museum
Open: Early May-Sep: Daily 11:30am-6:30pm and by
             appointment.
Address.   10820 Lappvik
Phone: (019) 244 3068, 231 301
Internet: www.hanko.fi/

Linnoitusmuseo – Fortress Museum
Open: May-Aug: Tue-Sun 11am-4pm, Thu also 6pm-7pm,
             Sep-Apr: Wed-Thu, Sat-Sun 1pm-3pm, Thu also
             6pm-7pm
Address: Nycanderinkatu 4
             10900 Hanko
Phone: (019) 220 3228, 220 3223
Fax: (019) 220 3261

Bengtskärin majakka – Bengtskär Lighthouse
Open: Jun-Aug: Daily 10am-8pm
Phone: (02) 466 7227, 050 353 6933, 050 528 7410
Fax: (02) 466 7227
Internet: www.fma.fi/lighthouses
             www.rosita.fi/ saarikoh
             www.travel.fi/fin/saaristomeri

Hauensuolen kalliomaalaukset – Hauensuoli Rock Paintings
             Daily by waterbus from the east Harbor during the
             summer months.
Phone: (019) 220 3411

TAMMISAARI – EKENÄS
Tammisaaren museo – Tammisaari Museum
Open: Mid May-mid Aug: Daily 11-5pm,
             Mid Aug-mid May: Tue-Thu 6-8pm, Fri-Sat 12-4pm
             and by appointment.
Address: Kustaa Vaasankatu 11
             10600 Tammisaari
Phone: (019) 263 2240, 263 3161
Fax: (019) 263 3150
E-mail: ekenasmuseum@ekenas.fi
Internet: www.ekenas.fi

Raaseporin linna – Raasepori Castle
Open: May and Aug 16-31: Daily 10am-5pm, Jun-Aug
             15:Daily 10am-8pm, Sep: Sat-Sun 10am-5pm
             and by appointment.
Address: 10710 Snappertuna
Phone: (019) 23 4015
Internet: www.kulturfonden.fi/raseborg

Tenholan kirkko – Tenhola Medieval Church
Open: Mid Jun-late Aug: Daily 10am-6pm, Late Aug-mid
             Jun: Mon-Thu 10am-12
Address: Gamla vägen 11
             10520 Tenhola
Phone: (019) 245 0550

Fax: (019) 245 0552
Internet: www.evl.fi/tenhola

POHJA – POJO
Fiskarsin ruukki – Fiskars Ironworks
Phone: (019) 299 504
Fax: (019) 277 230
E-mail: fiskars.info@fiskars.fi
Internet: www.fiskarsvillage.net

Fiskarsin museo – Fiskars Museum
Open: May-Sep: Daily 11am-4pm, Oct-Apr: Sun 1pm-3pm
               and by appointment.
Address: Museomäki
               10470 Fiskars
Phone: (019) 237 013, 237 023
Fax: (019) 237 013
E-mail.   lokalhistoriska.arkivet@kolumbus.fi
Internet: www.stn.fi/x/fiskarsmuseum

Billnäsin ruukki – Billnäs Ironworks
Address: 10330 Pinjainen
Phone: Apr-Sep: (019) 237 041, Oct-Mar: (019) 26 611
Fax: (019) 266 1200
Internet: www.probillnas.fi

Billnäsin Museovoimalaitos – Billnäs Museum Power Plant
Open: Jun-Aug: Daily 10am-6pm, May and Sep 1-15:
               10am-4pm and by appointment.
Address: Vasarasepäntie 28
               10330 Billnäs
Phone: (019) 233 079, 0500 603 435
Fax: (019) 238 8411, 2771

Pohjan kirkko – Pohja Medieval Church
Open: Jun-Aug: Mon-Fri 9am-3pm and by appointment.
Address: Flemingintie 6
               10420 Pohjankuru
Phone: (019) 245 3266
Fax: (019) 245 3003

KARJAA – KARIS
Mustion linna – Mustio Manor
Open: May-Aug: Daily 12-5pm and by appointment.
Address: Mustion Linna
               10360 Mustio
Phone: (019) 36 231
Fax: (019) 362 3250
E-mail: myyntipalvelu@mustionlinna.fi
Internet: www.mustionlinna.fi

Karjaan kirkko – Karjaa Medieval Church
Open: By appointment.
Address: Keskuskatu 23
               10300 Karjaa
Phone: (019) 279 3055
Fax: (019) 279 3050

SAMMATTI
Paikkarin torppa – Paikkari Croft
Open: May-Aug: Sun-Fri 11am-6pm, Sat 11am-4pm,
               Sep: Daily 11am-5pm
Address: Paikkari, Haarjärvi
               09220 Sammatti
Phone: (019) 356 659
Fax: (09) 4050 0400
E-mail: lea.vartinen@nba.fi, erkki.pyokkimies@sammatti.fi
Internet: www.nba.museums/paikkari
               www.sammatti.fi

Sammatin kirkko – Sammatti Church
Open: Jun-mid Aug: Daily 10am-4pm and by appointment.
Address: 09220 Sammatti
Phone: (019) 356 900
Fax: (019) 356 900
Internet: www.sammatti.fi/skunta

LOHJA – LOJO
Tytyrin kalkkikaivosmuseo – Tytyri Limestone Quarry Museum
Open: Jun-Aug: Daily 11am-6pm May, Sep-Dec: Sat-Sun
               12-4pm
Address: Tytyrinkatu
               08100 Lohja
Phone: (019) 345 1765, 369 1309
Fax: (019) 369 1326
Internet: www.lohja/tytynew

Lohjan kirkko – Lohja Medieval Church
Open: Mid May-Aug: Daily 9am-4pm, Sep-mid May:
               10am-3pm and by appointment.
Address: 08100 Lohja
Phone: (019) 32 841
Fax: (019) 322 452
E-mail: lohja.kirkkoherranvirast@evl.fi
Internet: www.kolumbus.fi/lohjan.seurakunta.fi
               www.lohja.fi/stlauri

Lohjan museo – Lohja Museum
Open: Tue-Sun 12-4pm, Wed until 7pm
Address: Iso-Pappila
               08100 Lohja
Phone: (019) 369 4206
Fax: (019) 369 4203
Internet: www.lohja.fi/museo.htm

INKOO – INGÅ
Fagervikin ruukki ja kirkko – Fagervik Ironworks and Church
Open: By appointment.
Address: 10250 Fagervik
Phone: 040 589 7945, (019) 295 151

Inkoon kirkko – Inkoo Medieval Church
Open: Mid Jun-Jul: Daily 10am-4pm
               Ola Westmanin puistotie 12
Address: 10210 Inkoo
Phone: (09) 221 2101
Fax: 09) 296 1212
E-mail: inga.kansli@evl.fi

Degerby Igor -museo – Degerby Igor Museum
Open: Jun-Aug: Tue-Sat 10am-2pm and by appointment.
Address: 10160 Degerby
Phone: (09) 221 1912, 050 598 6526
Internet: www.inga.fi/~igor

SIUNTIO – SJUNDEÅ
Siuntion kirkko – Siuntio Medieval Church
Open: Early Jun-late Aug: Daily 10am-6pm and by
               appointment.
Address: Suitiantie 51
               02570 Siuntio
Phone: (09) 819 0910
Fax: (09) 813 4643
E-mail: ismo.turunen@evl.fi

Suitian kartanolinna – Suitia Fortified Manor
Open: By appointment.
Address: 02570 Siuntio
Phone: (09) 8190 8530, 256 1165

Fax: (09) 8190 8549
Internet: www.helsinki.fi/aikuiskoulutus/lum

KIRKKONUMMI – KYRKSLÄTT
Hvitträsk
Open: Jun-Aug: Daily 10am-6pm, Apr-May and Sep-Oct:
          Daily 11am-6pm, Nov-Mar: Daily 11am-5pm
Address: Hvitträskintie 166
          02440 Luoma
Phone: (09) 4050 9630
Fax: (09) 4050 9631
E-mail: hvittrask@luukku.com
Internet: www.nba.fi/museums/hvittr

KARKKILA – HÖGFORS
Suomen valimomuseo – Finland's Foundry Museum
Open: May-Aug: Wed-Sun 11am-6pm, Sep-Apr: Sat 11am-
          3pm, Sun 11am-6pm
Address: Tehtaanpuisto
          03600 Karkkila
Phone: (09) 2250 5261, 0400 938 337
E-mail: suomen.valimomuseo@co.inet.fi
Internet: www.karkkila.fi

**Karkkila-Högforsin työläismuseo – Karkkila-Högfors
Workers' Museum**
Open: Jun-mid Aug: Wed-Sun 12-6pm and by appointment.
Address: Fagerkulla
          03600 Karkkila
Phone: (09) 2250 52451, 0500 938 337
Fax: (09) 2250 5208
E-mail: tommi.kuutsa@karkkila.fi
Internet: www.karkkila.fi

3 KESKI-UUSIMAA – CENTRAL UUSIMAA

ESPOO – ESBO
Espoon kirkko – Espoo Medieval Church
Open: Daily 10am-6pm
Address: Kirkkopuisto 5
          02770 Espoo
Phone: (09) 8625 0236
Fax: (09) 8625 0215
Internet: www.evl.fi/espoo

Glimsin talomuseo – Glims Farmstead Museum
Open: May-Sep: Tue-Sun 11am-5pm, Oct-Apr: Tue-Fri
          10am-4pm, Sat-Sun 12-4pm and by appointment.
Address: Glimsintie 1
          02740 Espoo
Phone: (09) 863 2979
Fax: (09) 868165 7031
E-mail: mariliina.perkko@espoo.fi
Internet: www.espoo.fi/museo

Espoon kaupunginmuseo – Espoo City Museum
Open: Tue-Fri 10am-7pm, Sat-Sun 11am-6pm
Address: WeeGee Building
          Ahertajantie 5
          02100 Espoo
Phone: (09) 8165 7033
Fax: (09) 8165 7031
E-mail: mariliina.perkko@espoo.fi
Internet: www.espoo.fi/museo

Helinä Rautavaaran museo – Helinä Rautavaara Museum
Open: Tue-Fri 11am-5pm, Wed until 7pm, Sat-Sun 11am 4pm
Address: WeeGee Building

          Ahertajantie 5
          02100 Espoo
Phone: (09) 412 9439
Fax: (09) 412 9355
E-mail: etnomuseo@kolumbus.fi

Otaniemen kappeli – Otaniemi Chapel
Open: Jun-Aug: Mon-Fri 10am-3pm
Address: Jämeräntaival 8
          02150 Espoo
Phone: (09) 8625 0400
Fax: (09) 8625 0425
Internet: www.evl.fi/srk/espoo/tapiola

Gallen-Kallelan Museo – Gallen-Kallela Museum
Open: May 15-Aug: Daily 10am-6pm, Sep-May 14: Tue-Sat
          10am-4pm, Sun 10am-5pm
Address: Gallen-Kallelan tie 27
          02600 Espoo
Phone: (09) 541 3388
Fax: (09) 541 6426
E-mail: tarvaspaa@gallen-kallela.fi
Internet: www.gallen-kallela.fi

Suomen Kellomuseo – Finnish Museum of Horology
Open: Jul-Aug: Wed 2pm-8pm, Thu-Sun 12-4pm Sep-Jun:
          Wed 2pm-8pm, Sun 12-4pmand by appointment.
Address: Opinkuja 2
          02100 Espoo
Phone: (09) 452 0688
Fax: (09) 4520 5656
E-mail: tuulia.tuomi@kelloseppaliitto.fi
Internet: www.kelloseppaliitto.fi/museo

VANTAA –VANDA
Helsingin pitäjän kirkko – Helsinge Parish Medieval Church
Open: Jun-Aug: Mon-Fri 9am-8pm, Sep-May: Daily
          9am-12 and 1pm-3pm
Address: Kirkkotie 45
          01510 Vantaa
Phone: (09) 822 625
Fax: (09) 873 5063
Internet: www.vantaanseurakunnat.net

Vantaan kaupunginmuseo –Vantaa City Museum
Open: Wed-Sun 11am-4pm
Address: Tikkurila Old Station
          Hertaksentie 1
          01300 Vantaa
Phone: (09) 8392 4449
Fax: (09) 8392 3638
E-mail: jorma.uimonen@vantaa.fi
Internet: www.vantaa.fi/kaupunginmuseo

**Heureka Suomalainen Tiedekeskus – Heureka, the Finnish
Science Centre**
Open: Daily: 10am-6pm, Thu until 8pm
Address: Tiedepuisto 1
          01300 Vantaa
Phone: (09) 85 799
Fax: (09) 873 4142
E-mail: info@heureka.fi
Internet: www.heureka.fi

Suomen Ilmailumuseo – Finnish Aviation Museum
Open: Daily 11am-6pm
Address: Tietotie 3
          01530 Vantaa
Phone: (09) 8700 870

Fax: (09) 8700 8720
E-mail: info@suomenilmailumuseo.fi
Internet: www.suomenilmailumuseo.fi

Myyrmäen kirkko – Myyrmäki Church
Open: By appointment.
Address: Uomatie 1
            01600 Vantaa
Phone: (09) 830 6429, 830 6440, 8501 8724
Fax: (09) 830 6432

TUUSULA
Tuusulan kirkko – Tuusula Church
Open: Jun-Jul: Mon-Fri 10am-6pm, Sun 12-6pm
Address: Kirkkotie 34
            04310 Tuusula
Phone: (09) 875 960, 040 551 7687
Fax: (09) 8759 6271
E-mail: hilkka.palo@evl.fi
Internet: www.tuus.net

Tuusulan työläiskotimuseo – Worker's Home Museum
Open: May-Aug: Sat-Sun 12- 4pm, Jun-Aug: Wed also
            6pm-8pm
Address: Kirkkotie
            04300 Tuusula
Phone: (09) 272 1622, 0400 955 255
Internet: www.tuusula.fi/matkailu/nahtavyydet/tyolaiskoti

Klaavola – Klaavola Museum
Open: Jun-Aug: Tue-Fri 12-4pm, Sat-Sun 12-5pm,
            Sep-May: Tue-Fri 11am-4pm
Address: Klaavolantie 3
            04300 Tuusula
Phone: (09) 8718 3460
Fax: (09) 8718 3458
Internet: www.tuusula.fi/matkailu/nahtavyydet/klaavola

Kellokosken kirkko – Kellokoski Church
Open: By appointment.
Address: Männistöntie 5
            04500 Kellokoski
Phone: (09) 2790 5740, 040 540 3745
Internet: www.tuus.net

Halosenniemi – Halosenniemi Museum
Open: May-Aug: Mon 11am-5pm, Tue-Sun 11am-7pm,
            Sep-Apr: Tue-Sun 11am-4pm
Address: Halosenniemi, Rantatie
            04300 Tuusula
Phone: (09) 8718 3461
Fax: (09) 8718 3458
E-mail: halosenniemi@tuusula.fi
Internet: www.tuusula.fi/matkailu/nahtavyydet/halosenniemi

JÄRVENPÄÄ
Ahola
Open: May-Sep: Tue-Sun 11am-6pm
Address: Sibeliuksenväylä 57
            04400 Järvenpää
Phone: (09) 291 6685, 2719 2718
Fax: (09) 2719 2791
E-mail: matkailu@jarvenpaa.fi
Internet: www.jarvenpaa.fi, www.tuusulanrantatie.info

Järvenpään taidemuseo – Järvenpää Art Museum
Open: May-Sep: Tue-Sun 11am-6pm Mar-Apr: Thu 2pm-6pm
Address: Kirjastokatu 8
            04400 Järvenpää

Phone: (09) 2719 2827
Fax: (09) 2719 2791
E-mail: matkailu@jarvenpaa.fi
Internet: www.jarvenpaa.fi, www.tuusulanrantatie.info

Villa Kokkonen
Open: Jun-Aug: Thu-Sun 11am-6pm, May and Sep:
            Sat-Sun 11am-6pm
Address.   Tuulimyllyntie 5
            04400 Järvenpää
Phone: (09) 286 204, 2719 2718
Fax: (09) 2719 2791
E-mail: matkailu@jarvenpaa.fi
Internet: www.jarvenpaa.fi, www.tuusulanrantatie.info

Ainola
Open: May-Sep: Tue-Sun 10am-5pm
Address: Ainolantie
            04400 Järvenpää
Phone: (09) 287 22, 050 3819
Fax: (09) 2719 2791
E-mail: matkailu@jarvenpaa.fi
Internet: www.ainola.fi
            www.tuusulanrantatie.info
            www.nba.fi

KERAVA
Keravan museo – Kerava Museum
Open: Jun-Aug: Tue-Sun 12-5pm, Sep-May: Wed 12-6pm,
            Sun 12-5pm and by appointment
Address: Museopolku 1
            04200 Kerava
Phone: (09) 2949 2166
Fax: (09) 2949 2082
E-mail: leena.jarnfors@kerava.fi
Internet: www.kerava.fi/index2.htm

Keravan taidemuseo – Kerava Art Museum
Open: Tue-Sun 12-7pm
Address: Klondyke Building
            Kumitehtaankatu, Savio
            04260 Kerava
Phone: (09) 294 8090
Fax: (09) 294 8090
Internet: www.kerava.fi/palvelu/kulttuuri/taidemuseo

NURMIJÄRVI
Aleksis Kiven syntymäkoti – Birthplace of Aleksis Kivi
Open: Jun-Aug: Tue-Sun 11am-5pm, Wed until 7pm
            Mid May-May 31: Tue-Fri 9:30am-4pm, Sat-Sun
            11am-5pm
Address: Palojoentie 271
            01940 Palojoki
Phone: (09) 250 5609
Fax: (09) 2500 2503
E-mail: museo@nurmijarvi.fi
Internet: www.nurmijarvi.fi/kirku/museoak

HYVINKÄÄ
Suomen Rautatiemuseo – The Finnish Railway Museum
Open: Jun-Aug: Daily 11am-5pm, Sep-May: Tue-Sat 12-
            3pm, Sun 12-5pm
Address: Hyvinkäänkatu 9
            05800 Hyvinkää
Phone: 0307 25241
Fax: 0307 25240
E-mail: info@rautatie.org
Internet: www.rautatie.org

Hyvinkään taidemuseo – Hyvinkää Art Museum
Open: Tue-Fri 11am-7pm, Sat 10am-3pm, Sun 11am-5pm
Address: Hämeenkatu 3 D
           05800 Hyvinkää
Phone: (019) 459 4002
Fax: (019) 459 4001
Internet: www.hyvinkaa.fi/taidemuseo

MÄNTSÄLÄ
Alikartano – Alikartano Manor
Open: May 15-Aug 31: Daily 11am-5pm, Sep: by appoint-
           ment for groups.
Address: Nummistentie 48
           04660 Numminen
Phone: (019) 688 3398
Fax: (09) 405 0400
E-mail: lea.vartinen@nba.fi,
           kartanomatkat@kartanomatkat.fi
Internet: www.nba.fi/museums/alik
           www.mantsala.fi/kartanomatkat

Sälinkään kartano – Sälinkää Manor
Open: By appointment for groups.
Address: Kartanontie 20
           04740 Sälinkää
Phone: (019) 688 6263, 689 0275, 0400 612 575
Fax: (019) 687 3379
E-mail: kartanomatkat@kartanomatkat.fi
Internet: www.mantsala.fi/kartanomatkat

Saaren kartano – Saari Manor
Open: Jul: 8am-3pm by appointment, Aug-Jun: Mon-Thu
           8am-4pm, Fri 8am-3pm by appointment.
Address: Pohjoinen Pikatie 800
           04920 Saarentaus
Phone: (019) 529 500, 689 0275
Fax: (019) 687 3379
E-mail: maoinfo@keuda.fi, kartanomatkat@kartanomatkat.fi
Internet: www.mantsala.fi/kartanomatkat

Hirvihaaran kartano – Hirvihaara Manor
Open: By appointment for groups.
Address: Kartanonlenkki 56
           04680 Hirvihaara
Phone: (019) 688 8255, 689 0275
Fax: (019) 688 8158
E-mail: hirvihaara@hirvihaara.fi,
           kartanomatkat@kartanomatkat.fi
Internet: www.mantsala.fi

Sepänmäen käsityömuseo – Sepänmäki Handicraft Museum
Open: Jun-mid Aug: Tue-Sun 12-6pm
Address: Sepänmäki 10
           04680 Hirvihaara
Phone: (019) 688 8070, 689 0214
Fax: (019) 689 0212
E-mail: sepanmaki@mantsala.fi
Internet: www.mantsala.fi/english/tourism
           .

4 ITÄ-UUSIMAA – EASTERN UUSIMAA

PORVOO – BORGÅ
Hörbersgården Museum
Open: Midsummer-early Aug: Sun 12-3pm
Address: Österby
           07370 Pellinki
Phone: (019) 540 067, 540 105

Porvoon tuomiokirkko – Cathedral
Open: May-Sep: Mon-Fri 10am-6pm, Sat 10am-2pm, Sun
           2pm-5pm, Oct-Apr: Tue-Sat 10am-2pm, Sun 2pm-4pm
Address: Kirkkotori 1
           06100 Porvoo
Phone: (019) 661 11
Fax: (019) 583 487

Porvoon museo – Porvoo Museum
Open: May-Aug: Daily 11am-4pm, Sep-Apr: Wed-Sun 12-
           4pm and by appointment.
Address: Old Town Hall
           Välikatu 11
           06100 Porvoo
Phone: (019) 5747580
Fax: (019) 582 283
E-mail: info@porvoonmuseo.fi/matkailijanporvoo/museot
Internet: www.porvoo.fi

Edelfelt-Vallgren museo – Edelfelt-Vallgren Museum
Open: May-Aug: Daily 11am-4pm, Sep-Apr: Wed-Sun 12-4pm
Address: Välikatu 11
           06100 Porvoo
Phone: (019) 574 7589
Fax: (019) 582 283
E-mail: info@porvoonmuseo.fi
Internet: www.porvoo.fi/matkailijanporvoo/museot

Albert Edelfeltin Ateljeemuseo – Albert Edelfelt Studio Museum
Open: Jun-Aug: Tue-Sun 10am-4pm May 15-31 and Sep 1-
           15: Tue-Sun 10am-2pm
Address: Edelfeltinpolku 3, Haikkoo
           06400 Porvoo
Phone: (019) 577 414
Internet: www.porvoo.fi/matkailijanporvoo/museot

J. L. Runebergin koti – Home of J. L. Runeberg
Open: Closed until 2004
Address: Aleksanterinkatu 3
           06100 Porvoo
Phone: (019) 581 330
Fax: (019) 582 283
Internet: www.porvoo.fi/matkailijanporvoo/museot

Walter Runebergin veistoskokoelman – Walter Runeberg's Sculpture Collection
Open: May-Aug: Mon-Sat 10am-4pm, Sun 11am-5pm,
           Sep-Apr: Wed-Sun 11am-3pm
Address: Aleksanterinkatu 5
           06100 Porvoo
Phone: (019) 582 186
Fax: (019) 582 283
Internet: www.porvoo.fi/matkailijanporvoo/museot

Yrjö A. Jäntin Taidekokoelma –Yrjö A. Jäntti's Art Collection
Open: Wed-Sun 12-4pm
Address: Papinkatu 19
           06100 Porvoo
Phone: (019) 524 5990
Fax: (019) 520 2440

Internet: www.porvoo.fi/matkailijanporvoo/museot
SIPOO – SIBBO

Sipoon vanha kirkko – Sipoo Medieval Church
Open: Jun-Aug: Daily 10am-8pm
Address: Brobölentie 68
            04130 Sipoo
Phone: (09) 239 1262

PERNAJA – PERNÅ
Suur-Sarvilahden kartano – Suur-Sarvilahti Manor
Open: By appointment for groups.
Address: 07930 Pernaja
Phone: (019) 533 212
Fax: (019) 533 252

Tervikin kartano – Tervik Manor
Open: By appointment for groups.
Address: 07740 Gammelby
Phone: (019) 634 206, 533 212
Fax: (019) 533 252

Rönnäsin saaristolaismuseo – Rönnäs Archipelago Museum
Open: Jun-mid Aug: Daily 12-5pm
Address: Idlax, Rönnäs
            07750 Isnäs
Phone: (019) 634 591, 635 747

Pernajan kirkko – Pernaja Medieval Church
Open: Mid May-mid Aug: Daily 12-4pm and by appointment.
Address: Pernajantie 330
            07930 Pernaja
Phone: (019) 521 0700
Fax: (019) 521 0730
E-mail: pernapernaja@evl.fi

LAPINJÄRVI – LAPPTRÄSK
Kirkot – The Churches
Open: Jun-Aug: Daily 10am-4pm
Address: 07800 Lapinjärvi
Phone: (019) 530 720

LOVIISA – LOVISA
Svartholman linnake – Svartholm Island
Open: Exhibition: Jun-Aug: Daily 12-5pm
            Boats leave from Laivasilta Harbor,
phone: (019) 555 445.

Loviisan kaupunginmuseo – Loviisa Town Museum
Open: Jun-Aug: Tue-Sun 11am-4pm, Sep-May: Sun 12-4pm
Address: Puistokatu 2
            07900 Loviisa
Phone: (019) 555 357
Fax: (019) 555 357
Internet: www.loviisa.fi

Loviisan Merenkulkumuseo – Museum of Seafaring
Open: Jun-Aug: Mon-Sun 10am-6pm and by appointment.
Address: Laivasilta 8
            07900 Loviisa
Phone: (019) 533 188, 533 037, 040 718 9897
Internet: www.ita-uudenmaanmuseot.com/
            loviisanmerenkulkumuseo

RUOTSINPYHTÄÄ – STRÖMFORS
Strömforsin ruukki – Strömfors Ironworks Village
Open: Jun-Aug 15: Daily 10am-6pm, Sep-May: Daily 8am-4pm
Address: Ruotsinpyhtään Ruukkialue
            Puistokuja 10 A

            07970 Ruotsinpyhtää
Phone: (019) 618 474
Fax: (019) 618 475
E-mail: ruotsinpyhtaa.ruukkialue@co.inet.fi
Internet.   www.kolumbus.fi/ruotsinpyhtaa

Ruotsinpyhtään kirkko – Ruotsinpyhtää Church
Open: Mid Jun-late Aug: Daily 10am-6pm
Address: Ruukintie 11
            07970 Ruotsinpyhtää
Phone: (019) 618 151
Fax: (019) 618 475

5 VARSINAIS-SUOMI – FINLAND PROPER

TURKU – ÅBO
**Turun linna ja Turun kaupungin historiallinen museo –
Turku Castle and Turku City Historical Museum**
Open: Apr 16-Sep 15: Daily 9am-8pm, Sep 16-Apr 15: Daily
            9am-7pm
Address: Linnankatu 80
            20100 Turku
Phone: (02) 262 0300
Fax: (02) 262 0314
E-mail: maakuntamuseo@turku.fi
Internet: www.turku.fi/museo
            www.nba.fi/

Turun tuomiokirkko – Turku Cathedral
Open: Apr 16-Sep 15: Daily 9am-8pm, Sep 16-Apr 15: Daily
            9am-7pm
Address: Tuomiokirkkotori 20
            20100 Turku
Phone: (02) 261 7101
Fax: (02) 261 7102
Internet: www.turunsrk.fi/kirkot

Turun synagoga – Turku Synagogue
Open: By appointment.
Address: Brahenkatu 17 b
            20100 Turku
Phone: (02) 231 2557
Fax: (02) 233 4689

**Luostarinmäen käsityöläismuseo – Luostarinmäki
Handicrafts Museum**
Open: Apr 16-Sep 15: Daily 10am-6pm, Sep 16-Apr 15:
            Tue-Sun 10am-3pm
Address: Kalastajankatu 4
            20100 Turku
Phone: (02) 262 0350
Fax: (02) 262 0352
E-mail: maakuntamuseo@turku.fi
Internet: www.turku.fi/museo

**Apteekkimuseo Ja Qwenselin talo – Pharmacy Museum
and Qwensel House**
Open: Apr 16-Sep 15: Daily 10am-6pm, Sep 16-Apr 15:
            Tue-Sun 10am-3pm
Address: Läntinen Rantakatu 13
            20100 Turku
Phone: (02) 262 0280
Fax: (02) 262 0444
E-mail: maakuntamuseo@turku.fi
Internet: www.turku.fi/museo

**Aboa Vetus & Ars Nova -museot – Aboa Vetus &
Ars Nova Museums**
Open: May-mid Sep: Daily 11am-7pm,

Mid Sep-November: Thu-Sun 11am-7pm, Dec
Sun 11am-7pm, Jan-Apr: Thu-Sun 11am-7pm
Address: Itäinen Rantakatu 4-6
           20700 Turku
Phone: (02) 250 0552
Fax: (02) 279 4909
Internet: www.aboavetusarsnova.fi
E-mail: info@aboavetusarsnova.fi

Turun taidemuseo – Turku Art Museum
Open: Tue-Sun 10am-4pm, Thu until 7pm
Address: Puolalanpuisto
           Aurakatu 26
           20100 Turku
           Located temporarily in the Observator in
           Vartiovuorenmäki Hill
Phone: (02) 274 7570
Fax: (02) 274 7599
E-mail: info@turuntaidemuseo
Internet: www.turuntaidemuseo.fi

Wäinö Aaltosen museo – Wäino Aaltonen Museum
Open: Tue-Sun 11am-7pm
Address: Itäinen Rantakatu 38
           20810 Turku
Phone: (02) 262 0850
Fax: (02) 262 0862
E-mail: wam@turku.fi
Internet: www.wam.fi

Sibelius-museo – Sibelius Museum
Open: Tue-Sun 11am-4pm, Wed also 6pm-8pm
Address: Piispankatu 17
           20500 Turku
Phone: (02) 215 4494
Fax: (02) 251 8528
E-mail: sibeliusmuseum@abo.fi
Internet: www.sibeliusmuseum.abo.fi

Forum Marinum
Open: May-Aug: Mon-Thu 10am-6pm, Fri-Sun 10am-4pm,
           Sep-Apr: Tue-Sun 10am-6pm
Address: Linnankatu 72
           20100 Turku
Phone: (02) 282 9511
Fax: (02) 282 9515
E-mail: pekka.paasio@forum-marinum.fi
Internet: www.forum-marinum.fi

Turun Biologinen museo – Turku Biological Museum
Open: Apr 16-Sep 15: Daily 10am-6pm, Sep 16-Apr 15:
           Tue-Sun 10am-3pm
Address: Neitsytpolku 1
           20810 Turku
Phone: (02) 262 0340
Fax: (02) 262 0342
E-mail: maakuntamuseo@turku.fi
Internet: www.turku.fi/museo

Kuralan Kylämäki – Kurala Kylämäki Museum
Open: Jun-Aug: Daily 10am-6pm
Address: Jaanintie 45
           20540 Turku
Phone: (02) 262 0420
Fax: (02) 262 0429
E-mail: maakuntamuseo@turku.fi
Internet: www.turku.fi/museo
           www.elamystenmaa.fi

Kuusiston piispanlinna ja kartano – Kuusisto Castle Ruins and Estate
Open: Mid May-Aug: Wed-Sun 12-6pm
Address: Linnanrauniontie 508
           21620 Kuusisto
Phone: (02) 255 7038, 040 521 4979
Internet: www.nba.museums/kuuskart

Kuusiston kirkko – Kuusisto Church
Open: By appointment.
Address: Linnanrauniontie 157
           21620 Kuusisto
Phone: (02) 255 7083, 255 7540
Fax: (02) 255 7088
Internet: www.kaarinansrk.fi

Liedon Vanhalinna – Vanhalinna Museum
Open: May-mid Aug: Tue-Fri 11am-6pm, Sat 11am-4pm,
           Mid Aug-Apr: Sun 1pm-4pm and by appointment.
Address: Vanha Härkätie 111
           21410 Vanhalinna
Phone: (02) 489 6700, 040 706 3796
Fax: (02) 489 6711
E-mail: vanhalinna@utu.fi
Internet: www.liedonvanhalinna.fi

Liedon kirkko – Lieto Medieval Church
Open: Jun-mid Aug: Daily 11am-8pm
Address: Kirkkotie 14
           21420 Lieto
Phone: (02) 489 4146
Fax: (02) 489 4148
E-mail: liedonkhranvirasto@evl.fi
Internet: www.liedonseurakunta.fi

Nousiasten kirkko – Nousiainen Church
Open: Jun-mid Aug: Daily 12-6pm
Address: 21270 Nousiainen
Phone: (02) 431 8589, 050 565 1940
Fax: (02) 431 7201

Maskun kirkko – Masku Medieval Church
Open: By appointment.
Address: 21250 Masku
Phone: (02) 434 8400
Fax: (02) 432 9614
Internet.   www.henrikin.fi/masku

Naantalin museo – Naantali Museum
Open: May 15-Aug: Daily 12-6pm, Dec 21-Jan 1: 2pm-6pm
           and by appointment.
Address: Katinhäntä 1
           21100 Naantali
Phone: (02) 434 5324
Fax: (02) 434 5433

Kultaranta
Open: Late Jun-Aug 15: by appointment.
Address: Kultaranta
           21100 Naantali
Phone: (02) 435 0850
Fax.   (02) 435 0852
Internet: www.travel.fi/naantali

Naantalin luostarikirkko – Naantali Medieval Convent Church
Open: May: 10am-6pm, Jun-Aug: Daily 10am-8pm
Address: Nunnakatu 2
           21100 Naantali
Phone: (02) 437 5411
Fax: (02) 435 1215
Internet. www.naantalinscurakunta.fi

RAISIO – RESO
Raision museo- ja kulttuurikeskus Harkko – Museum and Cultural Centre Harkko
Open: Jun-Aug: Tue-Fri 10am-6pm, Sat-Sun 12-5pm, Sep
           May: Tue-Fri 12-4pm, Wed until 7pm, Sat-Sun
           12-3pm
Address: Nallinkatu 2
           21200 Raisio
Phone: (02) 434 3381, 040 778 7160
Fax: (09) 434 3876
E-mail: mika.torma@raisio.fi
Internet: www.raisio.fi/harkko

Raision kirkko – Raisio Medieval Church
Open: Early Jun-late Aug: Daily 9am-8pm and by
           appointment.
Address: Kirkkotie 2
           21200 Raisio
Phone: (02) 436 0300
Fax: (02) 436 0301
E-mail: virasto.raisio@evl.fi
Internet: www.raisionseurakunta.fi

LEMU – LEMO
Lemun kirkko – Lemu Medieval Church
Open: By appointment.
Address: Kirkkotie 143
           21230 Lemu
Phone: (02) 431 4709
Fax: (02) 431 4709

ASKAINEN –VILLNÄS
Louhisaaren kartanolinna – Louhisaari Castle
Open: May 15-Aug: Daily 11am-5pm, Sep: by appointment
           for groups.
Address: Louhisaarentie 244
           21240 Askainen
Phone: (02) 431 2555
Fax: (02) 435 8056
E-mail: lea.vartinen@nba.fi
Internet: www.nba.fi/museums/louhi

Askaisten kirkko – Askainen Church
Open: Daily 9am-5pm
Address: Askaistentie 38
           21240 Askainen
Phone: (02) 431 2555, 431 4709
Fax: (02) 431 4709
E-mail: lemu-askainen@ecl.fi

MERIMASKU
Merimaskun kirkko – Merimasku Church
Open: By appointment.
Address: Killaistentie
           21160 Merimasku
Phone: (02) 436 9654
Fax: (02) 439 9918

RYMÄTTYLÄ
Rymättylän kirkko – Rymättylä Medieval Church
Open: By appointment.

Address: 21140 Rymättylä
Phone: (02) 252 1216
Fax: (02) 252 1231

MYNÄMÄKI
Mynämäen kirkko – Mynämäki Medieval Church
Open: Early Jun-late Aug: Daily 11am-5pm
Address: 23100 Mynämäki
Phone: (02) 430 6480, 050 595 6083
Fax: (02) 430 6628

TAIVASSALO – TÖVSALA
Taivassalon kirkko – Taivassalo Medieval Church
Open: Jun-Aug: Daily 9am-6pm
Address: 23310 Taivassalo
Phone: (02) 878 198
Fax: (02) 878 628

KUSTAVI – GUSTAVS
Isonkarin majakka – Isokari Lighthouse
Open: Jun-Aug: tours by appointment from Kustavi and
           Uusikaupunki.
Address: Isokari
Phone: (02) 841 5091, 050 556 1113, 040 584 5587, 8451 5209
Fax: (02) 841 5038, 841 2887
E-mail: elava.saaristo@wakkanet.fi
Internet: www.kustavi.fi
           www.rosita.fi

PIIKKIÖ – PIKIS
Pukkilan kartano- ja ajokalumuseo – Pukkila Estate and Vehicle Museum
Open: Jun-Aug 15: Daily 11am-5pm, May, Aug 16-Sep 30:
           by appointment for groups
Address: Littoistentie 114
           21500 Piikkiö
Phone: (02) 479 5320
Fax: (09) 405 0400
E-mail: lea.vartinen@nba.fi
Internet: www.nba.fi/museums/pukkila

PAIMIO – PEMAR
Paimion parantola – Paimio Sanatorium
Open: May-Aug: tours daily at 10am and 2pm
Address: Alvar Aallon tie 275
           21530 Paimio
Phone: (02) 261 4239, 261 1129, 474 5440
Fax: (02) 474 5202
E-mail: helena.kaartinen@paimio.fi
Internet: www.alvaraalto.fi

SAUVO – SAGU
Sauvon kirkko – Sauvo Medieval Church
Open: By appointment.
Address: 21570 Sauvo
Phone: (02) 473 0222
Fax: (02) 473 0222

PARAINEN – PARGAS
Paraisten kirkko – Parainen Medieval Church
Open: Mid Jun-late Aug: Daily 10am-6pm
Address: Kirkkoesplanadi 3
           21600 Parainen
Phone: (02) 454 7754, 040 516 0312
Fax: (02) 454 7766
Internet: www.paraistensuom-srk.fi/

NAUVO – NAGU
Nauvon kirkko – Nauvo Church

Open: By appointment.
Address: 21660 Nauvo
Phone: (02) 465 1412
Fax: (02) 465 1481

Nötön kirkko – Nötö Church
Open: By appointment.
Address: 21680 Nötö
Phone: (02) 465 1412
Fax: (02) 465 1481

Seilin hospitaali ja kirkko – Seili Church and Hospital
Open: By appointment.
Address: Seili
            21660 Nauvo
Phone: (02) 465 6110
Fax: (02) 465 6100
E-mail: ilppovuo@utu.fi
Internet: utu.fi/erill/saarmeri/eng

KORPPOO – KORPO
Korppoon kirkko – Korppoo Medieval Church
Open: By appointment.
Address: 21710 Korppoo
Phone: (02) 463 1186
Fax: (02) 463 1041

Utön majakka – Utö Lighthouse
            Regular boat traffic from Pärnäs in Nauvo
Address: 21740 Utö
Phone: 0400 190 959, (02) 465 7175, 465 1000, 050 365 0141
Fax: 0401 190 959

HOUTSKARI – HOUTSKÄR
Houtskarin kirkko – Houtskari Church
Open: By appointment.
Address: 21760 Houtskär
Phone: (02) 463 3530
Fax: (02) 463 3205

KEMIÖ – KIMITO
Kemiön kirkko – Kemiö Medieval Church
Open: By appointment.
Address: 25700 Kemiö
Phone: (02) 421 056
Fax: (02) 421 885

Sagalundin Museo – Sagalund Museum
Open: Jun-Aug: Daily 11am-6pm, Sep-May: Mon-Fri
            9am-3pm and by appointment.
Address: Museotie 7
            25700 Kemiö
Phone: (02) 421 738
Fax: (02) 421 847
E-mail: info@sagalund.fi
Internet: www.sagalund.fi

DRAGSFJÄRD
Hiittisten kirkko – Hiittinen Church
Open: By appointment.
Address: 25940 Hiittinen
Phone: (02) 466 6605
Fax: (02) 466 6605

Rodeborgin viikinkikeskus – Rodeborg Viking Center
Open: Late Jun-Jul: Daily 10am-8pm, May-late Jun and
            Aug: Daily 10am-6pm
Address: 25950 Rosala
Phone: (02) 466 7300, 050 353 6933

Bengtskärin majakka – Bengtskär Lighthouse
Open.   Jun-Aug: Daily 10am-7pm and by appointment
Address: Bengtskär
            25950 Rosala
Phone: (02) 466 7227, 050 353 6933, 050 528 7410
Fax: (02) 466 7227
Internet: www.fma.fi/lighthouses
            www.rosita.fi/ saarikoh
            www.travel.fi/fin/saaristomeri

Taalintehtaan ruukki – Taalintehdas Ironworks
Address: 25900 Taalintehdas
Phone: (02) 466 2200

**Taalintehtaan ruukkimuseo – Taalintehdas
Ironworks Museum**
Open: Jun-Aug: Tue-Sun 12-6pm and by appointment.
Address: Norrbacken
            25900 Taalintehdas
Phone: (02) 466 1496, 040 721 9535
E-mail: hans.ginlund@dragsfjard.fi

Björkbodan ruukki – Björkboda Ironworks
Address: 25860 Björkboda
Phone: (02) 424 199, 0400 424 198

Söderlångvikin museo – Söderlångvik Museum
Open: May 15-Aug: Daily 11am-6pm
Address: 25870 Dragsfjärd
Phone: (02) 424 662, 0500 507 526
Fax: (02) 6844 4622
E-mail: museum@amosanderson.fi
Internet: www.amosanderson.fi

PERNIÖ – BJÄRNÅ
Perniön museo – Perniö Museum
Open: Jun-Aug: Wed, Thu, Sun: 11am-4pm and by
appointment.
Address: Museotie 9
            25500 Perniö
Phone: (02) 775 9383
Fax: (02) 775 9301
E-mail: arja.niinisto.alanne@pernio.fi
Internet: www.pernio.fi

Perniön kirkko – Perniö Medieval Church
Open: Mid May-mid Aug: Mon-Sat 12-4pm
Address: 25500 Perniö
Phone: (02) 735 8611
Fax: (02) 735 8630

Teijon ruukki – Teijo Ironworks
Address: 25660 Mathildedal
Phone: (02) 736 3801, 0205 64 4700
Fax: (02) 736 6810
E-mail: webmaster@meri-teijo.com, teijo@metsa.fi
Internet: www.meri-teijo.com, www.metsa.fi

HALIKKO
Rikalanmäki – Rikalanmäki Hill
Open: Late May-Aug: Tue-Sun 12-6pm and by
            appointment.
Address: Linnanmäentie 74
            24800 Halikko
Phone: (02) 774 3266
Fax: (02) 774 3333
E-mail: aila.niinisto@halikko.fi
Internet: www.halikko.fi

Vuorentaan kartano – Vuorentaka Estate
Open: By appointment for groups.
Address: Vuorentaka estate
          24910 Halikko
Phone: (02) 736 4018, 040 565 1786
E-mail: vuorentaka.armfelt@pp.inet.fi

Wiurilan kartano – Wiurila Estate
Vaunumuseo – Wagon Museum
Open: May-Aug: Tue-Sun 11am-4pm and by appointment.
Address: Wiurilantie 13
          24910 Halikko
Phone: (02) 724 4382, 044 555 5458
Fax: (02) 736 4129
E-mail: anneaminoff@hotmail.com
Internet. www.wiurila.com

Halikon museo – Halikko Museum
Open: Jun-Aug: Tue-Sun 11am-4pm, Sep-May: Sun 11am-
          4pm and by appointment.
Address: Kirkkorinne 7
          24800 Halikko
Phone: (02) 774 3320
Fax: (02) 774 3333
E-mail: aila.niinisto@halikko.fi
Internet: www.halikko.fi/matkailu/english

Trömperin kestikievarimuseo – Trömperi Inn Museum
Open: Jun-Aug: Tue-Sun 12-6pm
Address: Vanha Turuntie
          25240 Hajala
Phone: (02) 728 3288
Fax: (02) 774 3333
E-mail: aila.niinisto@halikon-kunta.inet.fi
Internet: www.halikko.fi/matkailu/english

SALO
Veturitalli - Salon taidemuseo – Round House Salo Art Museum
Open: Tue-Fri and Sun 11am-7pm, Sat 11am-5pm
Address: Mariankatu 14
          24240 Salo
Phone: (02) 778 4892
Fax: (02) 778 4891
E-mail: veturitalli@salo.fi
Internet: www.salo.fi/taidemuseo/englanti

UUSIKAUPUNKI – NYSTAD
**Uudenkaupungin kulttuurihistoriallinen museo –
Uusikaupunki Museum of Cultural History**
Open: Early Jun-early Aug: Mon-Fri 10am-4pm, Wed until
          7pm, Sat-Sun 12-3pm, Early Aug-Early Jun: Tue-Sun
          12-3pm
Address: Ylinenkatu 11
          23500 Uusikaupunki
Phone: (02) 8451 5447
Fax: (02) 8151 5157
E-mail: mari.jalava@uusikaupunki.fi
Internet: www.kpi.uusikaupunki.fi/sivistys

Pyhämaan uhrikirkko – Pyhämaa Votive Church
Open: Jun-Aug 15: Mon-Sat 11am-5pm, Sun after the
          service until 5pm.By appointment: Tue 4pm-6pm, Fri
          9am-12
Address: 23930 Pyhämaa
Phone: (02) 840 4200, 0400 538 775
Fax.   (02) 840 4219

Kalannin kirkko – Kalanti Medieval Church
Open: Jun-Aug: Daily 9am-5pm and by appointment.

Address: 23600 Kalanti
Phone: (02) 874 271, 840 4410
Fax: (02) 840 4419

Männäisten ruukki – Männäinen Ironworks
Open: By appointment only.
Address: 23600 Kalanti
Phone: (02) 874 175

Kalannin kotiseutumuseo – Kalanti Local History Museum
Open: Early Jun-mid Aug: Tue-Fri 11am-3pm, Sat-Sun 12
          3pm, Rest of Aug: Sat-Sun 12-3pm and by
          appointment.
Address: Kuriirikuja 1
          23600 Kalanti
Phone: (02) 874 118
Fax: (02) 8451 5457
Internet: www.kpi.uusikaupunki.fi/matkailu

LAITILA
Laitilan kirkko – Laitila Medieval Church
Open: Jun-Aug: Daily 10am-6pm
Address: Untamontie
          23800 Laitila
Phone: (02) 856 539
Fax: (02) 856 541

Kauppilan umpipiha – Kauppila Farmstead
Open: Jun-mid Aug: Tue-Sat 12-4pm, Sun 12-6pm
          and by appointment.
Address: Koukkela
          23800 Laitila
Phone: (02) 855 208, 050 593 0470
Internet: www.laitila.fi

6 SATAKUNTA

PORI – BJÖRNEBORG
Keski-Porin kirkko – Keski-Pori Church
Open: Jun-Aug: Daily 9am-6pm Sep-May: Mon-Fri 10am-1pm
Address: Yrjönkatu, Kirkkopuisto
          28100 Pori
Phone: (02) 633 2955
Fax: (02) 623 8718
Internet: www.porievl.fi/

Reposaaren kirkko – Reposaari Church
Open: Jun-Aug: Daily 10am-3pm and by appointment.
Address: Kirkkokatu
          28900 Pori
Phone: (02) 638 4023, 638 4613
Fax: (02) 628 4023

Ahlaisten kirkko – Ahlainen Church
Open: May-Jul: Mon-Fri 9am-4pm, Sat-Sun 9am-6pm
Address: Ahlaistentie
          29700 Ahlainen
Phone: (02) 548 6017
Fax: (02) 548 6017

Satakunnan Museo – Satakunta Museum
Open: Tue-Sun 11am-5pm
Address: Hallituskatu 11
          28100 Pori
Phone: (02) 621 1078
Fax: (02) 621 1061
E-mail: satakunnanmuseo@pori.fi
Internet: www.pori.fi/smu

Porin taidemuseo – Pori Art Museum
Open: Tue–Sun 11am-6pm, Wed until 8pm
Address: Eteläranta
            28100 Pori
Phone: (02) 621 1080
Fax: (02) 621 1091
E-mail: taidemuseo@pori.fi
Internet.   www.pori.fi/art/satakunta/pori

Juselius-mausoleumi – Juselius Mausoleum
Open: May-Aug: Daily 12-3pm, Sep-Apr: Sun 12-2pm
Address: Käppärä Cemetery
            Maantiekatu
            28120 Pori
Phone: (02) 623 8746
Fax: (02) 623 8718

ULVILA
Ulvilan kirkko – Ulvila Medieval Church
Open: Jun-Aug: Daily 11am-7pm
Address: Kirkkotie, Vanhakylä
            28400 Ulvila
Phone: (02) 535 0600
Fax: (02) 535 0636

KULLAA
Leineperin ruukki – Leineperi Ironworks
Address: 29320 Leineperi
Phone: (02) 5591 244, 5591 551
Fax: (02) 5591 344

NOORMARKKU
Villa Mairea
Open: By appointment.
Address: 29600 Noormarkku
Phone: 010 888 4460
Fax: 010 888 4462
E-mail: anna.hall@a-ahlstrom.fi
Internet: www.alvaraalto.fi

KANKAANPÄÄ
Kankaanpään kaupunginmuseo – Kankaanpää Town Museum
Open: May 15-Aug: Daily 11am-6pm, Sep-May 14: Sat-Sun
            12-6pm and by appointment.
Address: Museokatu 10
            38840 Niinisalo
Phone: (02) 578 7454
Fax: (02) 578 7459
E-mail: kaupunginmuseo@kankaanpaa.fi
Internet: www.kankaanpaa.fi/museo

KARVIA
Karvian kirkko – Karvia Church
Open: By appointment.
Address: 39930 Karvia
Phone: (02) 544 1004
Fax: (02) 544 1665

RAUMA – RAUMO

Vanha Rauma – Old Rauma

Pyhän Ristin kirkko – Church of the Holy Cross
Open: Jun-Aug: Daily 9am-6pm, Sep: Mon-Sat10am-5pm,
            Sun 9am-5pm
Address: Luostarinkatu 1
            26100 Rauma
Phone: (02) 837 751

Fax: (02) 822 9568
Internet: www.rauma.seurakunta.net

Rauman museo – Rauma Museum
Open: May 15-Aug: Daily 10am-5pm, Sep-May 14: Tue-Fri
            and Sun 10am-5pm, Sat 10am-2pm
Address: Kauppakatu 13
            26100 Rauma
Phone: (02) 834 2532
Fax: (02) 834 3524
E-mail: rauman.museo@rauma.fi
Internet: www.rauma.fi/museo

Marela
Open: May 15-Aug: Daily 10am-5pm, Sep-May 14: Tue-Fri
            and Sun 10am-5pm, Sat 10am-2pm
Address: Kauppakatu 24
            26100 Rauma
Phone: (02) 834 2528
Fax: (02) 834 3524
E-mail: rauman.museo@rauma.fi
Internet: www.rauma.fi/museo

Rauman taidemuseo – Rauma Art Museum
Open: Jun-Aug: Mon-Thu 10am-6pm, Fri 10am-4pm, Sat
            Sun 11am-4pm, Sep-May: Tue-Thu 10am-6pm, Fri
            10am-4pm, Sat-Sun 11am-4pm
Address: Kuninkaankatu 37
            26100 Rauma
Phone: (02) 822 4346
Fax: (02) 822 2183
E-mail: rtm@raumantaidemuseo.inet.fi
Internet: www.rauma.fi

**Teresia ja Rafael Lönnströmin kotimuseo – The Teresia and
Rafael Lönnström Home Museum**
Open: Jun-Aug: Wed and Sun 12-4pm Apr-May and Sep:
            Sun 12-4pm, Oct-Mar: by appointment.
Address: Syväraumankatu 41
            26100 Rauma
Phone: (02) 8387 4700
Fax: (02) 8387 4742
E-mail: helka.ketonen@lonnstromintaidemuseo.fi
Internet: www.lonnstromintaidemuseo.fi

Lönnströmin taidemuseo – The Lönnström Art Museum
Open: Mid Jun-Aug: Mon 12-4pm, Tue-Thu 12-6pm, Fri
            Sun 12-4pm Sep-mid Jun: Tue-Thu 12-6pm, Fri-Sun
            12-4pm
Address: Valtakatu 7
            26100 Rauma
Phone: (02) 8387 4700
Fax: (02) 8387 4742
E-mail: katikivimaki@lonnstromintaidemuseo.fi
Internet: www.lonnstromintaidemuseo.fi

HARJAVALTA
Emil Cedercreutzin museo – Emil Cedercreutz Museum
Open: May-Aug: Sun-Fri 11am-6pm, Sat 11am-4pm, Sep-
            Apr: Daily 12-4pm, Thu and Sun until 6pm
            and by appointment.
Address: Museotie 1
            29200 Harjavalta
Phone: (02) 535 1200
Fax: (02) 535 1220
E-mail: cedercreutzin.museo@harjavalta.fi
Internet: www.harjavalta.fi/museo

NAKKILA
Nakkilan kirkko – Nakkila Church
Open: Jun-Aug: Daily 9am-4pm
Address: 29250 Nakkila
Phone: (02) 537 9300
Fax: (02) 537 9301

KOKEMÄKI
Pyhän Henrikin saarnahuone – St. Henrik's Preaching House
Open: Jun-Jul: Thu-Fri 2pm-6pm, Sat-Sun 12-4pm
Address: Risteentie 28
          32800 Kokemäki
Phone: (02) 540 6111
Fax: (02) 540 6110

EURA
Luistarin kalmisto ja näyttely – Luistari Burial Ground and Exhibition
Open: Mid May-mid Aug: Tue-Sun 12-6pm
Address: Luistarintie
          27500 Kauttua
Phone: (02) 8399 0269, 0500 626 738
Fax: (02) 8399 0330
E-mail: esihistoria@eura.inet.fi
Internet: www.eura.fi/esihistoria

Esihistorian opastuskeskus Naurava Lohikäärme – The Laughing Dragon Information Centre of Prehistory
Open: Mid May-mid Aug: Tue-Sun
Address: Eurantie 18
          27510 Eura
Phone: (02) 8399 0269, 0500 626 738
Fax: (02) 8399 0330
E-mail: esihistoria@eura.inet.fi
Internet: www.eura.fi/esihistoria, www.personal.inet.fi/
          palvelu/esihistorian.eura

Kauttuan ruukki – Kauttua Ironworks
Kauttua Factory Museum
Open: By appointment.
Address: Ruukinpuisto
          27500 Kauttua
Phone: (02) 8392 2561, 0500 626 738
Fax: (02) 8399 0330

LAPPI

Sammallahdenmäen kalmisto – Sammallahdenmäki Burial Ground

Address: Sammallahdenmäki
          27230 Lappi
Phone: (02) 838 7211, 050 320 5060, (02621 1069
Fax: (09) 4050 9262
Internet: www.nba.fi/archaeol/sammallahti/eng

EURAJOKI
Vuojoen kartano – Vuojoki Manor
Open: By appointment.
Address: Kartanontie 28
          27100 Eurajoki
Phone: (02) 869 4336
E-mail: hanna.tuominen@eurajoki.fi
Internet: www.eurajoki.fi

Irjanteen kirkko – Irjanne Church
Open: By appointment.
Address: 27110 Irjanne
Phone: (02) 868 0021

Fax: (02) 868 0532

HUITTINEN
Huittisten museo – Huittinen Museum
Open: Jun-Aug 15: Tue-Fri 12-5pm, Sat-Sun 12-4pm, Aug
          16-May: Sat-Sun 12-4pm and by appointment.
Address: Kirkkotie 4
          32700 Huittinen
Phone: (02) 560 4319
Fax: (02) 560 4215
E-mail: museo@huittinen.fi
Internet: www.huittinen.fi/nahtavyydet/museo

PUNKALAIDUN
Talonpoikaismuseo Yli-Kirra – Yli-Kirra Peasant Museum
Open: May-Sep 15: Daily 10am-5pm and by appointment.
Address: Rasintie
          31900 Punkalaidun
Phone: (02) 767 4111
Fax: (02) 767 4225

7 ÅLAND – AHVENANMAA

MARIEHAMN – MAARIANHAMINA
Mariehamn kyrka – Mariehamn Church
Open: By appointment.
Address: 22110 Mariehamn
Phone: (018) 5360
Fax: (018) 15 337

Sjökvarteret – Maritime Quarter
Open: Jun 15-Aug 15: Daily 10am-6pm, Aug 16-Jun 14:
          Mon-Thu 9am-11am and by appointment.
Address: Eastern Harbor
          22100 Mariehamn
Phone: (018) 16 033, 040 528 3899
Fax: (018) 16 034
E-mail: sjokvarteret@aland.inet.fi
Internet: www.sjokvarteret.com

Ålands museum – Åland Museum
Open: May-Aug: Daily 10am-4pm, Tue until 8pm
          Sep-Apr: Tue-Sun 10am-4pm, Tue until 8pm
Address: Stadhusparken
          22100 Mariehamn
Phone: (018) 25 426
Fax: (018) 17 440
E-mail: info@aland-museum.aland.fi
Internet: www.aland-museum.aland.fi

Ålands konstmuseum – Åland Art Museum
Open: May-Aug: Daily 10am-4pm, Tue until 8pm,
          Sep-Apr: Tue-Sun 10am-4pm, Tue until 8pm
Address: Stadhusparken
          22100 Mariehamn
Phone: (018) 25 426
Fax: (018) 17 440
E-mail: ingela.lonngren@ls.aland.fi
Internet: www.aland-museum.aland.fi/konst

Ålands sjöfartsmuseum – Åland Maritime Museum
Open: Jul: Daily 9am-7pm, May-Jun and Aug: Daily 9am-
          5pm Sep-Apr: Daily 10am-4pm
Address: Hamngatan 2
          22100 Mariehamn
Phone: (018) 19 930
Fax: (018) 19 936
E-mail: staff@maritime-museum.aland.fi
Internet: www.maritime-museum.aland.fi

Museifartyget Pommern – Museum Ship Pommern

Open: Jul: Daily 9am-7pm, May-Jun and Aug: Daily 9am-
5pm, Sep-Oct: Daily 10am-4pm

Address: Western Harbor
22100 Mariehamn

Phone: (018) 531 423, 531 421

Fax: (018) 531 479

E-mail: pommern@mariehamn.aland.fi

Internet: www.pommern.aland.fi

JOMALA

Jomala kyrka – Jomala Medieval Church

Open: By appointment.

Address: 22150 Jomala

Phone: (018) 31 004

Fax: (018) 31 853

Önningebymuseet – Önningeby Museum

Open: Early May-mid Aug: Daily 10am-4pm, Thu also 6pm
9pm, Mar-Apr and late Aug-late Oct: Sun 12-4pm
and by appointment.

Address: Önningeby 31
22100 Mariehamn

Phone: (018) 33 710

Fax: (018) 33 804

E-mail: kjell.ekstrom@aland.net

Internet: www.aland-museum.aland.fi/onningeby/museum
www.artistvillages.net

HAMMARLAND

Hammarland kyrka – Hammarland Medieval Church

Open: By appointment.

Address: 22240 Hammarland

Phone: (018) 36 029

Fax: (018) 37 873

ECKERÖ

Eckerö Post och Tullhus – Eckerö Mail and Customs House

Open: Mid May-mid Sep: Daily 10am-4pm, Tue and Wed
also 6pm-8pm

Address: 22270 Storby

Phone: (018) 38 689

Fax: (018) 38 089

E-mail: postvagen@turist.aland.fi

Internet: www.postvagen.aland.fi

Postrotemuseet – Mail Boat Museum

Open: Jun-Aug 15: Daily 10am-4pm

Address: 22270 Storby

Phone: (018) 39 462

Fax: (018) 38 262

E-mail: info@eckerolinjen.fi

Ålands Jakt- och Fiskemuseum – Åland Hunting and Fishing Museum

Open: May-Aug: Daily 10am-5pm, Wed until 8pm,
Apr and Sep: Sat-Sun 10am-5pm

Address: Fiskeläge 37
22270 Eckerö

Phone: (018) 38 299, 050 524 4099

Fax: (018) 38 289

E-mail: jakt-fiske.museum@aland.net

Internet: www.home.aland.net/m04315/index

Eckerö kyrka – Eckerö Medieval Church

Open: By appointment.

Address: 22270 Eckerö

Phone: (018) 38 387

FINSTRÖM

Finström kyrka – Finström Medieval Church

Open: By appointment.

Address: 22300 Finström

Phone: (018) 42 330

Fax: (018) 42 330

SALTVIK

Saltvik kyrka – Saltvik Medieval Church

Open: By appointment.

Address: 22430 Saltvik

Phone: (018) 43 260

Fax: (018) 43 268

Långbergsöda stenåldersby – Långbergsöda Stone Age Village

Open: All year. Guidance: Late Jun-mid Aug: Daily 11am-
6pm, Mid Aug-mid Sep: Daily 11am-3pm

Address: 22430 Saltvik

Internet: www.arkeologi.aland.fi

SUND

Kastelholms slott – Kastelholm Castle

Open: May-Sep: Daily 10am-5pm, guided tours only

Address: 22520 Kastelholm

Phone: (018) 432 150

Fax: (018) 43 2126

E-mail: kastelholm@aland-museum.aland.fi

Internet: www.aland-museum.aland.fi/kastelholm

Jan Karlsgårdens friluftsmuseum – Jan Karlsgården Open-Air Museum

Open: May-Sep: Daily 9:30am-5pm

Address: 22520 Kastelholm

Phone: (018) 432 150

Fax: (018) 432 126

E-mail: kastelholm@aland-museum.aland.fi

Internet: www.aland-museum.aland.fi/kastelholm

Fängelsemuseet Vita Björn – Vita Björn Prison Museum

Open: May-Sep: Daily 10am-5pm

Address: 22520 Kastelholm

Phone: (018) 432 150

Fax: (018) 432 126

E-mail: kastelholm@aland-museum.aland.fi

Internet: www.aland-museum.aland.fi/kastelholm

Sund kyrka – Sund Medieval Church

Open: By appointment.

Address: 22530 Sund

Phone: (018) 43 930

Bomarsundsmuseet – Bomarsund Museum

Open: Jul-mid Aug: Daily 10am-5pm, May-Jun: Daily
10am-3pm

Address: Prästö
22530 Sund

Phone: (018) 44 032

Fax: (018) 43 210

E-mail: kastelholm@aland-museum.aland.fi

Internet: www.aland-museum.aland.fi/kastelholm

LEMLAND

Lemböte kapellruin – Lemböte Chapel Ruins

Open: All year

Address: 22610 Lemland

Phone: (018) 39 000

Fax: (018) 39 230

Internet: www.arkeologi.aland.fi

Pellas Skeppargård – Pellas Shipmaster's House
Open: Mid Jun–mid Aug: Daily 12–4pm, Wed 12–7pm
           and by appointment.
Address: Granboda
           22610 Lemland
Phone: (018) 16 620, 045 7313 4012
Fax: (018) 16 901
E-mail: peter.darby@aland.net

Lemland kyrka – Lemland Medieval Church
Open: By appointment.
Address: 22610 Lemland
Phone: (018) 34 042
Fax: (018) 34 590

KUMLINGE
Kumlinge kyrka – Kumlinge Medieval Church
Open: By appointment.
Address: 22820 Kumlinge
Phone: (018) 55 407
Fax: (018) 55 466

Museigården Hermas – Hermas Farm Museum
Open: Jul: Mon–Fri 9am–7pm, Jun and Aug: Mon–Fri 9am–
           4pm and by appointment.
Address: 22830 Enklinge
Phone: (018) 55 334, 040 556 5984

BRÄNDÖ
Skärgårdsmuseet – Lappo Archipelago Museum
Open: Late Jun–mid Aug: Daily 10am–12, 2pm–4pm
           and by appointment.
Address: 22840 Lappoby
Phone: (018) 56 621, 040 566 7397
Internet: www.kulturfonden.fi/skargardsmuseet

KÖKAR
Kökar kyrka – Kökar Church
Open: Jun–Aug: Daily 9am–9pm and by appointment.
Address: 22730 Kökar
Phone: (018) 55 998
Fax: (018) 55 998
Internet: www.arkeologi.aland.fi

8 KANTA-HÄME

HÄMEENLINNA – TAVASTEHUS
Hämeen linna – Häme Castle
Open: May–Aug 14: Daily 10am–6pm,
           Aug 15–Apr: Daily 10am–4pm
Address: Kustaa III:n katu 6
           13100 Hämeenlinna
Phone: (03) 675 6820
Fax: (03) 616 6379
E-mail: hlinna@nba.fi
Internet: www.nba.fi/castles/tavast

Tykistömuseo – Artillery Museum
Open: May–Sep: Daily 10am–6pm, Oct–Apr: Sat–Sun
           12–5pm and by appointment.
Address: Linnakasarmi
           13100 Hämeenlinna
Phone: (03) 682 4600
Fax: (03) 682 4601

**Hämeenlinnan kaupungin historiallinen museo –
Hämeenlinna Historical Museum**
Open: Daily 11am–5pm
Address: Kustaa III:n katu 8

           13100 Hämeenlinna
Phone: (03) 621 2979
Fax: (03) 621 2851
E-mail: marja-liisa.ripatti@hml.htk.fi
Internet: www.hameenlinna.fi/hkhm

Vankilamuseo – Prison Museum
Open: Daily 11am–5pm
Address: Kustaa III:n katu 8
           13100 Hämeenlinna
Phone: (03) 621 2977
Fax: (03) 621 2960
E-mail: marja-liisa.ripatti@hml.htk.fi
Internet: www.hameenlinna.fi/hkhm

Palanderin talo – Palander House
Open: Jun–Aug: Daily 12–3pm, Sep–May: Sat–Sun 12–3pm
           and by appointment.
Address: Lukiokatu 4
           13100 Hämeenlinna
Phone: (03) 621 2967
Fax: (03) 621 2904
E-mail: marja-liisa.ripatti@hml.htk.fi
Internet: www.hameenlinna.fi/hkhm

Sibeliuksen syntymäkoti – Birthplace of Sibelius
Open: May–Aug: Daily 10am–4pm, Sep–Apr: Daily 12–3pm
Address: Hallituskatu 11
           13100 Hämeenlinna
Phone: (03) 621 2755
Fax: (03) 621 2806
E-mail: marja-liisa.ripatti@hml.htk.fi
Internet: www.hameenlinna.fi/hkhm

Korttien talo – House of Cards
Open: Jun–Aug: Daily 10–4pm, Sep–May: Tue–Sun 10am–
           4pm and by appointment for groups.
Address: Niittykatu 1
           13100 Hämeenlinna
Phone: (03) 616 9502
Fax: (03) 616 9602

Hämeenlinnan taidemuseo – Hämeenlinna Art Museum
Open: Closed for renovation. Will open in 2004.
Address: Viipurintie 2
           13200 Hämeenlinna
Phone: (03) 621 2669
Fax: (03) 621 2860
Internet: www.htk.fi/hml/artmuseum

Hämeenlinnan kirkko – Hämeenlinna Church
Open: Jun–Aug: Daily 11am–5pm May and Sep: Daily
           11am–3pm Oct–Apr: 10am–1pm
Address: Linnankatu
           13100 Hämeenlinna
Phone: (03) 626 4281, 0500 711 141
Fax: (03) 626 4293
E-mail: hameenlinna.seurakunta@evl.fi
Internet: www.hameenlinna-evl.fi

Vanajanlinna – Vanajanlinna Manor
Address: Vanajanlinnantie 485
           13330 Harviala
Phone: (03) 610 20
Fax: (03) 610 2210
E-mail: vanajanlinna@vanajanlinna.fi
Internet: www.vanajanlinna.fi

Vanajan kirkko – Vanaja Medieval Church
Open: Jun-Aug: Daily 10am-6pm May-Sep: Daily 10am-
              3pm and by appointment.
Address: 13101 Hämeenlinna
Phone: (03) 626 4220, 050 344 1945
Fax.   (03) 626 4294
E-mail: hameenlinna.seurakunta@evl.fi
Internet: www.hameenlinna-evl.fi

HATTULA
Pyhän Ristin kirkko – Church of the Holy Cross
Open: May 15-Aug 15: Daily 11am-5pm
              and by appointment.
Address: 13806 Hattula
Phone: (03) 631 1520
Fax: (03) 631 1542
E-mail: hattula.seurakunta@evl.fi
Internet: www.evl.fi/kirkko/srk

Panssarimuseo – The Finnish Armour Museum
Open: May-Aug: 10am-6pm, Sep: Sat-Sun 10am-5pm
              and by appointment for groups.
Address: Hattulantie 334
              13700 Parolannummi
Phone: (03) 1814 4524
Fax: (03) 1814 4522
E-mail: toimisto@panssarikilta
Internet: www.panssarikilta.fi

KALVOLA
Iittalan lasitehtaan museo – Iittala Glass Museum
Open: May-Aug: Daily 10am-6pm Sep-Apr:
              Daily 10am-5pm
Address: Iittalan Lasitehdas
              14500 Iittala
Phone: 0204 39 6230
Fax: 0204 39 3516
E-mail: iittala.museum@designor.com
Internet: www.designor.com

RENKO
Rengon kirkko – Renko Medieval Church
Open: Mid Jun-late Aug: Daily 11am-6pm
              and by appointment.
Address: Rengonraitti
              14300 Renko
Phone: (03) 652 7104
Fax: (03) 652 7304

RIIHIMÄKI
Riihimäen kaupunginmuseo – Riihimäki Town Museum
Open: Wed and Sun 12-6pm and by appointment.
Address: Öllerinkatu 3
              11130 Riihimäki
Phone: (019) 741 7202
Fax: (019) 741 7830
E-mail: kaupunginmuseo@riihimaki.fi
Internet: www.riihimaki.fi/kaupmuseo

Suomen lasimuseo – Finnish Glass Museum
Open: May-Aug: Daily 10am-6pm, Sep-Apr:
              Tue-Sun 10am-6pm Closed in Jan.
Address: Tehtaankatu 23
              11910 Riihimäki
Phone: (019) 741 7495
Fax: (019) 741 7555
E-mail: glass.museum@riihimaki.fi
Internet: www.riihimaki.fi/lasimus

Suomen Metsästysmuseo – Finnish Hunting Museum
Open: Apr-Sep: Daily 10am-6pm, Oct-Mar: Tue-Fri
              9am-4pm, Sat-Sun 10am-6pm Closed in Jan.
Address: Tehtaankatu 23 A
              11910 Riihimäki
Phone: (019) 722 294
Fax: (019) 719 378
E-mail: metsastysmuseo@kolumbus.fi
Internet: www.kolumbus.fi/metsastysmuseo

Riihimäen taidemuseo – Riihimäki Art Museum
Open: May-Aug: Daily 10am-6pm,
              Sep-Apr: Tue-Sun 10am-6pm
Address: Temppelikatu 8
              11100 Riihimäki
Phone: (019) 741 7333
Fax: (019) 741 7655
E-mail: riihimaen.taidemuseo@riihimaki.fi
Internet: www.riihimaki.fi/taidemus

LOPPI
Lopen vanha kirkko – Loppi Old Church
Open: Mid Jun-early Aug: Daily 12-6pm
Address: Pilpalantie 27
              12700 Loppi
Phone: (019) 426 4171
Fax: (019) 441 179
Internet: www.saunalahti.fi/lopensrk

Marskin Maja – The Hunting Lodge of Marshall Mannerheim
Open: Jun-Aug 15: Daily 11am-5pm and by appointment.
Address: Marskintie 216
              12700 Loppi
Phone: (019) 449 400, 040 548 0525
E-mail: teuvo.zetterman@marskinmaja.com
Internet: www.marskinmaja.com

FORSSA
Lounais-Hämeen museo – Southwest Häme Museum
Open: Mid Aug-May: Sun-Wed and Fri 12-4pm
              and by appointment.
Address: Wahreninkatu 12
              30420 Forssa
Phone: (03) 435 5998
Fax: (03) 435 5993
Internet: www.forssa.fi/museot

Forssan museo – Forssa Museum
Open: Mid Aug-May: Sun-Wed and Fri 12-4pm
              and by appointment
Address: Uittotie 2
              30100 Forssa
Phone: (03) 435 5998
Fax: (03) 435 5993
Internet: www.forssa.fi/museot

TAMMELA
Mustialan maanviljelysopisto – Mustiala Agricultural Instute
Address: Mustialantie 105
              31310 Mustiala
Phone: (03) 646 5519
Fax: (03) 646 5500
E-mail: mustiala@hamk.fi
Internet: www.mustiala.hamk.fi

JOKIOINEN
**Jokioisten Museorautatie – Jokioinen Museum Railway
and Narrow Gauge Museum**
Open: Museum: Jun-mid Aug: Daily 11am-6pm

Museum train operates on summer Sundays
Address: Minkiö Station
             Kiipuntie 49
             31630 Minkiö
Phone: (03) 433 3235, 050 504 7212
Fax: (03) 0042 586 1976
E-mail: info@jokioistenmuseorautatie.fi
Internet: www.jokioistenmuseorautatie.fi

Jokioisten kartano – Jokioinen Manor
Open: By appiointment.
Address: 31600 Jokioinen
Phone: (03) 4188 2203
Fax: (03) 4188 3449
E-mail: inkeri.koskela@mtt.fi
Internet: www.mtt.fi

9 PÄIJÄT-HÄME

LAHTI
Lahden kaupungintalo – Lahti Town Hall
Open: Tours on Fri at 2pm and by the appointment.
Address: Harjukatu 31
             15100 Lahti
Phone: (03) 814 2221
Fax: (03) 814 2244

Lahden historiallinen museo – Lahti Historical Museum
Open: Mon-Fri 10am-5pm, Sat-Sun 11am-5pm
Address: Lahdenkatu 4
             15110 Lahti
Phone: (03) 814 4534
Fax: (03) 814 4535
E-mail: museo@lahti.fi
Internet: www.lahti.fi/kulttuuri/museot/historia

Lahden taidemuseo ja julistemuseo – Lahti Art Museum and Poster Museum
Open: Mon-Fri 10am-5pm, Sat-Sun 11am-5pm
Address: Vesijärvenkatu 11
             15140 Lahti
Phone: (03) 814 4547
Fax: (03) 814 4545
E-mail: museo@lahti.fi
Internet: www.lahti.fi/kulttuuri/museot/taide

Radio- ja tv-museo – Radio and TV Museum
Open: Mon-Fri 10am-5pm, Sat-Sun 11am-5pm
Address: Radiomäki
             15100 Lahti
Phone: (03) 814 4511
Fax: (03) 814 4515
E-mail: museo@lahti.fi
Internet: www lahti.fi/kulttuuri/museot/radio

Hiihtomuseo – Ski Museum
Open: Mon-Fri 10am-5pm, Sat-Sun 11am-5pm
Address: Sports Center
             15110 Lahti
Phone: (03) 814 4520
Fax: (03) 814 4525
E-mail: museo@lahti.fi
Internet: www.lahti.fi/kulttuuri/museot

Ristinkirkko – Church of the Cross
Open: Daily 10am-3pm
Address: Kirkkokatu 4
             15110 Lahti
Phone: (03) 891 290

Fax: (03) 891 326
Internet: www.alvaraalto.fi

HOLLOLA
Hollolan kirkko – Hollola Medieval Church
Open: May-Aug: Daily 10am-6pm, Sep-Apr: Sun
             11am- 4pm and by appointment.
Address: Rantatie 917
             16710 Hollola kk
Phone: (03) 524 6600, 788 1351
Fax: (03) 524 6655

Pyhäniemen kartano – Pyhäniemi Manor
Open: Mid Jun-mid Aug: Daily 11am-6pm
Address: Pyhäniemi Manor
             Hollola
             16730 Kutajärvi
Phone: (03) 788 1466, 0400 496 770
Fax: (03) 788 1474
Internet: www.festivals.fi/pyhaniemi

ORIMATTILA
Orimattilan taidemuseo – Orimattila Art Museum
Open: Jun-mid Aug: Tue-Sun 12-6pm, Mid Aug-May: Tue
             Fri 12-4pm, Sat 10am-2pm, Sun 12-5pm
Address: Lahdentie 65
             16300 Orimattila
Phone: (03) 888 1370
Fax: (03) 888 1333
Internet: www.orimattila.fi/kaupunki/matkailu/taidemuseo

ASIKKALA
Urajärven kartanomuseo – Urajärvi Manor
Open: Jun-Aug: Daily 11am-5pm
Address: Kartanotie
             17150 Urajärvi
Phone: (03) 766 7191
Fax: (03) 405 0442
E-mail: lea.vartinen@nba.fi
Internet: www.nba.fi/museums/ura

Vääksyn kanava ja Vääksyn vesimylly- ja piensähkö-laitosmuseo – Vääksy Canal and Watermill Museum
Open: Jul: Tue-Fri, Sun 12-8pm, Sat 12-4pm Jun, Aug:
             Sat 12-4pm, Sun 12-6pm May and Sep:
             by appointment for groups.
Address: 17200 Vääksy
Phone: (03) 766 0860, 049 491 672

HEINOLA
Heinolan kaupunginmuseo – Heinola Town Museum
Open: Tue-Sun 12-4pm, Wed until 8pm
Address: Kauppakatu 14
             18100 Heinola
Phone: (03) 849 3651
Fax: (03) 715 2137
E-mail: museo@heinola.fi
Internet: www.heinola.fi/museo

Heinolan taidemuseo – Heinola Art Museum
Open: Tue-Sun 12-4pm, Wed until 8pm
Address: Kauppakatu 4
             18100 Heinola
Phone: (03) 849 3651
Fax: (03) 715 2137
E-mail: museo@heinola
Internet: www.heinola.fi/museo

Lääninkivalteri Aschanin talo – The Aschan Residence
Open: May 15-Sep 15: Tue-Sun 12-4pm, Wed until 8pm
Address: Kauppakatu 3 b
           18100 Heinola
Phone: (03) 849 3655
Fax: (03) 715 2137
E-mail: museo@heinola.fi
Internet: www.heinola.fi/aschan

SYSMÄ
Suvi-Pinx
Open: Early Jun-early Aug: Daily 11am-6pm
Address: Suopellontie 644
           19700 Sysmä
Phone: (03) 717 0581, (09) 454 8084
Fax: (03) 717 0559, (09) 454 8085

Sysmän kirkko – Sysmä Medieval Church
Open: Early Jun-early Aug: Daily 11am-5pm
Address: Kirkkotie 1
           19700 Sysmä
Phone: (03) 882 670
Fax: (03) 882 6734

HARTOLA
Itä-Hämeen Museo – Eastern Häme Museum
Open: Jun-Aug: Daily 11am-6pm, Sep-May: Daily 12-4pm
           and by appointment.
Address: Koskipää
           19600 Hartola
Phone: (03) 716 1252
Fax: (03) 716 1252
E-mail: ihmuseo@cc.jyu.fi
Internet: www.cc.jyu.fi/ihmuseo

10 PIRKANMAA

TAMPERE – TAMMERFORS
Tampereen tuomiokirkko – Tampere Cathedral
Open: May-Aug: Daily 9am-6pm, Sep-Apr: Daily 11am-3pm
Address: Tuomiokirkonkatu 3
           33100 Tampere
Phone: (03) 219 0214
Fax: (03) 219 0395

Museokeskus Vapriikki – Museum Centre Vapriikki
Open: Tue, Thu-Sun 10am-6pm, Wed 11am-8pm
Address: Veturiaukio 4
           33100 Tampere
Phone: (03) 3146 6966
Fax: (03) 3146 6839
E-mail: vapriikki@tampere.fi
Internet: www.tampere.fi/vapri

Tampereen taidemuseo – Tampere Art Museum
Open: Tue-Sun 10am-6pm
Address: Puutarhakatu 34
           33210 Tampere
Phone: (03) 3146 6577
Fax: (03) 3146 6584
E-mail: tamu@tampere.fi
Internet: www.tampere.fi/tamu

Sara Hildénin taidemuseo – Sara Hildén Art Museum
Open: Tue-Sun 11am-6pm
Address: Särkänniemi
           33230 Tampere
Phone: (03) 214 3134

Fax: (03) 222 9971
E-mail: sara.hilden@tampere.fi
Internet: www.tampere.fi/hilden

Hiekan taidemuseo – Hiekka Art Museum
Open: Tue-Thu 3pm-6pm, Sun 12-3pm and by appointment.
Address: Pirkankatu 6
           33210 Tampere
Phone: (03) 212 3975
Fax: (03) 212 3973
E-mail: hiekantm@vip.fi
Internet: www.vip.fi/~hiekantm

Willa Mac
Open: Wed, Sat and Sun: 12-5pm
Address: Palomäentie 23
           33230 Tampere
Phone: (03) 263 4244
Fax: (03) 263 4250
E-mail: mac-art@mac-art.net
Internet: www.snt-group.net/willamac/

Työväen keskusmuseo – Central Museum of Labour
Open: Tue-Sun 11am-6pm and by appointment.
Address: Werstas, Väinö Linnan aukio 8
           33210 Tampere
Phone: (03) 253 8800
Fax: (03) 253 8850
E-mail: info@tkm.fi
Internet: www.tkm.fi

**Amurin työläismuseokortteli – Amuri Museum
of Workers' Housing**
Open: Early May-mid Sep: Tue-Sun 10am-6pm
Address: Makasiininkatu 12
           33230 Tampere
Phone: (03) 3146 6771
Fax: (03) 3146 6808

Lenin-museo – Lenin Museum
Open: Mon-Fri 9am-5pm, Sat-Sun 11am-4pm
Address: Hämeenpuisto 28
           33200Tampere
Phone: (03) 276 8100
Fax: (03) 276 8121
E-mail: lenin@sci.fi
Internet: www.tampere.fi/culture/lenin

Nukke- ja pukumuseo – Museum of Dolls and Costumes
Open: Apr-Sep: Tue-Sun 11am-5pm and by appointment.
Address: Hatanpään puistokuja 1
           33900 Tampere
Phone: (03) 222 6261
Fax: (03) 222 6201
E-mail: haihara@sgic.fi
Internet: www.sgic.fi/~haihara/

Vakoilumuseo – Spy Museum
Open: Mon-Fri 12-6pm, Sat-Sun 10am-4pm
           and by appointment for groups.
Address: Hatanpään puistokuja 32
           33100 Tampere
Phone: (03) 212 3007
Fax: (03) 223 6989
E-mail: prologia@sci.fi
Internet: www.vakoilumuseo.fi

Kalevan kirkko – Kaleva Church
Open: May-Aug: Daily 9am-6pm, Sep-Apr: 11am-3pm

Address: Liisanpuisto 1
              33540 Tampere
Phone: (03) 219 0111
Fax: (03) 219 0200

Tampereen pääkirjasto Metso – Metso Tampere City Library
Open: Jun-Aug: Mon-Fri 9:30am-7pm,
              Sep-May: Mon-Fri 9:30am-8pm, Sat 9:30-3pm
              Reading room also: Sun 12-6pm
Address: Pirkankatu 2
              33100 Tampere
Phone: (03) 314 614
Fax: (03) 3146 1400
E-mail: tampereen.kaupunginkirjasto@tampere.fi
Internet: www.tampere.fi/kirjasto

Muumilaakso – Moominvalley
Open: Jun-mid Aug: Mon-Fri 9am-5pm, Sat-Sun
              10am-6pm, Mid Aug-May: Tue-Fri 9am-5pm,
              Sat-Sun 10am-6pm
Address: Hämeenpuisto 20
              33100 Tampere
Phone: (03) 3146 6578
Fax: (03) 3146 6567
E-mail: muumi@tampere.fi
Internet: www.tampere.fi/muumi

Kivimuseo – Mineral Museum
Open: Tue-Fri 9am-6pm, Sat-Sun 10am-6pm
Address: Hämeenpuisto 20
              33100 Tampere
Phone: (03) 3146 6046
Fax: (03) 3146 6808
Internet: www.tampere.fi/kivimuseo

YLÖJÄRVI
Museo Villa Urpo – Museum Villa Urpo
Open: By appointment. Closed Jul 1-mid Jul.
Address: Urpontie
              33450 Siivikkala
Phone: (03) 3142 4100
Fax: (03) 3142 4122
E-mail: villaurpo@yritys.soon.fi
Internet: www.villaurpo.com

KANGASALA
**Mobilia, Auto- ja tiemuseo – Mobilia Automobile
and Road Museum**
Open: May-Aug: Daily 10am-8pm,
              Sep-Apr: Mon-Fri 10am-3pm, Sat-Sun 12-6pm
Address: Kustaa Kolmannentie 75
              36270 Kangasala
Phone: (03) 3140 4000
Fax: (03) 3140 4050
E-mail: mobilia@mobilia.fi
Internet: www.mobilia.fi

LEMPÄÄLÄ
Kuokkalan museoraitti – Kuokkala Museum Road
Open: Jun-Aug: Daily 11am-5pm and by appointment.
Address: Kuokkalantie
              37550 Moisio
Phone: (03) 375 2643, 050 326 7557
Fax.   (03) 374 4216
E-mail: ritva.makela@sci.fi
Internet: www.lempaala.fi/matkailu/hakkari

TOIJALA
Veturimuseo – Locomotive Museum

Open: May 20-Aug 20: Mon-Sat 12-4pm, Sun 11am-6pm
              and by appointment.
Address: Ryödintie
              37800 Toijala
Phone: (03) 542 4585, 040 763 3087
Internet: www.toijala.fi/vapaa-aika

VALKEAKOSKI
Sääksmäen kirkko – Sääksmäki Medieval Church
Open: Mid Jun-mid Aug: Daily 8am-6pm
              and by appointment.
Address: Kirkkovainiontie 10
              37700 Sääksmäki
Phone: (03) 574 1200
Fax: (03) 574 1264

Myllysaaren museo – Myllysaari Museum
Open: Tue-Fri and Sun 12-6pm and by appointment.
Address: Kanavanranta 3
              37600 Valkeakoski
Phone: (03) 571 8100
Fax: (03) 571 8138
Internet: www.vlk.fi/museot

Kauppilanmäen museo – Kauppilanmäki Museum
Open: Jun-Aug: Tue-Sun 12-5pm and by appointment.
Address: Kauppilankatu 11-13
              37600 Valkeakoski
Phone: (03) 584 4014
Fax: (03) 571 8138
Internet: www.vlk.fi/museot

Visavuoren museo – Visavuori, Emil Wikström Museum
Open: Jun-Aug: Mon 11am-5pm, Tue-Sun 11am-7pm,
              Sep-May: Sun 11am-5pm and by appointment.
Address: Visavuorentie 80
              37770 Tarttila
Phone: (03) 543 6528
Fax: (03) 543 6528
E-mail: info@visavuori.com
Internet: www.visavuori.com

URJALA
Nuutajärven lasitehdas – Nuutajärvi Glass Museum
Open: Jun-Aug: Daily 10am-6pm,
              Sep-May: Sat-Sun 10am-5pm
Address: Nuutajärven lasikylä
              31160 Nuutajärvi
Phone: 0204 39 6504
Fax: 0204 39 6515

VAMMALA
Tyrvään kirkko – Tyrvää Medieval Church
Open: Under renovation
Address: 38200 Vammala
Phone: (03) 511 2609
Fax: (03) 511 4580

ORIVESI
Purnu
Open: Mid Jun-late Aug: Daily 11am-6pm
Address: Mustasaari 63
              35100 Orivesi as.
Phone: (03) 335 4323, 0400 501 065
Internet: www.oriseutu.fi/purnu

Oriveden kirkko – Orivesi Church
Open: Mid Jun-late Aug: Daily 10am-6pm
              and by appointment.

Address: Keskustie 17
             35300 Orivesi
Phone: (03) 335 2711, 3140 2515
Fax: (03) 335 1927

JUUPAJOKI
Kallenaution kievari – Kallenautio Inn
Open: Mid May-Aug: Daily 10am-8pm
Address: Kallenautiontie
             35540 Juupajoki
Phone: (03) 335 8915

RUOVESI
Kalelan taiteilijakoti – Kalela Artist's Home
Open: Late Jun-mid Aug: Daily 10am-5pm,
             Early Jun: by appointment for groups.
Address: Ruhala, Pöytäniementie
             34600 Ruovesi
Phone: (03) 486 1388, 476 0623
Fax: (03) 486 1444

Ruoveden kirkko – Ruovesi Church
Open: Jun-Aug: Daily 12-6pm and by appointment.
Address: 34600 Ruovesi
Phone: (03) 476 2221
Fax: (03) 476 2188

KURU
Kurun kirkko – Kuru Church
Open: Mid Jun-late Aug: Daily 10am-6pm
Address: Kirkkotie
             34300 Kuru
Phone: (03) 473 0500
Fax: (03) 473 0533

Kurun ulkomuseo – Kuru Open-Air Museum
Open: Mid Jun-early Aug: Tue-Sun 12-6pm
Address: Pokeluksentie 100
             34300 Kuru
Phone: (03) 483 911
Fax: (03) 483 9211

MÄNTTÄ
Gösta Serlachiuksen taidemuseo – Gösta Serlachius Museum of Fine Arts
Open: Jun-Aug: Tue-Sun 11am-6pm, Sep-May: Sat-Sun
             12-5pm and by appointment.
Address: Joenniemi Manor
             35800 Mänttä
Phone: (03) 474 5500
Fax: (03) 474 8260
E-mail: museum@serlachiusartmuseum.fi
Internet: www.serlachiusartmuseum.fi

G. A. Serlachius museo – The G. A. Serlachius Museum
Open: Late May-Aug: Tue-Sun 11am-6pm, Sep-May: Wed
             2pm-8pm, Thu-Sun 12-5pm and by appointment.
Address: R. Erik Serlachiuksenkatu 2
             35800 Mänttä
Phone: (03) 488 6832
E-mail: museum@serlachiusartmuseum.fi
Internet: www.serlachiusartmuseum.fi/gas

Honkahovi Art Center – The Honkahovi Art Center
Open: Mid Jun-mid Aug: Daily 10am-6pm
             and by appointment.
Address: Johtokunnantie 11
             35800 Mänttä
Phone: (03) 474 7005
Fax: (03) 474 6272

E-mail: ansali@mantta.fi
Internet: www.mantankuvataideviikot.fi

VIRRAT
Virtain perinnekylä – The Heritage Village
Open: Mid May-Aug: Daily 11am-6pm and by appointment.
Address: Herrasentie 16
             34800 Virrat
Phone: (03) 472 8100
Fax: (03) 472 8163
Internet: www.virrat.fi/perinnekyla

11 KESKI-SUOMI – CENTRAL-FINLAND

JYVÄSKYLÄ
Työväentalo – Worker's Club
Open: By appointment.
Address: Väinönkatu 7
             40100 Jyväskylä
Phone: (014) 624 903, 619 952
Fax: (014) 619 009
E-mail: foundation@alvaraalto.fi
Internet: www.alvaraalto.fi

Kulttuuri- ja hallintokeskus – Cultural and Administrative Center
Open: City Theater: Tue-Sat 12-7pm
             Office Building: Mon-Fri 8am-4pm
Address: City Theater: Vapudenkatu 36
             Office Building: Hannikaisenkatu 17
             40100 Jyväskylä
Phone: (014) 624 903
Fax: (014) 214 393
E-mail: foundation@alvaraalto.fi
Internet: www.alvaraalto.fi

Taulumäen kirkko – Taulumäki Church
Open: Jun-mid Aug: Daily 11am-8pm and by appointment.
Address: Lohikoskentie 2
             40320 Jyväskylä
Phone: (014) 338 7323
Fax: (014) 338 7333
Internet: www.evl.fi/srk/jyvaskylanmaaseurakunta

Jyväskylän yliopisto – University of Jyväskylä
Open: Main building: Jun-Aug: Mon-Fri 7:30am-4pm,
             Sep-May: Mon-Fri 7:30am-6pm
Address: Seminaarikatu 15
             40100 Jyväskylä
Phone: (014) 260 1152
Fax: (014) 260 1041
E-mail: ttimonen@admiral.jyu.fi
Internet: www.jyu.fi/english/geninfo1

Keski-Suomen museo – Museum of Central Finland
Open: Tue-Sun 11am-6pm
Address: Alvar Aallon katu 7
             40100 Jyväskylä
Phone: (014) 624 930
Fax: (014) 624 936
E-mail: ksmuseo.info@jkl.fi
Internet: www.jkl.fi/ksmuseo

Alvar Aalto -museo – Alvar Aalto Museum
Open: Tue-Sun 11-6pm
Address: Alvar Aallon katu 7
             40600 Jyväskylä
Phone: (014) 624 809
Fax: (014) 619 009

E-mail: pia.vainio@alvaraalto.fi
Internet: www.alvaraalto.fi

Jyväskylän taidemuseo – Jyväskylä Art Museum
Open: Tue-Sun 11am-6pm
Address: Kauppakatu 23 and Kilpisenkatu 8
           Galleria Harmonia: Hannikaisenkatu 39
           40100 Jyväskylä
Phone: (014) 626 856
Fax: (014) 624 814
E-mail: taidemuseo@jkl.fi
Internet: www.jkl.fi/kulttuuri/taidemuseo

Suomen käsityön museo – The Craft Museum of Finland
Open: Tue-Sun 11am-6pm
Address: Kauppakatu 25
           40100 Jyväskylä
Phone: (014) 624 946
Fax: (014) 624 947
E-mail: craftmuseum@jkl.fi
Internet: www.craftmuseum.fi

**Keski-Suomen Ilmailumuseo – Central Finland
Aviation Museum**
Open: Jun-mid Aug: Daily 10am-8pm
           Mid Aug-May: Daily 11am-5pm
Address: Tikkakoskentie 125
           41160 Tikkakoski
Phone: (014) 375 2125
Fax: (014) 375 3620
E-mail: keski-suomen.ilmailumuseo@kolumbus.fi
Internet: www.jiop.fi/ksimuseo

Säynätsalon kunnantalo – Säynätsalo Town Hall
Open: Jun-Aug: Mon-Fri 7:30am-3:30pm, Sat-Sun 1pm-
           4pm Sep-May: Mon-Fri 7:30am-3:30pm
           Library: Mon-Thu 2pm-7pm, Fri 11am-4pm
Address: Parviaisentie 9
           40900 Säynätsalo
Phone: (014) 623 801
Fax: (014) 623 802
E-mail: alvar.aalto-museo@jkl.fi
Internet: www.alvaraalto.fi

Muuratsalon koetalo – Muuratsalo Experimental House
Open: By appointment Jun-mid Sep: Mon, Wed,
           Fri 1:30pm-3:30pm.
Address: Säynätsalo
Phone: (014) 624 809
Fax: (014) 619 009
E-mail: pia.vainio@alvaraalto.fi
Internet: www.alvaraalto.fi

MUURAME
Muuramen saunakylä – Muurame Sauna Village
Open: Jun-Aug: Daily 10am-6pm
Address: Isolahdentie
           45950 Muurame
Phone: (014) 373 2670, 659 611
Fax: (014) 659 600
Internet: www.muurame.fi

PETÄJÄVESI

Petäjäveden vanha kirkko – Old Petäjävesi Church

Open: Jul-Aug: Daily 11am-7pm and by appointment.
Address: Vanhankirkontie

           41900 Petäjävesi
Phone: 040 582 2461, (014) 859 511, 447 1400
Fax: (014) 447 1421
E-mail: petajaveden.info@petajavesi.fi
Internet: www.petajavesi.fi

KEURUU
Keuruun museo Kamana – Kamana Keuruu Museum
Open: Jun-Aug: Daily 10am-6pm,
           Sep-May: Mon-Fri 10am-6pm, Sat-Sun 10am-4pm
Address: Kamana
           Kangasmannilantie 4
           42700 Keuruu
Phone: (014) 751 2541
Fax: (014) 751 2542
E-mail: anna-riikka.hirvonen@keuruu.kaupunki.fi
Internet: www.keuruu.fi/matkailu/kamana

Keuruun vanha kirkko – Old Keuruu Church
Open: Jun-Aug: Daily 11am-5pm and by appointment.
Address: Keuruuntie 1
           42700 Keuruu
Phone: (014) 774 4211, 751451
Fax: (014) 774 4224
E-mail: matkailu@keuruu.fi
Internet: www.keuruu.fi

Pihlajaveden vanha kirkko – Old Pihlajavesi Church
Open: Jun-Aug: All day
Address: Valkeajärvi
           42700 Keuruu
Phone: (014) 774 4211
Fax: (014) 774 4224
E-mail: matkailu@keuruu.fi
Internet: www.keuruu.fi

**Haapamäen höyryveturipuisto – Haapamäki Steam
Engine Park**
Open: Jun-mid Aug: Daily 10am-8pm Mid Aug-Aug:
           Sat-Sun 10am-6pm and by appointment.
Address: Veturipeistontie
           42800 Haapamäki
Phone: (014) 733 111
Fax: (014) 733 101
E-mail: veturipuisto@yritys.soon.fi
Internet: www.yritys.soon.fi/veturipuisto

HANKASALMI
Pienmäen talomuseo – Pienmäki Farm Museum
Open: Jun-Aug: Wed-Sun 12-7pm and by appointment.
Address: 41490 Niemisjärvi
Phone: (014) 845 497, 624 919
Fax: (014) 624 936
E-mail: ksmuseo.info@jkl.fi
Internet: www.jkl.fi/ksmuseo/pmaki

SAARIJÄRVI
Saarijärven museo – Saarijärvi Museum
Open: Jun-mid Aug: Daily 12-7pm, Mid Aug-May: Wed-
           Sun 12-7pm and by appointment for groups.
Address: Herajärventie 2
           43100 Saarijärvi
Phone: (014) 429 1412
Fax: (014) 455 117
E-mail: museo@saarijarvi.fi
Internet: www.saarijarvi.fi/museo

Säätyläiskotimuseo – Gentry Home Museum
Open: Late Jun-Jul: Wed-Sun 12-6pm

Address:	43250 Kolkanlahti
Phone:	(014) 439 688
Fax:	(014) 455 117
E-mail:	museo@saarijarvi.fi
Internet:	www.saarijarvi.fi/museo

Kivikauden kylä – Stone Age Village

Open:	Late Jun-Jul: Daily 12-7pm,Early Jun-late Jun: 12-7pm, Mid May-early Jun: Mon-Fri 10am-4pm, Aug: Tue-Sun 10am-4pm, by appointment for groups.
Address:	Summassaari
	43101 Saarijärvi
Phone:	(014) 422 873, 040 540 3642
Fax:	(014) 455 117
E-mail:	museo@saarijarvi.fi
Internet:	www.saarijarvi.fi/museo

KANNONKOSKI
Kannonkosken kirkko – Kannonkoski Church

Open:	By appointment.
Address:	Kirkkotie 13
	43300 Kannonkoski
Phone:	(014) 451 007
Fax:	(014) 451 249
Internet:	www.kannonkoski.fi

LUHANKA
Peltolan mäkitupalaismuseo – Peltola Croft Museum

Open:	Jun-Aug: Daily 10am-6pm
Address:	19910 Tammijärvi
Phone:	(014) 877 108

12 ETELÄ-SAVO – SOUTH SAVO

SAVONLINNA
Olavinlinna – Olavinlinna Castle

Open:	Jun-Aug 15: Daily 10am-5pm, Aug 16-May: Daily 10am-3pm
Address:	57150 Olavinlinna
Phone:	(015) 531 164
Fax:	(015) 510 585
E-mail:	olavinlinna@nba.fi
Internet:	www.nba.fi/castles/olof

Pikkukirkko – Savonlinna Little Church

Open:	Mid Jun-late Aug: Daily 11am-6pm
Address:	Olavinkatu 29
	57130 Savonlinna
Phone:	(015) 576 8012
Fax:	(015) 576 8011
Internet:	www.evl.fi/srk/savonlinna-saaminki

Savonlinnan tuomiokirkko – Savonlinna Cathedral

Open:	Mid Jun-late Aug: Daily 11am-7pm
Address:	Sotilaspojankatu 6
	57100 Savonlinna
Phone:	(015) 576 8012
Fax:	(015) 576 8011
Internet:	www.evl.fi/srk/savonlinna-saaminki

Rauhalinnan huvila – Rauhalinna Villa

Open:	Jun-early Aug: Mon-Sat 11am-8pm, Sun 11am-6pm, Early Aug-mid Aug: Mon-Sat 11am-6pm, Sun 11am-4pm and by appointment.
Address:	Lehtiniemi
	57310 Savonlinna
Phone:	(015) 517 640

Savonlinnan maakuntamuseo – Savonlinna Provincial Museum

Open:	Jul: Daily 11am-6pm Aug-Jun: Tue-Sun 11am-5pm
Address:	Riihisaari
	57130 Savonlinna
Phone:	(015) 571 4712
Fax:	(015) 571 4717
E-mail:	museo@savonlinna.fi
Internet:	www.savonlinna.fi/museo

Museolaivat – The Museum Ships

Open:	Mid May-Jun: Tue-Sun 11am-5pm, Jul-Aug: Daily 11am-6pm
Address:	Savonlinna harbor
Phone:	(015) 571 4712
Fax:	(015) 571 4717
E-mail:	museo@savonlinna.fi
Internet:	www.savonlinna.fi/museo

Savonlinnan taidemuseo – Savonlinna Art Museum

Open:	Jul: Daily 11am-6pm Aug-Jun: Tue-Sun 11am-5pm
Address:	Olavinkatu 40
	57130 Savonlinna
Phone:	(015) 571 4719
Fax:	(015) 571 4717
E-mail:	museo@savonlinna.fi
Internet:	www.savonlinna.fi/museo

PUNKAHARJU
Putikon kartano – Putikko Manor

Open:	Mid Jun-Aug: Daily 10am-6pm
Address:	Ylätalontie 47
	58550 Putikko
Phone:	(015) 645 322
Fax:	(015) 645 322
Internet:	www.putikonkartano.fi

Lusto Suomen metsämuseo – Lusto Finnish Forest Museum

Open:	Jun-Aug: Daily 10am-7pm, May and Sep: Daily 10am-5pm Oct-Apr: Tue-Sun 10am-5pm
Address:	Lustontie 1
	58450 Punkaharju
Phone:	(015) 345 1030
Fax:	(015) 345 1050
E-mail:	lusto@lusto.fi
Internet:	www.lusto.fi

Taidekeskus Retretti – Retretti Art Center

Open:	Jul: Daily 10am-7pm, Jun and Aug: Daily 10am-6pm
Address:	58450 Punkaharju
Phone:	(015) 775 2200
Fax:	(015) 644 314
E-mail:	retretti@retretti.fi
Internet:	www.retretti.fi

KERIMÄKI
Kerimäen kirkko – Kerimäki Church

Open:	Jun and early Aug: Daily 10am-6pm, Jul: Daily 10am-7pm Late Aug: 10am-4pm and by appointment.
Address:	Puruvedentie 65
	58200 Kerimäki
Phone:	(015) 578 9123, 578 9111
Fax:	(015) 578 9128
Internet:	www.kolumbus.fi/kerisrk/

MIKKELI
Mikkelin maaseurakunnan kirkko – Mikkeli Parish Church

Open:	Mid Jun-mid Aug: Daily 10am-5pm

and by appointment.
Address: Otavankatu 9
             50100 Mikkeli
Phone: (015) 201 0400
Fax: (015) 368 253

Mikkelin tuomiokirkko – Mikkeli Cathedral
Open: Jun-Aug: Daily 10am-6pm, Sep-May:
             Mon-Fri 10am-11am
Address: Ristimäen puisto
             50100 Mikkeli
Phone: (015) 20 101
Fax: (015) 201 0205
Internet: www.evl.fi/srk/mikkelitksrk

Savilahden kivisakasti – Savilahti Medieval Stone Sacristy
Open: Late Jun-early Aug: Daily 10am-4pm
             and by appointment.
Address: Porrassalmenkatu 32 a
             50100 Mikkeli
Phone: (015) 194 2424
Fax: (015) 366 161
E-mail: museot@mikkeli.fi
Internet: www.mikkeli.fi/museot/englanti

Suur-Savon museo – Suur-Savo Museum
Open: May-Aug: Tue-Fri 10am-5pm, Sat 2pm-5pm,
             Sep-Apr: Wed 10am-5pm, Sat 2pm-5pm
             and by appointment.
Address: Otavankatu 11
             50100 Mikkeli
Phone: (015) 213 606
Fax: (015) 366 161
E-mail: museot@mikkeli.fi
Internet: www.mikkeli.fi/museot/englanti

Mikkelin taidemuseo – Mikkeli Art Museum
Open: Tue- Fri and Sun 10-5pm, Sat 10am-1pm
Address: Ristimäenkatu 5
             50100 Mikkeli
Phone: (015) 194 2424
Fax: (015) 366 161
E-mail: museot@mikkeli.fi
Internet: www.mikkeli.fi/museot/englanti

Päämajamuseo – Headquarters Museum
Open: May-Aug: Daily 10am-5pm Sep-Apr: Fri-Sun 10am
             5pm and by appointment.
Address: Päämajankuja 1-3
             50100 Mikkeli
Phone: (015) 194 2427
Fax: (015) 366 161
E-mail: museot@mikkeli.fi
Internet: www.mikkeli.fi/museot/englanti

Viestikeskus Lokki – Communications Center Lokki
Open: May-Aug: Daily 10am-5pm, and by appointment.
Address: Naisvuori Hill, corner Vuorikatu and Ristimäenkatu
             Streets
Phone: (015) 194 2429
Fax: (015) 366 161
E-mail: museot@mikkeli.fi
Internet: www.mikkeli.fi/museot/englanti

Jalkaväkimuseo – Infantry Museum
Open: Jun 15-Aug 14: Daily 10am-5pm, May 15-Jun 14 and
             Aug 15-Sep 14: Tue-Sun 10am-5pm, Sep 15-May 14:
             Wed, Sat-Sun 12-5pm
Address: Jääkärinkatu 6-8

             50100 Mikkeli
Phone: (015) 369 666
E-mail: jalkavakimuseo.mikkeli@luukku.com
Internet: www.mikkeli.fi

Kenkäveronniemi pappila – Kenkäveronniemi Parsonage
Open: Mon-Fri and Sun 10am-6pm, Sat 10am-4pm
             and by appointment.
Address: Kenkävero
             Pursialankatu 6
             50100 Mikkeli
Phone: (015) 162 230
Fax: (015) 162 211
E-mail: kty.mikkeli@kolumbus.fi
Internet: www.travel.fi/kenkavero

HIRVENSALMI
Kissakosken tehdas – Kissakoski Factory
Open: Jun-Aug: Daily 10am-5pm and by appointment.
Address: Vahvamäentie 42
             52550 Hirvensalmi
Phone: (015) 652 810, 050 525 9712
Fax: (015) 652 803

RISTIINA
Ristiinan kirkko – Ristiina Church
Open: Mid Jun-late Aug: Daily 11am-6pm
Address: Kissalammentie 2
             52300 Ristiina
Phone: (015) 661 264

Pien-Toijolan talonpoikaismuseo – Pien-Toijola Farmstead Museum
Open: Jun-Mid Aug: Tue-Sun 10am-4pm
Address: 52360 Someenjärvi
Phone: (015) 52 360

Astuvansalmen kalliomaalaukset – Astuvansalmi Rock Paintings
Phone: (015) 740 1226, 040 584 9210
Fax: (015) 661 760
E-mail: kristiina.kilpijarvi@pp.inet.fi
Internet: www.internetix.ofw.fi/

MÄNTYHARJU
Taidekeskus Salmela – Salmela Art Center
Open: Early Jun-mid Aug: Daily 11am-6pm
             and by appointment for groups.
Address: Mäntyharjuntie 25
             52700 Mäntyharju
Phone: (015) 464 526, (05) 387 370
Fax: (05) 387 374
E-mail: taidekeskus.salmela@co.inet.fi
Internet.   www.taidekeskussalmela.fi

PIEKSÄMÄKI
Kulttuurikeskus Poleeni – Poleeni Cultural Center
Open: Mon-Fri 11am-7pm, Sat 9am-3pm
Address: Savontie 13
             76100 Pieksämäki
Phone: (015) 788 2435, 040 509 2008
Fax: (015) 788 2910
E-mail: info@mail.pieksamaki.fi
Internet: www.pieksamaki.fi

HEINÄVESI
Heinäveden kirkko – Heinävesi Church
Open: Early Jun-late Aug: Daily 11am-6pm
Address: Kirkkotie 19

```
                    79700 Heinävesi
Phone:      (017) 555 8400
Fax:        (017) 555 8420
```

Valamon luostari – Valamo Monastery
```
Open:       Daily 8am-9pm. Daily services are open to the visitors.
Address:    Valamontie 42
            79850  Uusi-Valamo
Phone:      (017) 570 1504
Fax:        (017) 570 1510
E-mail:     valamo@valamo.fi
Internet:   www.valamo.fi
```

13 POHJOIS-SAVO – NORTH SAVO

KUOPIO

Kuopion kulttuurihistoriallinen museo – Kuopio Museum of Cultural History
```
Open:       May-Aug: Mon-Sat 9am-4pm, Wed until 8pm, Sun
            11am-6pm, Sep-Apr: Mon-Fri 9am-4pm, Wed until
            8pm, Sun 11am-6pm
Address:    Kauppakatu 23
            70100 Kuopio
Phone:      (017) 182 603
Fax:        (017) 182 600
E-mail:     kuopionmuseo.kut@kuopio.fi
Internet:   www.kulttuuri.kuopio.fi/
```

Kuopion luonnontieteellinen museo – Kuopio Museum of Natural History
```
Open:       May-Aug: Mon-Sat 9am-4pm, Wed until 8pm, Sun
            11am-6pm, Sep-Apr: Mon-Fri 9am-4pm, Wed until
            8pm, Sun 11am-6pm
Address:    Kauppakatu 23
            70100 Kuopio
Phone:      (017) 182 111
Fax:        (017) 182 654
E-mail:     kuopionmuseo.kut@kuopio.fi
Internet:   www.kuopio.fi/ymp/ympmuseo
```

Kuopion korttelimuseo – Old Kuopio Museum
```
Open:       May 15-Sep 15: Daily 10am-5pm, Wed until 7pm
            Sep 15-May 15: Tue-Sun 10am-3pm
Address:    Kirkkokatu 22
            70100 Kuopio
Phone:      (017) 182 625
Fax:        (017) 182 630
E-mail:     tapio.laaksonen@kuopio.fi
Internet:   www.kulttuuri.kuopio.fi/korttelimuseo
```

VB Valokuvakeskus – The VB Photographic Centre
```
Open:       Jun-Aug: Mon-Fri 10am-7pm, Sat-Sun 11am-4pm
Address:    Kuninkaankatu 14-16
            70100 Kuopio
Phone:      (017) 261 5599
Fax:        (017) 261 5844
E-mail:     vb.valokuvauskeskus@co.inet.fi
Internet:   www.vb.kuopio.fi
```

J.V. Snellmanin kotimuseo – J.V. Snellman Home Museum
```
Open:       May 15-Aug: Daily 10am-5pm, Wed until 7pm,
            Sep-May 14: by appointment for groups
Address:    Snellmaninkatu 19
            70100 Kuopio
Phone:      (017) 182 624
Fax:        (017) 182 630
Internet:   www.kulttuuri.kuopio.fi/korttelimuseo
```

Kuopion taidemuseo – Kuopio Art Museum
```
Open:       Mon-Sat 9am-4:30pm, Wed until 8pm, Sun 11am-6pm
Address:    Kauppakatu 35
            70100 Kuopio
Phone:      (017) 182 633
Fax:        (017) 182 642
E-mail:     aija.jaatinen@kuopio.fi
Internet:   www.kulttuuri.kuopio.fi/taidemuseo
```

Suomen Ortodoksinen kirkkomuseo – The Orthodox Church Museum of Finland
```
Open:       May-Aug: Tue-Sun 10am-4pm
            Sep-Apr: Mon-Fri 12-3pm, Sat-Sun 12-5pm
Address:    Karjalankatu 1
            70110 Kuopio
Phone:      (017) 287 2220
Fax:        (017) 287 2211
E-mail:     kirkkomuseo@ort.fi
Internet:   www.ort.fi/kirkkomuseo
```

Kuopion tuomiokirkko – Kuopio Cathedral
```
Open:       Mid Jun-mid Aug: Daily 10am-6pm, Wed and Fri
            10am-midnight, Mid Aug-mid Jun: Daily 10am-3pm
Address:    Vuorikatu 17
            70100 Kuopio
Phone:      (017) 158 401
Fax.        (017) 158 402
Internet:   www.evl.fi/srk/kuopio
```

Männistön kirkko – Männistö Church
```
Open:       Mon-Fri 12-3pm and by appointment.
Address:    Kellolahdentie 8
            70420 Kuopio
Phone:      (017) 158 562
Fax:        (017) 158 563
```

RAUTALAMPI

Rautalammin kirkko – Rautalampi Church
```
Open:       Jun-Aug 15: Daily 9am-3pm
Address:    77700 Rautalampi
Phone:      (017) 530 008
```

Rautalammin museo – Peura Museum
```
Open:       Mid May-Sep: Tue-Fri, Sun 11am-4pm, Sat 11am-
            2pm and by appointment.
Address:    Kuopiontie 26
            77700 Rautalampi
Phone:      (017) 530 014
Fax:        (017) 530 014
```

KARTTULA

Riuttalan talonpoikaismuseo – The Riuttala Peasant Museum
```
Open:       Early Jun-mid Aug: Daily 11am-4pm
            and by appointment.
Address:    Riuttalantie 719
            72100 Karttula
Phone:      (017) 362 8108, 050 539 0835
Fax:        (017) 495 4958
Internet:   www.savonia.net/riuttala
```

VESANTO

Vesannon torpparimuseo – Vesanto Croft Museum
```
Oen:        Jun-Jul: Daily 11am-5pm and by appointment.
Address:    72300 Vesanto
Phone:      (017) 650 191
```

NILSIÄ

Paavon pirtti – Paavo's Cabin
```
Open:       Daily 8am-8pm. Regular boat traffic Jun-mid Aug
Address:    73890 Aholansaari
```

Phone: (017) 464 1117, 0500 585 544
Fax: (017) 481 061
E-mail: aholansaari@tahko.com
Internet: www.tahko.com

JUANKOSKI
Juankosken tehtaan- ja työväenmuseo – Juankoski Ironworks and Workers Museum
Open: Jun-late Aug: Tue-Fri 10am-6pm, Sat-Sun 12-4pm
            and by appointment.
Address: Juankoskentie
            73500 Juankoski
Phone: (017) 612 055
Fax: (017) 616 377
Internet: www.juankoski.fi

VIEREMÄ
Salahmin ruukki – Salahmi Ironworks
Open: Guided tours.
Address: Kiuruvedentie 30
            74230 Salahmi
Phone: (017) 716 112, 040 504 6800
Fax: (017) 716 153

SONKAJÄRVI
Jyrkkäkosken ruukki – Jyrkkäkoski Ironworks
Open: Guided tours.
Address: Tölppäsenniementie 30
            74380 Jyrkkä
Phone: (017) 765 626, 0400 656 122
Internet: www.sonkajarvi.fi

MAANINKA
Vanha Viannon kanava ja Ahkiolahden kanava – Old Vianno Canal and Ahkiolahti Canal
Phone: (017) 382 5219

Korkeakosken putous – Korkeakoski Falls
Phone: (017) 875 240

LAPINLAHTI
Halosen museo – The Halonen Museum
Eemil Halosen museo ja Lapinlahden taidemuseo – Eemil Halonen Museum and Lapinlahti Art Museum
Open: Mid Jun-Jul: Sun-Fri 10am-6pm, Sat 10am-5pm,
            Aug: Daily 11am-5pm,
            Sep-May: Tue-Sun 12-5pm, Wed until 7pm
Address: Suistamontie 3
            73100 Lapinlahti
Phone: (017) 732 288, 040 549 1484
Fax: (017) 733 178
E-mail: lltm@eemil.inet.fi
Internet: www.halostenmuseosaatio.fi

Väisälänmäen kulttuuri- ja luontopolku – Väisälänmäki Culture and Nature Trail
Open: Jun-Aug: Daily 12-8pm, May and Sep: Sun 12-8pm
            and by appointment.
Address: Väisälänmäki, Lapinlahti
Phone: (017) 768 0280, 040 532 5930
            050 589 3845
            guide (017) 768 0334, 733 722
Fax: (017) 182 630
E-mail: sirpa.tarkkinen@lapinlahti.fi

IISALMI
Koljonvirran multimediateatteri – Koljonvirta Multimedia Theater
Open: Guided tours.

Address: Olvi Hall
            Tehtaantie 1
            74100 Iisalmi
Phone: (017) 822 872
Fax: (017) 818 411
E-mail: koljonvirta@saunalahti.fi
Internet: www.koljonvirta.fi

Juhani Ahon museo – Juhani Aho Museum
Open: May-Aug: Daily 10am-6pm
Address: Ouluntie 37
            74120 Iisalmi
Phone: (017) 817 771, 830 3248
Fax: (017) 830 3248
Internet: www.iisalmi.fi/kulttuur/kulttuuritoimi/juhaniaho

Iisalmen vanha kirkko – Iisalmi Old Church
Open: Mid Jun-late Aug: Daily 11am-6pm
            and by appointment.
Address: Kirkkotie 20
            74120 Iisalmi
Phone: (017) 83 351
Fax: (017) 833 5233
Internet: www.evlsrk.iisalmi.fi

Evakkokeskus – Evacuation Center
Open: Daily 9am-6pm
Address: Kirkkopuistonkatu 28
            74100 Iisalmi
Phone: (017) 816 441, 812 244, 0500 271 163
Fax: (017) 814 941
E-mail: iisalmi@ort.fi

Iisalmen ortodoksinen kirkko – Iisalmi Orthodox Church
Open: Daily 10am-4pm and by appointment.
Address: Kyllikinkatu 8
            74100 Iisalmi
Phone: (017) 816 441

VARKAUS
Varkauden museo –Varkaus Museum
Open: Wed 12-7pm, Thu 10am-4pm, Fri 10am-2pm,
            Sun 10am-6pm
Address: Wredenkatu 5 A
            78250 Varkaus
Phone: (017) 579 4440
Fax: (017) 579 4441
E-mail: museo@vrk.varkaus.fi
Internet: www.varkaus.fi/museo

Varkauden taidemuseo –Varkaus Art Museum
Open: Tue-Fri, Sun 11am-6pm, Sat 11am-3pm
Address: Ahlströminkatu 17
            78250 Varkaus
Phone: (017) 579 4538
Fax: (017) 579 4679
E-mail: taidemuseo@vrk.varkaus.fi
Internet: www.varkaus.fi/taidemuseo

Mekaanisen Musiikin "Museo" – "Museum" of Mechanical Music
Open: Jul: Daily 11am-8pm Jun and Aug: Tue-Sun 11am
            6pm, Mar-May, Sep-Dec: Tue-Sat 11am-6pm, Sun
            11am-5pm
Address: Pelimanninkatu 8
            78850 Varkaus
Phone: (017) 558 0643, 0400 126 048
Fax: (017) 556 6566
E-mail: pawel.kempf@mekaanisenmusiikinmuseo.inet.fi

14 KYMENLAAKSO – KYMIJOKI RIVER VALLEY

KOTKA
Sunilan tehtaat – Sunila Factory
Phone: (05) 229 8231
Fax: (05) 229 8277
E-mail: paivi.totterman@sunila.fi
Internet: www.alvaraalto.fi

Kotkan kirkko – Kotka Church
Open: Jun-Aug: Sun-Fri 12-6pm
Address: Kirkkokatu 26
           48100 Kotka
Phone: (05) 225 9300
Internet: www.kotkanseurakunnat.fi

Maretarium
Open: Jul-mid Aug: Daily 10am-8pm,
           Jun and mid Aug-Sep: Daily 10am-6pm
Address: Sapokankatu 2
           48100 Kotka
Phone: (05) 234 4030
Fax: (05) 234 4040
E-mail: info@maretarium
Internet: www.maretarium.fi

Haapasaari Island
Open: Regular boat traffic and cruises to Haapasaari Island
           leave from Sapokanlahti Quay.
Phone: (05) 225 9300

Kyminlinna – Kyminlinna Castle
Open: By appointment.
Adress: Kyminlinna
Phone: (05) 1816 7111

Ruotsinsalmen linnoitus – Ruotsinsalmi Fortifications
Open: Regular boat service from Sapokanlahti Quay
Phone: (05) 234 4424
Fax: (05) 234 4407
E-mail: matkailu@kotka.fi
Internet: www.kotka.fi/matkailu

Kymenlaakson maakuntamuseo – The Provincial Museum of Kymenlaakso
Open: Tue-Fri 12-6pm, Sat-Sun 12-4pm
Address: Kotkankatu 13
           48100 Kotka
Phone: (05) 234 4433
Fax: (05) 234 4277
E-mail: museo@kotka.fi
Internet: www.kotka.fi/museo/english

Museolaivat – Museum Ships
Open: Mid May-Aug: Mon-Fri 10am-6pm,
           Sat-Sun 10am-4pm
Address: Rantasatama
Phone: (05) 234 4717
Fax: (05) 234 4277
E-mail: museo@kotka.fi
Internet: www.kotka.fi/museo/english

Kotkan ortodoksinen kirkko – St. Nicholas Orthodox Church
Open: Jun-Aug: Tue-Fri 12-3pm, Sat-Sun 12-6pm
           and by appointment.
Address: Isopuisto
           48100 Kotka
Phone: (05) 212 490, 234 4424
Fax: (05) 216 449

Langinkosken keisarillinen kalastusmaja – Langinkoski Imperial Fishing Lodge
Open: May-Aug: Daily 10am-7pm,
           Sep-Oct: Sat-Sun 10am-7pm and by appointment.
Address: Langinkoski
           48230 Kotka
Phone: (05) 228 1050
Fax: (05) 228 3300
Internet: www.kotka.fi/matkailu

HAMINA
Haminan kirkko – Hamina Church
Open: Early Jun-mid Aug: Daily 10am-5pm
Address: Raatihuoneentori
           49400 Hamina
Phone: (05) 730 1721
Fax: (05) 730 1728

Haminan kaupunginmuseo – Hamina Town Museum
Open: May-Aug: Tue-Sun 10am-4pm,
           Sep-May: Wed-Sat 11am-3pm, Sun 12-5pm
Address: Kadettikoulunkatu 2
           49400 Hamina
Phone: (05) 749 5242
Internet: www.hamina.fi/english/museot

Haminan kauppiaantalomuseo – Merchant's House Museum
Open: Jun-Aug: Tue-Sun 10am-4pm,
           Sep-May: Wed-Sat 11am-3pm, Sun 12-5pm
Address: Kasarminkatu 6
           49400 Hamina
Phone: (05) 749 5244
Internet: www.hamina.fi/english/museot

ANJALANKOSKI
Anjalan kartanomuseo – Anjala Manor
Open: May 15-Aug 15: Daily 11am-5pm
           and by appointment for groups.
Address: Ankkapurhantie 7
           46910 Anjalankoski
Phone: (05) 367 4994
Fax: (09) 405 0442
E-mail: lea.vartinen@nba.fi
Internet: www.nba.fi/museums/anjala

Anjalan kirkko – Anjala Church
Open: Jun-Jul: Daily 11am-6pm
Address: Anjalantie 2
           46910 Anjalankoski
Phone: (05) 750 8200
Fax: (05) 750 8255

ELIMÄKI
Elimäen kirkko – Elimäki Church
Open: Mid Jun-mid Aug: Mon-Fri 10am-4pm
Address: Vanhamaantie
           47200 Elimäki
Phone: (05) 741 4100
Fax: (05) 741 4115
E-mail: elimaki@evl.fi

Moision kartano – Moisio Manor
Open: Mid May-Aug: Mon-Fri 11am-6pm, Sat 11am-3pm,
           Sun 11am-6pm, Sep-mid May: Tue-Fri 11am-6pm,
           Sat 11am-3pm, Sun 11am-4pm
Address: Moisiontie 163
           47200 Elimäki
Phone: (05) 377 6331
Fax: (05) 377 6332

E-mail: moision.kartano@elimaki.inet.fi

Mustilan arboretum – Arboretum Mustila
Open: All year
Address: 47200 Elimäki
Phone: (05) 377 6678
Fax: (05) 377 7600
E-mail: arboretum@mustila.com
Internet: www.mustila.com

PYHTÄÄ
Pyhtään kirkko – Pyhtää Church
Open: Mid Jun-mid Aug: Daily 10am-6pm
Address: Harjuntie 11
            49270 Pyhtää
Phone: (05) 343 1921
Fax: (05) 343 1924

Kaunissaari Island
            Regular boat traffic from the Pyhtää center, Siltakylä
            village and Sapokanlahti Quay in Kotka

KOUVOLA
Kouvolan kaupunginmuseo – Kouvola Town Museum
Kouvolan apteekkimuseo – Kouvola Pharmacy Museum
Open: Jun-Aug: Tue-Fri 11am-6pm, Sat-Sun 12-5pm,
            Sep-May: Sun 12-5pm and by appointment.
Addresses: Varuskuntakatu 9
            45100 Kouvola
Phone: (05) 829 6586
Fax: (05) 375 1605
E-mail: heli.kaukiainen@kouvola.fi
Internet: www.kouvola.fi/palvelut/kulttuuri

Kouvolan Putkiradiomuseo – Kouvola Tube Radio Museum
Open: Jun-Aug: Tue-Fri 12-7pm, Sat-Sun 12-5pm
            Sep-May: Sun 12-2pm,Tue 1pm-4pm
            and by appointment.
Address: Pajaraitti 1
            45100 Kouvola
Phone: (05) 829 6558
Fax: (05) 829 6587
E-mail: kari.soininen@fimet.fi
Internet: www.kouvola.fi/palvelut/kulttuuri

Rautatieläiskotimuseo – Museum of Railway Worker's Home
Open: Jun-Aug: Tue-Fri 11am-6pm, Sat-Sun 12-5pm
Address: Veturimiehenraitti 5
            45100 Kouvola
Phone: (05) 829 6323
Fax: (05) 375 1605
E-mail: heli.kaukiainen@kouvola.fi
Internet: www.kouvola.fi/palvelut/kulttuuri

Kouvolan taidemuseo – Kouvola Art Museum
Open: Tue-Fri 11am-6pm, Sat-Sun, 12-5pm
Address: Varuskuntakatu 11
            45100 Kouvola
Phone: (05) 829 6565
Fax: (05) 375 1605
E-mail: heli.kaukiainen@kouvola.fi
Internet: www.kouvola.fi/palvelut/kulttuuri

KUUSANKOSKI
Työväenasuntomuseo – Worker's Museum
Open: May-Sep: Wed-Fri 11am-5pm, Sat 11am-3pm
Address: Rinnetie
            Kettumäki

            45700 Kuusankoski
Phone: (05) 740 4306

VALKEALA
Verlan kalliomaalaukset – Verla Rock Paintings
Access: The rock paintings are close to the Verla Mill Museum
            on the Valkeala side, but visible from Jaala side.
Address: 47850 Verla

JAALA

Verlan tehdas – Verla Mill

Verlan tehdasmuseo – Verla Mill Museum
Open: Mid May-Aug: Tue-Sun 10am-6pm
Address: 47850 Verla
Phone: 020 415 2170
Fax: 020 415 2186
E-mail: helena.mauno@upm-kymmene.com
Internet: www.upm-kymmene.com/verla

MIEHIKKÄLÄ
Salpalinja-museo – Salpa Line Museum
Open: Jun-Aug: Daily 10am-6pm
Address: Taavetintie 215
            49700 Miehikkälä
Phone: (05) 74 901, 374 7383
Fax: (05) 749 0219
E-mail: miehikkala@miehikkala.fi
Internet: www.miehikkala.fi/smudex

VIROLAHTI
Virolahden graniittilouhokset – Virolahti Granite Quarry
Phone: (05) 758 111
Address: Pyterlahti
            49900 Virolahti
Fax: (05) 347 1867

Salpa Line Fortifications
Open: Jun-Aug: Daily 10am-8pm and by appointment.
Address: Yläpihlaja
            49960 Ala-Pihlaja
Phone: (05) 758 111

15 ETELÄ-KARJALA – SOUTH KARELIA

LAPPEENRANTA
Lappeenrannan linnoitus ja Ratsuväkimuseo –
Lappeenranta Fortress and Cavalry Museum
Open: Jun-Aug: Mon-Fri 10am-6pm, Sat-Sun 11am-5pm,
            Sep-May: by appointment
Address: Fortress, Kristiinankatu 2
            53500 Lappeenranta
Phone: (05) 616 2257
Fax: (05) 616 2911
E-mail: soile.rinno@lappeenranta.fi
Internet: www.lappeenranta.fi/museot

Etelä-Karjalan Museo – South Karelian Museum
Open: Jun-Aug: Mon-Fri 10am-6pm, Sat-Sun 11am-5pm,
            Sep-May: Tue-Sun 11am-5pm
Address: Fortress, Kristiinankatu 15
            53900 Lappeenranta
Phone: (05) 616 2255, 616 2261
Fax: (05) 616 2911
E-mail: museot@lappeenranta.fi
Internet: www.lappeenranta.fi/museot

Etelä-Karjalan taidemuseo – South Karelian Art Museum
Open: Jun-Aug: Mon-Fri 10am-6pm, Sat-Sun 11am-5pm,
            Sep-May: Tue-Sun 11am-5pm
Address: Fortress, Kristiinankatu 8-10
            53900 Lappeenranta
Phone: (05) 616 2256
Fax: (05) 616 2253
E-mail: museot@lappeenranta.fi
Internet: www.lappeenranta.fi/museot

Wolkoffin talomuseo – Wolkoff House Museum
Open: Jun-Aug: Mon-Fri 10am-5pm, Sat-Sun 11am-5pm,
            Sep-May: Fri-Sat 11am-5pm
Address: Kauppakatu 26
            53100 Lappeenranta
Phone: (05) 616 2258
Fax: (05) 616 2911
E-mail: museot@lappeenranta.fi
Internet: www.lappeenranta.fi/museot
            Guided tours only.

Lappeenrannan ortodoksinen kirkko – Lappeenranta Orthodox Church
Open: Jun-mid Aug: Tue-Sun 10am-6pm
            and by appointment for groups.
Address: Kristiinankatu 3
            53900 Lappeenranta
Phone: (05) 4515 511, 0400 933 287

Lappeen kirkko – Lappee Church
Open: Jun-Aug: Daily 10am-8pm
Address: Kirkkokatu
            53100 Lappeenranta
Phone: (05) 612 6350
Fax: (05) 612 6236

Saimaan Kanavamuseo – Saimaa Canal Museum
Open: Mid Jun-mid Aug: Daily 12-6pm
Address: Sulkuvartijankatu 16
            53300 Lappeenranta
Phone: 020 448 3115
Fax: 020 448 3110
E-mail: paivi.vattulainen@fma.fi
Internet: www.fma.fi/saimaacanal/kanavamuseo

Lemin kirkko – Lemi Church
Open: By appointment.
Address: 54710 Lemi
Phone: (05) 414 6012
Fax: (06) 414 6372

SUOMENNIEMI
Lyytikkälän talo – Lyytikkälä Farmstead
Open: Jun-Aug 15: 12-6pm
Address: Pajulahdentie 17
            52830 Suomenniemi
Phone: (015) 417 157
Fax: (015) 735 7740

IMATRA
Imatran taidemuseo – Imatra Art Museum
Open: Jun-Aug: Tue-Fri 12-7pm,
            Sep-May: Tue-Fri 11am-7pm, Sat 11am-3pm
Address: Virastokatu 1
            55100 Imatra
Phone: (05) 681 6702
Fax: (05) 681 6628
Internet: www.imatra.fi/palvelut/kulttuuri/museot/taidemuseo

Valtionhotelli
Address: Torkkelinkatu 2
            55100 Imatra
Phone: (05) 688 8850
Fax: (05) 688 8888
E-mail: imatra@scandic-hotels.com
Internet: www.scandic-hotels.com

Vuoksenniskan kirkko –Vuoksenniska Church
Open: Jun-Aug: Daily 9am-8pm, Sep-May: Daily 10am-3pm
Address: Ruokolahdentie 27
            55800 Imatra
Phone: (05) 682 7211, 473 1610, 473 1236
Fax: (05) 682 7700
Internet: www.seurakunta.org/imatra

16 POHJOIS-KARJALA – NORTH KARELIA

JOENSUU
Utran kirkko – Utra Church
Open: Jun-early Aug: Daily 11am-6pm
Address: Väisälänkatu 2
            80170 Joensuu
Phone: (013) 896 808
Internet: www.evl.fi/srk/joensuu

Pohjois-Karjalan museo – North Carelian Museum
Open: Mon-Fri 9am-5pm, Sat-Sun 11am-4pm
Address: Carelicum
            Koskikatu 5
            80100 Joensuu
Phone: (013) 267 5222
Fax: (013) 267 5320
E-mail: auli.patjas@jns.fi
Internet: www.pohjoiskarjalanmuseo.fi

Joensuun taidemuseo – Joensuu Art Museum
Open: Tue-Sun 11am-6pm, Wed 11am-8pm
Address: Kirkkokatu 23
            80100 Joensuu
Phone: (013) 267 5388
Fax: (013) 267 5390
E-mail: annika.waenerberg@jns.fi
Internet: www.jns.fi/taidemuseo

KONTIOLAHTI
Jakokosken museokanava – Jakokoski Museum Canal
Open: Mid Jun-mid Aug: Daily 12-7pm
Address: Kesäteatterintie 17
            81220 Jakokoski
Phone: 020 448 3914
Fax: 020 448 3110
E-mail: paivi.vattulainen@fma.fi
Internet: www.fma.fi/saimaacanal/kanavamuseo

OUTOKUMPU
Outokummun kaivosmuseo – Outokumpu Mining Museum
Open: Jun-mid Aug: Daily 10am-6pm, Mid Aug-May: Sun
            and Wed 12-4pm and by appointment.
Address: Kaivosmiehenpolku 1
            83500 Outokumpu
Phone: (013) 555 356, 050 346 1193
Fax: (013) 555 294
E-mail: kaivosmuseo@co.inet.fi
Internet: www.personal.inet.fi7koti7kaivosmuseo

ILOMANTSI
Ilomantsin luterilainen kirkko – Ilomantsi Lutheran Church
Open: Late Jun-mid Aug: Daily 11am-6pm, Jul until 8pm

and by appointment.

Address: Henrikintie 1
82900 Ilomantsi
Phone: (013) 881 455
Fax. (013) 881 547
E-mail: ilomantsi.seurakunta@evl.fi
Internet: www.evl.fi/kirkko/srk

Ilomantsin ortodoksinen kirkko – Ilomantsi Orthodox Church
Open: Mid Jun-mid Aug: Mon-Sat 11am-6pm, Sun 11:30am-6pm. Also during the services.
Address: 82900 Ilomantsi
Phone: (013) 881 084, 881 707
Fax: (013) 883 270

Hattuvaaran ortodoksinen rukoushuone – Hattuvaara Orthodox Prayer House
Open: Late Jun-Jul: Tue-Sun 12-6pm and by appointment.
Address: 82967 Hattu
Phone: (013) 881 084, 881 707
Fax: (013) 883 270

Möhkön ruukkimuseo – Möhkö Ironworks Museum
Open: Jun-mid Aug: Sun-Fri 10am-6pm, Sat 10am-4pm and by appointment.
Address: Möhköntie 209
82980 Möhkö
Phone: (013) 844 111
Fax: (013) 883 270
Internet: www.pogosta.com/mohkonruukki

TUUPOVAARA
Koskenniskan mylly- ja kievarimuseo – Koskenniska Mill and Inn Museum
Open: Late Jun-early Aug: Sun-Fri 12-6pm, Sat 12-4pm and by appointment.
Address: Koskenniskantie 14
82750 Öllölä
Phone: (013) 685 2243
Fax: (013) 685 2240

Pörtsämön erämaakalmisto – Portsämo Wilderness Cemetery
Address: Öllölä
Phone: (013) 685 2265
Fax: (013) 685 2270

LIEKSA
Luontokeskus Ukko – Heritage Centre Ukko
Open: Mid Jun-mid Aug: Daily 9am-7 pm,
Mid Aug-mid Jun: Daily 10am-5pm
Address: Ylä-Kolintie 39
83960 Koli
Phone: (013) 688 8400
Fax: (013) 688 8401
E-mail: ukko@koli.inet.fi
Internet: www.metla.fi

Pielisjärven kirkko – Pielisjärvi Church
Open: Jun-Aug 15: Daily 11am-6pm and by appointment.
Address: Kirkkokatu 1
81700 Lieksa
Phone: (013) 417 7410
Fax: (013) 417 7440
Internet: www.evl.fi/srk/lieksa

Pielisen museo – Pielinen Museum
Open: May 15-Sep 15: Daily 10am-6pm,

Sep 16-May 14: Tue-Fri 10am-3pm and by appointment.
Address: Pappilantie 2
81720 Lieksa
Phone: (013) 689 4151
Fax: (013) 689 4916
E-mail: museo@lieksa.fi
Internet: www.lieksa.fi/lieksa/matkailu/museo

Kuvanveistäjä Eva Ryynäsen studio ja Paaterin kirkko – Sculptor Eva Ryynänen's Studio and Paateri Church
Open: Mid May-mid Sep: Daily 10am-6pm
Address: Paateri, Vuonisjärvi
Phone: (013) 520 2400, 543 223
Fax: (013) 526 438
E-mail: maitkailu@lieksa.fi
Internet: www.lieksa.fi/matkailu

JUUKA
Myllymuseo – Juuka Mill Museum
Open: Jun-mid Aug: Tue-Sun 11am-5pm
Address: Huttulantie
83900 Juuka
Phone: (013) 470 773
Fax: (013) 472 015
E-mail: matkailu@juuka.fi
Internet: www.juuka.fi/juuka

NURMES
Ikolan museo – Ikola Museum
Open: Jun-Aug: Tue-Fri and Sun 12pm-6pm, Sat 10am-3pm
Address: Kotiniementie 2
75530 Nurmes
Phone: (013) 689 5152
Fax: (013) 689 5902
E-mail: rauni.laukkanen@nurmes.fi
Internet: www.nurmes.fi/kulttuuri/museo/msivut/museo

VALTIMO
Murtovaaran talomuseo – Murtovaara House Museum
Open: Jun 1-mid Aug: Wed-Sun 11am-7pm and by appointment.
Address: Murtovaarantie 260 A
75700 Puukari
Phone: (013) 450 989

17 ETELÄ-POHJANMAA – SOUTH OSTROBOTHNIA

SEINÄJOKI
Lakeuden ristin kirkko – Cross of the Plain Church
Open: Late May-Aug: Daily 10am-8pm
Address: Koulukatu 24
60100 Seinäjoki
Phone: (06) 418 4111
Fax. (06) 418 4300
E-mail: seinajoen-kaupunki@seinajoki.fi
Internet: www.alvaraalto.fi, www.seurakunta.seinajoki.fi

Kaupungintalo – Town Hall
Open: Mon-Fri 9am-3pm
Address: Kirkkokatu 6
60100 Seinäjoki
Phone: (06) 416 2111
Fax: (06) 416 2506
E-mail: seinajoen-kaupunki@seinajoki.fi
Internet: www.alvaraalto.fi

Kirjasto – City Library
Open: Mon-Fri 10am-7pm, Sat 11am-3pm

Address: Kaulukatu 21
             60100 Seinäjoki
Phone: (06) 416 2318
Fax: (06) 416 2315
E-mail: kirjasto.seinajoen-kaupunki@seinajoki.fi
Internet: www.alvaraalto.fi

Kaupunginteatteri – City Theater
Open: By appointment.
Address: Alvar Aallon katu 12
Phone: (06) 416 2600
Fax: (06) 414 1333
E-mail: seinajoen.teatteri@seinajoki.fi
Internet: www.alvaraalto.fi

Etelä-Pohjanmaan maakuntamuseo – Provincial Museum of South Ostrobothnia
Open: Wed 12-6pm, Thu-Fri 12-4pm, Sun 12-4pm
             and by appointment.
Address: Törnäväntie 23
             60200 Seinäjoki
Phone: (06) 416 2642, 0500 669 249
Fax: (06) 416 2646
E-mail: e-pohj.maakuntamuseo@seinajoki.fi
Internet: www.sjk.fi/english/sights

Suojeluskunta-talo ja Lotta Svärd -museo – Civil Guard House and Lotta Svärd Museum
Open: Wed 12-6pm, Thu-Fri 12-4pm, Sun 12-4pm
             and by appointment.
Address: Kauppakatu 17
             60100 Seinäjoki
Phone: (06) 416 2734
Fax: (06) 416 2646
E-mail: e-pohj.maakuntamuseo@sjk.fi
Internet: www.sjk.fi/english/sights

ILMAJOKI
Yli-Lauroselan talomuseo – Yli-Laurosela Farmhouse Museum
Open: May-Aug: Daily 11am-5pm,
             Sep-Apr: Sat-Sun 10am-4pm
Address: Könnintie 2
             60800 Ilmajoki
Phone: (06) 424 6719, (09) 4050 9576
Fax: (06) 424 6739
E-mail: mikael.agren@pp.inet.fi, lea.vartinen@nba.fi
Internet: www.nba.fi/museums/lauro

Ilmajoen museo – Ilmajoki Museum
Open: Jun-Aug: Daily 11am-5pm and by appointment.
Address: Ilkantie 16
             60800 Ilmajoki
Phone: (06) 424 8474
Internet: www.ilmajoki.fi

JALASJÄRVI
Jalasjärven museo – Jalasjärvi Museum
Open: Jun-mid Aug: Mon-Fri 10am-4pm, Sat-Sun 12-4pm
             and by appointment.
Address: 61600 Jalasjärvi
Phone: (06) 456 0332

KAUHAJOKI
Hämes-Havusen talo – Hämes-Havunen Farmstead
Open: Jun-Aug: Sun 12-4pm
Address: Koskenkyläntie 312
             61800 Kauhajoki
Phone: (06) 233 4204, 040 755 9305

Internet: www.kauhajoki.fi/hames-havunen

ISOKYRÖ
Isonkyrön kirkko – Isokyrö Medieval Church
Open: Late May: Mon-Fri 9am-4pm Jun-mid, Aug: Mon-Fri
             11am-6pm, Sat 12-4pm, Sun 12-6pm
Address: Museotie
             61500 Isokyrö
Phone: (06) 471 5800
Fax: (06) 471 5820
Internet: www.evl.fi/srk/isokyro

VÄHÄKYRÖ
Vähäkyrön kirkko – Vähäkyrö Church
Open: By appointment.
Address: 66500 Vähäkyrö
Phone: (06) 478 4021
Internet: www.vahakyrosrk.fi

LAPUA
Lapuan tuomiokirkko – Lapua Cathedral
Open: Early Jun-mid Aug: Mon-Fri 10am-6pm
Address: Kosolankatu 3
             62100 Lapua
Phone: (06) 438 5230
Fax: (06) 438 5270
Internet: www.evl.fi/srk/lapuantuomiokirkko

Vanha Paukku -kulttuurikeskus – Vanha Paukku Cultural Center
Open: Mon 11am-8pm, Tue-Fri 11am-7pm, Sat 11am-3pm,
             Sun 12-6pm
Address: Kustaa Tiituntie 1
             62100 Lapua
Phone: (06) 438 4580, 050 592 5385
Fax: (06) 438 4588
E-mail: esa.sivonen@city.lapua.fi
Internet: www.lapua.fi

KAUHAVA
Iisakki Järvenpään puukkotehdas, museo – Puukko Factory Iisakki Järvenpää, the museum
Open: By appointment
Address: Passinraitti 32
             62200 Kauhava
Phone: (06) 434 0135, 0400 931 548
Fax: (06) 434 0919
Internet: www.kolumbus.fi/iisakki.jarvenpaa, www.kauhava.fi

YLIHÄRMÄ
Ylihärmän kirkko – Ylihärmä Church
Open: By appointment.
Address: 62375 Ylihärmä
Phone: (06) 484 6023

KUORTANE
Kuortaneen kirkko – Kuortane Church
Open: Daily 9am-4pm
Address: Kirkkotie
             63100 Kuortane
Phone: (06) 525 4116
Fax: (06) 525 3006

LEHTIMÄKI
Lehtimäen kirkko – Lehtimäki Church
Open: By appointment.
Address: 63510 Lehtimäki
Phone: (06) 527 1107
Fax: (06) 527 1187

ÄHTÄRI

Pirkanpohjan Taidekeskus – Pirkanpohja Art Centre
Open: May-Aug: Daily 10am-6pm, Sep-Apr:
Fri-Sun 12-5pm and by appointment.
Address: Ähtärintie 36
63700 Ähtäri
Phone: (06) 531 8321, 533 0314
Internet: www.pirkanpohja.fi

ALAJÄRVI

Suojeluskuntatalo – Civil Guard Building
Open: Mon-Fri 8am-4pm
Address: 62900 Alajärvi
Phone: (06) 5577 7255
Fax: (06) 5577 7299

Alajärven hallintokeskus – Alajärvi Municipal Center
Open: Mon-Fri 8am-4pm
Address: Alvar Aallon tie 1
62900 Alajärvi
Phone: (06) 5577 7255
Fax: (06) 5577 7299

Nelimarkka-museo – Nelimarkka Museum
Open: Sun-Fri 12 -6pm, Sat 12-4pm
Address: Pekkolantie 123
62900 Alajärvi
Phone: (016) 557 2129
Fax: (016) 557 3889
E-mail: mial@japo.fi
Internet: www.nelimarkka-museo.fi

VIMPELI

Vimpelin kirkko – Vimpeli Church
Open: Mid Jun-late Aug: Daily 10am-6pm
Address: Patruunanatie 28
62800 Vimpeli
Phone: (06) 569 0000
Fax: (06) 569 0029
Internet: www.personal.inet.fi/yritys/vsrk

Vimpelin Suksitehdasmuseo – Ski Museum
Open: Jun-Aug: Tue-Sun 1pm-6pm and by appointment.
Address: Kangastie 7
62800 Vimpeli
Phone: (06) 565 1231, 565 9200
Fax: (06) 565 1732
E-mail: vimpelin.kunta@vimpeli.fi

Suomen pesäpallomuseo – Museum of Finnish Baseball
Open: Jun-Aug: Tue-Sat 12-6pm, Sun 11am-6pm
and by appointment.
Address: Kangastie 7
62800 Vimpeli
Phone: (06) 565 1231, 565 9200
Fax: (06) 565 1732
E-mail: vimpelin.kunta@vimpeli.fi

KORTESJÄRVI

Suomen Jääkärimuseo – The Jäger Museum of Finland
Open: Mid Jun-mid Aug: Daily 11am-6pm, Mid Aug-mid
Jun: Mon-Fri 8am-3:30pm, Sun 11am-6pm
Address: Jääkärintie 80
62420 Kortesjärvi
Phone: (06) 483 2228
Fax: (06) 483 2209
E-mail: tellervo.suoranta@kortesjarvi.japo.fi
Internet: www.kortesjarvi.japo.fi

KAUSTINEN

Kansantaidekeskus – Museum of Traditional Folk Instruments
Open: Mon-Fri 9am-6pm, Sat-Sun 12-6pm
Address: Folk Art Center
Jyväskyläntie 3
69600 Kaustinen
Phone: (06) 860 4111
Fax: (06) 860 4222
E-mail: folk.art@kaustinen.inet.fi
Internet: www.kaustinen.fi/ktk/museo

ULLAVA

Vionoja-galleria – Vionoja Gallery
Open: Jun-Aug: Tue-Fri 12-7pm, Sat-Sun 12-6pm
and by appointment.
Address: Haapala
68380 Yli-Ullava
Phone: (06) 889 193, 889 730

18 POHJANMAA– OSTROBOTHNIA

VAASA – VASA

Mustasaaren kirkko – Mustasaari Church
Open: May-Aug: Daily 9am-4pm
Address: 65610 Mustasaari
Phone: (06) 326 1209
Fax: (06) 326 1299
Internet: www.vaasaevl.fi

Vanhan Vaasan museo – The Wasastjerna House
Open: Mid Jun-mid Aug: Daily 11am-5pm
Address: Kauppiaankatu 10
65380 Vaasa
Phone: (06) 356 3800
Fax: (06) 325 3784
E-mail: pohjanmaan.museo@vaasa.fi
Internet: www.vaasa.fi/pohjanmaanmuseo

Pohjanmaan museo – Ostrobothnian Museum
Open: Daily 10am-5pm, Wed until 8pm
Address: Museokatu 3
65100 Vaasa
Phone: (06) 325 3800
Fax: (06) 325 3784
E-mail: pohjanmaan.museo@vaasa.fi
Internet: www.vaasa.fi/pohjanmaanmuseo

Tikanojan taidekoti – The Tikanoja Art Museum
Open: Tue-Sat 11am-4pm, Wed until 8pm, Sun 12-5pm
Address: Hovioikeudenpuistikko 4
65100 Vaasa
Phone: (06) 325 3916
Fax: (06) 325 3918
E-mail: tikanojan.taidekoti@vaasa.fi
Internet: www.vaasa.fi/cult/tikanoja

Nandor Mikola Museo – Nandor Mikola Museum
Open: Jun-Aug: Tue-Sun 12-4pm,
Sep-May: Wed 2pm-6pm, Sat-Sun 12-4pm
By appointment for groups.
Address: Sisäsatama
65100 Vaasa
Phone: (06) 317 2745, 0400 337 733
Fax: (06) 317 2725
E-mail: info@mikolamuseo.com
Internet: www.mikolamuseo.com

Bragen ulkomuseo – The Brage Open-Air Museum
Open: Jun-Aug: Tue-Fri 1pm-6pm, Sat-Sun 12-2pm
           and by appointment.
Address: Hietalahden puisto
           65100 Vaasa
Phone: (06) 312 7166
Internet: www.museum.svof.fi/eng/brage

MUSTASAARI – KORSHOLM
Stundarsin käsityöläiskylä – Stundars Handicrafts Village
Open: May 20-Aug 15: Daily 12-6pm and by appointment.
Address: Stundarsvägen 5
           65450 Solf
Phone: (06) 344 2200
Fax: (06) 344 2201
E-mail: stundars@agrolink.fi
Internet: www.korsholm.fi

Sulvan kirkko – Sulva Church
Open: By appointment.
Address: 65450 Sulva
Phone: (06) 344 0026
Fax: (06) 344 0296

KORSNÄS
**Korsnäsin pappilamuseo – The Korsnäs
Parsonage Museum**
Open: Jun-Aug: Tue-Sun 1pm-5pm
Address: 66290 Harrström
Phone: (06) 364 5242
Internet: www.museum.svof.fi/eng/prast

Korsnäsin kotiseutumuseo – Korsnäs Local History Museum
Open: Late Jun-mid Aug: Tue-Sun 1pm-5pm
           and by appointment.
Address: Kyrkovägen 32
           66200 Korsnäs
Phone: (06) 364 1339
Fax: (06) 347 9140
Internet: www.museum.svof.fi/eng/hemkors

NÄRPIÖ – NÄRPES
**Närpiön kirkko ja kirkkotallit – Närpiö Church and
Church Stables**
Open: By appointment.
Address: 64200 Närpes
Phone: (06) 220 4200
Fax: (06) 220 4235

KRISTIINANKAUPUNKI – KRISTINESTAD
Ulrika Eleonoran kirkko – Ulrika Eleonora Church
Open: By appointment.
Address: 64100 Kristiinankaupunki
Phone: (06) 221 1073
Fax: (06) 221 2801

Lebellin kauppiaantalo – Lebell Merchant House
Open: Mid May-mid Aug: Tue-Sun 12-4pm
Address: Rantakatu 51-53
           64100 Kristiinankaupunki
Phone: (06) 221 2159, 040 508 525
Fax: (06) 221 6241
Internet: www.museum.svof.fi/eng/lebell

Kristiinankaupungin merimuseo – The Maritime Museum
Open: Jun-mid Aug: Tue-Sun 12-4pm
Address: 64100 Kristiinankaupunki
Phone: (06) 221 2859
Fax: (06) 331 6241

Internet: www.museum.svof.fi/eng/sjofart

Kiilin kotiseutumuseo – Kiili Local History Museum
Open: Jun-Mid Aug
Address: Kiilintie 90
           64490 Siipyy
Phone: (06) 222 5611
Fax: (06) 222 5615
E-mail: kilen@kiili.inet.fi
Internet: www.museum.svof.fi/eng/kilen

VÖYRI – VÖRÅ
Vöyrin kirkko – Vöyri Church
Open: By appointment.
Address: 66600 Vöyri
Phone: (06) 383 2004
Fax: (06) 383 2003

Myrbergsgården – Myrbergsgården Local History Museum
Open: Jul-Aug: Sun 1pm-5pm
Address: Bertby-Lålaxvägen 18
           66600 Vörå
Phone: (06) 383 0033
Internet: www.museum.svof.fi/eng/myrberg

MAKSAMAA – MAXMO
Klemetsintalot – Klemetsgårdarna Museum
Open: Jun-Aug: Daily 10am-9pm
Address: Kärklaxintie 308
           66640 Maksamaa
Phone: (06) 345 0122, 0500 363 681
Fax: (06) 345 0279
E-mail: maxmo@multi.fi
Internet: www.museum.svof.fi/eng/brage

ORAVAINEN – ORAVAIS
Vänrikki Stoolin keskus – Fänrik Stål Center
Open: Jun-Aug: Tue-Sun 12-6pm and by appointment.
Address: Slagfältsvägen 139
           66800 Oravainen
Phone: (06) 385 0714, 050 585 9555
E-mail: (06) 385 0810
Internet: www.oravais.fi/ohif

Kimon ruukki – Kimo Ironworks
Open: Jun-Aug: Tue-Sun 12-6pm
Address: Bruksgatan 34 and 268
           66810 Kimo
Phone: (06) 384 0369, 384 0355
Fax: (06) 384 0298
E-mail: gunvor.haggman@multi.fi
Internet: www.oravais.fi/kimobruk

Oravaisten kirkko – Oravainen Church
Open: Jun-late Aug: Daily 11am-6pm
Address: Kimontie 19
           66800 Oravainen
Phone: (06) 385 0011
Fax: (06) 385 0912
Internet: www.evl.fi/srk/oravais

UUSIKAARLEPYY – NYKARLEBY
Uudenkaarlepyyn kirkko – Uusikaarlepyy Church
Open: Jun-Aug: Daily 10am-6pm
Address: 66900 Uusikaarlepyy
Phone: (06) 722 0006
Fax: (06) 781 0021

Kuddnäs
Open: Jun-Jul: Daily 10am-5pm Aug: Daily 12-5pm,
           May: Daily 10am-4pm Sep: Sun 12-4pm
           and by appointment.
Address: Pietarsaarentie 22
           66900 Uusikaarlepyy
Phone: (06) 785 6111, 785 6482
Fax: (06) 785 6499
E-mail: kuddnas@nykarleby.fi
Internet: www.nykarleby.fi/eng/hemeng

LUOTO – LARSMO
Luodon kirkko – Luoto Church
Open: Jun-late Aug: Daily 10am-6pm
Address: 68570 Luoto
Phone: (06) 728 1555
Fax: (06) 728 1555

KRUUNUPYY – KRONOBY
Torgaren pappila – Torgare Parsonage
Open: Jun 15-Aug 15: Daily 12-6pm
Address: Torgarentie 22
           68500 Kruunupyy
Phone: (06) 834 3000
Internet: www.museum.svof.fi/eng/torgare
           www.kronoby.fi

PIETARSAARI – JAKOBSTAD
Pietarsaaren kirkko – Pietarsaari Church
Open: Jun-Jul: Mon-Fri 9am-4pm, Sun 9am-12
Address: Kirkkokatu 3
           68600 Pietarsaari
Phone: (06) 723 6517, 050 554 5737
Fax: (06) 785 8199
Internet: www.pedesoreprosteri.fi

Jakobstads Wapen
Open: Mid Jun-mid Aug: Mon-Fri 9 am-5pm
Address: Vanhan satamantie
           68600 Pietarsaari
Phone: (06) 723 7233
Fax: (06) 723 7233
E-mail: gamla.hamn@multi.fi
Internet: www.multi.fi/wapen

Pietarsaaren kaupunginmuseo – Pietarsaari Town Museum
Malmin talo – Malm House
Open: Daily 12-4pm
Address: Isokatu 2
           68600 Pietarsaari
Phone: (06) 785 1111
Fax: (06) 785 1440
E-mail: jakobstads.museum@jakobstad.fi
Internet: www.jakobstad.fi

Arktinen museo Nanoq – The Arctic Museum Nanoq
Open: Jun-Aug: Daily 12-6pm, Sep-May: Mon-Fri 11am-
           5pm and by appointment.
Address: Fäboda
           68600 Pietarsaari
Phone: (06) 729 3679
Fax: (06) 729 3679
Internet: www.museum.svof.fi/eng/nanoq

Pedersören kirkko – Pedersöre Church
Open: Mid Jun-mid Aug: 10am-6pm
Address: Vaasantie 118
           68600 Pietarsaari

Phone: (06) 785 8126
Fax: (06) 785 8198

KOKKOLA – KARLEBY
K. H. Renlundin museo – K. H. Renlund Museum
Taidemuseo – The Art Museum
Open: Jun-Aug: Tue-Sun 12-5pm Sep-May: Tue-Fri 12-3pm,
           Thu also 6pm-8pm, Sat-Sun 12-5pm
Address: Pitkänsillankatu 39
           67100 Kokkola
Phone: (06) 828 9475
Fax: (06) 828 9575
E-mail: paula.hyttinen@kokkola.kpnet.fi
Internet: www.museo.kokkola.fi

Historiallinen museo – The Historical Museum
Open: Jun-Aug: Tue-Sun 12-5pm,
           Sep-May: Tue-Fri 12-3pm, Thu also 6pm-8pm, Sat-
           Sun 12-5pm
Address: Pitkänsillankatu 28
           67100 Kokkola
Phone: (06) 828 9574
Fax: (06) 828 9389
E-mail: paul.stenman@kokkola.kpnet.fi
Internet: www.museo.kokkola.fi

Kaarlelan kirkko – Kaarlela Church
Open: Mid Jun-late Aug: Daily 10am-6pm
Address: Kruunupyyntie 1
           67700 Kokkola
Phone: (06) 829 6111
Fax: (06) 829 6200
Internet: www.kokkola.fi/seurakuntayhtyma

LOHTAJA
Lohtajan kirkko – Lohtaja Church
Open: Mid Jun-late Aug: Daily 11am-3pm
Address: Kirkkotie 2 B
           68230 Lohtaja
Phone: (06) 877 085
Fax: (06) 877 085

19 POHJOIS-POHJANMAA – NORTH OSTROBOTHNIA

OULU – ULEÅBORG
Oulun tuomiokirkko – Oulu Cathedral
Open: Jul: Daily 11am-9pm Jun and Aug: Daily 11am-8pm
           and by appointment.
Address: Kirkkokatu
           90100 Oulu
Phone: (08) 311 2516
Fax: (08) 311 6353
Internet: www.oulunseurakunnat.fi

Puolivälinkankaan kirkko – Puolivälinkangas Church
Open: By appointment.
Address: Mielikintie 3
           90550 Oulu
Phone: (08) 347 551, 531 4600
Fax: (08) 531 4620

Pohjois-Pohjanmaan museo – Museum of North Ostrobothnia
Open: Mid May-Aug: Tue-Sun 11am-6pm, Wed until
           8pm,Sat-Sun 11am 6pm Sep-Mid May: Tue-Fri
           10am-6pm,, Wed until 7pm
Address: Ainola
           90100 Oulu
Phone: (08) 5584 7150

```
            (08) 5584 7199
E-mail      ppm@ouka.fi
Internet:   www.ouka.fi
```

Oulun taidemuseo – Museum of North Ostrobothnian
```
Open:       Mid May-Aug: Tue-Fri 10am-6pm, Wed until 7:30pm,
            Sat- Sun 11am-6pm Sep-mid May: Tue-Fri 10am-
            6pm, Wed until 7pm, Sat-Sun 11am-6pm
Address:    Ainola
            90100 Oulu
Phone:      (08) 5584 7150
Fax:        (08) 5584 7199
E-mail:     ppm@ouka.fi
Internet:   www.ouka.fi/ppm
```

Oulun taidemuseo – Oulu City Art Museum
```
Open:       Tue-Sun 11am-6pm, Wed until 8pm
Address:    Kasarmintie 7
            90100 Oulu
Phone:      (08) 5584 7463
Fax:        (08) 5584 7499
E-mail:     keskus.taidemuseo@ouka.fi
Internet:   www.ouka.fi/taidemuseo
```

Turkansaaren ulkomuseo – Turkansaari Open-Air Museum
```
Open:       Late May-Aug: Daily 10am-8pm,
            Sep 1-15: Daily 11am-5pm
Address:    Turkansaarentie 165
            90310 Oulu
Phone:      (08) 5584 7154
Fax:        (08) 5586 7190
E-mail:     anneli.syrjanen@ouka.fi
Internet:   www.ouka.fi/ppm/turkansaari
```

KEMPELE
Kempeleen vanha kirkko – Kempele Old Church
```
Open:       Mid Jun-mid Aug: Mon-Fri 10am-6pm, Sat-Sun 12-6pm
Address:    90440 Kempele
Phone:      (08) 561 4500
Fax:        (08) 561 4555
```

LIMINKA
Limingan luontokeskus – Liminka Nature Center
```
Open:       Daily
Address:    Rantakurvi 6
            91900 Liminka
Phone:      (08) 562 0000, 0400 727 955
Fax:        (08) 562 0050
E-mail:     luontokeskus@merikoski.fi
Internet:   www.liminka.fi
```

Vilho Lampi -museo –Vilho Lampi Museum
```
Open:       Jun-Jul: Tue-Sun 12-6pm
Address:    Rantatie
            91900 Liminka
Phone:      (08) 381 578
Fax:        (08) 520 3612
E-mail:     raija.palsa@liminka.fi
Internet:   www.liminka.fi
```

Aabraham Ojanperän museo – Abraham Ojanperä Museum
```
Open:       Jul-Aug: Tue-Sun 12-6pm and by appointment.
Address:    Rantatie
            91900 Liminka
Phone:      (08) 520 3611
Fax:        (08) 520 3612
E-mail:     raija.palsa@liminka.fi
Internet:   www.liminka.fi
```

RANTSILA
Rantsilan kirkko – Rantsila Church
```
Open:       By appointment
Address:    92500 Rantsila
Phone:      (08) 250 143
```

RAAHE – BRAHESTAD
Raahen museo – Raahe Museum
```
Open:       Jun-Aug: Mon-Fri 12-6pm, Sat-Sun 12-4pm
            Sep-May: Tue-Fri 1pm-5pm, Sat 12-4pm,
Address:    Rantakatu 33
            92100 Raahe
Phone:      (08) 299 2446, 299 2445
Fax:        (08) 299 2427
E-mail:     eturunen@raahe.fi
Internet:   www.raahe.fi/
```

Soveliuksen talo – Sovelius House
```
Open:       Jun-Aug: Mon-Fri 12-6pm, Sat-Sun 12-4pm
            Sep-May: by appointment
Address:    Rantakatu 36
            92100 Raahe
Phone:      (08) 299 2446, 299 2445
Fax:        (08) 299 2427
E-mail:     eturunen@raahe.fi
Internet:   www.raahe.fi/
```

PYHÄJOKI
Annalan kotiseutumuseo – Annala Local History Museum
```
Open:       Jul: Mon-Fri 12-6pm, Sat-Sun 10am-6pm,
            Jun and Aug: Mon-Fri 12-6pm and by appointment.
Address:    Annalantie 20
            86100 Pyhäjoki
Phone:      (08) 439 0246
Fax:        (08) 439 0266
Internet:   www.pyhajoki.raaseu.fi/kunta/nahtavyydet/annala
```

KALAJOKI
Maakallan kirkko – Maakalla Church
```
Open:       By appointment.
Address:    Maakalla
            85106 Kalajoki
Phone:      (08) 464 0530
Fax:        (08) 463 684
```

NIVALA
**Kyösti ja Kalervo Kallion museo – Kyösti and Kalervo
Kallio Museum**
```
Open:       Jun-Aug: Tue-Sat 12-7pm, Sun 11am-7pm
            and by appointment.
Address:    Ruojantie 11
            85500 Nivala
Phone:      (08) 440 814
Fax:        (08) 443 9220
E-mail:     hanna.jarviluoma@nivala-lehti.fi
Internet:   www.nivala-lehti.fi
```

HAUKIPUDAS
Haukiputaan kirkko – Haukipudas Church
```
Open:       Mid Jun-mid Aug: 11am-6pm
Address:    Kirkkotie
            90830 Haukipudas
Phone:      (08) 547 1185
Fax:        (08) 547 5203
```

KIIMINKI
Kiimingin kirkko – Kiiminki Church
```
Open:       By appointment
Address:    90900 Kiiminki
```

Phone: (08) 816 1003
Fax: (08) 816 1010

YLI-II
Kierikkikeskus – Kierikki Stone Age Centre
Open: Mid May-Sep: Tue-Fri 10am-6pm, Sat 10am-4pm,
           Sun 10am-6pm Oct-Mid May: Tue-Sat 10am-4pm,
           Sun 10am-6pm
Address: Pahkalantie 447
           91200 Yli-Ii
Phone: (08) 817 0491
Fax: (08) 817 0494
E-mail: kierikki@kierikki.fi
Internet: www.kierikki.fi

20 LÄNSI-POHJA

KEMI
Kemin kulttuurihistoriallinen museo – Kemi Museum
Open: Tue-Fri 11am-5pm, Sat-Sun 12-6pm
Address: Sauvonsaarenkatu 11
           94100 Kemi
Phone: (016) 259 366
Fax: (016) 258 248
E-mail: historiallinenmuseo@kemi.fi
Internet: www.kemi.fi

Kemin taidemuseo – Kemi Art Museum
Open: Tue-Fri 11am-6pm, Sat 12-7pm, Sun 12-4pm
Address: Marina Takalon katu 3
           94100 Kemi
Phone: (016) 258 247
Fax: (016) 258 243
E-mail: pekka.ronkko@kemi.fi
Internet: www.kemi.fi

KEMINMAA
Keminmaan vanha kirkko – Kemimaa Old Church
Open: Early Jun-mid Aug: Mon-Sat 10am-6pm,
           Sun 11am-8pm, Mid Aug-end of Aug: Mon-Fri
           10am-4pm, Sun 11am-4pm
Address: 94450 Keminmaa
Phone: (016) 226 0200
Fax: (016) 271 686
Internet: www.keminmaa.seurakunta.net

Valmarin museo – Valmari Museum
Open: Jun-Aug: Mon-Sat 10am-6pm, Sun 11am-6pm
Address: Jokisuuntie 79
           94450 Keminmaa
Phone: (016) 271 038
Internet: www.kemi.fi/kulttuuri

TERVOLA
Tervolan vanha kirkko – Tervola Old Church
Open: Mid Jun-late Aug: Daily 10am-4pm
Address: 95300 Tervola
Phone: (016) 215 4500
Fax: (016) 435 134

TORNIO
Tornion vanha kirkko – Tornio Old Church
Open: Mid Jun-early Aug: Mon-Fri 9am-7pm, Sun
           11:30am-5pm, Late May-mid Jun and early Aug-mid
           Aug: Mon-Fri 9am-5pm and by appointment.
Address: Kirkkokatu
           95400 Tornio
Phone: (016) 430 632
Fax: (016) 482 231

Alatornion kirkko – Alatornio Church
Open: Jun-mid Aug: Mon-Fri 9am-3pm
           and by appointment.
Address: 95420 Tornio
Phone: (016) 441 493
Aineen taidemuseo – The Aine Art Museum
Open: Tue -Thu 11am-6pm, Fri-Sun 11am-3pm
Address: Torikatu 2
           95400 Tornio
Phone: (016) 432 438
Fax: (016) 432 437
E-mail: aine.taidemuseo@tornio.fi
Internet: www.tornio.fi/aine

**Tornionlaakson maakuntamuseo – Tornionlaakso Provincial
Museum**
Open: Tue-Fri 12-5pm, Sun 12-3pm
Address: Keskikatu 22
           95400 Tornio
Phone: (016) 432 452
Fax: (016) 432 453
E-mail: henri.nordberg@tornio.fi
Internet: www.tornio.fi/museo

YLITORNIO
Keisarinmaja – The Imperial Lodge
Open: Jun-early Aug 11am-5pm
Address: Aavasaksa
           95600 Ylitornio
Phone: (016) 578 314, winter 040 707 6794
E-mail: kruununpuisto@aavasaksa.inet.fi
Internet: www.aavasaksa.com

MUONIO
Muonion kotiseutumuseo – Muonio Local History Museum
Open: Jun-Aug: Tue-Sat 12-5pm
Address: Lahenrannantie
           99300 Muonio
Phone: (016) 534 311
Fax: (016) 534 320
E-mail: laila.nikunlassi@muonio.fi
Internet: www.muonio.fi

Kiela Naturium
Open: Mid Apr-Nov and early Jan-mid Feb: Mon-Fri 11am
           5pm, Sat-Sun by appointment for groups, Dec-early
           Jan and mid Feb-mid Apr: Daily 10am-8pm
Address: Kilpisjärventie 15
           99300 Muonio
Phone: (016) 532 280
Fax: (016) 532 284
E-mail: kiela@muonio.fi
Internet: www.kielanaturium.fi/eng, www.muonio.fi

21 KAINUU

KAJAANI
Kajaanin linnan rauniot – Kajaani Castle Ruins
Open: All year
Address: Kajaaninjoki, Linnansilta
Phone: (08) 615 5555
Fax: (08) 615 5664
E-mail: kajaani.info@kajaani.fi
Internet: www.kajaani.fi

**Ämmäkosken kanava "Lussitupa" – Ämmäkoski
Canal Museum**
Open: Jun 10-Aug 10: Tue-Sun 11am-5pm
Address: Ämmäkoski Rapids Shore

87100 Kajaani
Phone: (08) 615 5410, 0204 48 3515
Fax: 020 4483 3110
E-mail: paivi.vattulainen@fma.fi
Internet: www.fma.fi/ saimaacanal/kanavamuseo

Kajaanin kirkko – Kajaani Church
Open: Mid May-late Aug: Daily 10am-6pm
           and by appointment.
Address: Pohjolankatu
           87100 Kajaani
Phone: (08) 617 2200
Fax: (08) 617 2500
E-mail: kajaani.seurakunta@evl.fi
Internet: www.kajaaninseurakunta.fi

Kainuun museo – Kainuu Museum
Open: Mon-Fri 12-4pm, Wed until 8pm, Sun 12-5pm
           and by appointment for groups.
Address: Asemakatu 4
           87100 Kajaani
Phone: (08) 615 5407
Fax: (08) 615 5672
E-mail: antti.makinen@kajaani.fi
Internet: www.kajaani.fi/kainuunmuseo

Kajaanin taidemuseo – Kajaani Art Museum
Open: Mon-Fri 10am-4pm, Wed 10am-8pm, Sun 11am-5pm
Address: Linnankatu 14
           87100 Kajaani
Phone: (08) 615 5599
Fax: (08) 615 5581
E-mail: taidemuseo@kajaani.fi
Internet: www.kajaani.fi/taidemuseo

Paltaniemen kirkko – Paltaniemi Church
Open: Mid May-mid Aug: Daily 10am-6pm
           and by appointment.
Address: 88300 Paltamo
Phone: (08) 632 710
Fax: (08) 632 7117
E-mail: paltamo.khranvirasto@evl.fi
Internet: www.paltamonsrk.fi

KUHMO
Juminkeko – Juminkeko Cultural Center
Open: Jul: Daily 12-6pm, Aug-Jun: Sun-Thu 12-6pm
           and by appointment for groups.
Address: Kontionkatu 25
           88900 Kuhmo
Phone: (08) 653 0670
Fax: (08) 653 0673
E-mail: info@juminkeko.fi
Internet: www.juminkeko.fi

Kalevalakylä – Kalevala Village
Open: Early Jun-late Aug: Daily 10am-5pm,
           Jun 15-Aug 15: Guided tours,
           May and Sep: by appointment.
Address: Kalevalakylä, Hiitola
           88900 Kuhmo
Phone: (08) 652 0114, 0500 185 672
Fax: (08) 655 0246
E-mail: kalevala.kyla@kuhmonet.fi
Internet: www.kuhmonet.fi/kalevalakyla

Talvisotanäyttely – Winter War Museum
Open: Late Jun-mid Aug: Daily 9am-6pm, Mid May-late Jun
           and mid Aug-mid Sep: Daily 9am-4pm

and by appointment.
Address: Kalevalakylä, Hiitola
           88900 Kuhmo
Phone: (08) 655 6368
Fax: (08) 655 6368

HYRYNSALMI
Kaunislehdon talomuseo – Kaunislehto Farm Museum
Open: Jun-Aug: Wed-Sun 12-6pm
Address: Oravivaara
           89400 Hyrynsalmi
Phone: (08) 749 201, 749 455
Fax: (08) 742 086
Internet: www.hyrynsalmi.fi

SUOMUSSALMI
Jaloniemen Käsityötalo – Jaloniemi Handicratfs House
Open: Mid Jun-mid Aug: Mon-Fri 9am-7pm, Sat 9am-6pm,
           Sun 11am-7pm Mid Aug-mid Jun: Mon 9am-5pm,
           Sat 9am-4pm, Sun 11am-5pm
           and by appointment for groups.
Address: Jalonkaarre 3
           89600 Suomussalmi
Phone: (08) 7191 243
Fax: (08) 711 189
Internet: www.suomussalmi.fi

Raatteen portti – Raate Gate House Exhibition
Open: Jun-mid Sep: Daily 10am-6pm
           May and mid Sep-Oct: Fri-Sun 11am-5pm
           and by appointment.
Address: Raatteentie 2
           89800 Suomussalmi
Phone: (08) 721 450
Fax: (08) 711 189
E-mail: tourist.office@suomussalmi.fi
Internet: www.suomussalmi.fi/en/info/sights/talvisot/nayttel

Raatteen vartiomuseo – Raate Outpost Museum
Open: Jun-mid Aug: Mon-Fri 10am-8pm
           and by appointment.
Address: Raatteentie 185
           89800 Suomussalmi
Phone: (08) 719 1243
Fax: (08) 711 189
E-mail: tourist.office@suomussalmi.fi
Internet: www.suomussalmi.fi/en/info/sights/talvisot/nayttel

Värikallion kalliomaalaukset – Värikallio Rock Paintings
Phone: (08) 7191 243
Fax.   (08) 711 189
E-mail: tourist.office@suomussalmi.fi
Internet: www.suomussalmi.fi

VAALA
Lamminahon talo – Lamminaho Farm
Open: Jun-Mid Aug: Tue-Fri 12-6pm, Sat-Sun 12-4pm
           Mid Aug-end of Aug: Sat-Sun 12-4pm
           and by appointment.
Address: Lamminahontie 231
           91700 Vaala
Phone: (08) 536 3445, 536 0104
Fax: (08) 536 0181
E-mail: vaala@vaala.fi
Internet: www.vaala.fi

ROVANIEMI

Joulupukin Pajakylä, Napapiiri – Santa Claus Village, Arctic Circle
Open: Daily 10am-5pm
Address: 96930 Napapiiri – Arctic Circle
Phone: (016) 356 2096
Fax: (016) 356 2096
E-mail: marja.selin@napapiirin-infopalvelut.inet.fi
Internet: www.santaclausvillage.fi

Lapin Maakuntakirjasto – Regional Library of Lapland
Open: Jun-Aug: Mon-Thu 11am-7pm, Fri-Sat 11am-
            3pm, Sep-May: Mon-Thu 11am-8pm, Fri
            11am-5pm, Sat 11am-4pm
Address: Jorma Etontie 6
            96100 Rovaniemi
Phone: (016) 322 2463
Fax: (016) 322 3019
E-mail: rovaniemi@rovaniemi
Internet: www.rovaniemi.fi

Lappia-talo – Lappia Hall
Open: By appointment for groups.
Address: Jorma Etontie 8 A
            96100 Rovaniemi
Phone: (016) 322 2511
Fax: (016) 346 151
E-mail: rovaniemi@rovaniemi
Internet: www.rovaniemi.fi

Kaupungintalo – Town Hall
Open: By appointment for groups.
Address: Hallituskatu 7
            96100 Rovaniemi
Phone: (016) 322 2288
Fax: (016) 322 2992
E-mail: rovaniemi@rovaniemi.fi
Internet: www.rovaniemi.fi

Arktikum - Lapin maakuntamuseo ja Arktinen keskus – Arktikum - The Provincial Museum of Lapland and the Arctic Centre
Open: Jun 16-Aug 15: Daily 9am-7pm,
            Jun 1-Jun 15 and Aug 16-Aug 31: Daily 10am-6pm,
            Sep-Apr: Tue-Sun 10am-6pm,
            Late Nov-early Jan: also on Mon
Address: Pohjoisranta 4
            96200 Rovaniemi
Phone: (016) 322 2482
Fax: (016) 322 3091
E-mail: kimmo.kaakinen@rovaniemi.fi
Internet: www.rovaniemi.fi, www.arktikum.fi

Rovaniemen taidemuseo – Rovaniemi Art Museum
Open: Tue-Fri 10am-5pm, Sat-Sun 12-5pm
Address: Lapinkävijäntie 4
            96100 Rovaniemi
Phone: (016) 322 2820
Fax: (016) 322 3052
E-mail: hilkka.liikkanen@rovaniemi.fi
Internet: www.rovaniemi.fi/taide/taidemus

Rovaniemen kotiseutumuseo Pöykkölä – Rovaniemi Local History Museum Pöykkölä
Open: Jun-Aug: Tue-Sun 12-4pm
Address: Pöykköläntie 4
            96400 Rovaniemi
Phone: (016) 348 1095
Internet: www.rovaniemi.fi

SODANKYLÄ

Sodankylän vanha kirkko – Sodankylä Old Church
Open: Jun-mid Aug: Daily 9am-6pm,
            Mid Aug-late Aug: Fri-Sun 10am-6pm
Address: 99600 Sodankylä
Phone: (016) 611 018
Fax: (016) 611 057
E-mail: matkailu.neuvonta@sodankyla.fi
Internet: www.sodankyla.fi/english

Kultamuseo – Gold Prospector Museum
Open: Jun-Aug 15: Daily 9am-6pm,
            Aug 16-Sep: Daily 9am-5pm,
            Oct-May: Mon-Fri 10am-4pm and by appointment.
Address: Tankavaaran Kultakylä
            99695 Tankavaara
Phone: (016) 626 171
Fax: (016) 626 271
E-mail: tankavaara@saariselkä.fi
Internet: www.tankavaara.fi

Alariesto-galleria – Alariesto Gallery
Open: Jun-Aug: Mon-Sat 10am-5pm, Sun 12-6pm
            Sep-May: Mon-Fri 10am-5pm, Sat 12-4pm
Address: Jäämerentie 9
            99600 Sodankylä
Phone: (016) 618 643, 040 825 6562
Fax: (016) 612 093
E-mail: alariesto.galleria@pp.inet.fi
Internet: www.sodankyla.fi/engl

KITTILÄ

Särestöniemi-museo – Särestöniemi Museum
Open: Daily 10am-6pm
Address: Särestöntie 880
            99110 Kaukonen
Phone: (016) 654 480, 040 758 2085
Fax: (016) 654 489
E-mail: liisa.tervahauta-kauppala@kittilä.fi
Internet: www.kittila.fi/kuvat/sivukoe2

INARI

Saamelaismuseo Siida – Sámi Museum Siida
Open: Jun-Sep: Daily 9am-8pm Oct-Mar: Tue-Sun 10am-
            5pm, Open-Air Museum closed.
Address: Inarintie
            99870 Inari
Phone: (016) 665 212
Fax: (016) 671 486
E-mail: siida@samimuseum.fi
Internet: www.siida.fi

Pielpajärven kirkko – Pielpajärvi Church
Open: Early Jun-mid Aug: Daily 12-6pm
Address: 99870 Inari
Phone: (016) 675 0522
Fax: (016) 675 0540

UTSJOKI

Utsjoen kirkko – Utsjoki Church
Open: Late Jun-mid Aug: Daily 11am-6pm
Address: 99980 Utsjoki
Phone: (016) 677 107
Fax: (016) 677 172

INDEX

Photographs

Finnish National Gallery:
Central Art Archives: 2–3, 6
Jaakko Holm 21
Hannu Aaltonen 50, 62, 113, 145, 168, 214–215, 231
Janne Mäkinen 53
Jouko Könönen 54
Antti Kuivalainen 90
Jukka Romu 112, 182, 216
Janne Tuominen 127
Matti Janas 130, 211
Pirie Mykkänen 153

Otava Picture Archives:
15, 16 (both pictures, bottom Seppo Hilpo), 29, 31, 35, 41- 42, 44,
49, 54, 55 (both pictures), 56–57, 59, 64 (top and bottom), 65 (both
pictures, bottom Rauno Träskelin), 66, 75, 78, 86–87, 100 (both
pictures), 105 (both pictures), 114, 117, 124 (Ernst Ovesén), 126,
131, 138, 143–144, 151, 153, 167 (both pictures, top Cecil
Hagelstam), 170, 181, 184, 187, 190, 197, 199 (Matti Ruotsalainen),
223, 244, 251, 260, 268, 271, 273, 281

National Board of Antiquities:
13, 15, 25, 33, 46, 51, 60, 71, 82, 86, 96, 108, 120, 123, 132, 141, 156,
164, 166, 176 (P. Sarvas), 179, 193, 196, 205, 213, 222, 233, 236, 249,
258, 264, 267, 275

City Survey Division, Helsinki, 2003 14
Loviisa Maritime Museum 69
Pietarsaari Town Museum (Kaius Hedenström) 235
The Tikanoja Art Museum 237
Oulu Art Museum (Kaius Hedenström) 253
The Aine Pictorial Art Foundation, The Aine Art Museum, Tornio
(Kaius Hedenström) 264